Jews and the Ends of Theory

Jews and the Ends of Theory

Shai Ginsburg, Martin Land,
and Jonathan Boyarin
Editors

FORDHAM UNIVERSITY PRESS
New York 2019

Fordham University Press gratefully acknowledges financial assistance and support provided for the publication of this book by Cornell University and Duke University.

Fordham University Press also publishes its books in a variety of electronic formats. Some content that appears in print may not be available in electronic books.

Visit us online at www.fordhampress.com.

Library of Congress Cataloging-in-Publication Data

Names: Ginsburg, Shai, 1967– editor. | Boyarin, Jonathan, editor.
Title: Jews and the ends of theory / Shai Ginsburg, Martin Land, and Jonathan Boyarin, editors.
Description: First edition. | New York, NY : Fordham University Press, [2019] | Includes bibliographical references and index.
Identifiers: LCCN 2018011247| ISBN 9780823282005 (cloth : alk. paper) | ISBN 9780823281992 (pbk. : alk. paper)
Subjects: LCSH: Jews—Intellectual life—20th century. | Jews—Intellectual life—21st century. | Jewish literature—History and criticism—Theory, etc. | Critical theory. | Criticism (Philosophy)—History. | Jewish philosophy.
Classification: LCC DS113 .J57 2019 | DDC 909/.04924082—dc23
LC record available at https://lccn.loc.gov/2018011247

Printed in the United States of America

21 20 19 5 4 3 2 1

First edition

to the memory of

Helen Tartar z'l

and

Svetlana Boym z'l

CONTENTS

INTRODUCTION

Jews, Theory, and Ends

Shai Ginsburg, Martin Land, and Jonathan Boyarin

This book examines the intersections of three terms—*Jews*, *theory*, and *ends*. These intersections have informed strategies of scholarly and intellectual engagements with society, culture, history, and politics that, in the aftermath of World War II, informed the "human sciences" in Western and Central Europe and North America (and, given the military and economic dominance of the latter, in other regions of the world as well). Often, such strategies came to be grouped together under the monikers *criticism*, *theory*, or, at times, *critical theory*.

What would happen, we ask, when one turns to critical theory and evokes "the Jew": When, where, and why does this figure emerge and become visible? To what end, to what ends? At what—or at whose—expense? And what figure is it? Of nationality? Race? Ethnicity? Religion? Language? How do the spatial (geographical) and temporal (historical) coordinates of its emergence, alongside the perceptions of space and time to which it gave rise, shape our perspective of the present moment, its past, and future? Of our place in the world in relation to others? And what does the perspective of the present, marked by multiple intellectual, cultural, economic, and political crises and breaches—contribute to our understanding of these questions, their places and history? The ensuing dialogue accordingly traces, discontinuously as it may be, the figure of the Jew in the intellectual and scholarly corpora of the twentieth century.

The essays collected here endeavor to identify that figure, examine its sociological and rhetorical conditions of visibility, and chart, even if provisionally, its function within what has become known since the 1930s as "critical theory." The term, it should be recalled, is closely linked to the work of ambivalently Jewish intellectuals affiliated with what later came to be known as the Frankfurt School. Members of the Frankfurt School set "critical theory" over and against "traditional theory" to distinguish their own practice from what they deemed to be the prevalent approaches in the study of culture and society. One such bid to tell the terms apart is Max Horkheimer's 1937 programmatic "Traditional and Critical Theory."[1] Perceiving the world through the perspective of Descartes's *Discourse on Method*, traditional theory is "the sum-total of propositions about a subject, the propositions being so linked with each other that a few are basic and the rest derive from these."[2] It views facts, the conceptual apparatuses it deploys in interpreting these facts, and the role such apparatuses play in society as external to the theoretical activity and as independent of it. It thus plays a conservative role, buttressing existing social structures and relationships, and serving the political powers that be and their economic interests. Critical theory, in contrast, is "the unfolding of a single existential judgment."[3] Founding itself on Marx's critique of political economy, it views facts and the conceptual apparatuses that give them meaning as socially constructed. It turns attention to society itself and to the ways given social structures yield particular theoretical paradigms. By putting into relief the social constitution of knowledge and the interests it serves, critical theory sets itself as a mode of intervention in current social, economic, cultural, and political affairs. More than any "positive" approach, critical theory is, then, oppositional, in relation to traditional theory as well as to hegemonic cultural and political establishments. It suggests that things should not necessarily be as they are and that they could be changed.

Horkheimer's insistence on the distinctiveness of critical theory notwithstanding, however, the boundary lines between *theory* and *critical theory* have blurred in the academic parlance of the humanities and qualitative social sciences, and they are often treated as interchangeable. In what follows, we are less concerned with a rigorous deployment of these terms than with the question of how *opposition*—the *critical* gist of critical theory—is inflected by the figure of the "Jew."

One may begin tracing this question with the members of the Frankfurt School themselves. Neither in their writing nor in their everyday lives did they identify in the first instance as Jews; nor does their rhetoric assign a privileged status to the figure of the Jew. Still, the fact that they came to be identified ever more with this figure, even as their contribution to the broader discourse of theory is acknowledged, lies at the center of the phenomenon examined in this volume. We do not wish to emphasize exclusively the role that certain historical conjunctures explored in these pages might have played in the personal predicament of these intellectuals and in the "afterlife" of their writing in our day. Such restraint notwithstanding, we suggest that this rhetorical-sociological phenomenon—the specter of the Jew that looms behind the reception of the Frankfurt School—sheds light on a fundamental element of what we have come to identify as critical theory.

Tracing this spectral figure of the Jew in theory, the essays in this volume put forward "spectral reading," one that entails appellation: identification and naming.[4] Such reading charts a spectrum—social, conceptual, emotional—that stretches from materialization to disappearance, from confirmation to disavowal, from revulsion to love. It points at the generative power of pointing at "the Jew" alongside the destructive power of such gesture, the threats the Jew—with and without quotation marks—poses alongside those the Jew suffers.

Sociologically, such identification and naming reiterates a prior proclamation—"I am a Jew," "she or he is a Jew"—reiteration implicated in its antecedent, vacillating uncomfortably between approval and denouncement.[5] Even as it reproduces the violence the proclamation of one as Jew (both self-proclamation and the proclamation by another) entails, the significance of such reiteration nevertheless hinges substantially on whether one is the author of such proclamation or its willing or unwilling subject. The question of "will" points not only to the construction of subjectivity in its relationship to agency, a nexus central to our very understanding of theory in this context. It also brings to our attention the violence and abuse—verbal as well as physical, at times rising to the level of mortal danger—inherent in identification and naming. The latter asserts not only the authority to proclaim (and re-proclaim) one as "Jew," irrespective of his or her self-identification and experience; it also entails the power to superimpose categories of knowledge—sociological as well as theoretical—over one's understanding of oneself, even when one resists such categories. Such authority, that is, is not merely conceptual but, as history has repeatedly shown us, bodily as well.

Rhetorically, identification and naming serve to designate figures and categories as Jewish. There is no necessary linkage between the sociological and the rhetorical, or between the sociological and constructed subjectivity. And yet we have come to expect it, endeavoring to retrieve markers of sociological and rhetorical identity and perusing texts for the traces that would allow one to establish and make visible the sociological and the rhetorical for "what they are," namely, "Jewish." In this respect, the question of visibility is anything but simple: It requires attention not only to personal and institutional politics (of academic institutions alongside judicial, legislative, and executive ones), but also to the very structure of the scholarly discourse and, in particular, to what it lays bare alongside what it conceals. Attention to visibility implies, in fact, the opacity of the figure of the Jew (or, if you will, of the Jewishness of the figure), even its absence, precisely when one would have expected to encounter it: for instance, in the work of the Jewish members of the Frankfurt School during World War II. The question of "the Jew" is thus not merely one of proclamation, but of reading as well. "Reading," understood both in its everyday sense and as the wider search for markers to interpret, becomes an endeavor to salvage affiliation—Jewishness—and test its possible, plausible, and unwarranted terms even against the better judgment of the authors read. It is a quest for the specter of the Jew when she or he cannot be found in the flesh.

Spectral reading vacillates between mourning and the utopian, two key tropes that put forward a double perspective.[6] They figure prominently not only in key texts of the critical corpora we examine here and in their fast-growing academic scholarship, but also in their popular and semipopular renditions. The two tropes serve, in effect, as a Cartesian *glandula pinealis* of sort, sites of encounter—and crossover—between soul and flesh, between the virtual and the real, between criticism and history. These sites bid one face the histories that inform our present engagement. In light of the great catastrophes that have befallen Jews, which were often accompanied by the endeavor to extricate culture from the figure of the Jew and the Jewishness of the figure (endeavors that necessarily evoke profound aporias), spectral reading has often been an endeavor to excavate traces of a past that cannot be thought of but under the sign of violence. As such, it is a work of mourning. Simultaneously, however, this archaeological work has taken the form of territorialization (always conceived as reterritorialization, of claiming one's lawful abode): that is, it is not only a work of philology, but also the reclamation of a supposed polity. It marks the desire to shift immediately from the "no-longer-there" to the "not yet there" as a reassurance in the face of violence. That the present so harshly reveals the dystopian face of the major Jewish political experiments of our time brings to light the explosive aspect of the welding of mourning and the utopian, with which academic scholarship cannot pretend to have nothing to do. On the contrary, it is its obverse face.

Put otherwise, the two tropes of mourning and the utopian suggest the anxiety that hangs over this book. One may, in fact, suggest that it hangs over the very notion of critical theory from its inception, inasmuch as it laments a loss of certain modes of intellectual engagements and envisions new ones, carefully outlining their historical and political consequences. Indeed, one cannot dissociate the predicament of the figure of the Jew in theory from the endeavor to imagine a new European (and, by extension, global, though the transposition from Europe to globe has not been without its own critical conundrums) polity and history from the late eighteenth century on and, in particular, from the turn of the twentieth century. The association between that endeavor and Jews hinged on the perceived marginality of the latter, marginality that is not so much of the essence of historical societies but, rather, itself tropological.

Indeed, the marginal may be the most salient aspect of the Jew as a trope. In the intellectual world that critical theory helped build, we take for granted that to speak of power is to consider relationship—a relationship in which the power to name may be used to obscure the humanity of the subject of appellation. The "discovery" of the marginal as a worthy object of study and a source of creativity thus altered the role of Jews in post-Napoleonic Europe, both as figure and as individuals with something to say.

The affective power of the marginal owes much to the growing prominence of "progressive" ideologies in the humanities and social sciences. That power is, consequently, evinced by the growing unease in current theoretical debates in light of the perceived incongruity between that trope of marginality and the preeminence of Jews in the political, social, and economic formations that have emerged in the Euro-Atlantic world and in the Middle East in the aftermath of the Second World War. As Jews move (albeit always provisionally) from the margins of their respective societies to the center, the figure of the Jew in theory shifts from one of affiliation to one of indifference or even animus. This shift is informed, no doubt, by a sense of political as well as critical failure. The political failure consists in the inability to translate critical thinking into a substantive action that would yield different, inclusive politics. The critical failure is manifest in the difficulty of leaving the trope of the Jew behind, even as one acknowledges that it serves to buttress exclusive notions of politics and history against which it was originally evoked. The question becomes how to account, in theory, for shifting historical affiliations, for the nonidentity of identities through histories.

We are asking, then, whether such sociological shifts stand to bring to an end the rhetorical tradition of the Jew in theory, and, if so, what such theoretical eschatology would look like. Some scholars turn their attention ever more away from the pale of Jewish diasporas and seem content to let the trope of the Jew disappear without a whimper. Others, however, struggle as they endeavor to put that figure to rest, raising in the process the questions—surprisingly not always explicitly addressed—of how to do so, at what (and whose) expense, and what replaces it. One, it seems, cannot escape the theological character, and Christian at that, of this endeavor, as the salient approaches to this question reveal.[7] Since the late nineteen eighties, two figures have emerged as central to the efforts to think of Jews and theory at the turn of the twentieth century: Paul the Apostle and the jurist and political theorist Carl Schmitt.[8] The great divergence between the approaches to the one, the other, or to both notwithstanding, they all put into relief the tension between the universal and the particular, between rule and exception, between originary texts and their interpretations, that is, between word and history. To probe these terms with an eye to the questions that interest us in this volume is not merely to ask whether the "Jew" may be catholically transfigured without excluding the Jew and to account for the historical violence such exclusion entailed, but also to introduce refusal, renouncement, adamant rejection even. Critical theory is now to be tested through its regrets.

Badiou's and Agamben's engagement with these texts may serve as an example of how readings of Paul on the one hand and of Schmitt on the other reflect and engage the question of the Jew. Badiou attempts to overcome the Jew, whether as an intellectual opponent (in Levinas, whose ethics, so Badiou tell us, is no philosophy but, rather, theology), or as the paradigmatic figure of the victim, central to the contemporary modern liberal ethics of human rights. Tussling with the specter of Hannah Arendt, he turns to Paul in an attempt to undo the Jewish figure of modern politics, in which the Jew is seen as the prime example of the exclusion of the other from the modern state and its laws. Via Pauline Christianity, he seeks to read the Jew against the Jew and thereby overcome Jewish particularity. Badiou calls for a new ethics that would surpass the Levinasian "ethics of the Other," posing instead ethics of the event as surplus, of truth that—like Kuhn's structure of scientific revolutions—shatters earlier paradigms, and that would decenter the Jewish example. His obsession with the Jewish example, however, undercuts his attempt to overcome it.

Agamben, in contrast, embraces the figure of the Jew—of the incarcerated Jew, the Jew in the camp who is already not himself but something else, a figural "Muslim," as Gil Anidjar has reminded us.[9] For Agamben this camp Jew and his "bare life" are at the center—one would like to say absent center if it were not all too present—of the structure of sovereignty. Auschwitz becomes a panopticon of sorts which, through its focus on the Jewish body in the process of transubstantiation, allows us to see through it the working of the modern European state. Agamben's text is a call to arms, of course, resistance—a summons to search for opacity as a mode of resistance.

On that account, to raise the question of Jewishness in relation to critical theory is also to raise the question of secularism and religion, to contend that what is consistently understood to be a tension between religion and secularism characterizes not merely the social world, but critical discourse as well. It is to question the self-proclamation of the critical stance that it is indeed secular, that it is the main site where the secular is defiantly performed over and against religion. After all, criticism—and critical theory all the more so—emerged as a response to religion, as an attempt to distance one from religious identification, or at least from religion understood as grounded in uncritical faith in Revelation, and hence as "obscurantist." To speak of Jewishness, of Jews as religious subjects and as the subjects of religion, at the heart of critical theory is therefore to speak improperly, blasphemously as it were. We follow Talal Asad in turning our attention to the coordinates of the critical disciplines of present-day scholarship by asking whether one has the power to tear oneself away from religion, to mark a truly autonomous realm of criticism.[10] This question becomes a new anchor for a critical practice that remains committed to critical theory even as it undoes it.

Contemporary critical approaches thus invoke the specter of anti-Jewishness as a phenomenon of considerable theological significance. Not necessarily motivated by animus, their sociological context as well as their theoretical implications have to be pointed out: In part they seem to react to the collapse of universal figures of radical critique (perhaps most saliently, the universal working class). In the case of the Jew as a trope, that collapse has to do with the current sociology of Jews. The effort to (re)marginalize Jews rhetorically appears to us to be the result. Be that as it may, such quest continues to conceive the Jew primarily as figure and only secondarily (and rather abstractly) as living being. In other theoretical domains (women's studies and African American studies immediately come to mind) such approaches would be deemed intolerable today in light of the objectification and dehumanization implicit in them, and the marginal subject's demand to speak for herself or himself. The Jewish Question, the question of the Jew appears to operate by a different logic. But why should it?

The questions raised by the critical engagement with Jews, sociologically and rhetorically are manifold, but frequently circle back to one in particular: Can Jews speak, or is it always "the Jew" who speaks? The question of the Jew is thus also the question of speaking about the Jew, of the shift from the first-second person to the third person, or of the failure of that shift, the implication and framing of the first person by the third and vice versa.[11] Translation (from both experience and language, successful as failed, always suspected, always at a distance, either too abstract or too concrete) of first person experience into third person description is much of the work of theory. It suggests a certain commonality with more traditional sociocultural narratives that function to define and enforce collective boundaries, even as it calls these (at least "in theory") into question. Critical theory has found itself in a bind: On the one hand, it claims to interrogate its own theorizing as critically as it approaches its more traditional subject matter, doubling, splitting, or fracturing the third person so as to refract and reflect its modes of production. On the other hand, it facilitated an amalgamating shift—not inevitably a critical one—from the third person to the first, for the emergence of this modernist program. Those whose marginality made them the objects of theory may find that when modernism extends the opportunity to speak subjectively they are paradoxically left with no language uncorrupted by the semantics of their place as figure or trope in theory.

Indeed, critical theory offered an unprecedented opportunity for European Jews, in the first person, long aware that the narrative of Europe depended on a certain speaking about the Jew, in the third person, not entirely congruent with their experience, needs, or desires. Facing this prefiguration of the Jew, like a circus mirror that renders one visible but somehow unrecognizable to oneself, two strategies immediately present themselves: to reform the accepted narrative of non-Jews and Jews, or to dissociate oneself from the types defined in that narrative without subjecting them to explicit critique. Even the latter strategy further complicates the question of Jewish visibility, as it opens the possibility of reframing traditional concerns in a new language under some other rubric, rendering their identification as "Jewish" a matter of interpretation and critical judgment.

Finally, it is important to note that the question of exceptionalism—of Jews and Jewishness alike—seems to us misguided. For claims of exceptionalism often go hand in hand with the appellation, and at times denunciation, of the non-Jew. Violence repeatedly erupts in sites of such appellation, and it is not necessarily aimed at Jews. These days it may be directed toward those who are Other to Jews, and at Jewish Others by other Jews and Others who would speak in their name. This suggests that violence—not just symbolic, but at least potentially and often actually physical, and deadly—is inherent in the structures we are collectively examining here. We hope that such keen attention to violence may open the door to the exploration of its generative and destructive power.

The chapters that follow address the figure of the Jew as a special case for theory, a rich laboratory in which to test modern categorical types—nationality, race, ethnicity, religion—as a precise taxonomy whose universality would have been established had it been able to normalize the supernatural status assigned to Jews in earlier theological conceptions of Europe. The lack of definitive success in these efforts has reestablished the figure of the Jew as an outlier, a perennial wandering idea among a historical procession of momentarily rooted claims and conceptions. So despite the changed material circumstances of most Jews living in liberal democracies in recent generations, owing in some part to the influence of critical theory on social policy, the locus of the Jew within conventionally accepted types remains a proper subject of inquiry and redefinition to the present day.

This open-endedness in identifying Jews becomes even more ramified as we move to consider Jewish intellectuals, often said to be disproportionately represented in the discourse of critical theory. The stated disproportion suggests some means to posit a suitable proportion, a difficult task without some settled conception of who Jews are (in relation to whom) and who may be identified as a Jew. Deferring this questioning of the question, one nonetheless proceeds to ask what might account for this observed disproportion. Is it possible to consider some explanation not rooted in Jewishness as figure without rendering the observation itself meaningless? What then do we mean when speaking of "Jewish intellectuals" in the process of critically interrogating the figure of the "Jew" as a privileged subject in theory? Is the term "Jewish intellectuals" a two-word substantive, or does the word "Jewish" operate as an adjective modifying the word "intellectual"? Is the work of Jewish intellectuals affected by the baggage they bring as Jews, whether as a predisposition toward a type of explanation or concern with a type of question? Are there specifically Jewish concerns in critical theory, and who may designate them as such? Each of these questions, in some sense concretizing spectral reading, feeds back on the others in a tangle of nonlinear iterativity.

Jewish intellectuals have often been understandably reticent in regard to these questions. Members of the Frankfurt School were concerned that a search for Jewish influence in their work might be used to discount its general value, especially after Nazi propaganda joined the ideas of Marx, Freud, and Einstein as "Jewish science," foreign and degenerate, produced to destroy an intuitive Aryan connection to nature. Even short of such aggressive attack, ideas may be read as what Deleuze and Guattari call a communal action, seen as speaking primarily for the urges and agendas of a minority.[12] Then, on a certain view, the discovery of Jewish (qua minority) motifs in a work of general philosophy or social science would be no less damaging to its status as general scholarship than the denigration of Einstein's theory of relativity as Jewish physics. The imagined contamination is often ascribed to some Jewish mode of thought, not even reliance on source material of Jewish provenance (whose use is not limited to Jewish writers or necessarily intended to advance a minority agenda). But, of course, the theory of relativity is judged by its usefulness in describing the physical world within a given social context, not on one or another scientist's source of intuition. Similar criteria inform critical judgment throughout modern thought. As recommended by Einstein's work and practiced in critical theory, we regard the relativity of perception and intuition as an invitation to examine the role of perspective in the construction of intersubjective experience. Perhaps it is just this approach that anti-Semites have regarded as too Jewish.

The ensuing chapters treat both the figure of the Jew and the presence of Jews in certain disciplines under the title of an "end of theory." The latter is inevitably as broad as theory itself, and much in this discourse can be seen as routine editing, reassessing the field, and abandoning certain lines of inquiry that have run their course or found to be dead ends. But alongside this critique of critique, the "end of theory" also refers to certain efforts to reverse its accomplishments, in part by reestablishing the intellectual authority of traditional narratives and their "plain and commonsense" understandings.[13] What are the implications for Jews, as ambiguously privileged subjects and disproportionate practitioners of theory, if theory is closed off as a mode of inquiry? Resistance to theory seems to oppose the modernist program of improving life through the application of critical discourse to social action. Does it express, among other values, impatience with efforts to understand the figure of the Jews (and Jews) in its subtleties? Depending on how one understands the "Jew" in critical theory, as figure and as intellectual, the onset and structure of resistance to theory may appear resonant with earlier narratives in which political and economic reactions were accompanied by denigration of explicit or implicit Jewish concerns, encoded as suspicion of intellectuals.

Finally, the chapters bring a number of particular issues raised earlier into dialogic focus. Theory in the twentieth century challenged the notion of language as a neutral mode for transmission of ideas said to exist independently of their expression, pointing at the dependence of meaning on language. To account for this dependence, the study of any topic must include attention to the language of study and the processes by which its claims become accepted and repeated.[14] Is it coincidence that the close study of text and the detailed analysis of linguistic structures form the traditional approach to study and transmission of heritage for Jewish scholars since ancient times? In both cases, specialists developed and evolved a professional idiom intended to render the specifically linguistic insights mutually comprehensible and so distinguish speaking of speaking from conventional speaking. One particular style in the resistance to theory draws attention to the difficulty of acquiring facility in this mode of criticism and expresses a characteristic impatience that denies any value in making the effort. Does this specific manifestation of anti-intellectualism resonate with the style of a much older hostility to the complexities of rabbinic methods, reflected in the pejorative use of terms such as Talmudic for intricate logic[15] and Pharisee for hypocrite?

In asking what happens when one evokes "the Jew" in theory we have posed a cascade of ramifying questions that cannot be fully disentangled, let alone given definitive and complete answers, by us or by the contributors to this book. Some of the essays that follow engage directly with one or more of the issues we have raised, whereas others work to illuminate their context and pertinence, complicating our questions as formulated, rather than focusing their scope. Taken together, they put forward themes in a wide range of perspectives that defies neat classification, and one may perhaps sense in this mode of response the operation of another familiar Jewish trope. Nevertheless, before introducing the essays individually we briefly point to certain common approaches taken by the authors, and differences within them. In one sense or another, each of the essays illustrates what we have called "spectral reading." Each charts a quest for "the Jew" and "the Jewish" in scholarly texts whose authorship and cultural provenance are commonly understood to be not-merely-Jewish (or even not-Jewish). Indeed, all explore the problematics of designating "the Jew" and "the Jewish" and probating thematic inheritance, even as it becomes clear that the two terms remain ephemeral and indetermined. Or, which comes up to the same thing, subjectively, even momentarily, indeed also strategically determined in a complex—spectral, if you will—exchange between our contributors.

Explicitly seeking out Jewish sources in critical theory, Martin Jay discusses Leo Lowenthal and other founders of the Frankfurt School, examining their ambivalence toward the suggestion that their Jewish backgrounds and commitments might influence their intellectual work. In a similar way, James Porter reads the work of Erich Auerbach as a dismissal of Christian strategies of interpretation of the "Old Testament," suggesting a Jewish opposition that lurks behind Auerbach's authoritative work on Christianity. Further distancing Jewish self-identification from Jewish traditions of thought, Svetlana Boym locates certain Jewish impulses in the artistic priorities of the Russian formalist Victor Shklovsky and the Acmeist poet Osip Mandelshtam. Boym's essay raises yet another, key issue: that of Jews as figures of marginality or the periphery in critical theory as well as of the margins or periphery of the terrain purportedly covered by the endeavors to think "Jews in theory." She thus seeks to bring into consideration figures that thus far have been marginal to the discussion of Jews and Jewish identity. Martin Land tackles the issue of the complex relation between substantive Jewish culture and Jewish situation directly, exploring the relationship posited by theory between the Jews' marginality and their creativity. In light of society's notable ambivalence toward critique, he interrogates a history of misreadings of intellectual activity—Jewish and otherwise—up to the current moment. Hannan Hever offers a different "peripheral perspective," that of East European Hasidism. Focusing on the debate between Martin Buber and Gershom Scholem on how to understand Hasidic literature and its significance, Hever shows how this seemingly literary dispute was informed by debates on Jewish sovereignty and, in turn, informed these debates.

Whereas the center of gravity of most of the essays in this volume is Europe (specifically Western, Central, and Eastern) and North America, Andrew Bush and Yehouda Shenhav probe the topic from the perspectives of North Africa and the Middle East. Such geographical decentering poses significant challenges to theories of Jews grounded only in Ashkenazi Jewish experience. Bush turns to al-Andalus as a focus for Jewish identification, noting Derrida's comparison of al-Andalus to Yiddish as a portable home. Shenhav analyzes the politically motivated removal of Modern Hebrew away from its close linguistic ties to Arabic and the effective erasure of Mizrahi Jewish sources from contemporary intellectual life. Bush and Shenhav turn our attention to the power of language and translation, a theme with a long history in Jewish thought. Such attention is perhaps the sole element common to all of the essays, visible in the work of the contributors and in the works they discuss.

Sarah Hammerschlag shows how the relationship between these tropes of Ashkenaz and Sepharad is embedded in the discourse of modern European Jewish intellectual debates as simultaneously one of their anchors and points of contention. Examining the complex relationship between Emmanuel Levinas and Jacques Derrida, she shows how the two articulate divergent Jewish theories about Jews, a theme also present in the essays of Land, Porter, Bush and Shenhav. Elliott Wolfson, on his part, puts forward the reverse perspective when he reads the temporality of the Jewish eschaton in conjunction with Heidegger's rumination on temporality, pointing to their shared apperception. He thus not merely traces the specter of Heidegger—definitely a figure of resistance in the context of our volume—in premodern Jewish thought, but also reminds us that the boundaries erected by the figure of "the Jew" are indeed strategic and of the present moment.

Whereas most of the contributors to this volume underscore the gravity of its subject matter and its often fateful scholarly and political ramifications, Sergey Dolgopolski begins his philosophical exploration of the political by relating a joke. Dolgopolski shows how the Jewish motifs that haunt the joke illuminate the figuration of Jews in critical theory. Similarly opening with a joke, Jay Geller discusses the role of animals in literature as implicit surrogates for Jews, drawing a connection between this substitution and the theme of Jews in theory. In some sense, Dolgopolski and Geller distill the act of spectral reading to its minimal components, highlighting the challenges described earlier in locating Jewish thematic content by its explicit absence.

With all of this deployment of the notion of spectrality of Jewishness, "even" in the twenty-first century, it is not hard to imagine how complex the problem of Jewish visibility must have been for members of the Frankfurt School. Martin Jay exposes much of this complexity in presenting Leo Lowenthal as an exceptional case study. As we have noted, to point at the fact that many of the inner circle were Jewish—not just Jews by accident of birth—entails a kind of directed reading at odds, at least partially, with the members' account of their subjective experience. We may portray the search for traces of Jewish motifs and traditions in their work, in defiance of their explicit intentions, as exposing the founders of critical theory to the critical methods they developed. And yet, as Jay observes, these German intellectuals may have felt such reading as uncomfortably similar to the antisemitic practice of attacking their thinking as Jewish. Still, it may also be noted that a certain reluctance to recognize Jewish influences in the secular thinking of Jews is itself a historically familiar Jewish motif, partly in response to the anti-Semitic practice.

Jay's essay traces Lowenthal's early intellectual life through a series of passionate engagements with traditional and modernist Jewish thought that continued to find expression, in modulated form, in his work at the Institute for Social Research and, after 1933, in the United States. As a student in his twenties, Lowenthal was part of the community of young Jewish intellectuals surrounding Rabbi Nehemiah Anton Nobel, an adherent of German philosophy and Orthodox Judaism. During this period, Lowenthal explored the welding of mourning and the utopian expressed through the messianic. He was committed to the Weimar Jewish Renaissance, active in Jewish communal organizations and joined the psychoanalytic group around Erich Fromm and Frieda Reichmann, an observant Jew whose sanatorium served kosher meals and observed Jewish holidays. Adorno and Horkheimer did not share this enthusiasm for Jewish tradition and communal activity, but both Lowenthal and Fromm joined the Institute for Social Research, and began working in a milieu in which, as Jay observes, specifically Jewish themes, including anti-Semitism, were subsumed into questions of a wider scope. Still, Jay is able to locate the markers of distinctly Jewish concerns and sees Lowenthal as continuing to represent the Jewish Renaissance by negotiating a path between assimilation and parochial traditionalism. For example, unlike others of the Frankfurt School, Lowenthal portrayed Heinrich Heine's conversion as an attempt to express a type of Jewish identity. Here, Jay identifies the traces of Jewish identity in Lowenthal's reading of such traces in the life of Heine, engaging another historically familiar Jewish mode of inquiry. Lowenthal's Jewish visibility reflects both on Jewish sources in critical theory and the contributions of critical theory to the evolution of Jewishness.

Although various streams of Zionism have long disagreed—sometimes violently—over how to best normalize the political status of the Jews, all claim a commitment to normalizing the conditions of Jewish visibility, on some spectrum between assertion of state power and spiritual renaissance. Perhaps unsurprisingly, these conflicting claims reproduced within the Jewish communities assembling in Palestine varieties of stratification characteristic of the European Jewish experience. If Europe had conceived the Jews as an Oriental figure to be civilized by the West, Jews arriving from Europe announced themselves to be European Jews and constructed a figure of other Jews as Oriental.

Yehouda Shenhav begins his essay by discussing the efforts of the State of Israel to suppress both Palestinian assertion of state power and Palestinian spiritual renaissance. Much about these efforts can be understood from relatively recent Israeli legislation that prohibits certain types of discussion of the 1948 Nakba, the catastrophic exile of 750,000 Palestinians from towns, villages, and farms—quickly resettled by Jews—and the consequent uprooting of the social and cultural fabric of Palestinian society. Shenhav also reviews the evidence for the intentionality of the Nakba, which he connects to the martial law imposed on Palestinians of Israeli citizenship from 1948 to 1966, ending just months before the occupation of the West Bank and Gaza began the era of emergency rule that continues to this day. These events, and the debate surrounding censorship of the Nakba, center on questions of Palestinian visibility analogous to those previously raised in this introduction with respect to Jews: How does one characterize the figure of the Palestinian? Who may do so? What are the relationships among nationality, religion, and citizenship? In particular, Shenhav discusses the problem of reading as expressed through the relationship of Jewish Israeli society to Arabic, legally an official language of the state but practically deprecated in many circumstances and frequently defaced on public signage. He traces this relationship to the development of modern Hebrew, reborn as a spoken language during the twentieth century, and shows how political forces intervened to choose European languages rather than the linguistically closer spoken Arabic in modeling new vocabulary and grammatical structures. Quotations from Ze'ev Jabotinsky make clear the preference in certain circles for building the state-in-waiting as a European cultural entity in opposition to its Arab Middle Eastern location. This preference brings Shenhav back to the question of Jewish visibility in a personal sense, opening up an unavoidable political issue for a state that asserts the right to define Jewish visibility: What do the state and its underlying political philosophy say to the majority of Israeli Jews whose traditions were lived for centuries in Arabic? Can there be a peaceful resolution of the Middle East conflict without a peaceful resolution of the question of Palestinian visibility? Can there be peace within Israeli society without a peaceful resolution of the question of the visibility of Arab Jews?

In addressing Jewish identity outside of Ashkenaz, Shenhav draws on his family's background to the East in Baghdad. Andrew Bush similarly situates his analysis out of the Eurocenter. The way to his essay on Sephardic identity runs through the figure of Derrida. It concerns the pulls of Jewish communalism, discussing the experience of French-speaking Jews from the Maghreb, an Arabic word that indicates the west and shares a common linguistic root with the familiar Hebrew Ma'ariv (the name for prayers said at evening, toward sunset). As Bush observes, East/West in this context functions as code for a notion of South, in relation to Europe as North, a relation inseparable from colonialism. He examines a taxonomy of identities produced by Derrida, who enumerated the possible intersections of language and ethnicity, and argued that North African Jews stand outside of it. Bush develops this notion of otherness as distinct from the otherness carried in Yiddish—*mame loshn*—as a portable home, thus constituting an approach to a Sephardic version or taxonomy or theory. That approach would put "Ashkenazi-centrism in question by recognizing Sephardic, Levantine and other articulations of Jewish experience from beyond the literal and figurative pale as theoretical sources." By way of Gil Anidjar's *Our Place in al-Andalus*, he explores the experience of place, showing how al-Andalus can refer to a spatiotemporal context not defined on a map of European Spain. This experience of al-Andalus comes to us from a place already located as past centuries ago, and Bush highlights this pluperfect in parallel to Derrida's sense of loss in an urban Algeria where Ladino was no longer commonly spoken years before his birth. This received language of sadness and loss produces a version of mourning and utopia different from the spatial notions of home advocated by either Zionists or assimilationists in the Weimar Jewish Renaissance, pointing instead to a time and place whose boundaries are uncertain by conception, embodying a language that embraces such uncertainty without discomfort. Here Bush discusses Maimonides' *Guide for the Perplexed*, and follows Anidjar in exploring the original Arabic title, *dalālat al-hā'irīn*. Observing that the word *dalala*, rendered in the English title as guide, is closer in usage to sign or signifier, and invoking Benjamin's description of the irreducible uncertainty in the translator's task, Bush hints that Maimonides' title can be read as pointing to the place of perplexity as part of our place in al-Andalus. And perhaps, as Derrida has stated in much of his work, the embrace of a certain irreducible undecidability, at least with respect to European taxonomies, is a language of home that has been hospitable to Jews in the past and perhaps can be again.

In her reading of Derrida as a Jewish intellectual, Sarah Hammerschlag is less concerned with exposing Jewish motifs as the source of his thought than in locating in his work expressions of his identity as an intellectual and as a Jew. She applies insights from Derrida's philosophy of literature to his relationship with Emmanuel Levinas, probing the similarities and differences in their experience of these identities. Recounting a pair of anecdotes reported by Derrida, in which he revealed private comments made to him by Levinas, Hammerschlag finds in their very telling traces of the motifs Derrida observed in the texts he considered. She thus exposes in the closeness of their relationship the operation of secrecy and betrayal, the dissimulation present in representation, the movement from covenant to narrative, and the role of irony in constructing and subverting intimacy. In assessing these acts of exposure, she reveals by what means "Derrida used Levinas's words to perform the function he ascribes to literature." Here Hammerschlag finds evidence of a difference in their feelings toward Jewish community, arguing that Levinas used irony to establish cohesion while Derrida used it as a means of holding communitarian demands at arm's length. As she makes clear, Derrida's ambivalence toward Jewish community, in particular that aspect that imposes obligations and makes claims, was not separate from his awareness of familial overtones in his relationship with Levinas. Although Derrida discussed his Jewishness in various ways and contexts, it was through Levinas that he did and did not identify with the category of Jewish intellectual. This category cannot be fully distinguished from familial and communal considerations, especially when, as Hammerschlag shows, identity as Jewish intellectual (and the identity of the other to whom the Jew is other) diffracts into European and North African components—a point that engages with issues also raised by Shenhav and Bush. Having read these clues to identity from their philosophy and its enactment, Hammerschlag returns to the philosophical writings of Derrida and Levinas. With these insights into the ways that their respective relationships to Jewishness and Jewish community influenced their ideas, she enriches our grasp of their thinking about communitarianism and paternity, illuminating their underlying conceptions of truth and language.

Sergey Dolgopolski begins his essay with an anecdote that seemingly invites us to recognize its main figure as a Jew, to retrieve markers of sociological and rhetorical identity from his name and behavior, perhaps even to find confirmation of this reading in the absence of any explicit mention of his background. By refuting this act of designation, the essay draws our attention to habits of spectral reading and exploits the occasion to interrogate the idea of the political, from ancient to contemporary thought. But in the end, the Jewishness of the figure seems well established, and his actions are understood as embodying a well-known Talmudic mode of inquiry. What has perhaps changed, what is now "remembered better" in Dolgopolski's formulation, is our grasp of the figure of the Jew, the figure of the "human being," and, more generally, the visibility of the political in the traditions of European philosophy and Talmud. Central to both "grasp" and "figure" are various activities, mental and otherwise, with respect to representation, and Dolgopolski discusses the varieties of representation that play a role in perception, consciousness, and rationality. In this context, he presents the figure of the Jew as a type in European discourse, conceptually unrelated to ancient Jewish self-understanding and instead emerging as a fiction made necessary by the logic of Christian self-understanding. Bringing this type into the secularized modern world, with reference to Hannah Arendt's "The Jew as Pariah," he shows in what sense the Jew as a type required to preserve a certain set of ideas was transformed into the "human being" as a similarly required abstraction.

In Carl Schmitt's understanding of the political, the functioning of representation in consciousness of political authority becomes the representation of representation, that is, an act that produces a representation of authority (a perceived monopoly of power) through a secondary act that merely produces a representation of power in its direct and localized assertion. Dolgopolski's goal is to replace Schmitt's representation of representation with a notion of authority embodied in Talmudic discourse, which he calls refutation of refutation. Talmudic refutation is distinguished from negative dialectics by the detailed rules of discourse, proceeding systematically through a hierarchy of methodological confrontations, with no method invoked before demonstrating the insufficiency of simpler methods. The desired result is an iterative refinement of collective memory as locus of the reasoning process by which ideas are given shared value, with the goal of restoring openness and inventiveness to tradition and eliminating mechanical transmission. By way of refuting his earlier refutation of the figure in his anecdote, Dolgopolski refines our earlier recognition of some Jewishness in the behavior of that figure.

The key role played in that essay by a Russian Jewish joke suggests that the increasing silence of theory may be tied to an increasing inability to laugh. Seriously. Seriously? Put another way, what is to be learned if we address the questions that guide this volume playfully, via jokes, linking our inquiry to the great tradition of Jewish humor? This is what Jay Geller, again following Derrida, offers to do. He accordingly sets out his inquiry from the famous joke on "the elephant and the Jewish question," whose prominence is attested by its many iterations not only in collections of Jewish jokes but also in works of philosophy and theory. This joke allows Geller to explore two questions in their tantalizing interrelation. The relationship between theory and Jews, he suggests, is not unlike the relationship between Jews and animals. The joke unsettles the boundary lines that allow us to define these terms clearly. Drawing together two seemingly unrelated terms such as Jews and elephants and pointing at their close proximity, jokes do not merely comment on the preposterous character of the "rumor about the Jews" that there is an inherent relationship between Jews and nonhuman animals, and a certain category of animals—vermin, no less. The joke also points to what escapes theory and calls out its limitations, for theory takes the Jew as well as the animal as categories, singular as they might be, that can be comprehended only vis-à-vis universals: "Here is how the Jew is deployed, here how the Animal, here how the Jew like the Animal, or here how the Animal like the Jew." Theory fails, however, to interrogate the modes and idioms in which a particular Jew is figured as a particular animal, is performing as a particular animal, particularly when our ability to think in (theoretical) categories and maintain the distinction between them—between Jews and animals, between humans and animals, between Jews and humans—is challenged. In the fiction of Franz Kafka Geller finds an instance of how Jewish authors have called into question the human-(nonhuman) animal divide in their struggle to think through European modernity. In that modernity, the comparison between nonhuman animals and human beings—to Jews we could add people of color, people of other sexualities, the mentally challenged, and many more—has been central, with both surprising and disastrous consequences.

Svetlana Boym, of blessed memory, shares Geller's disaffection with theory and similarly looks for an alternative approach to the by now well-trodden theoretical path of theory and its ends. In her search, she turns to figures not commonly noted in the discussion on the relationship between theory and Jews: the Russian literary critic Victor Shklovsky and poet Osip Mandelshtam. She explores their autobiographical narratives to articulate what she calls the off-modern turn. That turn is a zigzag movement that defies the demands of systematic thinking and that does not follow any of the popular "isms" of Jewish intellectual engagement of the day: idealism, Marxism, nationalism, or messianism. Boym elaborates on Shklovsky's key term of estrangement. She maintains that Shklovsky intended estrangement not *from* the world, but *for* the world. Faced with historical catastrophes, that attitude insists on political and artistic engagement while maintaining critical distance from immediate, topical political demands. It thus puts into relief the complexity of historical and political circumstances and the human plurality within ourselves as well as in others. Both Shklovsky and Mandelshtam, she shows, look for artistic, political, and existential practices that defy theoretical conceptions along with their hierarchies and logics, for modes of art and thinking that undercut prescribed rules. Such practices bear the promise of freedom, of seeing the world anew, of a new beginning.

Alongside Yehouda Shenhav's and Andrew Bush's essays in this volume, Boym's essay points at gaping lacunae in our common consideration of theory in general and of the relationship of Jews and theory in particular. Weighted heavily toward English, French, and German intellectual production, such consideration fails to account for the intellectual traditions of Eastern Europe, the Middle East, and North Africa, home to the largest Jewish communities until these were uprooted and destroyed by the great upheavals of the twentieth century: the two world wars and the civil and regional conflicts that accompanied the establishment of nation-states in their aftermath. From the perspective of Jewish demography, the marginalization of the East-European intellectual tradition is particularly notable. At the turn of the twentieth century, about half of world Jewry lived in the western regions of the Russian Empire, mainly in what is today Lithuania, Belarus, Poland, Moldova, Latvia, Ukraine, and parts of western Russia. One should think of the off-modern not merely temporally, but geographically as well, as an attempt to incorporate regions excluded in and by theory.

Like Shklovsky and Mandelshtam, the German literary critic Erich Auerbach also wrote in response to the historical upheaval of the mid-twentieth century, not over and against history, but as a form of historical engagement. Looking at his work, James Porter asks how we can distinguish between Jewish and Christian interventions in these questions. Though a Jew, Auerbach became a leading authority on Western Christian traditions. Porter argues that notwithstanding his lifelong preoccupation with the theological and philosophical debates that informed Western Christianity, his perspective was Jewish, not Christian. In his work, Auerbach endeavors to portray the evolution of historical consciousness in the West and the discovery of the human and social worlds it yielded. He reflects on this evolution in relating the narrative of *realism*. In this account, realism is not a literary genre, but rather the evolving recognition of human consciousness of its own conditions, the growing awareness, that is, that reality and the real inhere in the sensuous, the mundane, and the human. And at the center of this narrative, Porter contends, Auerbach places Judaism and its heritage rather than Christianity. For Auerbach, history and historical consciousness first appear in the Jewish biblical stories, which provide in turn the structure and the framework for all subsequent expressions of historical thought and experience. In relating the history of realism, Auerbach shows the persistence of Jewish thought throughout Western literature. From this perspective, his treatment of the Christian *figura*—the key term for Auerbach—gains a different meaning than the one commonly attributed to it by critics. Figural reading does not recover biblical meaning. Rather, it is the manifestation of anxiety in the face of the inscrutability of the biblical narrative and its account of faith. In the biblical narrative, reality emerges as God breaches space and time, rendering them insignificant (contrary to our own conceptions of the real) and thus allowing for human activity in all its significance to come forth. Figural reading, on the other hand, anxiously endeavors to fill out this breach, transforming in the process space and time and investing them with meaning. Yet such reading fails to provide the messianic deliverance it promises and to overcome the Jewish inheritance of history: not as a given but, rather, as a painful awareness of conflict and antagonism and the discovery of contingency that cannot fully be grasped with the intellect.

One of the key questions hovering above all the contributions to this volume is the relationship between theory and politics, and more specifically between the role played by Jews in theory, whether as its subjects, objects, or figures, and the unfolding catastrophe in Israel-Palestine. Alongside Shenhav, Hannan Hever tackles this question most explicitly. In his chapter, Hever looks at one of the most famous and significant debates in Jewish studies, between Gershom Scholem and Martin Buber over the character of Hasidism. On the face of it, the debate was a literary one, centering on the significance of the Hasidic tale and its role in the interpretation of the Hasidic movement. Whereas Buber strove to incorporate the Hasidic tale into the canon of modern Jewish literature, Scholem saw it as a thing of the past, with little pertinence to the present. Consequently, whereas Buber focused exclusively on Hasidic storytelling and translated, edited, and anthologized Hasidic tales so they would be made part of the canon, Scholem stressed the integrity of the original texts and sought to understand them within the wider corpus of Hasidic homiletics. These two divergent literary approaches lent themselves to two interpretive paradigms: first, the historical-philological approach of the *Wissenschaft des Judentums* to which, regardless of his critique, Scholem saw himself as heir; and second, Buber's phenomenological approach, which treats history creatively so it can serve contemporary needs. It was a debate between two conceptions of Hasidism, one as a system of theological concepts, and the other as a way of life. Yet, as Hever shows, this debate was not merely historicist, but topical and political as well (or, perhaps, in the first instance). For in this debate, Buber and Scholem negotiated the question of Jewish sovereignty and endeavored to determine the desired relationship between Jews and the state. Buber extrapolated on the biblical sovereignty of God and turned to the figure of the Hasid as embodying the proper relationship between the sovereign and his subject; Scholem, in contradistinction, followed Carl Schmitt in underscoring human sovereignty, which, though initially established by analogy to God, effectively usurps divine authority. His is a human world in which man is judged in the historical context of Jewish law. Ultimately, the two positions served as the foundation of their appraisal of the Zionist project in Israel-Palestine and the State of Israel. Based on his conception of theocratic sovereignty, Buber repudiated the notion of a "Jewish State" and advocated a binational state. Scholem, in contrast, perceived the Second World War as a political state of emergency and so came to "embrace the State of Israel as an attempt for Jewish intervention in history."

The weakened link between the figure of Jews and that of theory might, one imagines, have something to do with the dominance of American culture in the decades following World War II, and the concurrent "whitening" and integration of Jews into "middle-class" American society. Martin Land's investigation of what happens as critique loses ground focuses on the ideological history of that process. He begins by tracing the assertions that link the predominance of Jews in critical discourses to Jewish marginality to a 1919 essay by Thorstein Veblen. Veblen does not argue that creativity and innovation thrive on the margins but, rather, that marginal groups like the Jews are better able than their European contemporaries to hold to a position of detachment and alienation from tradition and received wisdom, transforming their marginality into a critical perspective from which they are able to question, as it were, both themselves and the European social and economic systems. Recent critics of Veblen such as David Hollinger and Paul Burstein have pointed at his blindness toward the cultural and economic characteristics of Jewish communal life. In their critique, however, they take the disproportionate success of American Jews as their prime measure, supplanting Veblen's intellectual value (of scientific and social criticism) with monetary value. From this perspective, Jews are no longer marginal but, on the contrary, central to the ever-expanding social order of capital. It is within this shift to economic triumphalism that Land views the resistance to theory: the death of irony as an organizing trope of public discourse, the celebration of comforting certainties over taxing doubts, and the dismissal of intellectual pursuits that do not affirm beliefs held in advance. Here, Land turns to the work of the eccentric British psychoanalyst Wilfred Bion and his study of delusion in psychosis. Unlike Freud, Bion understood psychosis to be a form of disrupted perception, in which the mind seeks to protect itself from painful knowledge. Knowledge, Bion argued, is not simply an impression imprinted on our brain, but a willingness to acknowledge links between external objects and to establish an emotional relationship between ourselves and these observed links. He views the failure to recognize links not as a passive deficiency but, rather, as an active avoidance of knowledge and denial of the other, with ethical and political consequences. In short, such refusal disrupts one's ability to question oneself alongside the presuppositions of the existing social, cultural, economic, and political orders. This entails in turn the refusal of the paradigm that links Jews and critical thinking, and hence, its end.

Elliot R. Wolfson concludes this volume with the most direct philosophical meditation on the end. He interweaves mediations on temporality, human experience, and our inability to speak of the end. Wolfson points, in fact, at the co-dependence of our conceptions of end and of beginning. Following Martin Heidegger closely, he suggests that to comprehend the beginning one must think of it from the perspective of futurity, from the perspective, that is, of the ultimate end. Consequently, the beginning lies not in the past but, rather, in the future: It is initiated as beginning by the vision of what is to come, which endows it with its significance. Wolfson then brings this mode of philosophizing to bear on the way we understand Jewish eschatology, which lies at the center of Jewish theorization about time. As he notes, in Jewish eschatology what is yet to come is understood as what has already happened, whereas what has happened is derived from what is yet to come. Heidegger has indeed dismissed Judaism as a religion that by its very nature cannot experience temporality authentically. Yet his own understanding of temporality accords well with rabbinic conceptions of temporality and later kabbalistic eschatologies. They all seem to share the same notion of tradition as it is constructed by their respective notions of temporality.

And with that, perhaps it is time to begin the end(s).

NOTES

1. Max Horkheimer, "Traditional and Critical Theory" and "Postscript," in *Critical Theory: Selected Essays* (New York: Continuum, 1972), 188–252.

2. Ibid., 188.

3. Ibid., 227.

4. Our approach is obviously inspired by Jacques Derrida's *Specters of Marx: The State of the Debt, the Work of Mourning, and the New International* (New York: Routledge, 1994), but also by Avery Gordon's *Ghostly Matters: Haunting and the Sociological Imagination* (Minneapolis: University of Minnesota Press, 1997).

5. Here one should think not only of Louis Althusser's "Ideology and Ideological State Apparatuses," in *Lenin and Philosophy, and Other Essays* (New York: Monthly Review Press, 1971), 85–126; but also of Émile Benveniste's *Problems in General Linguistics* (Coral Gables, Fla.: University of Miami Press, 1971) and, in particular, of his discussion on the nature of the pronouns (217–22).

6. Gershom Scholem's interpretation of Jewish mysticism is central to the welding of these two tropes. See, for instance, *Major Trends in Jewish Mysticism* (New York: Schocken Books, 1961).

7. Most recently, Cynthia M. Baker has pointed to the dependence of the appelation *Jew* on Christian worldview. "*The Jew*," she writes, "serves instrumentally to name the key *other* out of which and over against which the Christian *self* was and is constituted. . . . *Jew*(s)—signifier and signified, word and connotations—has become a constant element not only in the historical formation and formulation of Western (Christian and post-Christian) identities but also the categories by which contours of identity are articulated" (*Jew* [New Brunswick, Rutgers University Press 2017], 23–24).

8. Here one might name, among many others, Giorgio Agamben's *State of Exception* (Chicago: University of Chicago Press, 2005) and *The Time That Remains: A Commentary on the Letter to the Romans* (Stanford: Stanford University Press, 2005); Alain Badiou, *Saint Paul: The Foundation of Universalism* (Stanford: Stanford University Press, 2003); Daniel Boyarin's *A Radical Jew: Paul and the Politics of Identity* (Berkeley: University of California Press, 1994); Judith Butler, *Parting Ways: Jewishness and the Critique of Zionism* (New York: Columbia University Press, 2012); Jean-François Lyotard and Eberhard Gruber's *The Hyphen: Between Judaism and Christianity* (Amherst: Humanity Books, 1999); Jacob Taubes's *The Political Theology of Paul* (Stanford: Stanford University Press, 2004); Slavoj Žižek's *The Puppet and the Dwarf: The Perverse Core of Christianity* (Cambridge, Mass.: MIT Press, 2003), and *Violence: Six Sideways Reflections* (New York: Picador, 2008).

9. Gil Anidjar, *The Jew, the Arab: A History of the Enemy* (Stanford: Stanford University Press, 2003).

10. See Talal Asad, *Formations of the Secular: Christianity, Islam, Modernity* (Stanford: Stanford University Press, 2003); Talal Asad, Wendy Brown,

Judith Butler, and Saba Mahmood, *Is Critique Secular? Blasphemy, Injury, and Free Speech* (New York: Fordham University Press, 2013).

11. Once again, Benveniste is central to our argument.

12. Gilles Deleuze and Félix Guattari, *Kafka: Toward a Minor Literature* (Minneapolis: University of Minnesota Press, 1986).

13. Martin Jay has surveyed the argument against theory in "For Theory," in *Cultural Semantics: Keywords of Our Time* (Amherst: University of Massachusetts Press, 1998), 15–30.

14. Michel Foucault explores this argument in *The Archeology of Knowledge* (London: Routledge, 2002).

15. A similar move in the modern European thought wars of religion may be seen in the use of "Jesuitical" as a pejorative name for somehow-illegitimate casuistry.

CHAPTER 1

Leo Lowenthal and the Jewish Renaissance

Martin Jay

On January 24, 1922, the twenty-one-year-old Leo Lowenthal,[1] then recovering from a bout of tuberculosis at the Black Forest spa of Menzenschwand, received some shattering news from his friend Siegfried Kracauer in Frankfurt. That morning Rabbi Nehemiah Anton Nobel (1871–1922), at the height of his powers and the inspiring leader of a generation of young German Jews, had suddenly and unexpectedly died at the age of only fifty-one. At that moment, Lowenthal, who had been temporarily estranged from his father, was being supported at the spa by Rabbi Nobel.[2] "I know," Kracauer wrote,

> how profoundly sad you will be, how much you have lost with him, and extend to you my hand in deepest friendship. I was also indescribably shaken by the sudden death of this man, because I had honored and loved him, even if I knew him only from afar. . . . He was entirely spirit—what others had taught, he *was*. I loved his *essence*, his wonderfully mild and unassuming goodness, which surrounded him like an atmosphere, yes, even radiated out from him to all—both deserved and undeserved. In an era of extreme skepticism and disbelief, he was to me

> the revelation of a genuine religious personality. . . . Was he one of the thirty Zaddikim who live in every generation?[3]

The powerful impact of Nobel's death was felt by others in the close-knit community of his young admirers, among them Franz Rosenzweig, who wrote to Martin Buber on the following day:

> You will already have read in the newspaper of the terrible blow that has struck us here. Part of the basis of my life has been snatched from underfoot. We never know our future, but we can nevertheless see before us the beginning of the road that leads into the future. At least we call them fortunate who can see this beginning of the road before them. And until yesterday morning, I would have called myself thus.

Alluding to a "dark and seemingly hopeless conversation" he had had with Buber only shortly before Nobel's death, Rosenzweig pleaded, "Stay with us, stay in this world for me!"[4]

As evidenced by this level of heartfelt anguish, Nobel was clearly no ordinary rabbi. He was instead the charismatic leader of an extraordinarily gifted group of young German Jewish intellectuals, who were to make their mark in the Weimar Republic and gain even more fame during their exile to America and Palestine after 1933. He boasted the cultural *Bildung* of a German mandarin—his death came just after he gave the second of three planned lectures on Goethe—and the rigorous training of a professional philosopher, who had written a dissertation in Bonn on Schopenhauer's theory of beauty before going to Marburg to study with Hermann Cohen.[5] But he was also a spell-binding speaker, who astounded audiences with his oratorical power. Writing to a friend after High Holy Day services in 1921, Rosenzweig groped for words to describe how moved he had been:

> Nobel's sermons were incredibly magnificent. . . . It's impossible to describe. . . . I have nothing to compare it with. Only the very greatest can be measured alongside of it. I, too, might have the ideas, after all, and many men have the rhetoric, but something else is involved here, a final quality, a rapture of the whole man, so that one wouldn't be surprised if he took wing in the end and disappeared. Nothing would be too audacious for him to risk saying at such moments, and there's nothing that would not be true coming from such a mouth.

After reminding his correspondent of his characteristic skepticism about all that Nobel represented—conservative Judaism, Zionism, mysticism, idealism—Rosenzweig nonetheless concluded:

> He prays the way one thinks of people praying only thousands of years ago when the great prayers originated; he speaks to the people as one thinks only the prophets should have been allowed to speak. It's really the Spirit as "cloudburst."[6]

For those in his thrall, Nobel was clearly a life-changing experience, and his premature departure truly traumatic. Lowenthal had found in him a permissive and nurturing father figure, to whom he could turn to legitimate his rebellion against his secular, assimilated, liberal father, a doctor with no patience for the more observant practices embraced, at least for a while, by his son.[7] In an essay he contributed to *Der jüdische Student*, Lowenthal wrote, "This death hit me with the force and unexpectedness of a great cosmic event, no, like the fall of an entire cosmos. Later this initial feeling revealed itself to me—as the thought of a space won back from wordless pain—as a key to understanding transience [*das Dahingegangene*]."[8] A half century later, he could still vividly recall the rabbi's impact, if now with a touch of ironic distance. Nobel, he told his interviewer Helmut Dubiel, was

> a curious mixture of mystical religiosity, philosophical rigor, and quite likely also a more or less repressed homosexual love for young men. It really was kind of a "cult community." He was a fascinating speaker. People flocked to hear his sermons. He kept his house open to all, and people would come and go as they pleased. Of course that was a godsend, especially in the chaotic years after World War I.[9]

Nobel's appeal, it is clear in retrospect, was enhanced not only by his remarkable personal magnetism and silver tongue, but also by the ability of his followers to see in him what they needed in a turbulent period of rapid and frightening change. He was an adherent of Orthodox Judaism, having studied rabbinics with German Orthodoxy's leading figure, Ezriel Hildesheimer, in Berlin, and a critic of the overly assimilationist Reform or liberal alternative that had attracted many adherents in the Wilhelmine period.[10] And yet he was also uneasy with the Orthodox establishment of his day, personally tolerant of all variants of Judaism, and able to maintain close friendships with more liberal figures like Leo Baeck.[11] A fervent defender of the German war effort and supporter of Hermann Cohen's optimistic claim that German culture and Judaism were fully compatible—he even designed the inscription in Hebrew and German for Cohen's tombstone in Berlin's Weissensee Cemetery—Nobel nonetheless identified with the Zionist project of a Jewish homeland. In 1904, in fact, he had been elected vice president of the orthodox Zionist organization known as Mizrachi, which sought to counter religious hostility to the establishment of a Jewish state before the coming of the messiah.[12]

A strong believer in the importance of strictly observing Jewish law, Nobel was anything but an embodiment of the "dry legalism" alleged by many gentile critics from Kant on who accused Judaism of lacking devotional intensity and experiential immediacy. Instead, he was open to the recovery of mystical currents in Jewish thought, which were so tempting for many in the interwar era.[13] It was thus possible for figures like Buber, still not entirely past the romantic *Erlebnismystik* of his early years, and Rosenzweig, whose "new thinking" spurned the Idealist rationalism of Cohen, to find him an inspiration.[14] Despite Buber's initial qualms about Nobel's defense of Orthodoxy, he joined Rosenzweig and thirteen other young admirers in presenting a Festschrift in 1921 to Rabbi Nobel to mark his fiftieth birthday.[15] It was a worthy monument to a figure who made a singular contribution to what became known as the Weimar "Jewish Renaissance."[16]

The distinguished roster of contributors to Nobel's Festschrift included Buber, Kracauer, Ernst Simon, Rudolf Hallo, Richard Koch, Eduard Strauss, Eugen Mayer, Max Michael, Joseph Prager, Bruno Strauss, Robert Weiss, and Leo Lowenthal. Lowenthal's contribution had originally been prepared for a seminar at the University of Heidelberg in 1920 directed by no less a figure than Karl Jaspers, who was then known as a psychologist more than a philosopher. Contemptuous of what he saw as Jaspers's "scientistic positivism," Lowenthal audaciously directed his fire at the chapter on the demonic in Jaspers's recently published book *The Psychology of Worldviews* (1919), which he saw as "the devil incarnate." Preferring Goethe's understanding of the demonic as a link between the poet's genius and the divine, he disdained the reductionism he saw in Jaspers's account.[17] As Lowenthal recalled years later, "At that time, I was in a mystical, radical, syncretic mood, a mixture of revolutionary radicalism, Jewish messianism, infatuation with an ontologically conceived phenomenology, acquaintance with psychoanalysis. . . . All of this was blended together to form a very missionary-messianic Bloch-like rapturous philosophy."[18] As might be expected, Ernst Bloch, whose recently published *Spirit of Utopia* had been a major influence on the young Lowenthal, later admired the essay, but Jaspers was less tolerant, indeed as Lowenthal remembered it, he was "furious, even aggressive and insulting. He showed no pedagogical understanding for this young student who had just let these ideas pour out. After Jaspers's outburst, I stood up, bowed to my fellow students, and left the seminar room, slamming the door."[19]

Despite the qualms of Rosenzweig and Kracauer, "The Demonic: Draft of a Negative Philosophy of Religion" appeared in the Festschrift for Nobel.[20] It is clearly the work of a talented, ambitious, and overwrought young man, written in a florid style, syncretic in its adoption of arguments from many different sources, and typical of the early Expressionist years of the Weimar Republic. Even Edvard Munch's *The Scream* makes an appearance as an example of the "deep psychological secret of modern agony."[21] Like many other young Jews who were increasingly ambivalent about the mandarin ideology of *Bildung*, which had captivated assimilating German Jews for generations, Lowenthal looked for more radical solutions to the ills of modernity wherever he could find them.[22] In the words of Michael Löwy, who included Lowenthal in his admiring history of "Jewish libertarian thought in Central Europe," "The Demonic" "sketched the foundations of a negative theology that drew on Marx, Lukács, and Bloch to argue that we are living in a world without God and without redemption, a cold world handed over to despair, a space between paradise and the Messiah which seeks God without finding him."[23] Citing Kierkegaard and Bloch, who argue that the demonic must ultimately be overcome, the work concludes: "At the end lies the ruin of all demonology, for the bright messianic light signifies the principled negation and destruction of all that is tenebrous. And the useful role of the demonic as that which interrogates without remainder is over in a final, all-comprehensive '*unio mystica*' which finds its peace in God the Lord."[24] Many years later Lowenthal himself would look back on the essay with the skepticism of maturity, calling it sarcastically "an almost unreadable 'master work'" and admitting, "I barely understand a word of it now."[25] The exasperated Jaspers, it turns out, may have been right all along.

When it appeared in Nobel's Festschrift, Kracauer wrote a delicately phrased, ambivalent letter, in which he acknowledged the personal depths out of which Lowenthal had composed the essay, admitting that he himself lacked the religious passion, "philosophical eros," and metaphysical urgency that he saw in the piece (and the work of other writers like Lukács). But he also criticized Lowenthal's undisciplined tone, which smacked too much of Bloch's histrionics.[26] Recalling a remark of Scheler's about Bloch, that his thought was "a running amok to God" (*Amoklauf zu Gott*), Kracauer said the characterization fit the piece as well. Reacting to Lowenthal's world-negating theological stance, he told his young friend: "Frankly, I *don't believe in the messianic time* (the 'fulfilled time' of Lukács means something different). I don't believe in *this* God, and when only *this* desperado attitude is religious, then am I an entirely unreligious man and will remain so."[27]

Although there remain echoes of his apocalyptic inclinations in the dissertation he wrote in 1923 on the Catholic mystic Franz von Baader,[28] Lowenthal seems to have been sobered by his friend's critique, whose sentiments Kracauer more or less repeated even more vehemently a few years later in a letter following a reading of Rosenzweig's *Star of Redemption*.[29] Kracauer's disdain for what he saw as religious *Schwärmerei* [rapturous effusion] anticipated the more public break with other members of the Nobel circle he announced in a spirited attack in 1926 in the *Frankfurter Zeitung* on the initial volume of the translation of the Hebrew Bible by Buber and Rosenzweig.[30] But whereas Kracauer rarely again returned to Jewish themes—and when he did so, as in his 1937 biography of Jacques Offenbach, it was in banal terms that dismayed friends like Adorno and Benjamin[31]—Lowenthal continued to be actively involved in Jewish culture for the better part of the decade.

Serving on the Advisory Board for Jewish Refugees (Beratungstelle für Ostjüdische Flüchtlinge) and frequently lecturing to audiences at Jewish adult education centers, Lowenthal also wrote for community newspapers such as the *Bayerische Israelitische Gemeindezeitung*, along with Hannah Arendt and Gershom Scholem, and was co-editor with Ernst Simon of the *Jüdische Wochenzeitung*. But he grew progressively disaffected by the latter's unreflective support of Jewish settlements on Arab land in Palestine.[32] His allegiance to Zionism had in fact always been ambivalent. Although he joined a Zionist movement while a student in Heidelberg, he had reassured his parents in 1920: "I am not—perhaps still not—a Zionist. I am a searcher [*Suchender*], a problematic man. I will never be satisfied with a formula."[33] Yet he found other ways to affirm his Jewish identity. For example, Lowenthal remained an active member of the psychoanalytic circle around Frieda Reichmann, to whom he had been introduced by his wife Golde and introduced in turn to Erich Fromm, her future husband. She was an observant Jew, as well as a Zionist, whose practice was sometimes called "Torahpeutic." Her sanatorium in Heidelberg, Lowenthal remembered, "was a kind of Jewish-psychoanalytic boarding school and hotel. An almost cultlike atmosphere prevailed there. Everyone, including me, was psychoanalyzed by Frieda Reichmann. The sanatorium adhered to Jewish religious laws; the meals were kosher, and religious holidays were observed. The Judeo-religious atmosphere intermingled with the interest in psychoanalysis." And then he significantly added, "Somehow, in my recollection I sometimes link this syncretic coupling of the Jewish and the psychoanalytic traditions with our later 'marriage' of Marxist theory and psychoanalysis at the Institute, which was to play such a great role in my intellectual life."[34]

Before, however, turning to the meaning of that parallel, it is necessary to attend to another aspect of Lowenthal's continued involvement with Jewish issues in the 1920s, the series of lectures he composed on a number of eminent German Jewish thinkers and intended to turn into a book called *Judaism and Jewishness in Recent German Philosophy*.[35] As early as 1922 in an essay he wrote jointly with Ernst Simon, Erich Fromm, Fritz Goethin, and Erich Michaelis, he had bemoaned the anti-intellectual celebration of Hasidism espoused by naïve followers of Martin Buber, who knew nothing of the deeper intellectual resources in the German Jewish tradition.[36] In a series of talks, given at the Frankfurt Lehrhaus and other Jewish venues in western Germany, Lowenthal explored the contributions of a number of major European intellectuals with Jewish backgrounds, from Maimonides, Moses Mendelssohn, Salomon Maimon, and Heinrich Heine to Karl Marx, Ferdinand Lassalle, Hermann Cohen, and Sigmund Freud.[37] Lowenthal was careful to include figures who were both identified and not identified with specifically Jewish themes, figures from Western Germany alongside of those who had Eastern origins (the latter having to be understood more in terms of their biographical struggles than the former), and those struggling with emancipation into bourgeois society as well as those struggling to escape from it.

The first thing that strikes the contemporary reader of these talks is the depth of Lowenthal's mastery of the work and lives of a very wide range of difficult thinkers. These do not seem the tentative exercises of a beginner still in his mid-twenties, but rather very much the reflections of someone who has been immersed in the material over a long career. Deftly interweaving intellectual and personal elements into the stories he tells, Lowenthal explores the challenges facing Jews moving from traditional identities into the modern world, bourgeois, secular, and assimilated, but without leaving behind the still potent legacy of their religious heritage. He probes the attempts from Maimonides to Cohen to reconcile Judaism and rationality, the dialectic in Judaism between obedience to the law and vital experience, and the tension between national assertion and universal ideals.

Perhaps Lowenthal's most vivid portrait is of Heine, which begins with the blunt question "Why did Heine become a Christian?" Tacitly resonating with the reason for Heine's disillusionment, he argues that the poet was deeply alienated from the watered-down Reform Judaism in the Germany of his day, which had left behind its creative period in the time of Mendelssohn and turned into a veiled version of Christianity, the pseudo-faith of what he called the "Sunday Jews."[38] Rather than returning to an earlier version of Judaism, which he mistakenly identified with dogmatic fanaticism and wan legalism, he chose baptism, but not only, as his famous explanation had it, as an entry ticket to European culture. By adopting Christianity, Heine, as Lowenthal described him, was really struggling to realize the redemptive mission of Judaism, understood in universal terms. "Heine had submitted to Christianity in order to be able to destroy it in a messianic rage. . . . To Heine European culture means the Europe of the French Revolution, it means the possibility of a joyful, free and full life. . . . It is a horrible historical irony that this specifically Jewish side of Heine, this love for a worthy life of free persons, is what drove him out of Judaism."[39] Judaism, especially in its prophetic tradition, was thus the source of a more universal impulse that survived Heine's self-exile from a version of it that failed to realize its most ambitious goals.

Something similar informed Lowenthal's reading of Marx. The disturbing expression of anti-Semitism in Marx's notorious essay "On the Jewish Question," whose odiousness Lowenthal does not try to deny, is attributed to Marx's "profound ignorance of Jewish cultural values." But he then adds, "There remains in spite of it all, the twofold nature of his claim—on the one hand, the protest against the fact that Judaism can be the symbol of capitalism; on the other, the Jewish-universalist manner in which the protest is carried out."[40] Likewise, in the final essay of the series, which dealt with Sigmund Freud a few weeks after he received Frankfurt's Goethe Prize, an honor Lowenthal had done much to assure, he squeezed out of Freud's Jewish background a very general lesson: "If we want to speak of Freud's relation to Judaism . . . we must direct our attention to those qualities he displays in the whole of life. . . . Help and reconstruction for individuals and for society as a whole—that is the star that illumines Freud's life and work."[41]

By the time of that final essay in the series, Lowenthal's overtly Jewish commitments had palpably waned. Perhaps he had absorbed some of Kracauer's sourness about the enthusiasms of his youth; perhaps he was reflecting the general turn in Weimar culture against the apocalyptic messianism of the early Expressionist years; perhaps he was over his rebellion against his parents and their values. Whatever the cause, he had already joined the third of the outsider intellectual communities—the first two being Nobel's circle and the psychoanalytic group around Fromm-Reichmann—that would become a more permanent resting place for his contrarian and utopian strivings: the Institute for Social Research. He had been introduced to Max Horkheimer by his school-time friend Felix Weil, whose wealthy father's generosity had financed the institute's founding in 1924. Horkheimer had himself never been in the thrall of Rabbi Nobel, remembering many years later that "I must say emphatically that I did not belong to that circle, I did not know the Rabbi, I had never seen him. . . . I didn't belong already for the reason that this Rabbi was the complete opposite of liberal Judaism, he represented conservative Judaism."[42] Adorno, three years younger than Lowenthal and also a protégé of Kracauer, had even less use for Nobel and his circle, although he may have found some indirect inspiration in Rosenzweig's ideas as conveyed by Benjamin and Scholem.[43] Only half-Jewish in origin—his mother was from a Catholic background—and raised by a fully assimilated father who displayed a "somewhat ostentatious aversion to everything that was consciously Jewish,"[44] Adorno was never drawn to the *Ostjuden* or had much respect for their champions like Martin Buber. Nor did he ever consider, let alone try to realize, a return to Orthodox practice as a rebuke to his parents (in fact, he never really rebelled against his parents at all).[45] Lowenthal and Fromm, he dismissively remarked to Horkheimer, were "professional Jews."[46] As his influence in the institute grew and Fromm's diminished, the palpable residues of Jewish themes were attenuated.

Assessments of the Frankfurt School's debts, often reluctantly acknowledged, to Jewish sources, have been attempted a number of times.[47] Although it is clear that anti-Semitism became a focal point of their work, especially in the wake of the Holocaust, they often tended to subsume specifically Jewish themes and issues under larger rubrics.[48] The most egregious example of this approach was Horkheimer's 1939 essay "The Jews and Europe," which occasioned a violent condemnation by Scholem in the last letter he ever sent to Benjamin before the latter's suicide.[49] Despite its title, the essay virtually ignored Jewish issues and concentrated on the relationship between fascism and capitalism.

Lowenthal was, however, a partial exception to this rule. He seems, for example, to have remained convinced that Heine's Jewish identity was central to his cosmopolitan redemptive project. In 1947, he published a translation of his Weimar essay in *Commentary*, the major organ of the liberal Jewish intelligentsia in America, then edited by Elliot Cohen.[50] In his recent account of the institute's American years, Thomas Wheatland focuses on the role of this essay in cementing relations between Horkheimer's circle and the New York intellectuals of that era. It was, he writes, "a powerfully crafted example of the kind of Jewish exploration that Cohen and the rest of the editorial board of *Commentary* were encouraging. The figure of Heinrich Heine functioned for Lowenthal as a symbol for the problems faced by the entire New York intellectual community and by many German-Jewish exiles as well."[51] Rather than being a way station to full conversion or assimilation and the loss of any residual Jewish identification, Heine's journey ended with his disillusionment with Christianity and was best understood as a cautionary tale. "Thus through Heine," Wheatland concludes, "was Lowenthal able to discover a distinctly Jewish identity consistent with Critical Theory and the prewar political impulses that gathered the Horkheimer circle together. . . . In the wake of the war, Heine stood as a symbol—perhaps all Jewish exiles could return home."[52]

But when other members of the school turned their attention to figures like Heine after the Holocaust, they did not adopt Lowenthal's earlier focus on his Jewish roots. Thus, for example, Adorno's powerful talk for the Heine centenary in 1956, "Heine the Wound," refers to them only obliquely and not as a legacy worth preserving.[53] Heine's romantic lyric poetry, he argues, was ultimately a failure, because it could not really attain the fluency in the German language it sought.[54] As such, it was an expression of the failure of Jewish emancipation, which now has become emblematic of a more general human condition of homelessness. "There is no longer any homeland other than a world in which no one would be cast out any more, the world of a genuinely emancipated humanity. The wound that is Heine will heal only in a society that has achieved reconciliation."[55] Here the conclusion drawn by Adorno was diametrically opposed to the more optimistic lesson that, if Wheatland is right, was implied in Lowenthal's piece.

In Jürgen Habermas's 1986 essay "Heinrich Heine and the Role of the Intellectual in Germany," even less attention is paid to his Jewish background, as Heine is portrayed as a critical Enlightenment "intellectual"—a word with negative connotations in Germany—who was marginalized by the mandarin *Geistigen* who dominated German letters until after World War II.[56] It is Heine the hedonist, the democrat, the politically engaged thinker who nonetheless defended artistic autonomy, rather than Heine the self-questioning Jew, who is at the center of Habermas's analysis. Although noting in passing that "the hatred that battered Heine as a Jew and an intellectual all his life made him well aware of the double-edged nature"[57] of German nationalism, Habermas ignored any positive legacy that Heine might have taken from the Jewish tradition.

Lowenthal himself, it has to be admitted, for a long time after the publication of his essay in *Commentary* was inclined to do the same. Perhaps because the ethnic identities of institute members had so often been evoked by its enemies, he and his colleagues were reluctant to give them ammunition for the slurs.[58] Although sharing the Frankfurt School's frequent identification of the Jewish taboo on picturing God with their own reluctance to spell out what utopia might look like, he distanced himself from what he dismissively called the later Horkheimer's adoption of "concrete religious symbolism."[59] Only in the interviews he gave near the end of his life did he acknowledge that he had underestimated the importance of Jewish motifs in his work and those of his colleagues at the institute:[60]

> I do believe that a Jewish element, if you want to call it that, was alive in most of us, consciously or unconsciously, in the sense of "it is yet to come," that is, of hope, of the unspeakable, which cannot be named but only sensed, which can only be negatively determined. And that I want to acknowledge even today, for it does unite in a certain way, the hope, now seriously compromised, for a life of dignity for every person with the thought that that will probably not happen and that a tragic element is bound irrevocably to our life.[61]

But if one can say that Lowenthal's Jewish impulses—and those of Fromm, Benjamin, and in a more attenuated way, most of his other institute colleagues—found their way into Critical Theory, what about his contribution to the Weimar Jewish Renaissance itself? In many ways his participation was typical of his generation, rebelling against parental authority and conventional mandarin academic life, looking for a new community of belief, often led by a charismatic leader.[62] Although some of the other young Jews who came of age during or after World War I and were swept up in the apocalyptic mood of those years remained more or less in its thrall, Lowenthal moved quickly on. His Zionism, such as it was, was already a thing of the past by 1925, and he never contemplated migration to Palestine. Nor did his writing retain any marks of the Expressionist rapture that had entranced Bloch—and appalled Kracauer—in his early essay "The Demonic." The inspiration for his personal attempt to live an orthodox life did not long survive the death of Rabbi Nobel, and by the mid-twenties he had cast his lot with the materialists around Horkheimer at the institute.[63]

In retrospect, Lowenthal's trajectory looks as if it moved him past the Jewish Renaissance and back into another version of the universalist assimilationism, albeit no longer of the liberal variety, that he had spurned in his father's generation. But if we take a more capacious view of the ways in which Jewish life renewed itself during that era, perhaps another conclusion might suggest itself. To reach it, let me return to the expressions of sorrow greeting Rabbi Nobel's sudden death by Lowenthal and Franz Rosenzweig, both of which evidenced the profound loss they felt. Significantly, however, only a short while after the rabbi's death, Rosenzweig presented a far more nuanced picture to his friend Joseph Prager:

> You evidently don't know how I stood with Nobel. More particularly, you are unaware of the negative side of our relationship. I respected only the Talmudic Jew, not the humanist, only the poet, not the scholar, only the prophet, not the philosopher. I rejected the qualities I did reject because, in the form in which he had them, they were deeply un-Jewish. At least this is what I always felt. All my veneration and love never blinded me to this toying with Christian and pagan ideas. True, it couldn't do me any harm, since I am armored against this kind of temptation as perhaps no Jew in *galut* [exile] has been before me. But in the effect he had on others I was always aware of the poison mixed with the medicine. . . . Had I met him sooner, say ten years ago, he might *possibly* have driven me away from Judaism, more likely he would have completely ruined me.[64]

And then he added, with a touch of arrogance, "What I have learned from Nobel is that the soul of a *great* Jew can accommodate many things. There is danger only for the little souls."[65]

From Rosenzweig's perspective, Lowenthal's later development away from his Jewish commitments would seem to corroborate this fear. Nobel's inspiration in his case did allow for an openness to the broader currents of German thought, if still intermingled with residues of the Jewish. But whether or not this trajectory can be taken as evidence of a "little soul" is something else. Rosenzweig may have had a very exclusivist notion of what constituted unpolluted Jewish purity, but we need not follow his lead. As David Biale has recently shown in his masterly study of the tradition of Jewish secular thought, there has been a robust alternative to normative definitions of "authentic" Jewish identity, whether understood religiously or culturally.[66] Rather than niggling over the proper credentials for inclusion in a club of the righteous, it has opened its doors to a wide range of people whose debts to and identifications with the rich legacy of Jewish experience and textual reflections on it are not homogeneous. Ironically, even those figures like Lowenthal who did not tarry with the religious identities they once fashioned in rebellion against their assimilated parents must be accounted full-fledged participants in that narrative.

At the end of his study of the Weimar Jewish Renaissance, Michael Brenner turns to the towering figure of the Hebrew novelist and Nobel Prize laureate Schmuel Yosef Agnon. "In contrast to most German-Jewish authors," he writes, "Agnon abstained from both stigmatizing German-Jews as assimilated 'non-Jewish Jews' and idealizing 'authentic' East European Jews. . . . Agnon demonstrated his respect for the multifaceted achievements of German Jews."[67] The young Leo Lowenthal would not have agreed with this verdict, but as he matured and left behind—or more correctly, tempered—the apocalyptic intransigence and messianic yearnings of his early years, he would surely have come to recognize its wisdom. Indeed, only through his remarkable capacity to absorb impulses from many different sources, no matter their religious or cultural pedigree, did Lowenthal develop into the genuine Renaissance Man that those of us privileged to have known him remember so well.

NOTES

1. Lowenthal dropped the umlaut from his name when he emigrated to America in 1934, but it is retained in his German language publications. This essay will use the former spelling, except where references are made to German works.

2. Rachel Heuberger, "Die Entdeckung der jüdischen Wurzeln," in *Das Utopische soll Funken schlagen . . . zum hundertsten Geburtstag von Leo Löwenthal*, ed. Peter-Erwin Jansen (Frankfurt, 2000), 67. See also her informative essay "Leo Löwenthal und Erich Fromm: Die 'jüdischen' Juden der Frankfurter Schule," in *Die Frankfurter Schule und Frankfurt: Eine Rückkehr nach Deutschland*, ed. Monika Boll and Raphael Gross (Frankfurt, 2009). For a general account of Lowenthal's early period, see Alfons Söllner, "Der junge Leo Lowenthal: Vom neoorthodoxen Judentum zur aufgeklärten Geschichtsphilosophie," in *Gesellschaft—Gewalt—Vertrauen: Jan Philipp Reemtsma zum 60. Geburtstag*, ed. Ulrich Beilefeld, Heinze Bude, and Bernd Greiner (Hamburg, 2012). For a comparison of his Jewish experiences with those of his colleagues in the Frankfurt School, see Jack Jacobs, *The Frankfurt School, Jewish Lives and Antisemitism* (Cambridge, 2014). See also Doris Maja Krüger, "Leo Löwenthal und die jüdische Renaissance in der Weimarer Republik," in *Das Kulturerbe deutschsprachiger Juden: Eine Spurensuche in den Ursprungs-, Transit- und Emigrationsländern*, ed. Eike-Vera Kotowski (Berlin, 2015).

3. Siegfried Kracauer to Leo Lowenthal, January 24, 1922, Frankfurt, in *In steter Freundschaft: Briefwechsel*, ed. Peter-Erwin Jansen and Christian Schmidt (Hamburg, 2003), 35. An allusion to the legend, based in Talmudic dicta, that in every generation thirty-six (rather than Kracauer's thirty,

as here) righteous souls sustain the world. See Gershom Scholem, "The Tradition of the Thirty-Six Hidden Just Men," in *The Messianic Idea in Judaism* (New York, 1995).

4. Franz Rosenzweig to Martin Buber, January 25, 1922, Frankfurt, in *The Letters of Martin Buber*, ed. Nahum N. Glatzer and Paul Mendes-Flohr, trans. Richard Winston, Clara Winston, and Harry Zohn (New York, 1991), 257. See also his memorial essay, "Der Denker: Nachruf auf A.N. Nobel," in *Der Mensch und sein Werk: Gesammelte Schriften, III: Zweistromland* (The Hague, 1984).

5. See Rachel Heuberger, "Orthodox versus Reform: The Case of Rabbi Nehemiah Anton Nobel of Frankfurt a. Main," in *Leo Baeck Yearbook*, 37 (London, 1992). She has expanded her discussion in *Rabbiner Nehemiah Anton Nobel: Die jüdische Renaissance in Frankfurt am Main* (Frankfurt, 2005).

6. Rosenzweig to Gertrud Oppenheim, October 5, 1921, in Nahum N. Glatzer, *Franz Rosenzweig: His Life and Thought* (New York, 1961), 104.

7. The depth of their attachment is evident in two postcards Nobel sent to Lowenthal in 1921 in which the rabbi worries about his health, gives him permission not to fast on Yom Kippur, says he is praying for him, and mentions sending money to his doctor. See Nobel to Lowenthal, October 10, 1921, and October 17, 1921, in *Das Utopische soll Funken schlagen . . . Zum hundertsten Geburtstag von Leo Löwenthal*, ed. Peter-Erwin Jansen (Frankfurt, 2000). Speaking of his own father, Lowenthal remembered that "it was a terrible disappointment for him that his son, whom he, the father, the true scion of the enlightenment, had raised so 'progressively,' was now being pulled into the 'nonsensical,' 'obscure' and "deceitful' clutches of a positive religion." Leo Lowenthal, *An Unmastered Past: The Autobiographical Reflections of Leo Lowenthal*, ed. Martin Jay (Berkeley, 1987), 20. Significantly, his father Victor refused to go to his wedding in December 1923 to Golde Ginsburg because she came from Königsberg and was thus uncomfortably close to being an *Ostjude*. As he told a later interviewer, "My parents' home symbolized, so to speak, everything I didn't want—bad liberalism, bad enlightenment, and two-sided morality." "'We Never Expected Such Fame': A Conversation with Matthias Greffrath, 1979," in *Communication in Society*, vol. 4, *Critical Theory and Frankfurt Theorists*, ed. Helmut Dubiel, trans. Don Reneau et al. (New Brunswick, N.J., 1989), 240. He did, however, also come to appreciate the positive role his father had played in his development, telling Helmut Dubiel: "Even today I feel very indebted to my father. He was a typical representative of the educated German-Jewish middle class. I was encouraged to read Goethe, Schopenhauer, and Darwin. I was encouraged to go to concerts and to the theater, to prepare myself for operas and the like. Later my father was very dissatisfied with me because I pursued my university studies without a

definite goal, changing from one faculty to another. Quite frankly, I studied everything but medicine. That certainly has to do with the just-mentioned Oedipus complex." *Unmastered Past*, 43.

8. Löwenthal, "Rabbiner Dr. N. A. Nobel, verschieden am 24. Januar 1922," *Der jüdische Student: Zeitschrift des Kartells jüdischer Verbindungen* 19, no. 2 (1922): 87–88.

9. Lowenthal, *Unmastered Past*, 21. The subdued erotic side of the "cult" can be read between the lines in the contribution Siegfried Kracauer was to make to the Festschrift for Nobel, which was the second half of his long essay *Über die Freundschaft*, ed. Karsten Witte (Frankfurt, 1974).

10. See David Ellenson, *Rabbi Ezriel Hildeshiemer and the Creation of a Modern Jewish Orthodoxy* (Tuscaloosa, Ala., 1990).

11. See the discussion in Albert H. Friedlander, *Leo Baeck: Teacher of Theresienstadt* (New York, 1968), 36–37.

12. For brief accounts of its role, see Walter Laqueur, *A History of Zionism* (New York, 1978), 481–84. Michael Stanislawski, *Zionism and the Fin de Siècle: Cosmopolitanism and Nationalism from Nordau to Jabotinsky* (Berkeley, 2001), 164–67.

13. See Michael Löwy, *Redemption and Utopia: Jewish Libertarian Thought in Central Europe*, trans. Hope Heaney (Stanford, 1992); Anson Rabinbach, *In the Shadow of Catastrophe: German Intellectuals between Apocalypse and Enlightenment* (Berkeley, 1997); and Benjamin Lazier, *God Interrupted: Heresy and the European Imagination between the World Wars* (Princeton, 2008).

14. For Buber's development during these years, see Paul Mendes-Flohr, *From Mysticism to Dialogue: Martin Buber's Transformation of German Social Thought* (Detroit, 1981); for a discussion of Rosenzweig's attitude toward Cohen, see Peter Eli Gordon, *Rosenzweig and Heidegger: Between Judaism and German Philosophy* (Berkeley, 2003), chap. 1.

15. *Gabe Herrn Rabbiner Dr. Nobel zum 50. Geburtstag*, by Martin Buber et al., (Frankfurt, 1921).

16. The term had, in fact, been coined by Martin Buber as early as 1901—see his "Jüdische Renaissance," in *Ost und West* (1901)—but was only realized after the war. For a general discussion, see Michael Brenner, *The Renaissance of Jewish Culture in Weimar Germany* (New Haven, 1996). He writes of Nobel, "A new type of rabbi, like Nehemias Anton Nobel of Frankfurt and Joseph Carlebach of Hamburg, reached out to non-orthodox Jewish students and intellectuals. By their new approaches toward Jewish mysticism or by their modern pedagogical techniques, those leaders of Weimar Orthodox Jewry were indeed able to awaken new interest in Judaism—although not necessarily in Orthodoxy—on the fringes of Jewish society" (54).

17. For a discussion of Goethe's celebration of the demonic, see Angus

Nicholls, *Goethe's Concept of the Daemonic: After the Ancients* (Rochester, 2006). In contrast, according to Wolfgang L. Zucker, Jaspers "relates genius and the demonic to the dialectic of the self; but true to his Kantian rejection of all theology, he does not see the problem in religious terms. For him both genius and the demonic are existentially experienced in the lonely dialogue of the self with itself. Both can be objectified and therefore mythologized as angels and devils, but precisely such otherness of genius and demon leads into untruth and inauthenticity where the self loses itself. They are the dialectical explications of the wholeness of the self, experienced as guides of the soul (the Greeks would have said *psychopompoi)*, in the process of self-illumination. They certainly are not the same in Jaspers's analysis; genius leads into the light of reality and permanence, it wants order and rationality, and raises its warning voice whenever the soul is in danger of getting lost. In contrast, the demonic leads to the depths, into the darkness that threatens, where the light ends; it beckons with the total catastrophe of existence not only as an always present possibility but as a luring temptation." "The Demonic: From Aeschylus to Tillich," *Theology Today* 26, no. 1 (1969): 47.

18. Lowenthal, *Unmastered Past*, 49.

19. Ibid.

20. It can now be found in Leo Lowenthal, *Schriften*, vol. 5, *Philosophische Frühschriften*, ed. Helmut Dubiel (Frankfurt, 1987), and in English translation in *The Frankfurt School on Religion: Key Writings of the Major Thinkers*, ed. Eduardo Mendieta (New York, 2005).

21. Lowenthal, "Demonic," 107. In *Unmastered Past* (49), Lowenthal alludes to suicide notes he had composed in 1920, an indication of his fragile and vulnerable state of mind when he composed this essay.

22. For an account of the fascination of German Jews for *Bildung*, see David Sorkin, *The Transformation of German Jewry, 1780–1840* (New York, 1987), and George Mosse, *German Jews beyond Judaism* (Bloomington, 1985); for a discussion of their disillusionment, see Steven E. Aschheim, "German Jews beyond *Bildung* and Liberalism: The Radical Jewish Revival in the Weimar Republic," in *Culture and Catastrophe: German and Jewish Confrontations with National Socialism and Other Crises* (New York, 1996).

23. Michael Löwy, *Redemption and Utopia: Jewish Libertarian Thought in Central Europe: A Study in Elective Affinity*, trans. Hope Heany (Stanford, 1992), 70. For more on this theme, see Micha Brumlik, "Messianic Thinking in the Jewish Intelligentsia of the Twenties," in *Wissenschaft vom Menschen / Sciences of Man*, vol., 2, *Erich Fromm und die Kritische Theorie* (Hamburg, 1991).

24. Lowenthal, "Demonic," 112.

25. Lowenthal, "Recollections of Adorno," in *Unmastered Past*, 204.

26. Kracauer's disdain for Bloch was made public in the review he wrote in the *Frankfurter Zeitung* on August 27, 1922, of *Thomas Müntzer als Theologe der Revolution*, which Bloch tried to rebut in *Durch die Wüste* (Berlin, 1923).

27. Kracauer to Lowenthal, December 4, 1921, in *In steter Freundschaft*, 31–32. For a discussion of Kracauer's more ambivalent attitude toward Nobel and the Frankfurt Lehrhaus, see Enzo Traverso, *Siegfried Kracauer: Itinéraire d'un intellectual nomade* (Paris, 1994), chap. 2. For a consideration of his complicated relationship with Rosenzweig in particular, see Matthew Handelman, "The Forgotten Conversation: Five Letters from Franz Rosenzweig to Siegfried Kracauer," *Scientia Poetica* 15 (2011).

28. Leo Löwenthal, "Die Sozietätsphilosophie Franz von Baaders: Beispiel und Problem einer religösen Philosophie" (PhD diss., University of Frankfurt, 1923). Sections were ultimately published in 1966 and 1967 in the *Internationales Jarhbuch für Religionsoziologie*. Lowenthal reports that Kracauer and Adorno mocked him for his interest in Baader and the expressionist style in which he wrote about him. See *Unmastered Past*, 207. It may be worth recalling that Baader had been very interested in the work of the earlier Christian mystic Jakob Boehme, about whom, along with Nicholas Cusa, Martin Buber wrote in his dissertation. Clearly, Jewish thinkers who were seeking to overturn conventional wisdom could find inspiration in heterodox Christian sources. For a discussion of Lowenthal's dissertation, see Söllner, "Der junge Leo Lowenthal," 311–17.

29. Kracauer to Lowenthal, August 31, 1922, in *In steter Freundschaft*, 46, where he calls the book "rubbish [*ein Schmarren*]. . . . I despise this type of philosophy which makes a system out of a hymn, and for the sake of this system concocts the craziest constructions (for example Rosenzweig's distinction between Judaism and Christianity) and blathers in tones of wonder about Creation, Revelation and Salvation, which would arouse the pity of a dog. Rosenzweig is and remains an Idealist, if not an over-Idealist, from which even his [Jewish Star] won't save him—just as I don't believe that his book will have great success in the future, in spite of Scholem and his brother Benjamin." As late, however, as 1924, it seems that Lowenthal was still considering a sequel to "The Demonic," in a project on "Religion and Magic," which was never realized. Kracauer wrote him a cautiously supportive response to the project statement, although commenting that it was too grandiose ever to be realized. See his letter of November 2, 1924, in *In steter Freundschaft*, 63.

30. Siegfried Kracauer, "The Bible in German," in *The Mass Ornament: Weimar Essays*, trans. and ed. Thomas Y. Levin (Cambridge, Mass., 1995). The dispute over the translation is discussed in Martin Jay, "Politics of Translation: Siegfried Kracauer and Walter Benjamin on the Buber-Rosenzweig Bible," in *Permanent Exiles: Essays on the Intellectual Migration from German*

to America (New York, 1985); Lawrence Rosenwald, "On the Reception of the Buber-Rosenzweig Bible," *Prooftexts* 14, no. 2 (1994); Klaus Reichert, "'It Is Time': The Buber-Rosenzweig Bible Translation in Context," in *The Translatability of Cultures*, ed. Sanford Budnick and Wolfgang Iser (Stanford, 1996); Leora Batnitzky, *Idolatry and Representation* (Princeton, 2000); Peter Eli Gordon, "Translation and Ontology: Rosenzweig, Heidegger, and the Anxiety of Affiliation," *New German Critique*, no. 77; Brian Britt, "Romantic Roots of the Debate on the Buber-Rosenzweig Bible," *Prooftexts* 20, no. 3 (2000).

31. Affirming Adorno's dismissive appraisal of Kracauer's *Jacques Offenbach und das Paris seiner Zeit* (Amsterdam, 1937), Benjamin wrote that the latter's apologetic inclinations are "especially flagrant in those passages which touch upon Offenbach's Jewish origins. For Kracauer, the Jewish element remains rooted in origins. He doesn't even dream of recognizing it in the work itself." Benjamin to Adorno, May 9, 1937, in Theodor Adorno and Walter Benjamin, *The Complete Correspondence, 1928–1940*, ed. Henri Lonitz, trans. Nicholas Walter (Cambridge, Mass., 1999), 186.

32. The public break came in an essay, written under the pseudonym "Hereticus," called "Die Lehren von Chinas," *Jüdisches Wochenblatt* 2, no. 25 (1925), in which he compared the events in China of his day, in which Westerners were buying up lands from rich landowners, with those in Palestine; in both cases, he predicted a rebellion of dispossessed peasants.

33. Lowenthal to his parents, June 17, 1920, in *Das Utopische soll Funken schlagen . . .*, ed. Jansen, 38. As Aschheim has noted, "The young Loewenthal's Zionism had little to do with Palestine. It was rather, as he wrote to Ernst Simon, a mode of consciousness, the most appropriate way the Jews could realize Bloch's *Spirit of Utopia*." "German Jews beyond *Bildung* and Liberalism: The Radical Jewish Revival in the Weimar Republic," 37.

34. Lowenthal, *Unmastered Past*, 26. In his memoir, *From Berlin to Jerusalem: Memories of My Youth*, trans. Harry Zohn (New York, 1980), Gershom Scholem had a somewhat more sour recollection: "Some of my best students and acquaintances from Zionist youth groups, such as Simon, Fromm and Leo Löwenthal, visited the sanatorium on an outpatient basis. With the exception of one person they all had their Orthodox Judaism analyzed away" (156).

35. Ibid., 112. The project was supported by Buber and Rosenzweig, but failed to get backing from the Moses Mendelssohn Foundation, possibly, Lowenthal conjectured, because of opposition from Leo Strauss.

36. Erich Fromm, Fritz Goethin, Leo Löwenthal, Ernst Simon, and Erich Michaelis, "Ein prinzipielles Wort zur Erziehungsfrage," *Jüdische Rundschau* 27, no. 102–3 (1922).

37. Lowenthal, "German Jewish Intellectual Culture: Essays from the 1920's," in *Communication in Society*, vol. 4. The 1925 essay on Maimonides, who of course was not German in origin, is not included in this selection, but can be fund in Jansen, ed, *Das Utopische soll Funken schlagen . . .*"

38. Lowenthal, "German Jewish Intellectual Culture," 18.

39. Ibid., 17.

40. Ibid., 34. The positive reference to "Jewish-universalist" values suggests the abiding importance of Hermann Cohen's neo-Kantianism for Lowenthal, which is emphasized in Söllner, "Der junge Leo Lowenthal."

41. Ibid., 45.

42. Cited from interviews given to Ernst von Schenk in John Abromeit, *Max Horkheimer and the Foundations of the Frankfurt School* (Cambridge, 2011), 64.

43. Susan Buck-Morss, *The Origin of Negative Dialectics: Theodor W. Adorno, Walter Benjamin, and the Frankfurt Institute* (New York, 1977), 5–7.

44. Stefan Müller-Doohm, *Adorno: A Biography*, trans. Rodney Livingstone (Malden, Mass., 2005), 19.

45. See the remarkably intimate and affectionate correspondence in Theodor W. Adorno, *Letters to His Parents, 1939–1951*, ed. Christoph Gödde and Henri Lonitz, trans. Wieland Hoban (Malden, Mass., 2003).

46. Cited in Müller-Doohm, *Adorno*, 20.

47. See, for example, the essays in the section "Frankfurter Schule und Judentum," in *Die Frankfurter Schule und Frankfurt*. ed. Boll and Gross; and Margarete Kohlenbach and Raymond Geuss, eds., *The Early Frankfurt School and Religion* (New York, 2005).

48. For a consideration of their work on anti-Semitism, see Lars Rensmann, *Kritische Theorie über Antisemitismus: Studien zu Struktur, Erklärungspotential und Aktualität* (Berlin, 1998).

49. Max Horkheimer, "Die Juden und Europa," *Zeitschrift für Sozialforschung* 8, no. 1/2 (1939). See Scholem to Benjamin, February [?], 1940, in *The Correspondence of Walter Benjamin and Gershom Scholem*, ed. Gershom Scholem, trans. Gary Smith and Andre Lefebvre (New York, 1989). For a more sympathetic reading, see Dan Diner, "Reason and the 'Other': Horkheimer's Reflections on Anti-Semitism and Mass Annihilation," in *On Max Horkheimer*, ed. Seyla Benhabib, Wolfgang BonÐand John McCole (Cambridge, Mass., 1993).

50. Leo Lowenthal, "Heine's Religion: The Messianic Idea of the Poet," *Commentary* 4, no. 2 (1947). *Commentary*, under the later editorship of Norman Podhoretz, would become a forum for neoconservative ideas, but in the years the institute was in New York, its outlook was more progressive.

51. Thomas Wheatland, *The Frankfurt School in Exile* (Minneapolis, 2009), 157.

52. Ibid., 158.

53. Theodor W. Adorno, "Heine the Wound," *Notes to Literature*, 2 vols., ed. Rolf Tiedemann, trans. Shierry Weber Nicholsen, vol. 1 (New York, 1991).

54. In his infamous antisemitic polemic *Judaism in Music*, Richard Wagner had also decried what he saw as the failure of Heine's German—its being built on a lie—but for Adorno, it was precisely Heine's achievement to resist ideological wholeness and open a wound that had universal implications.

55. Ibid., 85.

56. Jürgen Habermas, "Heinrich Heine and the Role of the Intellectual in Germany," in *The New Conservatism: Cultural Criticism and the Historians' Debate*, ed. and trans. Shierry Weber Nicholsen (Cambridge, Mass., 1989). Habermas, to be sure, also wrote an essay titled "The German Idealism of the Jewish Philosophers," in 1981, in which he detailed the vital role of Jewish thinkers in modern German culture. See Habermas, *Religion and Rationality: Essays on Reason, God, and Modernity*, ed. Eduardo Mendieta (Cambridge, Mass., 2002).

57. Habermas, "Heinrich Heine and the Role of the Jewish Intellectual in Germany," 82.

58. That his anxiety was by no means unwarranted is demonstrated by the antisemitic motifs in the recent allegations of right-wing conspiracy theorists who blame "cultural Marxism" and "political correctness" on the institute. For a discussion, see Martin Jay, "Dialektik der Gegenaufklärung: Die Frankfurter Schule im Verschwörungnarrativ extremistischer Randgruppen," *Westend: Neue Zeitschrift für Sozialforschung* 8, no. 1 (2011).

59. Lowenthal, "Walter Benjamin: The Integrity of the Intellectual," in *Communication in Society*, vol. 4, *Critical Theory and Frankfurt Theorists*, 83.

60. In his 1979 interview with Helmut Dubiel, Lowenthal admitted (much to my delight): "However much I once tried to convince Martin Jay that there were no Jewish motifs among us at the Institute, now, years later and after mature consideration, I must admit to a certain influence of Jewish tradition, which was codeterminative." *Unmastered Past*, 112.

61. Lowenthal, "We Never Expected Such Fame," 240–41.

62. According to Michael Brenner, "Like groups of non-Jewish intellectuals (the most famous being that of Stefan George), the Jewish groups were organized around one dominant figure. They included the study group of the charismatic Rabbi Nehemias Anton Nobel in Frankfurt, the Talmud study circle of Salman Baruch Rabinkow in Heidelberg, the private kosher psychoanalytic clinic in Heidelberg where Frieda Reichmann cultivated both Torah

and Freudian analysis, the wartime Berlin Volksheim of Siegfried Lehmann, and the Berlin group centered around an obscure scholar of Jewish mysticism, Oskar Goldberg." *The Renaissance of Jewish Culture in Weimar German*, 71. The pattern was, of course, not only followed by German Jews during a traumatic era in which patriarchal authority was challenged by the collapse of the Kaiserreich and the economic chaos of the postwar years. What the Austrian psychoanalyst Paul Federn called a "fatherless society" was experienced by many in central Europe during that era. See Paul Federn, *Zur Psychologie der Revolution: Die Vaterlose Gesellschaft* (Vienna, 1919).

63. It is important to acknowledge that from his adolescence, Lowenthal had been actively involved in socialist and pacifist causes, often involving political activity of one sort or another. See his account in *Unmastered Past*, 33–43.

64. Rosenzweig to Joseph Prager, end of January 1922, in *Franz Rosenzweig: His Life and Thought*, 106–7.

65. Ibid., 107.

66. David Biale, *Not in the Heavens: The Tradition of Secular Jewish Thought* (Princeton, 2011).

67. Brenner, *Renaissance of Jewish Culture in Weimar Germany*, 208.

CHAPTER 2

The Palestinian Nakba and the Arab-Jewish Melancholy: An Essay on Sovereignty and Translation

Yehouda Shenhav

> A tank and a heavy bulldozer made their way into the village, and started plowing the soil, until they arrived at the mosque where the old imam was waiting. A man in his seventies—blind and hunchbacked—who spoke classical Arabic with noticeable eloquence. The soldiers broke into the mosque and ordered the imam to raise his hands and surrender. After a quick search, they asked him to leave the mosque. He refused. The officer approached the man and yelled at him with all his might, until the mosque's walls started to tremble. He then shot a bullet in the air, and thick dust dropped off the ceiling. The blind man grabbed the officer's arm, pushed it down, and spit on his face. The officer wiped off his face, and ordered the soldiers to serve him "dinner." They carried him out and left. The bulldozer started uprooting the mosque's ramparts. The old Sheikh disappeared after that "dinner." The village of Um al-Zinat was wiped off the surface of the earth. Only the olive tree remained deeply rooted in the soil, awaiting the return of its landlords. The burning sun scorched the olive tree's trunk, and the dew drops snuggled among its leaves. It was undeniable evidence of the renewal of life.
>
> —SALMAN NATOUR, *The Life and Death of the Wrinkled-Face Sheikh*

The tale of Um al-Zinat (and for that matter of al-Ramla, al-Majdal, al-Lud, al-Birwe, Ein Koud, Safuri, Mi'ar, Ein Ghazal, Jaba, Ajzam, al-Hdt'ha, Bir alsba, Askalan—approximately five hundred Palestinian towns and villages that were wiped out in 1948) is a story that Hebrew culture and Israeli historiography prefer to conceal and forget. Despite partial democratization of Israeli historiography in recent decades, the majority of Israelis still deny the Nakba and subscribe to anachronistic myths—perpetuated by politicians, military personnel, historians, and self-appointed citizens—such as the ostensibly voluntary exodus of the Palestinians.[1] For many years Israelis treated the stories of the Nakba as top secret, hiding them as skeletons in the closet. They have refused to look at their past courageously and continue to believe that they live in a free and open society.

But now, following the adoption of a reckless but useful piece of legislation known as the Nakba Law (March 2011)—which imposes sanctions on organizations that mention the Palestinian tragedy—almost every household in Israel has become acquainted with the Arabic word: al-Nakba. By banning, sanctioning, and erasing, the Israeli legislature succeeded in achieving the exact opposite. This may be a perfect example of Max Weber's "unexpected consequence of human action." An editorial in the daily *Ha'aretz*, which usually focuses only on the injustices of the occupation beyond the Green Line, turned its gaze "inward" to the question of 1948: "Stop rewriting history. Without recognizing the Palestinian Nakba it is impossible to understand the sources of the Israeli-Arab conflict." *Ha'aretz* reprimanded the Israeli government for its feverish efforts to eliminate and remove the history of the Nakba from Israeli textbooks.[2] This editorial is no trivial matter given the depth of denial, organized silencing, and taboo on opening the Pandora's Box of 1948.

It is hard to grapple with the drama that took place in Palestine three years after the end of World War II. The exile of 750,000 people from their homes, while in the background the image (even if not a mirror image) of Jews being deported from Europe. Frantic children, women, and men embarking on boats and ships at the seaports of Haifa, Acre, and Jaffa—leaving their belongings and families behind. It is now clear that expulsions and massacres took place all over Palestine, not only in Dir Yasin, al-Lod, and al-Tantura. The ethnic cleansing of Palestine included the abolition of hundreds of Palestinian towns and villages, some immediately repopulated by Jews (and sometimes even other Palestinians) to prevent return. Add to that the confiscation of lands, houses, and property by the state, and the looting of removable objects by Jewish citizens—without any shame or disgrace.

To be sure, the ethnic cleansing of Palestine did not begin or end in 1948. It started back in the 1920s, with an aggressive acquisition and takeover of lands that reached a peak in 1948 and again in 1967. The ethnic cleansing continues in the present day by other means: the silent transfer in Jerusalem; the settlements and the expropriation of land in the West Bank; the communal settlements in the Galilee for Jews only; the new Citizenship decree (which bans Palestinian citizens from bringing their Palestinian spouses into Israel, thanks to the emergency laws); the "unrecognized Palestinian villages" constantly under the threat of destruction; the incessant demolition of Bedouin houses in the south; the omission of Arabic on road signs; the prohibition on importing literature from Arab countries, and many others. One telling example is the fact that not one Arab town or village has been established in Israel since 1948.

The materialization of an exclusively Jewish territorial sovereignty over 80 percent of historical Palestine would not have been possible without the enduring ethnic cleansing of the space. Rather than a state of its citizens in which Jews make a home for themselves, the State of Israel acts as an apparatus of granting privileges to Jews who are willing and able to accept the definition of the Zionist identity that the state wishes to impose. The Zionist decision to pursue a mono-ethnic Jewish state that monopolizes and controls territorial sovereignty (as opposed to bi-national or shared models of sovereignty) was first made in 1942 at the Biltmore Conference in New York and was ratified in Europe in 1946.[3] It was based on the seventeenth-century Westphalian model, which was founded on a politico-theological perspective, and state of exception.[4]

State of exception was developed in Roman law, in revolutionary and modern France, in the Weimar Republic and the Nazi regime, in Switzerland, Italy, England, and the United States. A typical historical example of scholarly thinking in this tradition is provided by Benjamin Constant, who already at the beginning of the nineteenth century recognized the menace associated with exceptions to the law, which he identified as more dangerous than overt despotism.[5] Whereas in traditional political theology the exception was defined in relation to temporality, in the case of Israel we observe a spatial dimension of emergency, which does not necessitate an expiration date.[6] The state uses emergency measures against its non-Jewish inhabitants and hence the absurd request to condition citizenship on loyalty to the Jewish nation.

The Westphalian form of sovereignty and the ethnic cleansing of Palestine were in part the realization on the ground of the "negation of the exile" ideology, developed in European Zionism. This is rather ironic: Jews who had just fled totalitarian emergency regimes in Europe accepted the same colonial emergency model in the Middle East, in order to distinguish between homeland and exile, and ostensibly protect the rights of the Jews. Thus, the emancipation of the Jews and protection of their rights are secured by these emergency legislations. On paper, Israel can turn in no time into one big Guantanamo Bay detention camp. Israeli law is anomalous, as are the territories under its control. Emergency regulations in Israel define exceptions to the law (martial law, curfews, preventive arrests, administrative detainees, political prisoners) that work effectively under the auspices of the law.[7]

Since its inception, the State of Israel has never ceased using emergency regulations to rule the Palestinians. Until December 1966 Israeli Palestinians lived under martial law, whereby they needed permits to move from one village to another, let alone to visit the big city. Economic activity was curtailed, fear was at its height, and the state waged demographic and spatial wars against its own Palestinian citizens. The system was abolished in December 1966, only to be reestablished in June 1967 to rule the West Bank and Gaza and to allow for Jewish settlements there. Israel inherited those emergency regulations from the British Empire, and renewed them without setting an expiration date. These measures enable an exclusively Jewish state cleansed of Arabs: a European state for European Zionist Jews outside of Europe—by denying the national rights of Israeli Palestinians and ignoring its Arab surrounding. Because the Israeli state has been unable to grant any cultural legitimacy to Arab culture and language, for Jews or others, Arab Jews can be regarded as inferior (or even disloyal to the Zionist project) for relying on inherited strengths. This state of suspicion stands in contrast to the relative willingness of contemporary society to accept the rejection of much "Israeli identity" by many immigrants from the former Soviet Union. Although I believe that Jews are entitled to live freely in the Middle East, their current presence is based on colonial relations with the Palestinians. It is startling and amazing that there is hardly any political thought today on the legitimacy of the Jewish existence in the Middle East beyond and outside these colonial emergency regulations.[8]

The denial of the Arab surrounding is manifested in various forms, and in this essay I mainly focus on language. From inception, and despite close etymology, the modern Hebrew language missed the opportunity to develop a close relationship with Arabic. There is ample evidence that modern Hebrew was constructed in contradistinction to Arabic, raising obstacles to communication and reconciliation between the two languages.[9] To be sure, language and sovereignty are tightly coupled. Language maps the cultural territory of the sovereign and construes its sources of legitimation. The sovereign is the one who speaks, dominates the discourse, and is able to conceal its violent roots. For this reason language also offers the opportunity to identify the fissures and fractures of sovereignty. This is best mirrored in the act of translation. At the etymological level the Arabic language resonates well with Hebrew, much more so than with English. Yet the rivalry that developed in the course of the last century between Arabic and Hebrew resulted in substantial linguistic and cultural barriers to moving between them. For such barriers Paul Ricoeur coined the term "the untranslatable."[10] In this context, the "untranslatable" is also a symptom of sovereignty barriers between languages.[11] Referring to the rivalry between Hebrew and Arabic, the late Muhammad Hamza Ghanaim described translation between Arabic and Hebrew as sitting on a sizzling tin roof. Rivalry shapes translation between the languages that grew apart despite their close linguistic affinity. This shapes translation between the two languages.

The Nakba according to the Wrinkled-Face Sheikh

I borrowed the short tale on the old sheikh at the outset from Salman Natour's novel: *The Life and Death of the Wrinkled-Face Sheikh*, which I translated from Arabic. The wrinkled-face Sheikh is a storyteller. He lays out a string of short fragments that describe the Nakba and the ethnic cleansing of Palestine from the point of view of its victims. In the early 1980s Salman Natour interviewed dozens of Palestinians who became refugees in their own lands. At first they refused to talk. Although the military regime had ended, fear still resided in their hearts. But once they talked, no one could have stopped them; they expressed pain and laughter. Stories are dried, condensed, pendulous, and often in the form of stream of consciousness. One story follows another, tragedy after tragedy, a chain of convoluted accounts of the Palestinian catastrophe.

While translating, I was swept up in the accumulation of testimonies, the distant and remote authorial voice, and the porous boundaries between literature and history that expand and shrink away, like the porous boundaries between Hebrew and Arabic.

Toward the end of translation I asked Natour about footnotes. Would he be interested in adding footnotes for Hebrew readers on the location of sites, chronology, and timetables, or references to events documented in historiography? Natour objected: "This is a novel and not a history book." True, but this is literature written as history. And history written as literature. Or a literary revisionist version of history. As Natalia Ginsburg put it in the preface to her *Family Lexicon*: "All places, events and characters in this novel are real. I did not invent anything. . . . [Yet] even though it is based on reality, I think that one needs to read it as a novel, without requiring anything more than what a novel can offer."[12]

The Wrinkled-Face Sheikh is a novel based on dozens of testimonies and autobiographies written and told by the victims. These testimonies and documents are absent in official historiography. Why? First, because testimonies are inferior to archival documents in the writing of history, and the defeated hardly ever have documents. Second, these testimonies were offered and written in Arabic, rather than Hebrew or English. These Arabic sources are hardly known to Israeli historians of the Nakba (e.g., Benny Morris wrote his major works on the Palestinian exodus without reading Arabic). Third, testimonies were given and written as literature in the Arabic language. This kind of evidence belongs to the bottom of the historiographical food chain. In contrast, revisionist Israeli historians took seriously—at least as a starting point—literary prose written in Hebrew on the Nakba, such as that by S. Izhar, Haim Guri, and Yoram Kaniuk. In an anthology titled *Tell Not in Gat*, Hannan Hever compiled representations of the Nakba in Hebrew poetry. He recites, for example, the famous poem by Natan Alterman who in the *Seventh Column* refers to war crimes perpetrated by Israeli soldiers five months after the massacre at Lod. This and other poems compiled in the anthology demonstrate how strong is the power of "fictional" poetry, and how it sheds light on the violent history that historiography tends to conceal.[13]

Melancholy

It is well known that no translation reaches completion. The translator faces untranslatable texts and incommensurable meanings, which are finally adjudicated arbitrarily. As literature on translation shows, it never reaches a satisfactory stopping point. Every stopping point is artificial, such as when the translation is published, and the translator knows deep down that the work is incomplete.

The untranslatable has enormous implications for the relationship between (Arabic) source and (Hebrew) destination. Add to that the changing states (both linguistically and ideologically) of the two languages between the time of writing and the time of translation, and not least the identity gaps between the author and the translator. The untranslatable is known to appear in every translation, but given the ideological war between Hebrew and Arabic, the untranslatable space breeds, increases, and expands. The translator knows that he or she was not really true to the original. This is the main reason behind the guilt and sense of betrayal among translators. This is where I was first introduced to the translator's melancholy.

For the translation of the *Life and Death of the Wrinkled-Face Sheikh* engulfed me with a familiar feeling of loss and betrayal, as Hebrew and Arabic did not agree in all respects. But this time, it was accompanied with something else: an obsessive urge to write and rewrite the text. Thankfully, Salman Natour has excellent command of Hebrew, and when he read the translation he gently defied my interventions. In the absence of a different name,

I call it melancholy. First, because it was impossible to put a finger on the lost object. Second, because I could not get rid of it. I was completely engulfed with the stories, walking around with moist eyes, telling everybody, those who wanted and those who did not, about my staggering experience. Indeed melancholia is about nameless loss. Indeed? What did I lose?

At the basic level there was sadness, sympathy with the victims, and possibly the attempt to cope with my guilt feelings. All these are clearly understood: morality, humanity, human rights, and the rights of minorities. I also have political reasons: I believe that no reconciliation or peace can be reached without a return to the 1948 tragedy.[14] No Jew can escape such a return. There is also the issue of Jewish property in Arab countries, which served as justification to confiscate Palestinian property. This is a long story, but disturbing enough to infuse one with a sense of depression.[15]

Then Amnon Raz-Krakotzkin posed a question to me: You spend most of your time translating literature on the Palestinian Nakba, which is important. Did you ask yourself why? Why aren't you working, for example, on Jewish Baghdadi texts written in Arabic at the beginning of the last century? Where does your urge come from? Here's the rub. Back to the story.

This is a story about the ethnic cleansing of Palestine from the perspective of its Palestinian victims. Hebrew culture denies the story because it raises questions about the morality of the Jewish state. One way or another, the cleansing of space and the establishment of homogeneous sovereignty enabled the binary distinction between the Jewish homeland and Arab exile. If the Nakba bestowed upon the Zionist European Jews a homeland, at the same time it destroyed the Arab-Jewish option in language and space. Admittedly, Zionism rejected all exilic life, but the legacy and memories of exilic Arab-Jewish life impeded the political and symbolic establishment of the "Jewish homeland" in quite specific and acute ways.

The ethnic cleansing of Palestine entailed the elimination of the Jewish-Arabic space and the rejection of a Jewish-Arab option of hybrid life. Yet there is no recognition in Israeli discourse for this loss, even if utopian. Perhaps this was the source of my melancholy. The striving for recognition of the Arab Jews was behind the urge to rewrite the story, as well as this (somewhat personal) essay.

Homeland/Exile

As in other cases (e.g., religion and secularism), the relationship between exile and homeland is mediated by an east/west dichotomy. It cuts one meaning "here" in the Middle East and another "there" in the West. For the European Zionist Jew there is a binary tension between exile and homeland: Exile is in Europe, and homeland is in the Middle East.[16] Yet although for the Zionist European Jew the distinction is binary, for the Arab Jew it is a sequel of spatial, linguistic, religious, and cultural fragments. Raz-Krakotzkin defined it as "exile within sovereignty," as it was materialized in the major Jewish centers in Safed, Tiberius, and Hebron, blurring the artificial distinction between exile and homeland.[17] I respond now to my urge to rewrite the story of the wrinkled-face sheikh from an Arab-Jewish point of view.

Saleh Shahrabani, my paternal grandfather, was an Arab Jew. He was a merchant who sold Iraqi dates in Palestine during the 1930s and 1940s. He made the trip four times a year, traveling from Baghdad via Syria to Northern Palestine: Haifa, Nazareth, and then to Jaffa. In Palestine he felt at home. He met with other Jews and donated to synagogues and other religious causes. In Haifa he unloaded the truck, spent a few days in town while the truck was circling around the Galilee, and then rode south to Jaffa, where he uploaded boxes of Jaffa oranges and shipped them to Baghdad and its vicinities. Apart from agricultural produce, he managed a business renting chairs for weddings in Baghdad. My grandfather was dark, lean, modest, God-fearing, allured by the holy land and its sanctity. He is not well known since the Arab Jews and the Arab-Jewish option were edited out of the Zionist lexicon. He was an ardent Jew who did not participate in any Zionist enterprise.

Saleh Shahrabani traveled throughout the Arab-Jewish space. He spoke Arabic there/here as it was common here/there. Each time he came to Palestine he stopped and met with the old sheikh under the olive tree in Um al-Zinat located on the way from Haifa to Jaffa. He even did business with people in the village. According to family stories he met the sheikh in March 1934 in the office building of Arab Agriculture Ltd. to sign an agreement for cooperation. Not between the Jew and the Arab, but between Palestine and Baghdad.

> He right away identified the place which lay on the western side of the entangled road that linked Ein Khoud with Ein Ghazal. All three sites were inscribed with dashed lines and black spots on the map of Palestine. Palestine of those days. When the buildings in Almaluk Street were owned by the Tbrawi family. When the building that now houses the police headquarters used to be the office building of Arab Agriculture Ltd., which was bordered on one side with Yafa Street and with the intersection of al-Salam Street on the other side.[18]

Saleh Shahrabani spoke the tongue of the old sheikh and loved his Arabic literary enunciation. The sheikh, for his part, liked the heavy Iraqi accent emanating from my grandfather's throat, and especially the deep guttural "Q" which was the custom in the desert. Once on the staircase, leaving the office building and led by his young assistant, the old sheikh turned to Saleh Shahrabani:

> A young guy from Um al-Zinat is heading to Baghdad to study engineering. Can he get a ride with you? Is it possible to get him a part-time job in your business in Baghdad? That would sustain him during the school year. He occasionally could come with you in your trips to Palestine, to visit his family. You'll love him. He is industrious and pious like you.

The Jewish merchant from Baghdad promised to take care of the young Palestinian student.

There is no doubt that Saleh Shahrabani yearned for Eretz Israel. This was the main reason he visited regularly in Palestine. In 1936, he even immigrated with his family to Palestine, but after nine months they returned to Baghdad. Is Baghdad homeland or exile? Is Palestine homeland or exile? I am doubtful whether these concepts were part of my grandfather's vocabulary. But when he thought about the space, he certainly did not envision a monopolistic territorial sovereignty with sealed borders. He certainly did not think about living in a Jewish ghetto with closed fences and barriers. He envisioned an open space where he did not have to choose between here/there there/here. A space that does not require the denial of the Arab surrounding. This was the option that allowed Saleh Shahrabani to visit Palestine, to immigrate to Palestine, to emigrate from Palestine, and to revisit time and again—as a never-ending multidirectional journey. As is the case with translation.

But Palestine was cleansed of Arabs and the Arabic language, and although Saleh Shahrabani lived in Israel at the end of his life, when he already had dozens of grandchildren, he felt like a stranger in the Jewish city, just like the wrinkled-face sheikh:

> A staircase dressed with chiseled stones separates Haifa of today from Haifa of yesterday. The past resides in downtown and the vibrant present takes place uptown. The sea retreated. The surrounding verdant mountains' peaks are growing balder, year after year. Haifa has turned pale, shrouded in the thick smoke of industry, and upset by the long cries of outgoing and incoming ships to the port. The Sheikh wakes up at sunrise and leaves home, wandering alone around the city's new

> streets: YL Peretz, The Prophets, Mendele the Bookseller, Father Abraham, Mother Sarah. Names and expressions that did not exist in the Arabic language. Even the soles of his shoes were barely accustomed to the city's new streets.[19]

Similar to the sheikh, Saleh Shahrabani woke up at sunrise and left home. He wandered alone in the streets and did not adapt to the new city. He encountered names and expressions whose meaning he did not understand. He sat down on a wooden bench and held in his fingers a white beaded string. After a short rest, he went to the town hall where none of the officials understood Arabic. He walked down to Wadi al-Nissnas, and found it empty and abandoned. He turned to Wadi al-Salib where he met David Ben Harush who spoke Moroccan Arabic. Finally, he headed to the Iraqi synagogue in the Hadar neighborhood, where everyone spoke Arabic with a deep accent.

Did I go too far with nostalgia? Certainly. First, my grandfather did not know the old sheikh. Second, the Arab-Jewish option is not without disagreements and conflicts. Is it possible that my grandfather left Palestine out of fear when the Arab Revolt started in 1936? There were enduring conflicts between Jews and Muslims, as there were between Sunnis and Shiites and between Druze and Christians. But nostalgia is not just popular folklore, however important. Nostalgia can turn into a cultural and political horizon. I believe that this is the only way available to Jews to settle in the region and even protect their rights. This is an option in which all Jews living in the region become Arab Jews.[20] It requires an alternative model of sovereignty.

Sovereignty is perhaps the only central concept in modern state theory that has not yet undergone serious deconstruction.[21] Sovereignty is a multifaceted phenomenon, heterogeneous and unstable in nature. It is always a perforated practice that contains ambiguous territorial and heterogeneous populations that cannot be integrated under the banner of one sovereignty. The Arab-Jewish option is not based on a monopolized or homogenized territory. It is founded on a pierced and porous space, without a sharp distinction between exile and homeland, at least not in the same manner as it is constructed in European Zionism. As Hannan Hever shows in his discussion of Hebrew literature, Jewish immigration from Arab countries was less ridden with utopian narratives as compared to Jewish immigration from Europe.[22] It is worth recalling the vocabulary of the Jewish Iraqi writer Shimon Balas, describing his account of the transition from Baghdad to Tel Aviv in 1950: "I never changed my native soil or homeland. I only moved from one place to another within the region. I am not in conflict with the Arab surrounding. I came from an Arab region, and remained in constant dialogue with it."[23]

Balas traveled in the region. Like my grandfather. Like my father. Like many Arab Jews. They have traveled on trucks, donkeys, or camels. Whatever was the routine movement from Baghdad to Palestine, and back. Saleh Shahrabani drove an old military truck from the leftovers of the British army. He traveled in a space where there was no sharp distinction between homeland and Diaspora. The Palestinian Nakba is therefore also the liquidation of the Arab-Jewish model. My urge to re-write the text, my melancholic urge to intervene, derived in part from this loss.

The Arab-Jewish Option

Elimination of the Arab-Jewish option and the shrinkage of the Arab space began years before the Nakba. The State of Israel has developed a phobia toward its Arab surroundings and toward the Arabic language. This phobia recently received a grotesque expression, when Israel banned entry of the Arabic translation of Amos Oz's *A Tale of Love and Darkness*, since it was printed in Beirut. One of the signs for this phobia is the tiny percentage of Jews who have a good command of Arabic. While approximately 92 percent of the Palestinians in Israel have a good command of Hebrew, only 2 percent of the Jews speak or understand Arabic (if we subtract the older generation of Arab Jews who were born in Arab countries). These scandalous differential rates attest primarily to the colonial relations between the languages and the phobia Israelis developed toward Arabic. The slim rate of Arabic speakers among the Jewish Israelis is a voluntary acceptance of the cleansing practices of the state.

Arabic speakers in Israel know how hard it is to exercise the right to language in the swelling Jewish space. Because it is perceived as inferior, there is no inclination to know and learn the language. It is specifically grim among the second and third generation Mizrahi Jews when Arabic is a source of ambivalence and conflict. Israel's policy on the issue is more than puzzling. It certainly does not suggest any intention or desire to accept and win acceptance from the Arab surrounding. It is the behavior of a stranger who comes to visit a region for a short spell. Someone called it a "villa in the jungle." Others have compared this to the behavior of the Crusaders. They too did not come to settle into the region, did not make an effort to integrate, did not speak Arabic, and developed a phobia toward Arabs. They eventually left.

By comparison, with the Arab conquests in the seventh century, Arabic Jewish language replaced Aramaic as the language of the Jews. Famous Jewish writers, among them Musa Ibn Maimon (Maimonides), Ibn Said Joseph Alafiomi (Saadia Gaon), and Abu al-Hassan Allawi (Yehuda Ha'Levi) wrote in this language. For this reason, intellectuals such as David Yellin, Joseph Meyuchas, and Shalom Yahuda begged in the early parts of the twentieth century to resume Hebrew in the medieval tradition, in the form of a symbiotic relationship with Arabic.

The meeting points between Hebrew and Arabic in the early days of Islam were based in part on theological dialogue between Judaism and Islam. The Muslims hardly betrayed the Jews as the European Christians did. However, in the context of Palestine/Israel, the renewal of the Hebrew language tagged along the Judeo-Christian tradition and the Protestant return to the Bible. It meant denial of the Arab-Jewish tradition, erasure of the history of the land from biblical time to the present, and the denial of Palestinian existence. The coupling of Jewish identity and Arabic identity became taboo in Hebrew, and the renewal of Jewish Arabic language (تعريب) was overlooked as a serious option in the revival of modern Hebrew.

Despite the closeness between the languages, Hebrew rejected the Arabic language, and saw in it a filthy remnant of exilic life. Initially Eliezer Ben-Yehuda understood the proximity between the languages and believed in its generative productivity, expanding the rather lean Hebrew vocabulary. He offered to import words not only from literary Arabic but also from the spoken language.[24] In so doing he offered an alternative to the model of enmity between the two languages. But apart from a handful of supporters, these recommendations were met with resistance, and the Arabic language was perceived as the language of the enemy and a hump on Hebrew's back.[25]

From its inception, the Hebrew Language Academy held discussions on the sources of the Hebrew language. A bone of contention was whether the Bible is the sole source of Hebrew, or whether they should rely on other sources such as the Talmud, Mishnah, Midrash, or Agada. This is how one question was formulated: "[Was] the Mishnah a natural living language [. . . or] an artificial jargon . . . which took upon itself a look of Hebrew but in fact is only broken Aramaic?"[26]

The return to the Bible was a theological act that implied the negation of Arabic and Arabs. The revival of Hebrew biblical language sought to purify these Arabic and Aramaic remains in Hebrew, and return to the language of the Holy enunciation. Arab and Arabic are seen as hunchbacks that developed after the destruction of the commonwealth. The

Jewish philosopher Gershom Scholem understood early on the power of the inevitable sacralization of the supposedly secular revived Hebrew language. In 1926, during the great cultural war for Hebrew as a spoken language in mandatory Palestine, Scholem wrote to fellow philosopher Franz Rosenzweig:

> The people here [in Palestine] do not understand the implications of their actions. . . . They think they have turned Hebrew into a secular language, that they have removed its apocalyptic sting. But this is not the case. . . . Every word that is not created randomly anew, but is taken from the "good old" lexicon, is filled to overflowing with explosives. . . . God will not remain mute in the language in which he has been entreated thousands of times to return to our lives.[27]

In 1929, when my grandfather Saleh Shahrabani traveled from Baghdad to Haifa and Jaffa, Ze'ev Jabotinsky explained to the committee for the renewal of the Hebrew language, that their Europeanness does not allow them to adapt an Eastern or Arabic accent: "There is no reason to believe that the ancient accent of the ק, ע, ט, ח should carry Arab pronunciation.[28] In renewing our language, we must determine the appropriate ringing which fits our musical taste, which is first and foremost European and not Eastern."[29]

Likewise, the committee for the renewal of the Hebrew language stated: "We recently arrived from Europe and our throats are unable to pronounce difficult Arab letters. How would we express the Arabic ט or ק in Arabic from the cavity of our throats?[30] The committee was completely oblivious to my grandfather and other Arab Jews.

The renewal of the Hebrew language was based in many cases on ideological contrast with Arabic, which was perceived as inferior and filthy compared to the biblical lexicon. This was realized in the rejection of words and expressions that were too close to Arabic. In so doing, European Zionism adopted a Christian doctrine that sought to renew the Bible in isolation from the Jewish tradition in exile, and in particular its proximity to the Arabic language. The rejection of Arabic added enormous impediments to the possibility of reconciliation between the languages.

Reconciliation between languages is the task of the translator. Translation as a cultural phenomenon undercuts the exclusivity of ethnic sovereignty. Translation develops from a mere technical esthetic artifact into a mode of existence. Translation of this kind does not have "source" or "destination." They co-develop as in shared sovereignty.

Reconciliation between Languages

In his essay "Task of the Translator" Walter Benjamin argued that the role of the translator is to bring us to an "ancient promised place, hitherto uninhabited by human beings, a place where reconciliation between languages is fully realized."[31] Perfect translation is a messianic act, since reconciliation between languages resides outside human history and lies in the realm of apocalyptic eschatology. According to Benjamin, reconciliation between the tongues means return. Return of "exile within sovereignty." A bilingual return that tolerates reunion between Arabic and Hebrew. It requires a new thought on sovereignty. A model which would be flexible enough to accommodate both languages, as in both people. Sovereignty which is based on sharing (לחלוק) rather than dividing (לחלק).[32] The first step is recognition of the Nakba.

In recent years, historiography has abandoned the old question that sought to clarify how many Palestinians were expelled and how many of them fled on their own initiative or at the initiative of their leaders. This has been futile and removed from the center of historiography. Today many historians, Jews and Palestinians, provide a revisionist formulation in which the Nakba is not just the expulsion and displacement of 1948, but especially the ban on return to homes and families immediately after the war and in fact to this date. According to this interpretation, the sovereign decision of the Israeli government to prevent the return of hundreds of thousands of people to their homes after the war is a formal act of ethnic cleansing.

Thus, the Nakba is not an event that ended in 1948, but a trauma that continues into the present as shown in the following brief episode, again from the *Life and Death of the Wrinkled-face Sheikh*. It deals with the skeletons that Israel keeps in the closet and with the return of the repressed. It also attests to the melancholy of the Jew, but this time, the European Jew. It suggests that the Arab-Jewish option is not a biological artifact and is not peculiar to Arab Jews. It is offered to every Jew who desires to live here in peace.

The Artists' Village

The village of Ayn Houd was transformed into a Jewish artists' colony known as Ein-Hod.[33] In the old days, there was there a grand mosque whose spire rose to several feet above the ground. In the artists' colony the mosque was converted into a highbrow restaurant. At the entrance stands a female host who caters to the artists' needs and their respectable guests.

A few years ago, a man arrived at the artists' colony from Siris, a village located in the Jennin district. He headed to a house inhabited by an artist who immigrated from Europe or America. The artist's wife who opened the door was startled at first, seeing the strange "rouge-head" staring at her. The man was silent as a stone, as he had never seen a half-naked woman opening the door of his house. The woman recovered quickly and gently invited the man inside. She summoned her husband, the artist, who was also apprehensive at first, seeing the Keffiyeh and the thick mustache of the visitor. But the artist also recovered quickly, particularly after he saw a smile spread across the visitor's face.

He asked the Arab man:

—What brings you here?

The Arab man answered without hesitation: I was born here. This is my home.

—This is your home?

His voice expressed great amazement, and he promptly invited the man to enter.

—What do you mean? Tell me what happened!

The guest seated himself on a comfortable armchair and told him the story from beginning to end. The artist welcomed him lavishly and served him a cup of coffee. He even offered him a glass of whiskey. He then apologized, sat down next to him and begged to hear the story. The artist believed every single word he heard. The Sheikh we are talking about sealed off the story:

> —The Arab man went back to his village in the West Bank. The artist, however, was seized by guilt, sadness and irritability. He decided to leave the house and moved to another. But the ghosts kept pursuing him to the new home. Every day he woke up waiting for another Arab man who would come to visit the house where he was born. Nightmares and ghosts never vanished and followed him everywhere, until he decided to leave the country altogether.

NOTES

1. See, for example, Shay Hazkani, "Catastrophic Thinking: Did Ben-Gurion Try to Rewrite History?" *Ha'aretz Magazine*, May 16, 2013. Hazkani shows how Ben Gurion asked the best Israeli orientalists to supply him with evidence the Palestinians were not expelled, but escaped from Palestine.

2. "Stop Rewriting History," *Ha'aretz* Editorial, May 19, 2013.

3. See Hannan Hever, "The Post Zionist Condition," *Critical Inquiry* 38, no. 3 (2012): 630–48.

4. See Shenhav Yehouda, "Imperialism, Exceptionalism and the Contemporary World," in *Agamben and Colonialism*, ed. Svirsky Marcelo and Simone Bignall (Oxford: Oxford University Press, 2012), 17–31.

5. B. Fontana, ed., *Constant: Political Writings* (Cambridge: Cambridge University Press, 1988), 143.

6. This territorial dimension is also backed up by the negation of rabbinic (exilic) tradition as consecrating time rather than space. This negation of exile is materialized by the "return" to the imagined biblical territory and time.

7. For elaboration see Yehouda Shenhav, Christopher Schmidt, and Shimshon Zelniker, eds., *State of Exception and State of Emergency* (Van Leer Jerusalem Institute and Hakibbutz Hameuchad, 2009). Hebrew.

8. See Amnon Raz-Krakotzkin, "The Six-Day State: Israel, the Occupation and the Bi-National Position," *Mahsom*, June 26, 2007 [Hebrew]; Amnon Raz Krakotzkin (2007), *Exil et Souverainete* (Paris: La Fabrique, 2007) [French]. For a review see Yehouda Shenhav, *Beyond the Two-State Solution: A Jewish Political Essay* (London: Polity Press, 2012).

9. This was also in the case of Yiddish, but in the case of Arabic, contradictions are particularly interesting since they had to "overcome" etymological identity.

10. Paul Ricoeur, *On Translation*, trans. Eileen Brennan (New York: Routledge, 2006); but see also Barbara Cassin, ed., *Dictionary of Untranslatables* (Princeton: Princeton University Press, 2015). Cassin suggests that the untranslatable never ceases (not) being translated and thus refers to a process that is never complete.

11. Shenhav Yehouda, "Sovereignty Gaps, the Exception and State of Exception," *Theory & Criticism* 29 (2206): 205–18. Hebrew.

12. Natalia Ginzburg, *Family Lexicon* (Hakibutz Ha'Meuchad, 2012), 5 (from Italian to Hebrew: Miriam Shusterman-Podavno and Menahem Pery).

13. Hever Hannan, *Tell Not in Gat—The Naqba in Hebrew Poetry 1948–1958* (Tel Aviv: Pardess Press, Zochrot, 2010, 2nd ed., 2012). Hebrew.

14. Shenhav, *Beyond the Two-State Solution*. See also Jonathan Boyarin, *Storm from Paradise: The Politics of Jewish Memory* (Minneapolis: University of Minnesota Press, 1992).

15. For detailed analysis see Yehouda Shenhav, *The Arab Jews: A Postcolonial Reading of Nationalism, Religion and Ethnicity* (Stanford: Stanford University Press, 2006), chaps. 4–5.

16. See Haggai Ram, *Iranophobia* (Stanford: Stanford University Press, 2009).

17. See Amnon Raz Krakotzkin, "Exile within Sovereignty: Toward Criticism of the "Negation of Exile" in Israeli Culture," *Theory & Criticism* 3 (1993): 23–55 (Hebrew); Amnon Raz Krakotzkin, "Exile within Sovereignty Part B," *Theory & Criticism* 4 (1994): 113–39. Hebrew.

18. Salman Natour, *The Life and Death of the Wrinkled-Face Sheik* (Tel Aviv: Resling, 2014). Translations from Arabic to Hebrew and English are mine. —YS.

19. Ibid.

20. See Shenhav, *Beyond the Two-State Solution*. Chapter 5 addresses the rights of the Jews.

21. For a few exceptions see Jens Bartelson, *A Genealogy of Sovereignty* (Cambridge: Cambridge University Press, 1995). See also Shenhav Yehouda, "Does Critical Theory Have a Color? Reflections on Post-Westphalian Sovereignty," in *Four Lectures on Critical Theory*, ed. Gil Eyal (Tel Aviv: Ha'kibbutz Ha'meuchad and the Vanleer Jerusalem Institute, 2012), 15–49 Hebrew.

22. See Hannan Hever, "'We Have Not Arrived from the Sea': A Mizrahi Literary Geography," *Social Identities* 10, no. 1 (2004): 31–51.

23. Ammiel Alcalay, "At Home in Exile: An Interview with Shimon Ballas," *Literary Review* 37, no. 2 (1994): 180–89.

24. Iair G. Or, "The Emergence of New Hebrew: Beliefs and Ideologies in the grammatical discussions of the Hebrew Language Committee, 1912–1928," Master's thesis (Tel Aviv: Tel Aviv University, 2014). Hebrew.

25. Shenhav Yehouda, "The Politics and Theology of Translation: How Do We Translate Nakba from Arabic to Hebrew," *Israeli Sociology* (Hebrew), 14 (2012): 157–84.

26. The Committee for the Hebrew language, *Memories and Minutes* (Jerusalem, 1929), 50.

27. Gershom Scholem, *One More Thing: Chapters in Heritage and Revival*, vol. B, (Tel Aviv, Am Oved, 1989), 59. Hebrew.

28. Arabic transliteration: ḥ = ח/ṭ = ט/q = ק/ʿ = ע

29. Zeev Jabotinsky, *Hebrew Pronunciation* (Tel Aviv, 1930), 25.

30. The Committee for the Hebrew language, *Memories and Minutes* (Jerusalem, 1929), 51.

31. Walter Benjamin, "The Task of the Translator," in *The Translation Studies Reader*, ed. Lawrence Venuti (London: Routledge, 2000).

32. In *Beyond the Two-State Solution*, I provide a more elaborate discussion of this idea.

33. This passage is from Natour, *Life and Death of the Wrinkled-Face Sheik*.

CHAPTER 3

The Ends of Ladino

Andrew Bush

I

Isak Papo, an engineer and university professor, compiled a selection of stories told in Ladino by several Jews from Sarajevo, including many of his own tales, published in 1994.[1] Here is his recollection of his childhood language lessons:

> A hundred years ago in the time of the Turks, there were no other schools for Jewish children aside from the *maldar*.
>
> Then when the Austrians came, the Jewish children went to school for four or eight years, afterwards they began to go off to the Gymnasium, also the wealthiest used to send their sons to Vienna.
>
> When "La Benevolencija" was founded, with the help of that institution young men would go to Vienna on scholarship.
>
> In the beginning, the *maldar* was located in a house at the bottom of Logavina Street, near the big synagogue and the *Hanizitju*.

The "bearer of the pen" (secretary) of the community of the Sephardim, Ham R. Bencion Pinto (called by the abbreviation HARBAC) was one of the organizers of the construction in Ćelmaluša (in the year 1903), where the administration moved, the Bet Din.

This house was called "The Talmud Torah" in which was also located the school for educating hazanim called "Degel Atora."

In the entrance of the Talmud Torah was written "Reshit Hochma Yeriat Adonay" in Hebrew letters, which means "The beginning of wisdom is fear of God" "Početak mudrosti je strah gospodnji" (Psalm 111:10).

In the *maldar*, my teacher was *Ham* Daniel Danon, who came to Sarajevo from Travnik. Here this esteemed teacher taught elementary Hebrew [*las primeras letras hebrejas*].

When we read clearly without "shegiyoth" [errors] he would make our faces golden passing with his "*sat*" [*el mus fazija la kara di oru pasandu kun su "sat"*] that he had hanging in his vest pocket.

This gesture pleased us very much and we could not forget [*i no pudijamus olvidar*], trying always to know the lesson we would prepare ourselves at home.

Ham Daniel remained in my memory for his humility and his behavior with the pupils.

Unfortunately, he was one of the sacrifices in the Jasenovac camp.[2]

The Austro-Hungarian annexation of Bosnia-Herzegovina dates to 1878, and so roughly forty years before Papo, born in 1912, went to his Hebrew lessons with Ham Daniel. The institution of the *maldar* persisted, therefore, despite the process of assimilation into a Westernized educational system to which Papo alludes in his opening paragraphs. Like the Ashkenazi institution of early learning known in Yiddish as the *cheder*, the term *maldar* is a loanword from Hebrew, a metathesis of the root that gives both *melamed* and *talmid*, teacher and student. The *maldar* is, then, a Hebrew school in several senses. *Maldar* (alternatively *meldar*) is also, strictly speaking, a verbal noun, which, as an infinitive, means "to read," sometimes "to pray," as when Papo says "Kvandu maldavamus klaru" (When we read clearly)—I shall have occasion to return to the grammar of such activated nouns at the close of my discussion.

Ham Daniel's gilding is also familiar from Ashkenazi settings as a variant of the stories of teaching, literally, the first Hebrew letters (*las primeras letras hebrejas*) by dipping a child's finger in honey and tracing the forms. Before one even learns the alphabet, one learns that learning is sweet. And it is easy to imagine the sweetness of the gesture, the hand of the humble Ham Daniel gently rubbing the smooth and shining surface of his pocket watch over the smooth and shining faces of his pupils. Is he also *timing* them (as one might say, gilding them), that is introducing them into the world of clock time at the very moment that he is opening the linguistic way into the traditional world of Bible and prayer? Is he passing time? The Ladino gesture (*gestu*) is indeterminate due to the absence of a direct object pronoun: a dangling participle of sorts, *pasandu*. Similarly, the construction of the subsequent phrase leaves some doubt as to whether it was the gesture or the lesson that the pupils could not forget. Unless, as I suppose, the gesture was the lesson, not so much another language lesson as the other of language lessons, the other of language. Smooth on smooth, this is important: Whatever we make of the *pasandu* (to construct a different kind of verbal noun of this gesture), it does not appear to be an inscription in the sense of the path-breaking *frayeur* of the deconstructive scene of writing, no breaking of the skin, a sealing of a covenant that is, however, not a cut. A scene of instruction, perhaps.[3]

There are many noteworthy elements in Papo's story aside from the pedagogy of sweetness. The text is at once a memoir and a chronicle—indeed, in that mixture Papo offers the *maldar* as an example of the hybrid formation of what Pierre Nora named a *lieu de mémoire*, a redoubt of memory, tradition, ritual, and continuity, within and as seen from the world of history and change. Thus, Papo also opens questions for historical research. For instance, what kind of "Jewish space" is the *Hanizitju* (the little *han*, or inn, of Turkish origin) that Zjena Čulić and Myrna Svičarević, the translators for the bilingual, Ladino-English edition of the stories, assimilate, too quickly perhaps, to the history of Jews in Western Christendom, with their term "ghetto"?[4] They also make the interesting decision to omit the final sentence referring to the sacrifices at Jasenovac, so that, for the English-language reader, the story never reaches the end, dehistoricizing and forgetting at once. The toponym *Jasenovac* locates Ham Daniel's death in the extermination center run by the Ustashe government of independent Croatia from 1941 to 1945 for the extermination of Jews, Serbs, and Roma. As chronicle, then, Papo's ending would frame the history of Ladino-speaking Jews in Sarajevo as the period between the Ottoman Empire, a haven for Jews following the Edict of Expulsion from the Iberian realms of the Catholic Monarchs in 1492, and the Holocaust. The end of the text speaks of the end of the Jews of Sarajevo, or of their traditional life, both represented by Ham Daniel. Papo's ending subordinates the homely gestures of Ladino-speaking-Ottoman-Austro-Hungarian-Croatian-Jews to the course of a history that eradicated that place; and yet it also commemorates a teacher precisely in such a gesture. Papo's ending closes off history but commits the *pasandu* to memory in an acknowledgment that the teaching lives on as an enduring bond.[5]

I shall take up these questions of the closure of history and the *durée* of memory in a tale of the end of Ladino as told by Jacques Derrida in *Monolingualism of the Other; or, The Prosthesis of Origin*, through which he would define "our place," an exceptional place for Jews in colonial Algeria.[6] I will be especially interested in the ways in which a certain kind of memory, a *hypermemory*, of Ladino disrupts his Ashkenazi-centric articulation of Jewish places and the place of Jews. I will be proposing a Sephardic version, a continuity beyond the purported end of Ladino; I will be listening for the echo of the *pasandu*.

For the moment, I underline one further detail in Papo's language lesson as a premonitory counterpoint to Derrida's hypothesis of monolingualism. In describing Ham Daniel's gesture, the word for the watch suspended from his waistcoat pocket remains lodged in Papo's memory in Bosnian as *sat*. From this watchword, as it were, one may reconstruct the complex language environment. Hebrew is the *langue d'arrivée* in the *maldar*, and Ladino, the predominant language of the text and, presumably, of instruction in the classroom, the *langue de départ*.[7] In a different sense, however, Hebrew too is the *langue de départ*, preceding the Ladino-speaking community and indeed Ladino itself, and crucial to the formation of both across the itinerary leading from Iberia to Sarajevo and beyond. But the *sat* would indicate that in addition to Hebrew and Ladino, Bosnian was also spoken in the *maldar*, even in connection with the most intimate, most memorable gesture of the *pasandu*. There is further evidence, of course, in the trilingual quotation in the more advanced language lesson of the Hebrew inscription on the facade of the Talmud-Torah, taken from verse *Resh* of the alphabetical acrostic Psalm 111.[8] Čulić and Svičarević leave out the Bosnian version, assuming perhaps that it would have been incomprehensible to the English-language readership of their translation. But Papo must have imagined readers, whether Jewish or non-Jewish, who would need help with the Hebrew, and would have found help in the Bosnian. This is not the occasion to take up the differences between the *imperial* history of the Balkans under Ottomans and Austro-Hungarians, on the one hand, and the *colonial* history of Algeria under the French, on the other, but Papo's story stands as a reminder that the Other may also be multilingual.

2

Derrida takes an autobiographical turn in *Monolingualism* familiar in his late work—most notably, his "Circumfession"[9]—drawing on his experience growing up as a Jew in colonial Algeria as an allegory of the aporia that deconstruction was invented to articulate, if not to resolve. He expresses the impasse succinctly in linguistic terms: "I only have one language; it is not mine" (*M*, 1). The argument, both historical and theoretical, concerns the place of Jews as a political anomaly and a deconstructive supplement to the binary construction of the colonizer and the colonized, and so represents an early effort to stage a conversation, with all of its attending difficulties, between Jewish studies and postcolonial theory.[10] It remains an enticing avenue for consideration, and no less politically fraught more than a decade later.

The postcolonial context of *Monolingualism* is adumbrated even before the text gets under way. A prefatory note refers to a shorter text, delivered orally at an "international and bilingual" conference titled "Echoes from Elsewhere"/"*Renvois d'ailleurs*," at Louisiana State University, Baton Rouge, in 1992, the year of the quincentennial commemoration of Columbus's first transatlantic voyage. The papers were to address the colonial expansion of the French language: "We were required to deal with problems of *francophonie* outside France, problems of linguistics or literature, politics or culture" (*M*, unnumbered). In the French text, the note follows immediately after the dedication to David Wills and immediately before the first epigraph from Edouard Glissant (and a second from Abdelkébir Khatibi), the conference organizers. Hence, it constitutes a *Gastgeschenk*, a guest's gift, that Derrida glosses as "acknowledgments and token of the guest who is giving thanks for received hospitality" (*M*, 82)—a point to which I will return.[11] It is within that context that Derrida offers a typology of conference participants against which he represents himself as the unique, excluded, and exemplary case. He classifies his colleagues as follows: (a) French citizens from France who were not North African; (b) *francophones* who were neither French nor North African; and (c) "French-speaking Maghrebians who are not and have never been French, meaning French citizens" (*M*, 12). His Moroccan-born friend Khatibi, for instance, fits into the last group. Jews born in colonial Algeria, however, are North Africans, not French from France; but unlike colonial Algerian Arabs and Berbers, they became French citizens as a result of the Crémieux decree of 1870, and remained so except for the time when they were stripped of citizenship by the Vichy government during World War II. The native Jews of colonial Algeria, therefore, are (d) none of the above.

As the representative of unclassifiable Algerian Jews at the conference, Derrida then claims, hyperbolically, that even in comparison to Khatibi, "between the two of us, I consider myself to be the *most* Franco-Maghrebian, and perhaps even the *only* Franco-Maghrebian here" (*M*, 12). Hyperbole, he will go on to reflect, is the way that a language that has no *at-home-ness* (*un "chez-soi,"* with Derrida's quotation marks, *M*, 54, translation altered) takes place, and takes its place among the other languages. It is, therefore, the characteristic trope of the language that has no place in Derrida's taxonomy of other native French speakers at the conference, and thus it is his characteristic trope as well: "In the end, I exaggerate. I always exaggerate" (*M*, 49, translation altered).[12]

Since he cannot be made to fit any of the geo-politico-linguistic classes that he had constructed, Derrida pauses to ask, "Where would I categorize myself then? What taxonomy should I invent?" (*M*, 13). His answer comes in a closer consideration of his situation as a Jewish, French-speaking, Maghrebian French citizen. Here he offers a new classificatory system based on "interdictions": (a) "dissociated" from the Arab or Berber language and culture; and (b) from the French (and hence, European) language and culture (*M*, 37–43). These first two conditions are not exclusively those of Algerian-born Jews. French-from-France were also generally dissociated from Arab and Berber language and culture; and all colonial subjects, Arabs and Berbers no less than Jews, would be estranged from the metropolitan language and culture. The distinctive feature of "indigenous Jews" (*M*, 53) was a third interdiction. Whereas Arabs and Berbers had access to their own languages and cultures—if not untrammeled by the colonial condition—Jews like the young Derrida did not:

> As for language in the strict sense, we could not even resort to some familiar substitute, to some idiom internal to the Jewish community, to any sort of language of refuge that, like Yiddish, would have ensured an element of intimacy, the protection of an "at-home-ness" against the language of official culture, a second auxiliary in different socio-semiotic situations. "Ladino" was not spoken in the Algeria I knew, especially not in the big cities like Algiers, where the Jewish population happened to be centered. (*M*, 54–55)

At this mention of Ladino, set off by quotation marks, the text itself is cut off or cut up. A note intervenes and *Monolingualism* splits into parallel texts, much as in the format of "Circumfessions." In the English-language edition, the note bears the number 9, setting it within a series of consecutive notes, and it is printed inconspicuously, like the others, at the end of the volume. In the French text, all the notes appear at the bottom of the page, but unlike the other numbered notes, here an asterisk marks a case that is *hors série*. The upper part of the page continues the ongoing conversation with postcolonial theory, contesting the colonial dichotomy with the supplement of a Jewish minority that, purportedly, has no language in which it is at home. The note sketches, rather, another, future project in Jewish studies, theorizing a Jewish ethics of language. It is an *outpouring* that runs across the lower register for many pages, beginning as a *supposition*, that is a placement beneath (*sub-ponere*): "Supposing [*À supposer*] that these modest reflections propose *to add* an example [*proposent de* verser *un exemple*, emphasis added]" (*M*, 78). *Verser*: tip over, pour out; a turning (Latin *versus*) that can also be an overturning (recall French *bouleverser*). The added example, he supposes, might turn things upside down, as indeed, he tries to show, above, in the main and ongoing argument, in which the example of the Jewish, French-speaking, Maghrebian French citizen is meant to overload and overcome the binary structure of colonialism.

Derrida already has the deferred project's "most ambitious" title in mind, *The Monolingualism of the* Hôte: *The Jews of the Twentieth Century, the Mother Tongue and the Language of the Other, on Both Sides of the Mediterranean* (*M*, 78, translation altered).[13] But the allusion to two-sidedness is misleading. Looking out "From the coast of this long note," Derrida follows the predominant perspective of the field of Jewish studies to find the sources of theory in Ashkenaz alone, on "the other shore of Judaism, on *another*, other coastline of the Mediterranean" from where he locates himself in his text (*M*, 78–79). Starting out from Rosenzweig, and proceeding through a sampler of twentieth-century Jewish types—Arendt, Scholem, and Levinas (and, glancingly, Benjamin and Adorno, Kafka and Celan)—he reports that "The best-known and the most justly famous among them are European by birth. And all of them 'Ashkenazim'" (*M*, 79). He stands at one of the ends of theory for Jews and Jewish studies, the Ashkenazi boundary, which, he recognizes, "already poses a number of problems" (*M*, 79). Theorizing in Jewish studies begins, again and again, with certain well-known and justly famous Ashkenazi figures, and just as often ends there. So another of the ends of theory—now in the sense of its goals—would be to put that Ashkenazi-centrism in question by recognizing Sephardic, Levantine, and other articulations of Jewish experience from beyond the literal and figurative pale as theoretical sources.[14]

At that end and to that end, Derrida asks, "What would be the '*Sephardic*' *version* (*le versant sépharade*) of this typology?" (*M*, 79, emphasis added and translation altered). In its Ashkenazi version, his disquisition on monolingualism as a Jewish condition with no home-language, the Jewish *hôte* is often ghost and always guest with nothing to give other than an acknowledgment of hospitality received—but never, it would appear, a host. But how, then, to account for the alternative experience of the *maldar* in yet another other Europe and all that the sweet pedagogy of Ham Daniel Danon has to offer?

3

Before pursuing Derrida's schema for an alternative *Monolingualism* to the end, I pause to return to the point where his text splits into the upper and lower registers, looking back from the coast of his long note and along the slant of the Sephardic *versant* (also a side or slope, including the sloping bank of a river or sea). I recall that Derrida turns to his supposition at the moment when he enunciates the third interdiction that fully distinguishes Algerian Jews from French colonizers and colonized Arabs and Berbers: No Ladino! At least not any more, at least not in Derrida's place in Algiers, "the Algiers I knew." The end of Ladino thus announced, however, is not so much a fact of linguistic history. Derrida does not comment on the possibility of Ladino speakers either in the Algiers that he did not know *or elsewhere*, for instance, in other postimperial and postcolonial settings, like Sarajevo. It is rather a rhetorical topos in a long-standing discourse in Jewish studies. Gil Anidjar recounts a Sephardic version of the lachrymose conception of Jewish history, to recall Salo Baron's famous formulation, in which Derrida's enunciation of the end of Ladino may be situated:

> Only the last in a series of "ends" that inform and provide coordinates for the representation of medieval Spain in modern Jewish historical and literary discourses, 1492 illustrates a major mode of appearance of the Iberian peninsula and of its contents. Like earlier "ends" of al-Andalus (Islamic Spain), such historical loci, or, more precisely, framing moments and movements, are constitutive of the peninsula's appearance. This is neither to say that everything has simply ended, that nothing remains, nor that what was has been entirely and purely lost and that it can thus be simply located in an unreachable beyond. Rather, as end, al-Andalus, medieval Spain, appears insofar as it declines and disappears.[15]

Or, in sum, "the end is the place and taking place of al-Andalus" (*OP*, 57). Anidjar then turns to Maimonides for a theoretical articulation of Jewish place and the taking place of language under the heading of "our place in al-Andalus" that sidesteps the mourning of Sephardic endings expressed in the "rhetoric of sadness" (*OP*, 105).

A brief survey of terms is in order. Al-Andalus is not Sepharad, since the two toponyms may overlap geographically but constitute different *lieux de mémoire*, different collective memories. And both "medieval Spain" and "Islamic Spain" are wholesale anachronisms. In the medieval period there was no geopolitical entity known as Spain, but rather a group of separate Muslim and Christian kingdoms with fluctuating alliances and enmities between them. To speak of medieval or Islamic Spain, therefore, is to construct yet another nationalistic *lieu de mémoire* in the deeply contested collective memories of the modern Spanish nation-state. Finally, Ladino, also called Djudezmo, was by no means the monolanguage of Jews in or from al-Andalus/Sepharad; Maimonides, for instance, wrote his works in Hebrew and in Arabic, but not in Ladino.

These confusions rather tally with than stand against Anidjar's reconstruction of Maimonides' theory of language, whose hallmark is the perplexity occasioned by a breach in signification and, therefore, in communication: the "taking place of language as an exposure to its limit" (*OP*, 43). Anidjar illustrates by reciting a parable from the Arabic of Maimonides' *Guide of the Perplexed*, which turns upon the term *dalāla* that Anidjar glosses as "a gesture pointing to a thing or to a direction: a 'signal,' 'sign-post,' 'indicator,' or 'indication,' to which we may now here add 'sign,' 'signification,' and 'demonstration'" (*OP*, 38). *Dalāla* is also the term in Maimonides' title that is usually translated as "guide."

Maimonides' parable, with Anidjar's emphases, reads as follows:

> Know that if one does not understand the language of a human being whom one hears speaking, one indubitably knows that he speaks, but without knowing what he intends to say. Something of even graver import may occur: sometimes one may hear in someone else's speech words that in the language of the speaker indicate a certain meaning, *tadullu 'alā ma'nā*, and by accident, *bi-l-'araḍ*, that word indicates, *tadullu*, in the language of the hearer, the contrary of what the speaker intended. Thus, the hearer will think that the signification, *dalāla*, that the word has for the speaker is the same as its signification, *dalāla*, for him. For instance [Ar. *maṯal*, Heb. *ke'ilu*] if an Arab hears a Hebrew man saying *'aba* [Heb. he wishes], the Arab will think that he speaks of an individual who was reluctant with regard to some matter and refused, *'abā*, it.[16]

It is easy to recognize here an exemplary tale of Derrida's opening premise in *Monolingualism of the Other*, cited above: "I have but one language, and it is not mine" (13). My language, whichever one or ones I mean by that, is always exposed to the limit of its signification. Homophony, in this case, gives evidence that the word one thinks one hears is not in one's own language, and, as a corollary, that where one may think to be at home in language, one may be a guest.

Anidjar observes that the common response to such a linguistic muddle is to seek to put an end to confusion and that the end is often achieved by the *determination* of a historical context that fixes meaning. Maimonides deliberately upended that contextualization when he spoke of "our place, in al-Andalus" from Cairo, after his exile from Iberia. Against the history of his own end in al-Andalus, Maimonides proposes a rhetorical structure of unending affiliation, or as Anidjar argues, Maimonides' "language unsettles its localization and repeatedly produces the disappearance of its context" (*OP*, 2). If *dalāla* may be understood as "signification," then, it is a sign in the sense that Hamid Dabashi has expounded: *Dalāla* does not signify (it is neither a signifier nor a signified), but rather *signates*.[17] One might almost say that for Anidjar, Maimonidean *dalāla* is a *de-signation*, the deconstructive aspect in *all* language.[18]

For Maimonides, however, *dalāla* is, first and foremost, a pedagogy, as he makes explicit from the outset of the *Guide* in the "Epistle Dedicatory," addressed to "My honored pupil Rabbi Joseph."[19] The well-prepared pupil who does not forget (*i no pudijamus olvidar*) the lessons of *dalāla* learns that at its limit, language is endless, defying the determinations of historical contextualization. Anidjar recalls the account by his own teacher, Amos Finkelstein, of the indeterminacy of Maimonides' language in the *Guide* as a case in point: "The ruling out of 'thoroughgoing determination' is constitutive of the 'very material structure of the world,' as well as of the 'language of man.' That this has been yet another reason for hermeneuts' and commentators' despair is not to be doubted. Yet, the 'work' of resistance and its articulation in Maimonides' writing offers itself as a taking place that *hardly calls for mourning*" (*OP*, 43, emphasis added). The absence of at-home-ness is not necessarily lamentable; but also, there may be real loss that elicits a response other than mourning, as I shall presently explore.

By treating the end of Ladino as a historical fact rather than a rhetorical structure, Derrida would contain its meaning within the confines of the familiar narration of the historical contexts of the ends of al-Andalus, that is a history of definitive turning points, variously located. But the very endlessness of the endings of al-Andalus, including the end of Ladino, to which Anidjar attests, suggests a compulsion to repeat that destabilizes Derrida's classificatory system. The slippage becomes apparent almost immediately after the asterisk comes to mark the split in the text. Derrida gives a summary of the psycholinguistic amputations suffered by the "community" (with his cautionary quotation marks) of Jews in colonial Algeria, corresponding to the three indictions: "(1) It was cut off (*coupée*) from both Arabic or Berber (more properly Maghrebian) language and culture. (2) It was also cut off from French, and even European language and culture, which, from its viewpoint, only constituted a distanced pole or metropole, heterogeneous to its history. (3) It was cut off, finally, or to begin with, from Jewish memory, and from the history and language that one must *suppose* (*on doit supposer*) to be their own, but which, at a given moment, no longer were" (*M*, 55, emphasis added and translation altered). I reiterate that it is the third historical condition that defines the specific place of Algerian Jews for Derrida. But the uprising of a *supposition* from the note to the text is itself a sign—a *dalāla*—that the story of the end of Ladino may be on edge, shaking the firm ground of history (what happens in a given moment) in "our place." Before the split, Derrida had assumed that Algerian Jews did have Ladino and it was theirs; now the moment of loss is predicated of a Ladino that they may not have ever had. For the monolingual, Franco-Maghrebian Jew:

> [a desire] springs forth and even sets itself up as a desire to reconstruct, to restore, but it is really a desire to invent a first language that would be, rather a prior-to-the-first language destined to translate that memory. But to translate the memory of what, precisely, did not take place, of what, having been (the) forbidden, ought, nevertheless, to have left a trace, a specter, the phantomatic body, the phantom-member—palpable, painful, but hardly legible—of traces, marks, and scars. As if it were a matter of producing the truth of what never took place by avowing it. What then is this avowal, and the age-old error or originary defect from which one must write? (*M*, 61)

The loss at the end is explained as a loss of beginnings. Historical skepticism has been stretched to a deconstructive argument that holds the lost language to be a myth of origins, a prosthesis (as the subtitle of *Monolingualism* has it) for a limb that never was, and therefore was never cut off in the first place.

The question of the compulsion (*il faut écrire*) is not merely rhetorical, however, nor is Derrida's skepticism uncontested in the text. He had in fact already begun to answer. The avowal is "the most difficult thing" (*M*, 60), a difficulty that he links to the scene in "Circumfession" in which he was "next to a mother who was dying while losing her memory, her speech, and her power of naming" (*M*, 60). The mother—his mother—is still alive, living on beyond the end of language, most particularly beyond the ability to call her son Jackie by name. Nevertheless, she elicits a "supplement of loyalty" (*M*, 60) that resists the cutting off of mother from son, and calls for further examination.

As she appears in "Circumfession," Derrida's mother is a limit case of language that he presents as the mad mother and the madness of the mother tongue in his discussion of Arendt (*M*, 87–89) in the long note under the asterisk in *Monolingualism*. For Arendt, "The forgetting of the mother tongue . . . would indeed be the effect of a repression," as she had confessed (*M*, 90). But other diagnoses are possible, other psychic formations than repression—cryptonomy, for instance—to account for a silencing that is the effect of shame.[20] In Freudian repression, the ego struggles against the wish of the repressed material to burst forth and reveal its own secrets; cryptophores are witnesses to shameful secrets that are not their own, and the cryptic drive is dedicated to preserving their secrecy. Cryptonomy is an extremely exacerbated case of the supplement of loyalty; its more familiar form is melancholia.[21]

Nicolas Abraham illustrates the workings of melancholia by way of a parable in much the same terms as Derrida's prosthesis of avowal. The melancholic would neither be like the amputee who refuses to accept the loss of a limb and so feels ghost pains in the missing member nor like the so-called psychically healthy amputee who accepts the loss, reconstitutes bodily integrity as a whole person-without-a-limb and receives the compensation of introjecting the loss by telling the story in the commemorations of a society of amputees in the work of mourning and of the addition of a prosthesis that is by no means originary. Instead, the melancholic amputee remembers the loss, knows the limb is forever after unavailable, and yet remains psychically attached to it, endlessly loyal to "another, new unity" now constituted as a combination of the present body and the absence of the limb.[22]

Derrida redescribes melancholia in *Monolingualism* under the heading of "the madness of a hypermnesia": An "anamnesis beyond the mere reconstruction of a given heritage, beyond an available past. Beyond any cartography, and beyond any teachable knowledge. At stake there is an entirely other anamnesis, and, if one may say so, even an anamnesis of the entirely other [*du tout autre*]" (*M*, 60, translation altered). Where memory defines the *available* past, melancholic hypermemory not only somehow remembers a past that has been lost and is *utterly* unavailable, but also maintains a continuous allegiance to it. One might think again of the *lieu de mémoire* as, more precisely, a hypermemory site: The continuous relationship that held a memory community together over the *longue durée* has been definitely cut off by historical change, but the memory of that continuity (not the continuity itself) can be revisited and commemorated at the *lieu de mémoire*. Derrida's tale has no *maldar*. Instead, he repeats the endless ending of al-Andalus as the end of Ladino, reconstituting Franco-Maghrebian Jews as a combination of their monolingual French and their absent Ladino in "expressions of longing and melancholic self-deprecation" (*OP*, 114). In the madness of hypermemory, however, the unheard Ladino would live on in an unheard-of French—a form of speaking in translation.[23] It would be as though whenever Derrida wrote of the trace and the *écart*, the cut, the shibboleth and the sign of circumcision, he was speaking a Judeo-Arabic he did not know and saying *dalāla*—and that the same were possible in a Sephardic version of French that retained the unspoken hypermemory of Ladino.

4

Historical skepticism is a defense against the difficulty of hypermnesia and the ongoing attachment to what was real but what is lost. Denying that Jews in the Algeria that Derrida knew ever spoke an originary Ladino may be easier than avowing allegiance to a mad mother tongue, an unspeakable Ladino that lives on beyond its purported end. Derrida gives a glimpse of that alternative, a Ladino that haunts the present as a monolanguage of the Ghost, in a peculiar, I would even say cryptic, textual formation. Having begun the supposition under the asterisk with his examination of Rosenzweig as the first of his three principal examples of *The Monolingualism of the* Hôte, Derrida interrupts his long note to include a parenthesis of some two pages in length in the English translation (*M*, 80–82). He begins the note-within-a-note by announcing another project to come, as he had at the outset of the long note: "I shall perhaps speak again elsewhere [*ailleurs*]" (*M*, 80).[24] A long note under an asterisk, that is elsewhere than the text, and now a long parenthesis representing an elsewhere within the note itself: These sites of enunciation of a project to come, beyond the ending of text and note alike, are a formal response to the task set by the conference organizers. They are *renvois d'ailleurs*, the writing of a monolingual who speaks only the *langue d'arrivée* of the place to which he (in this case) has not arrived. Derrida represents these "echoes from elsewhere" as the haunting of the present by the voice of the future. But the elsewhere may also be located in the past, as in the case of Maimonides' toponymic designation, "our place in al-Andalus," enunciated from Cairo.

In the note-within-the-note Derrida is discussing Scholem's supposition, in a letter to Rosenzweig, that modern, secularizing Hebrew is being built upon an abyss in which the ancient, sacred language lies buried, but buried alive. Scholem sees that linguistic formation as a volcano threatening to erupt, hence, like repression, whose force strives to break through to the surface. But, once again, it is also possible to conceive of a language—call it a monolanguage—that proclaims the end of its Other and buries it in a crypt, precluding any echo from elsewhere of the sacred. What would be the dream of that uncommon language? To this question, too, Derrida has an answer, but not before he completes his survey of the Ashkenazi coast.

Derrida will have already discussed Rosenzweig and Arendt as his first two principal types, with brief accompanying consideration of Scholem and Adorno, when he turns or overturns his taxonomy with the addition of a third type. The examples are Levinas, a native of Lithuania, who spoke and wrote in French as an adoptive language, and Kafka (Celan is also mentioned here), who wrote in German as a native speaker from an ethnic minority but not in the German of Germans and Germany (*M*, 90–93). In Derrida's schema, Rosenzweig represents the theoretical position that Jews have no *langue en propre*[25]—no language of their own, theirs as a property and perhaps no language that they speak quite properly; whereas for Arendt, language is the only property that Jews have, the only home in which they dwell, wherever they are. The example of Levinas, in particular, allows Derrida to make explicit the connection between language and place that is common to the otherwise opposed conceptions of Rosenzweig and Arendt. He quotes a comment by Levinas that represents French language as French soil, which leads Derrida to the following remark, whose edge is sharpened against the tacit allusion to the slogan of "blood and soil": "As the Heideggerian she remains in this respect, but like many Germans, Jewish or not, Arendt reaffirms the mother tongue, that is to say, a language upon which a virtue of originality is bestowed. 'Repressed' or not, this language remains the ultimate essence of the soil, the foundation of meaning, the inalienable property that one carries within oneself"—that is, like blood (*M*, 91). The postcolonial context of Derrida's conference complicates the linguistic-nation with the politics of the linguistic-state.

Levinas stands outside of the language community of the nation-state as a nonnative speaker. And although "Levinas speaks of an *acquired* familiarity" (*M*, 91), which implies property rights, the ethics of language that Levinas represents for Derrida is of an entirely different relation to and in language. Derrida states:

> There seems to be little solemn reference to a mother tongue in [Levinas's] works and no self-assurance assumed in proximity with it, except for the gratitude he expressed, on behalf of someone who declared that "the essence of language is friendship and hospitality," to the French language on each occasion, to French as an adopted or elected language, the welcoming language, the language of the *hôte*. (*M*, 91)

Derrida had already considered hospitality as a poisoned gift in his long note, immediately following the long parenthesis. It was still a matter of Scholem and Rosenzweig, though now, long after the latter's death, expressed in a letter to his co-translator, Buber. Scholem took their German version of the Hebrew Bible to be a *Gastgeschenk*, "with as much appropriate admiration as irony and skepticism," in Derrida's words, "toward the so-called 'Judeo-German' couple" (*M*, 83). More irony and even more skepticism, for the Holocaust had already all but exterminated the German-speaking Jewish population that would have been the readership of Rosenzweig and Buber's translation. Derrida comments:

> A translation of the Bible as a tombstone, a tombstone in the place of a gift from the guest or a gift of hospitality [*Gastgeschenk*], a funerary crypt given in thanks for a language, the tomb of a poem in memory of a language given, a tomb which contains several other ones, including all the ones from the Bible, including the one from the Scriptures (and Rosenzweig was never far from becoming a Christian), the gift of a poem as the offering from a tomb which could be, for all one will ever know, a cenotaph, what an opportunity to commemorate a monolingualism of the other! What a sanctuary, and what a seal, for so many languages! (*M*, 83)

In contrast, Levinas is neither ironic nor skeptical of hospitality, which is for him, rather, an enactment along the horizontal lines of an ethics of a holy, covenantal relationship. Nor is it so certain who is the guest and who is the host in Levinas's relation to language. His characteristic trope, if it is one, is the deployment of key terms for philosophy in French that translate the sacred force of an underlying biblical and rabbinic Hebrew. That relationship of French to Hebrew in his philosophical texts is made altogether explicit through the parallel project of Levinas's Talmudic lessons. Hebrew—not a modernizing, secular Hebrew, but the sacred Hebrew of Jewish tradition, the Hebrew of the Talmud-Torah—is the at-home language and French the *Gastgeschenk* in acknowledgment of the hospitality extended to philosophy.

5

As a language of philosophy, French (or Greek, as he will say more customarily) passes through a sacred, Jewish language for Levinas. But for a monolingual Franco-Maghrebian Jew, for whom Ladino, rather than Hebrew, represents the linguistic point of reference to an unavailable Jewish sphere, what would that passing sound like?

For Derrida the answer comes at the end of the long note, beyond the disruptive, if still Ashkenazi example of Levinas, beyond the brief fantasy of a mixed, but still Ashkenazi marriage of "the German of Arendt, with the German of Kafka" (*M*, 93):

> In this typo-topology, but also outside it, in this place of defiance for the distinction between Ashkenazim and Sephardim, I feel even less capable of a discourse that will measure up to another poetics of language, to an immense and exemplary event: in the work of Hélène Cixous, and in a miraculously unique way, another intersection is weaving *all* these filiations, regenerating them toward [*vers*] a future still without name. It is necessary to recall that this great-French-Jewish-woman-writer-from-Sephardic-Algeria, who is reinventing, among others, the language of her father, *her* French language, an unheard-of French language is also a German-Ashkenazic-Jewish-woman by her "mother tongue." (*M*, 93, translation altered)

Overdone by the last: The Ashkenazi typology cannot contain Cixous, nor can it ever be complete without her. In the face of her "immensity," her miraculous uniqueness, Derrida recovers his hyperbolic wit.[26] Her Sephardic slant reopens the canon of language theory in Jewish studies to the Maghrebian shore of the Mediterranean. At the end of the pile-up of her predicates, Cixous gives rise to a new toponym, *d'ailleurs*, for a Jewish dwelling in colonial and postcolonial Algeria: *Algérie-sépharade*, Sephardic Algeria.[27] Derrida need no more pledge allegiance and lament a lost Ladino, for Cixous has put an end to that ending. In Cixous's *inouïe langue française*, her unheard-of French, he now overhears the voice that speaks for and from the hypermnesic Algerian Jewish *lieu de mémoire—our place in Algeria*, Derrida's no less than Cixous's—that Cixous herself calls "my Algeriance."[28]

The full title of Cixous's auto-bio-geo-graphical text reads, "My Algeriance, in Other Words: To Depart Not to Arrive from Algeria," but it is the neologism *Algeriance* that remains the key. Neologism is as characteristic of Cixous's language practices as hyperbole is to Derrida (she might say, "I invent, I always invent"). *My Algeriance* is unheard of, and yet *proper*, morphologically correct French that extends the toponym, Algeria, beyond its orthographical end and exposes the language of location to its limits. The apparent fixity of a static, homogenous, and measurable geography is set in motion by giving the proper noun a form derived from the present participle of a verb. Cixous explains: "I like the progressive form and the words that end in *-ance*. So much so that if I headed *toward* France [*si je me suis dirigée* vers *la France*, my emphasis] without mistrust, it is perhaps because of this grammatical ending [*terminaison*] which gives the present participle its lucky chance" (*MA*, 227, translation altered). Mireille Calle-Gruber amplifies the point in her reading of the closely related neologism *passance* in "My Algeriance." Where Cixous writes, "The chance of my genealogy and history had arranged things in such a way that I would *stay passing*; in an originary way for me I am always passing by, in *passance*" (*MA*, 227), Calle-Gruber comments, "To be in '*passance*' thus designates *the state of movement*, the being-movement."[29] The *-ance* is a *dalāla* indicating the taking place of indeterminate action or a gesture pointing to a direction; and *passance*, more particularly, is the signpost of a *passing* that has never passed, much less passed away: the very *toward* of a movement.

It is very difficult, maybe the most difficult thing, this Algeri-ing, even this Fr-ancing:

> I went toward [*vers*] France, without having had the idea of arriving there. Once in France I was not there. I saw that I would never arrive in France. I had not thought about it. At the beginning I was disturbed, surprised, I had so wanted to leave that I must have vaguely thought that leaving would lead to arriving. Just as beginning would lead to ending. But not at all. Everything has always done nothing but leave and begin. In the first naïve period it is very strange and difficult to not arrive where one is. For a year I felt the ground tremble, the streets repel me, I was sick. Until the day I understood there is no harm, only difficulties, in living in the zone without belonging. (*MA*, 226–27)

Disturbed, surprised, *troublée*, *étonnée*, unsettled and perplexed, Cixous invents a fourth interdiction: no ending. The *vers*, too, is a *dalāla*, a guide to this Un-landing,[30] as Derrida glimpses from the coast of his long note, when he supposes that there must be a Sephardic version of Jewish pla-cing, a *vers*-ing, a toward-ing, a Sephardic *vers-ant*. Cixous's *dalāla* of the *-ance* is a *renvoi d'ailleurs* pointing to the Ladino that is unavailable to her, and yet, miraculously, she speaks in the translation of her unheard-of French.

An Unconcluding Pedagogical Postscript

This ghostly Ladino living on in Cixous's unheard-of French is "beyond cartography," as Derrida had supposed in his long note, insofar as it maps a location that is never here nor there—neither in Algeria nor in France, for example—but always elsewhere. Cixous's Ladino is a language native to a plac-ing, rather than a place. It would be more a little inn, a *hanizitju*, than a private house, a language of the *hôte* that makes her newly invented French feel at home precisely because it is always passing through. But is such a language of the *hôte* an "unteachable knowledge," as Derrida also *avers*?

I recall an introductory lesson, a language prior to the language of the text, Anidjar's prefatory acknowledgments page of *Our Place in al-Andalus*, where he declares, "This book was written in the wake of Amos Funkenstein's death. His teaching has been and continues to be a true gift." And how do we know the gift was true? What was the truth of the gift? That the teaching is continuous, that the learning is endless. And the student says, thank you.

And Ham Daniel was a teacher, unsettling the monolingualism of his pupils, lifting the interdictions that cut them off from the depths of their past, and therefore from themselves, welcoming them into language that is and is not theirs. And how did he say, you're welcome? Without a word, in a gesture of sweetness that is a language-prior-to-the-first-language and that is never lost. And his welcoming was his teaching. And Isak remembered.

Not so much a knowledge, then, this sacred, unspoken, even unspeakable language that suffuses the languages we learn to speak, and above all as an acknowledgment. Not something taught, but a *teach-ing*, which in the Hebrew of Ham Daniel's language lesson is *torah*. And Ham Daniel's *torah*, living on beyond the ends of Ladino, is his *pasandu*.

NOTES

1. Isak Papo, Rikica Ovidija, Gina Camhy, and Clarissa Nikoïdski, *Cuentos sobre los sefardies de Sarajevo/A Collection of Sephardim Stories from Sarajevo*, trans. Zjena Čulić and Myrna Svičarević (Split: Logos, 1994). In the Ladino text of the biographies of the authors, Papo is referred to as the editor of the volume (191).

2. Isak Papo, "La karitja di oru" ("The Little Face of Gold"), in Papo et al., *Cuentos*, 108, in my translation. I follow Papo in leaving more or less acclimatized Hebrew loan words (e.g., Bet Din, hazanim, Degel Atora [in its Ladino pronunciation]) as is, as well as in his idiosyncratic punctuation.

3. I find myself still, as I have for these several decades, between my two teachers, Jacques Derrida at his scene of writing and Harold Bloom at his scene of instruction, wishing, still, that they had continued that disjointed conversation, ever *à venir*. See Jacques Derrida, "Freud et la scène de l'écriture," in *L'écriture et la difference* (Paris: Éditions du Seuil, 1967), 293–340; and Harold Bloom, "The Primal Scene of Instruction," in *A Map of Misreading* (New York: Oxford University Press, 1975), 41–62; and "Wordsworth and the Scene of Instruction," in *Poetry and Repression: Revisionism from Blake to Stevens* (New Haven: Yale University Press, 1976), esp. 55.

4. The *Hanizitju* is also known in the Ladino of Sarajevo as *il Kortižo* (from Castilian *cortijo*, a manor house or farmhouse, a landed estate usually with corral or courtyard) and as *Velika avlija* (Great Yard) in Bosnian. Čulić and Svičarević translate the *kil grandi*, big synagogue (without capitalization in the text—in contrast to *Hanizitju*) as a reference to the "Great Temple," which would be the Sephardic synagogue built in 1932 and destroyed by the Nazis in 1941, rather than as a common noun. However, that synagogue was not built until long after Ham Daniel's lessons narrated in the memoir, though the lapse may be in Papo's memory. On the *Hanizitju*, see Muhamed Nezirovič, "The Sephardim of Bosnia," at http://esefarad.com/?p=61846 accessed 8/23/2016. On Jewish space in its theoretical and historical constructions, see Barbara E. Mann, *Space and Place in Jewish Studies* (New Brunswick, N.J.: Rutgers University Press, 2012).

5. See Quỳnh N. Phạm, "Enduring Bonds: Politics and Life Outside Freedom and Autonomy," *Alternatives: Global, Local, Political* 38, no. 1 (2013): 29–48.

6. Jacques Derrida, *Monolingualism of the Other; or, The Prosthesis of Origin*, trans. Patrick Mensah (Stanford: Stanford University Press, 1998), 1, henceforth cited parenthetically in the text as *M* and the corresponding page number. Where translations are altered, the French text is taken from Derrida, *Le monolinguisme de l'autre, ou la prothèse d'origine* (Paris: Galilée, 1996).

7. I ask the reader's indulgence. I am a language teacher. I cannot bring myself to speak of the language that my students are learning in the classroom as a *target* language. It's not a shooting gallery. On the *langue d'arrivée* and *langue de départ*, see *M* 61.

8. The Ladino text refers the passage erroneously to Psalm 110, corrected in the accompanying published translation.

9. Jacques Derrida, "Circumfession," in Derrida and Geoff Bennington, *Jacques Derrida*, trans. Bennington (Chicago: University of Chicago Press, 1993).

10. See also Albert Memmi's closely related Jewish supplement to his own *The Colonizer and the Colonized* (New York: Orion, 1965) in Albert Memmi, *Jews and Arabs*, trans. Eleanor Levieux (Chicago: John P. O'Hara, 1975).

11. In the same note, Derrida makes further acknowledgment of Christine Buci-Glucksmann, director of the International College of Philosophy, where he had delivered a still earlier "outline" of the paper. The name of Patrick Mensah, the translator of the text, appears among the acknowledgments in the English version of the note, but not in French.

12. Most notoriously, for Jewish studies, Derrida had referred to himself as "the last of the Jews" in "Circumfession," 190. In *Monolingualism*, he explicitly acknowledges that the earlier claim had been "above all the same hyperbole. . . . I take stock, believe me, of the ridiculousness and overkill of these puerile allegations (like the 'I am the last of the Jews' in *Circumfession*)" (*M*, 83).

13. I leave the keyword *hôte* to retain the ambiguity of the two principal significations in English—to wit, both *host* and *guest*—that is crucial to Derrida's usage. As he presently announces in the note, Derrida will continue to discuss the *hôte* under the heading of hospitality, for instance, in his essay, "Hostipitality," trans. Gil Anidjar, in *Acts of Religion*, ed. Anidjar (New York: Routledge, 2002), 356–420, as well as in Jacques Derrida and Anne Dufourmantelle, *Of Hospitality*, trans. Rachel Bowlby (Stanford: Stanford University Press, 2000). See also the related treatment of the figure of the ghost, related etymologically to *hôte*, e.g., Jacques Derrida, *Specters of Marx: The State of the Debt, The Work of Mourning and the New International*, trans. Peggy Kamuf (New York: Routledge, 1994).

14. See Andrew Bush, *Jewish Studies: A Theoretical Introduction* (New Brunswick, N.J.: Rutgers University Press, 2011), 40–49. The vigorous growth of Sephardic studies in recent years is encouraging.

15. Gil Anidjar, *"Our Place in al-Andalus": Kabbalah, Philosophy, Literature in Arab Jewish Letters* (Stanford: Stanford University Press, 2002), 57, cited henceforth parenthetically as *OP*.

16. The passage quoted on *OP* 10 is based on Moses Maimonides, *The Guide of the Perplexed*, trans. Shlomo Pines (Chicago: University of Chicago Press, 1963), 2 vols. Anidjar has supplied and so highlighted Maimonides' Arabic terms.

17. See, for instance, Hamid Dabashi, "In the Absence of the Face," in *The World Is My Home: A Hamid Dabashi Reader*, ed. Andrew Davison and Himadeep Muppidi (New Brunswick, N.J.: Transaction, 2011), 19–56, including his critique of Derrida in note 14.

18. I am aware of a certain circularity in this supposition: Given Anidjar's profound engagement with the work of Derrida, which predates "'Our Place in al-Andalus"—see especially *Acts of Religion*—it is as well to say that he reads Derridean deconstruction into Maimonides as to say that he discovers a Maimonidean trace in Derrida.

19. Maimonides, *Guide*, 1:3–4.

20. See Nicolas Abraham and Maria Torok, *The Wolf Man's Magic Word: A Cryptonomy*, trans. Nicholas Rand (Minneapolis: University of Minnesota Press, 2005), which includes Derrida's foreword, "Fors," a direct intervention in the elaboration of the theory of the crypt.

21. Abraham and Torok contest Freud's "Mourning and Melancholia," the latter in *The Standard Edition of the Complete Psychological Works of Sigmund Freud, Volume XIV (1914–1916): On the History of the Psycho-Analytic Movement, Papers on Metapsychology and Other Works*, 237–58. See Abraham and Torok, "Mourning *or* Melancholia: Introjection versus Incorporation," and other related papers on the crypt and the phantom in Nicolas Abraham and Maria Torok, *The Shell and the Kernel: Renewals of Psychoanalysis*, vol. 1, trans. Nicholas Rand (Chicago: University of Chicago Press, 1994). Drawing on Abraham and Torok, I have treated the question of melancholia as an alternative paradigm to historical consciousness in a very different setting (see Bush, *The Routes of Modernity: Spanish American Poetry from the Early Eighteenth to the Mid-Nineteenth Century* [Lewisburg, Pa.: Bucknell University Press, 2002], esp. 33–39)—then, as now, part of a lifetime of conversation with Nicholas Rand, dating back to his *Le cryptage et la vie des oeuvres* (Paris: Aubier, 1989), through his collaborations with Maria Torok, such as Nicholas Rand and Maria Torok, *The Secret History of Psychoanalysis* (Cambridge, Mass.: Harvard University Press, 1997) and continuing to the present day.

22. See Nicolas Abraham, "Notes du séminaire sur l'unité duelle et le fantôme [1974–75]," in *L'écorce et le noyau*, ed. Nicolas Abraham and Maria Torok (Paris: Aubier-Flammarion, 1978), 397–98.

23. I allude here—I can do no more than allude without an asterisk and a long note of my own—to a chain of tradition in theory that connects Anidjar's reading of the Maimonidean parable of fractured languages and indeed the whole working method of *"Our Place in al-Andalus"* to Walter Benjamin's theory of translation (see esp. *OP* 17 and 98–101). I suppose that I could sketch a project-to-come that would be a closely related alternative to Derrida's outline of the *Monolingualism of the* Hôte. The foundation would be the more than oft-cited essay by Benjamin, "The Task of the Translator," trans. Harry Zohn, in Walter Benjamin, *Selected Writings, Vol. 1, 1913–1926*, ed. Marcus Bullock and Michael W. Jennings (Cambridge, Mass.: Belknap Press of Harvard University Press, 1996), 253–63. Reading back from Benjamin to Buber and Rosenzweig's German translation of the Hebrew Bible (see the related texts in Martin Buber and Franz Rosenzweig, *Scripture and Translation*, trans. Lawrence Rosenwald and Everett Fox [Bloomington: Indiana University Press, 1994]), the itinerary would cross out of the Ashkenazi curriculum to a Sephardic version in Rosenzweig's reflections on his

translations of Halevi (see Barbara Ellen Galli, *Franz Rosenzweig and Jehuda Halevi: Translating, Translations, and Translators* [Montreal: McGill-Queen's University Press, 1995]); reading forward, one approaches Derrida's essay on Benjamin of 1985, "Des Tours de Babel," trans. Joseph F. Graham, in *Psyche: Inventions of the Other* (Stanford: Stanford University Press, 2007), 1:191–225, and "Living On/Border Lines," trans. James Hubert, in *Deconstruction and Criticism*, by Harold Bloom et al. (New York: Seabury, 1979), 75–176; and thence on to Anidjar again, especially his close consideration of Scholem in relationship to Benjamin under the heading of mourning (*OP* 102–65), and his subsequent work. I am beginning to pursue that project in relation to a still more recent link in the chain, Judith Butler's *Parting Ways: Jewishness and the Critique of Zionism* (New York: Columbia University Press, 2012) in conjunction with the poetry of Adrienne Rich. The politics of Butler's one-state solution in Israel-Palestine was a principal instigator of much of the discussion at the conference represented in the papers collected in the present volume. I consider instead her recourse to Benjamin's theory of translation, as she receives it along this chain (especially from Derrida), as a theory of Jewish studies.

24. This project was realized as Jacques Derrida, "The Eyes of Language: The Abyss and the Volcano" and "Secularizing Language: The Volcano, the Fire, the Enlightenment," trans. Anidjar, in *Acts of Religion*.

25. Mensah translates, "They have no language that is exclusively their own" (*M*, 79), but the derivation of exclusivity from property raises too many question to address here.

26. Derrida does not continue his reading of Cixous in the long note, but they have both written often and at length about each other's work. See, among others, Hélène Cixous, *Portrait of Jacques Derrida as a Young Jewish Saint*, trans. Beverley Bie Brahic (New York: Columbia University Press, 2004), and "The Strangejew Body," trans. Bettina Bergo and Michael B. Smith, in *Judeities: Questions for Jacques Derrida*, ed. Bettina Bergo, Joseph Cohen, and Raphael Zagury-Orly (New York: Fordham University Press, 2007), 52–77; and Jacques Derrida, *H.C. for Life, That Is to Say—*, trans. Laurent Milesi and Stefan Herbrecthter (Stanford: Stanford University Press, 2006), and *Geneses, Genealogies, Genres, and Genius: The Secrets of the Archive*, trans. Beverley Bie Brahic (New York: Columbia University Press, 2006).

27. There is a syntactic ambiguity in Derrida's exaggerated stringing together of qualifiers. A *grande-écrivain-française-juive-d'Algérie-sépharade* could be a Sephardic-*grande-écrivain-française-juive-d'Algérie*, and Mensah translates the compound that way: "this great-French-Sephardic-Jewish-woman-writer-from-Algeria" (*M*, 93). In contrast to the arrangement of "juive-ashkénaze-allemande," with Ashkenazi in the midst, however, the final adjective would

seem displaced, overflowing the ending, suggesting rather that Cixous is being characterized as a *grande-écrivain-française-juive*-from Sephardic Algeria.

28. Hélène Cixous, "My Algeriance, In Other Words: To Depart Not to Arrive from Algeria," trans. Eric Prenowitz, in *Stigmata: Escaping Texts* (London: Routledge, 1998), 204–31; cited henceforth parenthetically as *MA*, no less. Mireille Calle-Gruber provides ample excerpts from the French text, otherwise difficult to access, in "La langue des alliances. *Mon Algériance*," *Études littéraires* 33, no. 3 (2001); see especially 84–85 (http://www.erudit.org/revue/etudlitt/2001/v33/n3/501309ar.pdf, accessed 8/23/2016). I take my references to Cixous's original text from Calle-Gruber's excerpts.

29. Calle-Gruber, "La langue des alliances," 91.

30. Cixous is explicit in her undoing of the traditional language of the covenantal promise: "France was never the Promised Land," and she adds, "The sentence 'next year in Jerusalem' makes me flee. The desire, the necessity of arriving 'home,' I understand them and I do not share them" (*MA*, 227).

CHAPTER 4

The Last Jewish Intellectual: Derrida and His Literary Betrayal of Levinas

Sarah Hammerschlag

"The Son is a parasite as Literature," Derrida wrote in his 1999 essay "Literature in Secret."[1] Within the context of the essay this statement is a commentary on Kafka's letter to his father, which is itself treated in the essay as a commentary on the story of Abraham and Isaac. However, surreptitiously there is another father/son narrative that resonates in this text, and throughout Derrida's late corpus, the story of another betrayal between father and son, one which situates Derrida as the son, as the parasite, as the site of literature, even, and Emmanuel Levinas as the father.

Derrida's topic in the essay is not explicitly Emmanuel Levinas, or paternity, but the relationship between literature and religion. The essay was added as an addendum to *Gift of Death* (*Donner la mort*), and while Levinas plays a fairly central role in *Gift of Death*, his name appears in "Literature in Secret" only in the context of an anecdote. And the anecdote calls attention to itself only insofar as Derrida oversignified his efforts not to draw attention to it.

It appears within brackets and is prefaced with a disclaimer: "Although reporting this anecdote is not essential to what I am developing here . . . I remember how one day Levinas, in an aside, during a dissertation defense said to me, with a sort of sad humor and ironic protestation, 'Nowadays, when one says "God," one almost has to ask for forgiveness or excuse oneself: "God, if you'll pardon the expression."'[2] It would be easy to dismiss the comment. Derrida himself redoubled his indication that this is exactly what we *should* do.

After all, what would Levinas have to do with an essay whose primary theme is the relation between scripture and literature? The answer of course is everything.

Derrida, if we look closely, has already given himself away, for the phrase "God, if you'll pardon the expression," appears as the essay's epigraph, under the title and after the subtitle, "an impossible filiation." As an epigraph it appears without quotation marks, disconnected from its context, an unattributed citation, a fragment.

Pardon for Not Meaning to Say

The essay "Literature in Secret" itself concerns the process by which a word spoken between two can become quotation, a citation, and then a fragment. It considers what happens when a pledge or a secret is subject to representation. It argues that representation is always already a dissimulation and a betrayal of this relation. Explicitly at issue is the secret that stands between Abraham and Isaac in the Akeda, and the essay proposes that the story of Abraham's sacrifice of Isaac in the Hebrew Bible is already a betrayal of the pact between Abraham and God, as a recounting of what Abraham could not himself tell, what he could not tell Sarah or Isaac. It is the recounting of this story by a third party disseminated to anyone, for any reader.

This drift from covenant to narrative, from the second to the third person, reveals the connection between modern fiction and the story of Abraham. Modern fiction, Derrida argues, is the inheritor of a biblical betrayal. Moreover, it is something like a sequel, a repetition and reorientation of the religious fable. What separates it from the biblical testament is that it signifies as a request for pardon, a pardon for the betrayal of representation. By treating what it represents as fiction, literature refuses to offer up the secret as something revealed. "Pardon de ne pas vouloir dire," or "Pardon for not meaning (to say)." This fragment, according to Derrida in the essay, is the formula at the heart of modern literature. Fiction in particular is marked by the suspension of a "vouloir dire" insofar as it disrupts any transparent relation between what is represented and reality.

The suspension of the "vouloir dire" in language was a theme of Derrida's, beginning with *La voix et le phénomène* (1967). In *Voice and Phenomenon*, *vouloir dire*, or *Bedeutung*, is for Derrida, via his reading of Husserl, that element of meaning that expresses the will of the speaker. Its absence correlates to the lack of an animating spirit, or "the process of death at work in the signs."[3] In the text Derrida reverses the priority between Husserl's two concepts of the sign: expression and indication. Expression for Husserl, a sign with *vouloir dire*, a sign which means, is primary. Indication, a sign devoid of intention, but not thus void of signification, is secondary. Derrida's close reading of *Logical Investigations I*, particularly of Husserl's description of self-presence, reveals that expression is in fact secondary and an effect of indication, thus calling into question the sign's capacity to act as a pure expression. Derrida proceeds through an analysis of the function of the "living voice" in Husserl. Here "fiction" is already implicated in the making of meaning, for in speaking to myself, through an internal voice, which should be the site of a pure presence, Husserl suggests that I must proceed by way of a fiction,[4] for insofar as I speak to myself, I imagine that I use a sign, when in fact the very act of representation would be foreign to the perfect internal solitude of the self. Derrida argues that this necessary "fiction" around which "auto-affection" is imagined is indeed a fiction, but only insofar as he reverses the terms. The activity or movement of the self speaking to itself, which implies a self differing from itself, is the only means by which self-presence can be thought. "But this pure difference, which constitutes the self-presence of the living present reintroduces into it originarily all the impurity that we had believed we were able to exclude from it."[5] The illusion is thus the pure interiority of a self-presence that doesn't involve *re*-presentation, rather than the obverse. At the basis of the speaking subject, thus, there is already what Derrida called "archi-writing," which "is at work in the origin of sense." This dynamic would then implicate the very system of signification, its "meaning" making, which would now be characterized by what Derrida names "supplementarity":

> The structure of supplementarity is very complicated. Insofar as it is a supplement, the signifier does not first re-present merely the absent signified. It substitutes itself for another signifier, for another signifying order, which carries on another relation with the missing presence, another relation that is more valuable owing to the play of difference. . . . In this way the indication is not only the substitute which supplements the absence or the invisibility of the indicated. . . . The indicated also replaces another type of signifier, a signifier whose signified (the *Bedeutung*) is ideal.[6]

It would thus be fair to say that all discourse for Derrida is in fact compensating for an absence of "vouloir dire." Thus when Derrida speaks of the modern institution of literature, it is not to describe a dynamic of meaning that is any different from language in general but it is a means of inhabiting it differently. Literature, Derrida argues in "Literature in Secret," says *Pardon* for not having a *vouloir dire*. How so? As a genre, fiction is characterized by its obscuring the relationship between author and speaker. When a text is categorized as fiction, whatever its content, this designation complicates any ascription of intention to its author. A fictional story recounts; it moves the relation between two to the plane of representation, where it becomes a relationship *for* a third. In this sense it inherits the biblical task of revealing the secret, but it alters it, by presenting its material under new auspices. The circulation of literature opens up the relationship between two to anyone who can pick up and read. But it replaces the covenantal call with content whose status has itself been called into question by the fact of its context itself having been disrupted. What is key in "Literature in Secret" is that this replacement is a kind of repetition whose function is to undermine the dynamic of election without covering over its own problematic status as representation. At the same time, Derrida argues, literature reinstates the secret but on new ground, not as the site of a covenantal election, a between-two which can in fact be betrayed, but rather through an exposure to interpretation, and resignification, to a slippage in meaning that ironically guards its own secrecy by disrupting the relation between agent and meaning, such that a vertical relation of revelation is replaced by a horizontal drift. One could argue of course, as Derrida often does, that this quality is intrinsic to language itself. Thus what marks literature is its avowed parasitic position. It sucks the life out of the covenantal structure of religion but feeds off of its contractual tics. To emphasize his point, Derrida begins the essay by asking us to imagine the phrase "Pardon for not meaning to say" divorced from any context, discovered on a wall, or inscribed in a stone, such that "the average 'Hermeneut' would never know whether this request ever signified something in a real context."[7]

The Betrayal of Irony

With the context of the essay in mind, let us return to Derrida's anecdote. In retelling the story about Levinas, Derrida was betraying his own pact. The story is told of a moment when Levinas took Derrida into confidence. The act of its recounting not only betrays his confidence, it also reveals something of the transformative quality of representation. What we have here is a redoubled irony, for Levinas, who was himself being ironic, appears to have made the comment in a shared moment of intimacy with Derrida in which Derrida as addressee would appear to have been in collusion with Levinas. Here the irony, it seems, has the function of solidifying an unspoken agreement between two, a shared sense of incredulity that reference to the divine, to the sphere of religion, would be something for which one would have to excuse oneself. Here we can think of what Wayne Booth calls stable irony, in which the meaning of the utterance implies the confidence that both the speaker and the listener know the speaker's position and thus can share in the joke. This mode of irony, Booth notes, "is the key to the tightest bonds of friendship."[8] I would add that it marks the site of a secret. This is a consistent rhetorical technique employed by Levinas in his essays, one that seems to have the function of clearly drawing the line between insider and outsider.

In the very act of retelling the story, Derrida betrayed the secret, as well as the bond enforced by the rhetorical technique. This is even more apparent when we consider the context. The incident itself is relayed in the service of an argument claiming literature as that which "in naming God must ask forgiveness." The dynamic that Levinas seemed to be condemning, Derrida *defended* as the fundamental task of literature. Thus in telling the story, Derrida broke the pact set in place by the original ironic utterance. He resisted the gesture of inscription, which would have placed Derrida and Levinas on the inside of an understanding only by excluding all others present. In the process he, at least momentarily, established a new site of irony, between Derrida and the reader of or listener to Derrida's paper, such that Levinas would now be excluded, and indeed would become the object of the joke.

In so doing, Derrida exploited the fact that even the most stable of ironies always has the potential to be turned on its users. As even Booth concedes: "Irony in itself opens up doubts as soon as its possibility enters our heads, and there is no inherent reason for discontinuing the process of doubt at any point short of infinity. . . . It is not irony but the desire to understand irony that brings such a chain to a stop."[9] Whereas for Booth such a scenario would indicate the misuse of a powerful tool, for Derrida the capacity for instability to infect the communicative act points to the very essence of language. It is no surprise then that deconstruction has been read as the exemplary site of postmodern irony.[10]

By subverting Levinas's stable irony, a gesture used to solidify the complicity between the two thinkers, Derrida took the betrayal a step further.

In fact, Derrida used Levinas's words to perform the function he ascribes to literature, for in using the phrase as an epigraph: "Dieu, passez-moi l'expression," Derrida set in motion the representational drift. Insofar as the essay defines literature as scripture's bastard son, betraying its secret but reinscribing it through a slippage that disallows disclosure, Derrida turned his own covenantal secret into literature.

Proximity

The incident itself provides the formula for understanding Derrida's relationship to Judaism, in contrast to Levinas's. Neither was a stranger to irony, but for Levinas irony was a tool for developing communal cohesion, emphasizing mutual understanding. For Derrida it was the device by which one slips out of the community grip.[11]

Given that Derrida's avowed references to Judaism appear mostly in and through ironic utterances—signing his essays on Jabès Reb Risa and Reb Rida in *Writing and Difference*, calling himself the last Jew in "Circumfession," and a Marrano in many of his later texts, referring to himself as "the least and the last of the Jews [le seul et le dernier des Juifs]"—it is worth noting that he himself emphasized the parallels between himself and Levinas in their situation and relation to French philosophy.[12]

In response to an interviewer who insisted on their differences, Derrida in a 1986 interview commented:

> We share the same traditional heritage, even if Levinas has been engaged with it for a much longer time and with greater profundity. Therefore, the difference is not there either. This is not the only example, but I often have difficulty in placing these discrepancies otherwise than as differences of "signature," that is of idiom, of ways of proceeding, of history, and of inscriptions connected to the biographical aspect, etc. These are not philosophical differences.[13]

It is difficult not to read even this statement as bearing multiple levels of irony, for if there is one thing Derrida's work consistently communicated it is the impossibility of distinguishing the "philosophical" from the marks of the signature: from idiom, history, and biography. At the same time, however, Derrida never ceased asserting his proximity to Levinas, the factors of which were clearly both philosophical and circumstantial, as were their sites of difference.

The two thinkers shared in common that they both came to France from Jewish backgrounds, Levinas from Lithuania, Derrida from Algeria, and for each, philosophy, the philosophical canon, was the means by which they acclimated and assimilated into French culture. For both, France and its philosophical culture was a means of liberation. Levinas recounts in a 1987 interview with François Poirié that it was in his first course with Maurice Pradines, when Pradines described the Dreyfus affair as a moment in which ethics conquered politics, that Levinas chose to be a philosopher.[14] For Derrida, from the moment of his expulsion from the state-run Lycée Ben Aknoun in November of 1942 and his enrollment at the Lycée Maimonide, Judaism was associated for him with the procedures of communal inscription. From Derrida's perspective the act of anti-Semitism was mirrored in the reformulation of the Jewish community in its response to the Vichy race laws: "This reactive self-defense was certainly natural and legitimate, even irreproachable," he once said, "but I must have sensed that it was a drive, a gregarious *compulsion* that responded too symmetrically, that *corresponded* in truth to an *expulsion*."[15] Even after Derrida was allowed to return to the Lycée Ben Aknoun, the experience tainted his passion for school, and it was only the discovery of a vocation in philosophy that provided the avenue of transformation and transportation to an affiliation with the Metropole.

But Jewishness could not fully be sloughed off for Derrida even by changing continents. From the very first, it shadowed his relation to Levinas. Derrida and Levinas first met in 1964 in Levinas's class at the Sorbonne, but Benoit Peeters notes that Levinas could have come to know of him through other means, through the networks of the Jewish community. Jacques Lazarus, the Algerian representative to the World Jewish Congress, which sponsored the Colloque des intellectuels juifs de langue française, of which Levinas was one of the founding members and most important contributors, wrote to Derrida's father, Aimé Derrida, a few months after Derrida had begun attending Levinas's class, to tell him that he had told Professor Levinas about Aimé's son Jacques and Jacques's work on Husserl.[16] Levinas had replied to Lazarus that he would be very happy to be in touch with Derrida. Levinas's position as surrogate father was thus secured.

Another Irony, Another Betrayal

It is clear as well that Derrida had at least some affiliation with the Colloque des intellectuels juifs de langue française. He is listed among the invited participants throughout the 1960s, and at least twice in these years as one of the attendees (1964 and 1969). It was not until 1998, however, two and a half years after Levinas's death that Derrida spoke at the Colloque and there addressed Levinas's role in his previous attendance. As noted by Levinas's biographer, the Colloque was a place where Derrida would never be seen.[17] According to Derrida, writing in 1998, he attended the Colloque once before, in 1965 (the records suggest it was in fact 1964), as a participant who did not speak: "Close to Emmanuel Levinas, near him, perhaps together with him. In truth, I was here thanks to him, turned toward him. That is still the case today, differently."

Although such comments have been taken as evidence of Derrida's unconditional endorsement of Levinas, as is often the case with Derrida, the meat of what he had to say is in what he did not, for even if we resist calling it at a "philosophical difference" (though how could it not be?), the essay makes clear that the difference between them was not only a difference *of* "signature" or of idiom, but a difference concerning the *nature and function* of the "signature" and the idiom.

At the Colloque, Derrida never referred to himself as an "intellectual juif de langue française," except to note that this is exactly what his listeners at the Colloque would "call" him. The act of community inscription that is only intimated in the anecdote previously described, an act performed in and through irony, is here more directly referenced. It seems, at least from Derrida's description, that he was at the Colloque with Levinas and because of him. Derrida was thus informing the audience at the Colloque in 1998 of the role that Levinas played as his intermediary. Levinas was thus the link between Derrida and the figure of the "Jewish intellectual." Derrida framed his very appearance at the meeting in terms of his ambivalence toward community inscription, titling his talk "Avowing—the Impossible: 'Returns,' Repentance, and Reconciliation." The sense in which Derrida's presence at the Colloque in 1998, just a few years after Levinas's death, plays with and resists functioning as an avowal, a confession of identity, a return to the fold, was referenced in the talk without ever being a direct subject of discourse.

It is striking then, that in asserting his link to Levinas, Derrida reported at the meeting the story of another aside spoken by Levinas to Derrida, *another* moment of Levinasian irony, and once again enacted another betrayal: "I recall what Levinas told me in an aside." He once again begins, and this time rather than minimizing the incident's importance, he calls attention to it. He specifies that he would recount the incident in the present tense, in the style of the historian who uses the present to make his words more *sensible* to representation. Derrida's own irony here is palpable as it is exactly the possibility of such coincidence between speaker and listener that he aims to call into question. He continues: "André Neher is lecturing and Levinas whispers in my ear: You see he is the Protestant—me, I'm the Catholic." This time Derrida's audience was the Colloque itself, the audience from which this aside was kept secret. Recounting this moment was once again certainly an act of betrayal. Once again Derrida notes Levinas's irony and asks "What must a Jewish thinker be in order to use this language, with the depth of seriousness and the lightness of irony we hear in it?"[18]

This is a strange question: "What must a Jewish thinker be?" Derrida seems to be asking it under the assumption that the anecdote once again marked a moment of stable irony, a moment in which Levinas was able to call himself a "Catholic" without calling into question Derrida's own capacity to share in the joke. But of course Derrida would not let such an assumption of complicity remain—a further betrayal. Derrida asks,

> How can he remain a Jew together with himself, while opening himself to another, probable or improbable, Jew, in this case me, who has never felt very Catholic, and above all not Protestant? A Jew who, coming from another shore of Judaism than Neher and Levinas, a Mediterranean shore, immediately remarks in the abyss of these doubles or of this Judeo-Catholic-Protestant triangle, the absence of the Islamo-Abrahamic?[19]

Levinas's joke refers to the fact that Neher at these meanings gave the biblical interpretation and Levinas the Talmudic. Thus Neher, the crypto-Lutheran subscribed to the motto of *sola scriptura* while Levinas, the crypto-Catholic, insisted that within the Jewish tradition, the Torah could only be read and interpreted by the rabbis. Derrida by way of his comment situates himself apart from both of these perspectives. At the same time, he construes the joke otherwise, for the second time, having already told the story of the incident in his eulogy for Levinas, published as *Adieu to Emmanuel Levinas*, where he used it to point to the warm reception Levinas received among Catholics.

In "Avowing," he uses the incident instead to suggest that the very fact of such hybridization—Jewish-Catholic, Jewish-Protestant—ought to destabilize the very conditions for such a context of understanding. Derrida asks, "How could such a split or divided Jew [referring ostensibly to himself in the third person, but also to Levinas] have received this remark? How could he welcome its letter according to the spirit . . . that nothing of all these differences, dissociations, or indecisions could cut into the complicity of a certain 'living together.'" Derrida thus calls into question more directly the procedure of stable irony on which Levinas depended particularly in his Jewish writings. He calls it into question on two levels: questioning the assumption that there could be a contemporaneity between two people and furthermore that one could ever be contemporaneous to oneself. According to Derrida, the covenantal relation, the oath, and the secret are all already compromised the moment one opens one's mouth to speak or to respond to a call. This point had important consequences for Derrida concerning what it means to call oneself Jewish, insofar as Judaism serves as the exemplary covenantal religion.

Levinas's Irony

In Levinas's Jewish writings, irony appears often through rhetorical questions in which Levinas parrots a derogatory depiction of Judaism in order to afterward debunk it or parrots a position he finds pedestrian or indulgent only to demand more of his listener or reader. For example, in the essay "The State of Israel and the Religion of Israel," published in *Evidences*, a postwar French Jewish journal, Levinas begins,

> The idea that Israel has a religious privilege is one that exasperates everyone. Some see it as unjustifiable pride, while to others it looks like an intolerable mystification which in the name of a sublime destiny, robs us of earthly joys. To live like every other people on earth, with police and cinemas and cafés and newspapers—what a glorious destiny![20]

He concludes with an exclamation point, the ultimate ironic signifier. The point here as elsewhere is to use irony to undermine the perspective that he wants to discredit. This technique has the effect on the one hand of catching the reader sympathizing with the Zeitgeist, but then of reinscribing him or her into the circle so that after having been corrected, he or she can inhabit as well the ironic voice that distances him or her from "popular" opinion. The Jewish perspective thus serves as an interruption and an agitation to the common culture, but is only effective as interruption insofar as the reader is realigned in the process with Levinas's perspective. This effect is clearest perhaps in Levinas's ironic rendition of Heidegger in "Heidegger, Gagarin, and Us": "We must urgently defend against this century's technology. Man will lose his identity and become a cog in a vast machine . . . no one will exist for himself [*pour soi*]."[21]

"There is some truth in this declamation," Levinas continues, only to further denounce this position later in the essay as attributable to the "pagan recesses of our Western souls."[22] That Levinas could not fully master this irony, at least in some of its deployments, is evidenced by some of the interpretive disagreements that have surrounded his position on Zionism.[23] Nonetheless, it seems clear that he aimed to master it, that he depended on the clarity of an idea to shine through language, and was indeed often suspicious of indeterminacy even as he insists on an ethics founded on the opacity of the other. As Derrida puts it in "En ce moment même dans cet ouvrage me voici": "Apparently he likes the tear [*déchirure*] but detests contamination." Yet, Derrida insists, the dynamics of Levinas's project, its emphasis on futurity, would seem to defy that interpretive move.

> What holds his writing in suspense is that one must welcome contamination, the *risk* of contamination, in enchaining the tears and regularly *mending and resuming them* within the philosophical text or tissue of a *récit*. This *mending resumption* [reprise] is even the condition on which what is beyond essence may keep its chance against the enveloping seam of the thematic or dialectical. The tear must be saved, and to do so one must play off seam against seam. The risk of contamination must be regularly accepted (in a series) in order for the noncontamination of the other by the rule of the same to still have a chance.[24]

In the textual dynamics described here we can see both how and why irony was such an important rhetorical tool for Levinas as well as why it served as a means by which Derrida would himself "contaminate" Levinas's texts. As Derrida argues in "En ce moment," in order for the relation with the "Other" to inflect Levinas's text, Levinas requires a means of rending, or interrupting, the thematic flow of discourse. In order to signal that communication is always buttressed by what Levinas calls "Le dire," the saying, the text must bear the marks of the ethical relation. Irony would be one means of inflecting the text with that relation, for in order for irony to function, a meaning must appear that both crosses and supports the discursive plane. Or as Derrida puts it, "One must play off seam against seam." However, such an endeavor can take place only at the risk of contamination; that risk of an ironic subversion of one's irony is one of the stakes of the game.

It was the very drive toward subversion in Derrida's texts that Levinas found distasteful. In his 1973 essay on Derrida's *La voix et le phénomène*, "Tout autrement," Levinas delineated between his own critical project and Derrida's.

> The desertion of presence, carried out to the point of desertion of the true, to the point of meanings that are no longer held to respond to

> the summons of Knowledge. Truth is no longer at the level of eternal or omnitemporal truth—but this is a relativism beyond historicism's wildest dreams. An exile or casting adrift of Knowledge beyond skepticism, which remained enamored of truth, even if it did not feel itself capable of embracing it. Henceforth meanings do not converge on truth. Truth is not the main thing![25]

Once again we meet with the sarcastic exclamation point, used to reveal the absurdity of the position just outlined. How indeed could truth not be the main thing? Levinas demands in "Tout autrement." This essay continues the tradition between the two of working out a relation of proximity and critique. Like Derrida's "Violence and Metaphysics," it is simultaneously laudatory and scathing. It declares the radicality of Derrida's departure from the tradition, and then just as Derrida resituated Levinas within the philosophical tradition, Levinas resituates Derrida. Does Derrida represent a new Copernican revolution, akin to Kant's? Levinas asked. "Is it a new break in the history of philosophy? It would also show its continuity. This history of philosophy is probably nothing but a growing awareness of the difficulty of thinking."

That said, Levinas recognizes Derrida's accomplishment, declaring his "deconstruction" of Husserl devastating. "At the outset, everything is in place; after a few pages or paragraphs of formidable calling into question, nothing is left inhabitable for thought."[26]

But there is a double edge to this high compliment, for must not a thought be inhabitable if it is to represent a way forward? Even more ambivalent is the comment, "This is, all philosophical significance aside, a purely literary effect, a new *frisson*, Derrida's poetry." Even as it continued to serve Levinas as a source for philosophical reflection in the postwar era, as an end literature was suspect.[27] It seemed to give off the scent of a morbid frivolity.[28] Eighteen years earlier in an essay on Blanchot, Levinas had distanced himself from the literary vision as a response to philosophy's ills in similar terms. "The literary sphere into which Blanchot leads us . . . far from elucidating the world, exposes the desolate, lightless substratum underlying it, and restores to our sojourn its exotic essence, and to the wonders of our architecture, their function as makeshift desert shelters . . ." This world, he continued, "is not nihilistic. But, in it, justice does not condition truth."[29] He went further with Derrida, comparing his deconstruction to the 1940 evacuation of Paris, an event that preoccupied Levinas throughout the war, appearing repeatedly in his journals as a moment that signified "not only the end of illusion, but the end of meaning, when meaning itself appeared as an illusion." Derrida's own deconstruction of Husserl is like a military invasion, unforeseeable and ruinous: "Everything is torn down [*déconstruit*] and left desolate: the houses closed up or abandoned with their doors open or emptied of their inhabitants."

The implications are clear. Levinas did not contest the validity of Derrida's deconstruction, but he did wonder whether the metaphysics of presence, the edifice that Derrida tore down, hadn't been the intellectual foundation for civilization. Literature or poetry then would be akin to playing kick the can among the ruins.

Of course, Levinas's passion for certain literary texts is well known. He referred often to *The Brothers Karamazov* in his philosophical writings, and found much to admire in Proust.[30] Published in 2009, the *Carnets de captivité*, his journal from his time in a Nazi Lager during the war attest to this passion.[31] Not only did he quote literary texts extensively, there is also evidence among these that he was taking notes for at least two novels. At the same time, however, his own postwar project to find in the Talmud corroboration for his view that these ancient Jewish texts supported his vision of ethics requires him to insist on the texts' underlying philosophical meaning. The Talmud harbors philosophical arguments, he suggested, but hides them in "apologues" and "adages."[32] The reader must "retrieve the initial design of its force, even when it is enveloped and made more palatable by thoughts that want only to be pious." For the sake of retrieving the "essence" of the Talmud's meaning, he went so far as to borrow the Christian distinction between the letter and the spirit in order to claim that the spirit can be recovered from the Talmudic text and the dead letter sloughed off.

Turning Levinas

It is not surprising perhaps that Derrida was sensitive to the conception of textuality evinced in Levinas's work. In "Avowing," given at the 1998 Colloque and written near the time that "Literature in Secret" was written, Derrida quotes one of Levinas's Talmudic readings, given in 1963, also at the Colloque, on the tractate *Yoma*.

> The respect for the stranger and the sanctification of the name of the eternal form a strange equivalence. And all the rest is a dead letter. All the rest is literature. . . . The image of God is better honored in the right given to the stranger than in symbols. Universalism . . . bursts the letter apart, for it lay, explosive, within the letter.[33]

He quotes this passage however not in order to discuss the role of literature in Levinas's texts but rather to argue that Levinas saw the connection between Jewish universalism and respect for the other. He quotes it in the service of suggesting that there is a germ in Levinas's philosophy for understanding the very resistance to community inscription that Derrida felt so profoundly, particularly in Algeria in the 1940s. He quotes it in the service of counseling for a kind of vigilance

> against all the risks of the "living together" of the Jews, be they of a symbiotic type (naturality, birth, blood, soil, nation) or conventional (state juridical, in the modern sense): a certain communitarianism, a certain Zionism, a certain nationalism and all that can follow when the motifs of filiation through blood, appropriation of the place and the motif of election...[34]

That such a sentiment was far from Levinas's own concerns—Levinas who had devoted much of his energy in the postwar period toward cultivating Jewish communitarianism, lauding the return by Jewish youth to studying Judaism's great books, who chastised Vladimir Jankélévitch for not learning Hebrew—did not seem to trouble Derrida. The point of Derrida's misreading should now be clear: If indeed, "all the rest is literature" this is the very space that Derrida chose to inhabit by destabilizing the very foundation of interpretation that Levinas depended on, transforming his work *thus* into literature, in the sense described in "Literature in Secret" as a repetition that displaces and destabilizes the covenantal context. It is striking in fact that Derrida subtitled the essay "Avowing" "leçon," when Levinas himself repeatedly referred to his Talmudic readings as "Les leçons Talmudique." Derrida thus only omitted the "Talmudic" referent in his own text. He references Levinas's own function at the Colloque, situates his own work as a repetition, but omits the reference to a canonical source. In fact insofar as there is some kind of scriptural referent here it is clearly to Levinas. Levinas's own readings occupy the canonical position. In the passage quoted above, Derrida himself seems be imitating a rabbinic motif, for like the rabbis who often quote only a fragment of a proof text, leaving sometimes the most significant element of it implicit, Derrida too begins his citation of Levinas with an important omission. Levinas's paragraph begins, "To punish children for the faults of their parents is less dreadful than to tolerate impunity when the stranger is injured."[35] The child according to Levinas's reading of the Talmud passage *can* be held accountable for the sin of the parent. Or as Derrida no doubt read this line, the child can and will be reinscribed into the tribe to the point of suffering.

Derrida saw himself in the context of both the Colloque and the Jewish community more broadly as the child who was held accountable against his will, an Isaac figure if you will. This is a point he emphasizes throughout his presentation. He refers to himself repeatedly as "the Jewish child," and as "the child of whom I speak."

But even as he was very clearly resisting his reinscription into the community on one level, I want to emphasize that on another level there is a point upon which Levinas and Derrida agreed: Responsibility precedes accountability. If this is the centerpiece of Levinasian ethics, then Derrida was its most adamant supporter. And it is out of his loyalty to this Levinasian principle, in fact, that he ultimately called Levinas's communitarian allegiances into question.

At the same time, however, Derrida insisted on the violence of inscription, on the violence of the very act of election. Derrida's point thus seems to have been that without disavowing inscription one can occupy it differently, by mobilizing the element of betrayal that is already as proper to the covenantal relation as the act of inscription. For Derrida that is exactly the role of literature: "inheritor and traitor," as he writes in "Literature in Secret," parodying the very form of covenant or contract, as every act of literature does according to Derrida:

> Be it understood that literature surely inherits from a holy history within which the Abrahamic moment remains the essential secret (and who would deny that literature remains a religious remainder [reste un reste de religion], a link and a relay for what is sacrosanct in a society without God?), but it also denies this history, this appurtenance, this heritage. It denies that affiliation. It betrays it in the double sense of the word: it is unfaithful to it, it breaks with it at the moment of manifesting its "truth" and of unveiling its secret. To know its own filiation: impossible possibility. This "truth" rests on the condition of a condition of a denial whose possibility was already implied by the Binding of Isaac.

What I want to emphasize is the way in which this description of literature is equally a description of Derrida's own relation to Levinas: a betrayal, that was equally an act of fidelity, the sign of a *filiation* that marked Levinas as the father and Derrida as the son.

The role of paternity is key to Levinas's treatment of exteriority in his first magnum opus *Totality and Infinity* (1961), where it is considered under the theme of "fecundity," a category that Levinas opposes to the project. Where the project "emanates from a solitary head to illuminate and to comprehend . . . dissolves into light and converts exteriority into idea," fecundity, the son "comes to pass from beyond the possible, beyond projects," one "irreducible to the power over possibles."[36] Levinas thus considered paternity as a relation that allows for a true futurity, one not mastered by the subject, not describable in terms of actualization. "Paternity is a relation with a stranger who while being Other," Levinas wrote, "*is* me, a relation of the I with a self which yet is not me."[37] The relation with the son illustrates the capacity of the self for true transcendence, not a transcendence which would merely materialize the vision of the self, as in the work of art that I produce from my idea and thus would not be transcendent, but one in which the issue, the son, would be fully free of the issuer.

To take up the role of the son for Derrida was to take up the role of Levinas's successor, as well as the very theme of succession, but it was not to respect the distinction between the relation of paternity and that of artist or writer to his production, so key to Levinas's conceptualization.

Already in 1980 in the essay "En ce moment . . . me voici" Derrida argues that the distinction between the son and the work cannot be maintained. Like the son, Derrida counters, the work too is the future and has a future, one that is not reducible to the "power over possibles," one which cannot be protected from contamination, from *La difference*, a term whose feminine form was already a response to Levinas's masculine description of paternity.[38] In 1980 Derrida developed the implication of this *gendered* difference. He enacted the work's independence by showing the way in which the differential function of language always escapes the intention of the author. Merely by replacing Levinas's name with his initials, EL, its vocalization issues in the pronoun "elle." For Derrida this "reading otherwise" is the outgrowth of Levinas's philosophy, the only Levinasian response to the gift of Levinas's text, but it issues at the same time from the very working of textuality itself, is "the very process of the trace insofar as it makes a work in a making-work."[39] For Derrida the relation of the son to the father is also already the very movement of "the work," of textuality. In the text Derrida dramatizes this parallel by playing the role of the son/daughter and issuing a text whose betrayal, he suggests, was the only possible gesture of loyalty.

With this relation of filiation in mind, which marks a site both of a fidelity to Levinas and its site of betrayal we can finally return to consider the way in which Levinas served as a site of reference for Derrida's various expressions of Jewish identification.

In "Circumfession," for example, Derrida refers to himself as "the last of the Jews, the end of Judaism. . . . There are so few of us and we are so divided."[40] In other texts Derrida makes use as well of the notion of the Marrano, for which the very act of self-avowal already belies the claim to be one. This exercise of ironic self-description, declaring oneself "le dernier des juifs," the least and the last of the Jews," Derrida discloses in his 2001 "Abraham, l'autre," ties up with what he wants to say about literature in its relation to religion and to Judaism more particularly. It is equally, he insists, an expression of fidelity to "the site of a responsibility without limits," and thus we can infer an expression of fidelity to the Levinasian conception of election.

Given Levinas's own distrust of literary modes of expression, there might seem to be a tension here. But the tension is not between Levinas and Derrida, so much as it is within Levinas's own paradigm. It is a tension which Levinas fought to elide, and Derrida to mobilize.

What Levinas himself reveals in his treatment of ethical subjectivity is that the I in election is both noncoincident with itself and in the diachrony of the ethical relation, noncoincident with the other. It is Levinas as well who argues that the covenantal moment in Judaism is axiomatic of this very dynamic. It is out of fidelity to this insight that Derrida insisted that betrayal and fidelity always already coincide. But it is this very dynamic that Levinas seems to elide when he spoke from and toward a communitarian position.

In telling the story of one of Levinas's asides at the Colloque, Derrida describes his own reaction, "How could he [Derrida] welcome the letter according to the spirit of Levinas's comment?"

> that nothing of all these differences, dissociations or indecisions could damage [*entamer*] the complicity of a certain "living together" that had decided for *us* well before *us*—I name thus the supposed friendship, the affinity, the complicity, if not the shareable solidarity of Jews so different within themselves, so different from themselves within themselves and at their core, be they assured or not of a stable and decidable belonging to Judaism?[41]

How could Levinas, moreover, have insisted on the symmetry between the election of ethics and Judaism? How could he have used it to consolidate the communitarian "being together" of Jews, of Jewish intellectuals? How could he have defended Zionism, Jewish nationalism, the defensive postures that close ranks against those outside the fold?

When Derrida spoke of himself as "the last of the Jews" he insisted on the resonance that the very structure of election must have on identity. By destabilizing the irony of Levinas's own rhetoric, by enacting a betrayal that is already at the heart of Levinas's own thought, he asked for his pardon, "for not meaning to say."

NOTES

Portions of this essay were published as chapter one in Sarah Hammerschlag, *Broken Tablets: Levinas, Derrida, and the Literary Afterlife of Religion* (Columbia University Press, 2016).

1. Jacques Derrida, *Gift of Death and Literature in Secret* (Chicago: University of Chicago Press, 2008), 138.

2. Ibid., 148.

3. Jacques Derrida, *Voice and Phenomenon*, trans. Leonard Lawlor (Evanston, Ill.: Northwestern University Press, 2011), 34.

4. Ibid., 42.

5. Ibid., 73.

6. Ibid., 78–79.

7. Derrida, *Gift of Death*, 120.

8. Wayne Booth, *A Rhetoric of Irony* (Chicago: University of Chicago Press, 1974), 14.

9. Ibid., 59.

10. See Richard Rorty, *Contingency, Irony, and Solidarity*. (Cambridge: Cambridge University Press, 1989), 122–37. See also Simon Critchley's essay "Deconstruction and Pragmatism," in *Ethics, Politics, Subjectivity* (London, Verso, 1999). Critchley opposes Rorty's claim that deconstruction is apolitical by arguing that it is insofar as Derrida is loyal to a Levinasian ethics and produces a politics out of a dedication to the idea of infinite responsibility to the other that he gains his political cogency. I differ from Critchley here by arguing that it is only by betraying Levinas, in and through his destabilizing irony—that for which Rorty would disqualify Derrida as political—that his work gains its political force. For Derrida's response to Rorty, see "Deconstruction and Pragmatism," in *Ethics, Politics, Subjectivity*, 81–82. See also Hayden White, *Tropics of Discourse* (Baltimore: Johns Hopkins University Press, 1978), 281.

11. The theme of irony is in fact a common trope between them. A couple more examples: In Levinas's first letter to Derrida in 1964, he writes, "I must tell you of my great admiration for the intellectual power deployed in these pages, so generous even when they are ironic and severe," 22 October 1964. Benoit Peeters, *Derrida: A Biography*, trans. Andrew Brown (Cambridge: Polity, 2013), 140. In his eulogy for Levinas Derrida referred to Levinas's irony as a kind of trademark: "the gentle irony, so familiar to us." Jacques Derrida, *Adieu à Emmanuel Levinas*, trans. Pascale-Anne Brault and Michal B. Naas

(Stanford: Stanford University Press, 1999), 12. But given that we know from many sources that this irony was rarely gentle, one has to wonder whether Derrida was himself being ironic at this moment.

12. See Jacques Derrida, "Abraham, the Other," in *Judeities* (New York: Fordham University Press, 2007), 38, and Sarah Hammerschlag, *The Figural Jew* (Chicago: University of Chicago Press, 2010), 201–60.

13. Francis Guibal and Stanislas Breton, *Altérités* (Paris: Osiris, 1986), 75.

14. François Poirié, *Emmanuel Levinas, Qui etes-vous?* (Paris: La Manufacture, 1987), 70.

15. Jacques Derrida and Elisabeth Roudinesco, *For What Tomorrow* (Stanford: Stanford University Press, 2004), 111, Quoted in Benoit Peeters, *Jacques Derrida*, trans. Andrew Brown (Malden, Mass.: Polity Press, 2013), 21.

16. Peeters, *Derrida: A Biography*, 140.

17. Marie-Ann Lescourret, *Emmanuel Levinas* (Paris: Flammarion, 1994), 170.

18. Jacques Derrida, "Avouer—L'impossible," in *Comment Vivre Ensemble*, Acts du XXXVIIe Colloque des intellectuels juifs de langue française, ed. Jean Halpern and Nelly Hanson (Paris: Albin Michel, 2001), 185–86; Jacques Derrida, "Avowing," trans. Gil Anidjar, in *Living Together: Jacques Derrida's Communities of Violence and Peace*, ed. Elisabeth Weber (New York: Fordham University Press, 2013), 21.

19. Ibid., 186, 21.

20. Emmanuel Levinas, "État d'Israel et Religion d'Israel," *Evidences*, no. 20 (1951): 4–6.

21. Emmanuel Levinas, *Difficile liberté* (Paris: Albin Michel, 1963), 347; Emmanuel Levinas, *Difficult Freedom*, trans. Sean Hand (Baltimore: Johns Hopkins University Press, 1990), 231.

22. Ibid.

23. On this topic, see Howard Caygill, *Levinas and the Political* (London: Routledge, 2002), 159–99, and, more recently, Judith Butler, *Parting Ways* (New York: Columbia University Press, 2012), 54–68.

24. Jacques Derrida, *Psyché* (Paris: Galilée, 1987), 177; Jacques Derrida, *Psyche: Inventions of the Other I*, ed. Peggy Kamuf and Elizabeth Rottenberg (Stanford: Stanford University Press, 2007), 162.

25. Emmanuel Levinas, "Jacques Derrida: Wholly Otherwise," in *Proper Names* (Stanford: Stanford University Press, 1996), 57–58.

26. Ibid., 36.

27. See Emmanuel Levinas, "The Other in Proust," in *Proper Names*. Proust was clearly a source for Levinas's conception of the subject, particularly his descriptions of eros. At the same time in the final paragraph of the essay he includes a disclaimer: "But Proust's most profound teaching—if

indeed poetry teaches—consists in situating the real in a relation with what forever remains other" (105).

28. Jill Robbins in *Altered Reading: Levinas and Literature* (Chicago: University of Chicago Press, 1999) points out Levinas's emphasis on the way in which literature freezes the plasticity of the face.

29. Ibid., 139. For more on the relationship between Levinas and Blanchot, see Hammerschlag, *Figural Jew*, chap. 4.

30. We could include here many others: Shakespeare, Celan, Agnon, and Grossman, to name a few.

31. Emmanuel Levinas, *Carnets de captivité*, ed. Rodolphe Calin and Catherine Chalier (Paris: Imec/ Grasset, 2009).

32. Levinas, introduction to *Quatre lectures talmudiques* (Paris: Éditions de Minuit, 1968), 13.

33. Ibid., 61.

34. Derrida, "Avouer," 197; "Avowing," 29.

35. Levinas, *Quatre lectures talmudiques*, 60–61.

36. Levinas, *Totality and Infinity: An Essay on Exteriority*, trans. Alphonso Lingis (Pittsburgh: Duquesne University Press, 1969), 267.

37. Ibid., 277.

38. Derrida, *Psyche*, 179.

39. Ibid., 177.

40. Jacques Derrida, "Circumfession," in Geoffrey Bennington, *Jacques Derrida* (Chicago: University of Chicago Press, 1999), 145, 117, 160, 279. See Hammerschlag, *Figural Jew*, 243.

41. Derrida, "Avouer," 186, 22.

CHAPTER 5

Jews, in Theory

Sergey Dolgopolski

Let me follow a Talmudic tradition that suggests beginning with a joke or an anecdote. In the analysis in this essay, I will periodically return to and reevaluate the following story's power.[1]

It is 1970, Moscow, Red Square. Rabinovitch, who has a typical Jewish[2] surname, stands there distributing political leaflets. A KGB agent sees that. Wishing to arrest Rabinovitch, the agent grabs a leaflet, only to discover that there is nothing written on it. The leaflet is just a plain sheet of paper. The agent asks Rabinovitch: Why do you not have anything written on the leaflets? Now comes the punch line, which I will do my best to translate from Russian: "But isn't it all clear, nevertheless?" (Так ведь и так все понятно!).

Who is Rabinovitch? Does his act of political resistance define him specifically as a Jew or more generally as a human being, or perhaps, by a necessity to be explored in this essay, as inextricably both, or else, by another necessity to attend to, as neither, or perhaps again in some other way or capacity? To begin addressing these questions, questions of the political element at work in Rabinovitch's action, a precise theoretical lens is needed. I will both develop and focus this theoretical lens by applying, testing, and adjusting Carl Schmitt's theory of political representation and

Philippe Lacoue-Labarthe's theory of the role of fiction in the workings of reason in general and in political reason in particular. In other words, I will be using the Rabinovitch anecdote as a topos to think through the notions that animate the analysis in this essay and to afford a language making it possible to formulate its task.

The first notion is Carl Schmitt's definition of "political form" as the "representation of representation," and the second is the notion of the "fictioning essence of reason" in Philippe Lacoue-Labarthe's *Typography*.[3] I proceed first by mapping Schmitt's notion of the political form of representation onto the Rabinovitch anecdote. I probe a similar mapping of the Rabinovitch story vis-à-vis Lacoue-Labarthe's notion of a "type" (a technical term to be explained below), a notion in which Rabinovitch is seen as a necessary fiction needed for political reason (and by extension scientific, moral, and other forms of reason) to function. I use the results of these two mappings to assess the relationship between two "fictions" (in Lacoue-Labarthe's terms) or two "political forms" (Schmitt) in modern times: the "Jew" and the "human being."

My argument is that Rabinovitch (in Schmitt's terms) is a particular kind of representative. In terms of political form, he (or she—the gender is never made clear) exemplifies what Schmitt called the "representation of representation." In terms of content, Rabinovitch exemplifies the universal category "human being" and that the universal "human being," in turn, is inseparably a similar kind of representation of the Jew. Further (in Lacoue-Labarthe's terms), the inseparable dyad of Jew–human being is a necessary fiction, a "type," that modern political reason, by its very essence, must produce and maintain. I further suggest that both Schmitt's and Lacoue-Labarthe's approaches are necessary, but insufficient to grasp the political act that Rabinovitch commits in the story, an insufficiency that I attempt to redress using resources derived from the notion and practice of refutation in the Babylonian Talmud, which, as I argue, Rabinovitch enacts in the conversation with the KGB agent. Arriving at this understanding of the political as exemplified in the Rabinovitch story and what it can tell us about Jews, political reason, and the concept of the human and the Jew will require slowly working through the argument in several steps, beginning with Carl Schmitt's concept of "political form."

Rabinovitch, Schmitt, and "Political Form"

Rabinovitch's victory over the KGB agent both helps explain the necessity and shows the insufficiency of Schmitt's idea of "political form." The idea of "political form" is found in one of Schmitt's earlier works, *Roman Catholicism and Political Form* (1923)[4] in which Schmitt lays the conceptual groundwork for his later and more widely known theory of the political as the relation of friend to enemy, including the theory of the sovereign's proclamation of a state of emergency and/or exception from what otherwise would be the universal rule of law administered by the state. In this earlier work, he draws on the example of the Catholic Church as a model through which to think political form in general.

The polemical context in which the notion of the "political form" arose helps us understand that notion better. *Roman Catholicism and Political Form* is a polemic against the modern "anti-Roman temper." At the center of this polemic is a notion of political representation different from those associated with either a representative or a deputy. For Schmitt, there is an irreconcilable difference between an official, say, in the hierarchy of the Catholic Church and either a representative in a parliamentary democracy or a deputy in a dictatorship. The latter two represent what they themselves are not—either the electorate or the dictator. An official in the hierarchy of the Catholic Church, however, is a representative in a radically different sense. Schmitt writes:

> The Catholic Church is the sole surviving contemporary example of the medieval capacity to create representative figures—the pope, the emperor, the monk, the knight, the merchant. It is certainly the last of what a scholar once called four remaining pillars—the House of Lords, the Prussian General Staff, the Academie Française, and the Vatican. It stands so alone that whoever sees therein only external form mockingly must say it represents nothing more than representation.[5]

In this, Schmitt discovers what he both recognizes as correct and, at this early stage of his thought, dismisses as unacceptable—that the "representative figure" in question "represents nothing more than representation." G. L. Ulmen, in his translation of this passage, alleviates the difficulty of both that discovery and its formulation by inserting the word "idea" in the translation: The representative figure "represents the idea of representation."

Read according to the polemical tone of the essay, those who "mockingly" say this about Catholicism are those with the "anti-Roman temper." Schmitt want them to have a better understanding of what they argue against: The Catholic Church is founded on and exemplifies the representation of representation, rather than the representation of any pregiven content, as is the case in the modern point of view of either parliamentary or dictatorial representation. Representation in such modern institutions, including modern nation-states, even if commonly called "political," is in fact of merely a "techno-economical nature." In what Schmitt would later call "techno-economical" forms of rationality, means must match ends. In techno-economical rationality, one may have any desires, goals, or ends whatsoever. Realistic or not, these desires do not have to be rational; the only requirement is that the means to satisfy them must be "rationally calculated." For Schmitt, techno-economical rationality in fact involves no politics, although of course it might involve the state and its institutions. Political rationality, in contrast, requires the "rationality of goals" or a selective approach to differentiate worthy ends from unworthy ones. In *Roman Catholicism and Political Form*, Schmitt displays the celibate bureaucracy of the Catholic Church as the only surviving example of that rationality, which is a genuinely political form.

In these terms, Rabinovitch is clearly not a representative in a parliamentary system, nor is he a deputy in the Communist system. But in the story, Rabinovitch and his blank pamphlets nevertheless clearly represent some conception of the political. What, though? To answer this question, one has to look further into how Schmitt develops the notion of the representation of representation in distinction from that of such other conceptions of the representative.

Representation, as Schmitt understands it, involves an aesthetic dimension. For "whoever" mocks the external form of the church, the "representative figures" and the power to create them is foreign; it "stands so alone" because the representative figures represent no pregiven content—no electorate and no dictator. Yet by extension, that excludes representing any pregiven content at all—in the sense not only of political representation but also of aesthetic representation. The "medieval capacity" Schmitt highlights creates a representation that does not depend on the content it represents. It represents no content at all, a "mocking" critique would suggest. Yet for Schmitt, representing nothing but representation is not the same as representing nothing. The medieval capacity to create representative figures acts before these figures can come to represent any content. Therefore, the modern mockers of "the medieval capacity" have a point: The representation of representation is a form that does not follow from any particular content. But that means it therefore can embrace a wide variety of contents. That allows Schmitt to explain how the opponents of the Catholic Church could have "grasped completely the extent to which the Catholic Church is a complex of opposites, *complexio oppositorum*,"[6] as far as the content is concerned, without understanding the basis for it, both in terms of the political action of the church in different circumstances, which Schmitt addresses explicitly, and in terms of embracing noncontent-oriented, "abstract" art forms, along with art forms embracing a wide variety of the content, which I read here by implication.

Seen in those terms, Rabinovitch exemplifies something that Schmitt in this early polemic, merely attributing these insights to opponents of an institution that he was defending, did not yet see, but that underlies his later concept of political form: the representation of representation as such.[7] Like Rabinovitch's leaflets, it is a political form without any content whatsoever. Even in Schmitt's analysis of Roman Catholicism, the representation of representation precedes and grounds any representation of content, which therefore becomes a secondary representation. Rabinovitch's leaflets employ and exemplify the concept and the power of "representation of representation" because the absence of words shows that the primary representation, the representation of representation, works even if and precisely because the secondary representation, the referential content of the leaflets, is reduced to emptiness, or if you prefer, to the fullness of their empty pages. Empty of descriptions, they are still full of powerful political claims.

Beyond the leaflets, there is another, perhaps better-known example of the representation of representation and in particular of the power of such representation. This is the *ex cathedra* principle, or the principle of infallibility of everything the pope says "from the chair," as the Latin phrase has it, in Saint Peter's Cathedral in Rome.[8] What the pope represents is the representation of a rational goal, the divine good or the truth of the church, which is true because he pronounces it. Even if, as Schmitt can allow, the pope does not have to know exactly what that good is, his words *ex officio* count as representing it. He personally represents nothing beyond that representation.

However, unlike the pope, whose words are still means matching ends, Rabinovitch's act seems to be completely irrational from the techno-economical standpoint of the KGB agent. As a type of techno-economical rationality, the KGB agent, if taken to Rome, might still be able to understand the pope as a political type, in Schmitt's sense, because the pope seated in the chair of Saint Peter does not keep silent. However, the agent has a really hard time understanding Rabinovitch. I will come back to the difference between Rabinovitch and the pope later on. At this point, it suffices to highlight that emptiness of the leaflets, their being void of any content, has the power of creating the representative figure of primary representation, the representation of representation. As the leaflets show, one can be telling things even before one tells anything particular or specific.

Rabinovitch, Lacoue-Labarthe, and the Type

Yet the Rabinovitch story involves more than the representation of representation as the invocation of the form of the political. Rabinovitch argues about the empty pamphlets with the agent. But Rabinovitch is also a particular political actor within a specific political context. The story is about more than just the form of the political. So who is Rabinovitch? A woman? A man? A Jew? A human being in general? In which of these possible capacities does Rabinovitch act in the story? To articulate this complexity of the figure of Rabinovitch, I address that figure as a *type*, in the terms that Philippe Lacoue-Labarthe develops in his *Typography*. Applying and testing Lacoue-Labarthe's notion of type will help show that Rabinovitch is a very complex interplay of two modern types—the human being and the Jew. In light of this complex interplay, these strange leaflets can say or illustrate even more.

Lacoue-Labarthe's main thesis in *Typography* involves the "fictioning essence of reason." The claim is that reason must create fictions in order to operate[9] and that the way fictions are created changes in the course of history. The Rabinovitch anecdote can be understood as an illustration of this notion. Even the most obviously fictive representation, the empty leaflet, is still absolutely necessary for reasoning to occur between Rabinovitch and the agent. Without the leaflet (even if empty, which, as one might say, is the fiction in its fullest) reason, and its goal, the political act of protest, would not be available at all. Yet as we'll see as the result of a step-by-step exploration of Lacoue-Labarthe's argument, there are limitations that arise from that claim.

Is Man a Fiction?

The notion of the "fictioning essence of reason" appears in Nietzsche, is addressed in Heidegger, and analyzed in Lacoue-Labarthe's *Typography*. Minimally glossed, *Typography* is a work on Heidegger's reading of Nietzsche. For the purposes of this essay, I draw on Lacoue-Labarthe's analysis of the central point of Heidegger's polemics with Ernst Jünger: whether "man," and in particular the "worker," is the one who "bestows meaning" on the world through technology, as Jünger held, or whether "man" is no more and no less than a product or *type*, a fiction, produced, as Heidegger claimed, through the "essence of technology." For the latter thinker, that essence is, of course, "nothing technical," but instead is *Ge-stell.* This German word is much easier and much less useful to translate than it is to explain how it functions in Heidegger. One reason for this is that Heidegger's notion of *Ge-stell* is articulated in two contexts, the ancient Greek and the modern industrial.

If So, How Old?

The ancient form of *Ge-stell* is elucidated in Heidegger's reading of Plato's *ideas*, Lacoue-Labarthe argues. In that context, the "fictioning essence of reason" means that one can encounter reason, in this case *ideas*, through and only through fictions. Even true *doxa*, that is, opinions that do bespeak truth, are still opinions and thus fictions. Additionally, aesthetically, it is only through the looks of things (call them "appearances") that one can recognize the *ideas* that made those appearances possible. That leaves no possibility for encountering *ideas* directly. Facing the inevitability of fictions, we, together with Plato, first encounter the importance of theory as *theorein*, or the process of discovering *ideas* in and through appearances. That theory of *theorein* is important in order to eliminate any confusion: If *ideas* get confused in the process of recognition, it might lead to the mistaking of what seems to be for what is. *Theorein*, and the theory thereof, therefore has for Plato a moral value, as well: It both explains and helps avoid the nature of evil. Mistaking what seems to be for what is, is the root cause of evil. Evil corresponds to no idea, but only to the confusion between ideas. Therefore, even if evil does not truly exist, it deploys the power of confusion. Practicing theory in the form of dialogue helps us eliminate both the confusion and the evil that the latter creates.

That, of course, presumes a possibility of avoiding evil by eliminating confusion. If not confused in their recognition, the ideas bring forth good and only good, even if and unfortunately only through fictions. Reason must thus produce fictions, to "supply" *ideas*, to make them readily available, as the word *Ge-stell* (the German for a shelf, étagère, etc.) would suggest. Through these readily available fictions, one could recognize the reason, or for Plato, the *ideas*, in, through, and behind fictions, even if never leaving these fictions behind. This path through the fictioning of reason would, for Plato, be the only true and ethical way.

Things, however, change in the industrial stage. There, the fictioning essence of reason works with much greater complexity than it did when reason was understood as *ideas*. According to Lacoue-Labarthe, industrial (including postindustrial and, by extension, informational) *Ge-stell* no longer entails *ideas* in the Platonic sense, assuming instead a different form. The difference between *Ge-stell* as it works in Plato's *idea* and the modern *Ge-stell* has to do precisely with an even greater role of confusion in the industrial age. For Plato, confusion between *ideas* can still create appearances, alas faulty and evil. That evil and that confusion, Plato hoped, could be eliminated through the philosophical work of the dialogue, in which the philosopher can help the confused interlocutors think through and eliminate their confusion.

Modern Man Is Neither a Platonic Idea nor an Illusion to Dissipate

The luxury of eliminated confusion is no longer available in the fictioning of the industrial, postindustrial, and informational ages. In contrast to Plato's *idea*, Hegel's *Ge-stalt*, which is yet another word for an image and/or fiction, entails a confusion that one can recognize, but not eliminate. For example, while scientifically understood as illusions and thus as confusions, the images of sunrise and sunset do not cease shaping one's experience. A greater approximation comes from the example of Marx's political economy of value production. "Scientifically," that is, from the point of view of Marx's political economy, capitalism purchases the productive powers of the workers' labor, but pays only for the workers' time. As a result, the labor produces more value than the cost of the time of labor. The difference (and if you will, the confusion) between paid time and the productive power of labor, for Marx, is perceived neither by the capitalist nor the worker. However, that difference makes the capitalist-worker economy possible. What is more, failing to notice the difference between time and labor, for Marx, is practically unavoidable in capitalist society. That confusion entails a number of "inverted forms" in relationships between the capitalist and the worker. One such inverted form is the "form of commodity." In order for the capitalist economy to work, it *must seem*—for all parties involved—that value is a property of the commodity, rather than the product of labor. Gold and silver coins, for Marx, are "inverted forms" of commodity par excellence: Their value consists in displaying the value of a commodity regardless of the value a coin may have as a physical object. These and similar "inverted forms" are specters, which cannot be practically recognized as illusions, but which continue to inform how one practically accesses the appearances of the world and navigates one's way therein.

The "inverted forms" of Marx, along with other specters, or uncorrectable confusions, exemplify *Ge-stalt*[10] in its role as both fiction (which by Platonic definition is "what is not") and *idea* (which by that definition is "what is"). A confusion that cannot be eliminated is no longer a confusion in a classical Platonic sense, but rather, in Lacoue-Labarthe's terms, a *type*. Undermining Platonic distinctions, *Ge-stalt* is a fiction because it involves confusion, but it is also an *idea*, because it enables recognizing reason. A type, in these terms, is an illusion that must reside not only in fiction but also in theory, that is, must take part in reason and thus have the power of the real. Without jumping ahead of myself, I can only say at this point that modern Jews, as the title of this essay also suggests, belong to the realm of theory, that is, to the realm of types.

What is more, the *Ge-stalt*, or the specter, and thus the type, as well, cannot be recognized as an illusion to dissipate in practice and/or in experience. Rabinovitch's leaflets seem to exemplify such a conception of *Ge-stalt* well: Their empty pages are specters. The empty leaves of the leaflets do work that the KGB agent feels in experience, even if he cannot articulate it in theory. This is because he has encountered a type and thus has fallen into the logic of confusion with no escape.

We are now in a position to move from the leaflets to their distributor, Rabinovitch, as a Jew and a human being.[11]

Humans, Jews, and Other Ge-stalts *(not* Ideas*)*

An even closer approximation of a *Ge-stalt* is the *Mensch*, "man," or, if ungendered, "the human being." (Here, English affords more gender neutrality than German can. Rabinovitch is simply a person, as the story goes in original Russian—the gender of that human being and that Jew remains untold.) The logic of function (and of fiction) in the *Ge-stalt* of "man" or "the human being" has to do with bridging the differences between terms by making one of them the bridge. For example, the difference between man and woman has been bridged in the past by creating the fiction of both of them being a "man in general." In this logic of fictioning, any of the bridged terms could be used for the bridging. With "man" no longer politically correct, "woman" becomes a possibility. Along these lines, "gender" comes to be understood as pertaining not only to women, as before, but to men equally well. Yet the switch from "man" to "woman" as a universal[12] only repeats and reinforces the inevitability of having a specter, that is, the necessity of using one term of the difference to bridge that difference. As a result, modern "Mensch" or "man"/"human being" in general belongs to the terrain of specters and *Ge-stalts*, rather than Platonic *ideas*.

Following its "fictioning essence," reason must supply these *Ge-stalts* or types. Most important for understanding the relationships between the human and the Jew, the production of types entails an elision and/or suppression of classical Platonic mimesis. The (post)industrial and information age of types can no longer be reached by undoing mimesis, its mistakes and confusions. No clarity about the human or the Jew can be reached. Rather, even if and precisely because they are no longer even susceptible to the hope of being reached directly, contemporary rational thinking and acting must fight against the specters and types that such thinking also must create.[13] The specters include the specter of the human being, as well as the specter of the modern Jew. At stake therefore is the following question, "Is Rabinovitch human?"

A Human as a Jew

The modern industrial specter that is "a human" is much more closely connected to that of the Jew than it might seem. The spectral nature of these two figures becomes more clearly discernible if juxtaposed to other contexts in which the Jew functions as an image and/or a concept, but not as a specter. On the way from a territorial and/or tribal or moral and religious designation in the Bible, the term "Jew" in Christian theology emerges as a figure, an image, and if one prefers, an *idea*, but not a specter.[14] In the early Church Fathers, the figure of the Jew comes to replace/suppress that of the biblical "Israel," which the church annexed for itself as "Israel in spirit." That both created and left behind the other half of Israel, "Israel in the flesh," or carnal Israel.[15] Tangentially, at this point, "the Jew," at least if one assumes Lacoue-Labarthe's perspective, constituted no specter. It did not, even if in the theology of the early Church Fathers, "Jew" is already *a* figure of exception, if not *the* figure of exception par excellence. Indeed, these theologians could not have placed the Jews among the other others, such as either "pagans" or "heretics." "The Jew" could not be a heretic, for to be a heretic, one must be a Christian. Nor could "the Jew" be a pagan, because that would undermine the source from which the church theologically stems. In the Platonic view, such confusion in the idea of the Jew would perfectly explain why, within the Christian theology, the Jew became the figure of evil.

Yet notably, unlike what either Plato or Lacoue-Labarthe would suggest, the figure of the Jew already had something of the quality of a specter: Unlike the Platonic version of evil, this new form of "evil" could not be talked away by means of dialogue. Limited as the theological view was by the theological possibility, indeed necessity, of converting the "Jew" to Christianity, the figure of the Jew already had a degree of spectrality—precisely because, as the figure of the other, the Jew escapes the church's given stable set of *ideas* about the other others—pagans and heretics.[16]

The degree of spectrality intensified, for example, in Soviet Russia, where, among other places, religious conversion to Christianity no longer even intimated eliminating the status of the convert as a Jew. The latter no longer was considered a religious figure. And once religion is removed, "man" emerges. That is to say, the shift of the Jew away from a religious context happens at the same time, and as the result of the same process, that led to the emergence of the notion of a "human being."[17] Such radically different thinkers as the Russian Orthodox philosopher and theologian Pavel Florensky, on the one hand, and Hannah Arendt, on the other, help us understand the connection between the human and the Jew, as well as its role as the vehicle through which members of rabbinic communities assimilated into the larger society of "secular Christians" who no longer insisted on conversion as *conditio sine qua non* for both social and professional integration.

Despite the radical differences between these thinkers, Arendt and Florensky help explain the connection between the modern specters of Jew and "man" with much greater precision. Following anti-Judaic and indeed anti-Jewish motifs of Eastern Orthodoxy, Florensky[18] diagnoses the modern invention of the "human being" as Jewish. He radically refuses to accept the notion of the human, deeming it misleadingly egalitarian, and at the same time clearly recognizes its political power and "danger" for Russian Christian Orthodoxy. The dual move of refusing to accept the notion and recognizing its danger marks Florensky's notion of человек ("human being" or "man," but also "servant") as a specter, that is, as something that does not exist, but cannot be eliminated either. Florensky insistently warns against the dangers of the specter of the "human." From his point of view, the modern Jew and man, человек, give birth to each other: Having created the "human being," Jews, for him, proclaim themselves (and everybody else) human, which explains the theoretical spectrality, including the unavoidable practical misunderstanding, of both the Jew and the человек.

From a radically different position, Hannah Arendt illustrates the political danger that the specter of the "human being" represents for her as a Jew. Criticizing, as she does along with Schmitt and Heidegger, the liberal values of techno-economical rationality, she, not unlike Florensky, warns against abusing the notion of the human. She particularly demands, after having been persecuted as a Jew, not to be respected as a human, a member of "humankind." Rather, she insists that political respect be given to her as a Jew, that is, as someone who is both inside and outside of "humankind," the only position that, for her, makes the humanity of "humankind" possible.[19] Conceptually insisting on the "human being" as a specter, rather than either an image or a pure idea or concept, Arendt discerns the notion of the human as a function of the assimilationist utopia. Thus, in her *Jew as Pariah*,[20] she argues (once again in a manner not totally different from Florensky's) that the ideas of basic human rights, such as equality, the right to life, or to housing, a family, and so on, are only assumed to be universal, but in fact are fought for and recognized as universal paradigmatically by the Jewish pariahs seeking assimilation.

Both thinkers thus indicate a close connection between the human being and the Jew in the modern context. Following the logic of secularization, the concept of the "human being" makes possible a new modern operation disentangling the Jew from any "religious" context. This possibility also turns on racist and nationalist logics of (anti)assimilation. In turn, the Jew makes the "human being" possible by becoming the most concealed and the best-hidden singular beginning of the universality of "man." As a result, "human being" arrives on the stage as the vehicle of assimilation: The assimilating rabbinic Jews both promoted and ultimately fell prey to the modern concept of the human being.

In juxtaposing these two radically different thinkers, Florensky and Arendt, there thus lurks a new specter. That specter inextricably combines the Jew and the "human being," one as the function of the other. It is thus that Rabinovitch protests—simultaneously and inextricably as a human being and as a Jew.[21]

As Lacoue-Labarthe's framework of analysis suggests, the modern Jew and the "human being" are types, which, if reason is to remain reason, must elide mimetic representation. There of course remains an idea of "man" and the idea of Jew and even the idea of the two in one, so that Rabinovitch could be such a mimetic representation of the idea of a Jew, of a human being. Yet the fictioning power of reason, in its modern version, must radically and constantly elide such mimetic representations. The fictioning essence of reason must produce types as necessary fictions, rather than indulge in mimetic representations of Platonic *ideas*. In a sentence, Lacoue-Labarthe's diagnosis is that in order for the fictioning essence of reason to remain "of reason," the mimetic element of the fiction must be suppressed, even if it can never be fully removed. Elision of the mimetic representation of either the Jew or the human or both thus establishes the limit at which reason—rational thinking and acting—can produce fictions, but still remain rational.

However, the view of Rabinovitch as a double specter reaches, illuminates, and pushes that limit further, in the emptiness and at the same time in the necessity of the pamphlets. As Schmitt would have to argue, the inseparable unity of the two representations of representation in this story—of the modern "Jew" and the no less modern "human being"—provides a heuristic basis from which to begin to understand what the empty sheets do. Yet the theory of fictioning is necessary but not sufficient to understand the agency of the empty sheets. To compensate for that insufficiency, in what follows, I will begin applying and renegotiating these theoretical concepts to think about the political form of the Talmud, and in turn, apply that form to gaining an even better view of Rabinovitch as a political figure, beyond the types and typology of the human and the Jew in modernity.

The Political in the Talmud

So far, we have seen that Schmitt views the political sphere in terms of the representation of representation, and Lacoue-Labarthe views mimesis in representation as the limit of the *Ge-stell*, the foundation of modern specters, while Arendt views the Jew as a specter to be respected if one wants to guarantee the humanity of humankind. If these approaches can become collectively applicable to or at least heuristically important for addressing the question of the political form of the Talmud, then the question would be: Does the political form in the Talmud entail the representation of representation, or more specifically, representation as *Ge-stalt* limited, as Lacoue-Labarthe argued, by the suppression of mimesis, and does it therefore imply the humanity of the rabbis in the Talmud as Jews, as well (perhaps) as the Jewishness and/or rabbinic character of modern humans? The task of addressing this question consists in mapping out the political form in the Talmud in regard to representation in Schmitt's, Arendt's, and Lacoue-Labarthe's claims. That task calls for applying and renegotiating the concepts of representation, and in particular of type, *Gestalt*, in relationship to mimesis, including their configuration in the fusion of the concepts of the Jew and the human being in the figure of Rabinovitch.

The first step on the way to exploring this prospect of the analysis of political form in the Talmud is a comparative exposition of the Talmud in terms relevant for the task: the rhetoric of the Talmud and the status of refutation there, because what Rabinovitch stands for and does is a fundamental refutation of politics as it is situated in the context of the story. Here, I approach the political in the Talmud in the broader context of both Aristotle's and Quintilian's rhetorics, taken as synecdoches for the larger respective Greek and Latin rhetorical traditions and schools.

Aristotle's rhetoric entails three main parts: enthymeme ("rhetorical syllogism"), character, and example. The former can be understood logically as a shortened logical syllogism, as it was by Boethius. An alternative understanding would be expressionist: The implied, but not expressed, part of the enthymeme has a meaning that would be lost when explicated. In that understanding, the fact of being kept implicit has meaning of its own far beyond the meaning of what is implied. As I have argued elsewhere,[22] an expressionist understanding of the enthymeme provides a better, even if still not sufficient, approximation of how the enthymeme as a part of rhetoric is used, de facto, in rabbinic academies.

In turn, Quintilian's arts of rhetoric include: character (or delivery), refutation, memory (for words and for things), *inventio* (as both "invention" and "discovery" at the same time), and example.

The art of rhetoric displayed on the pages of the Babylonian Talmud redistributes these categories so that refutation comes to the fore in all parts of the rhetorical art. In the Talmud, refutation serves as a vehicle for memory. More technically, it helps both the "memory for things" and the "memory for words." An attempted and often ultimately failed refutation of the "memory for words" of or about earlier rabbinic authorities results in a better, that is more precise, "memory for things" involved in the teaching of these authorities. As a vehicle for remembering, the process of refutation by the same token becomes the process of invention: The "things" (enthymemes) to be remembered in the teachings or deeds of the earlier authorities are discovered and by the same token invented through heuristic refutation of their given verbal accounts. Refutation thus serves as the driving force of invention. Refutation also provides the truth criterion to judge the accuracy of the results: The account is true if there is a valid/considerable point that it refutes. The process of *inventio* is driven by refutation, because refuting and ultimately failing to refute an account of a teaching or a deed leads to inventing (discovering) a new memory (and new understanding) of that account, thus featuring an invention. Yet refutation is not only a way to produce/invent that new memory; it is also a criterion for judging the accuracy or truth of the resulting invention: One knows that the memory of a teaching is true if one knows/remembers what that teaching was supposed to refute or, in other words, what it was inventing in the first place. Thus, displayed on the pages of the Talmud is a process of *inventio* driven by refutation as both a truth criterion and a protocol of truth production. Refutation thus also becomes the main feature of the character and the definitive mode of delivery, which therefore are no longer individual or collective efforts, but rather both the refutation of and the search for refutations implied in the positions of the others.

Here, memory embraces and exceeds thinking, producing the authority of the open past, which is unlike the Platonic model, in which thinking and remembering coincide, thus sending us back not to the past, but rather to the eternity that Plato defines as "being," as opposed to "becoming." In the context of the present essay, the question would then be how the prominence of refutation (and in particular of the refutation of a refutation) in the Talmudic art of remembering informs our understanding of "political form" in the Talmud, and how understanding that form, if the Talmud indeed displays a "political form," translates into understanding the connection between the Jew and a human being in modernity, if we think that connection in terms of *Ge-stalt* as a modern form of *Ge-stell*.

In the Talmud, refutation subsumes the other parts of classical rhetoric—invention, delivery, and memory. To invent or find a novel idea or interpretation in a statement in the Talmud is to find what that statement refutes. Successfully making a point is done in the form of the explicit refutation of the position of an opponent, often by presenting the thesis of the opponent as self-refuting. To remember a given tradition better is precisely to find a novel idea or interpretation in it, or to discover what that tradition refutes.

This changes the position of refutation from one among several rhetorical techniques to the overarching mode of rhetorical thinking and acting. That change requires us to move beyond the marginal positions traditionally allowed for rhetorical schools within Aristotelian or Platonic philosophies and academies. This is why any return of the Talmudic refutations on the map of the tradition of rhetoric does not mean subsuming the Talmud into the tradition of philosophy. Instead, it signifies a movement that, using Schmitt's terms, one can define as a movement toward a new "political" or a new representative figure, the figure of the one who refutes in response to refuting. That means even more broadly that Talmud (without the "the" of the text), as an intellectual discipline, extends beyond rhetoric, moving toward a theory of the political that would not be a philosophy of the political.[23]

The three points made above—memory as both framing and exceeding the philosophical theory of being and/or eternity, refutation as subsuming other elements of rhetoric, and refutation as the form of remembering beyond the confines of rhetoric—collectively introduce the dimension of the truth production in Rabinovitch's political action.

Applying and/or renegotiating Schmitt's definition of "political form" as a pure representation of representation would mean that authority, including political authority in the Talmud, would feature something different from what it would for Schmitt. Of course, with empty leaflets in hand, the representation of representation can still go as far as to mean that there is no secondary representation at all. However unlikely the case might be, if the pope mounted the papal "chair" in Saint Peter's and said no words, thus representing no particular thing, the pope, according to Schmitt, still would represent representation; his silence *ex cathedra* would still be as infallible as any words. That is to say, the political form of primary representation (the representation of representation) would work even with a zero degree of secondary representation (the representation of "things"). Yet Rabinovitch does even more. However unlikely the case of the pope's silence *ex cathedra*, the empty (and in that limited sense "silent") leaflets do more than the pope's hypothetical silence would do.

They refute. They refute not only and not primarily the words and the techno-economical world of the KGB agent, but also and much more importantly, the leaflets undermine the very possibility of the zero degree of secondary representation. As Rabinovitch has it, they are not simply silent/empty. Rather, they make their point without words.

They do so because the infallibility principle works in the leaflets not on the grounds of representation, but rather on the grounds of refutation. If in the Talmud refutation is a truth criterion, then one is to speak or to write any words if and only if there is a point to refute. One therefore is not supposed to say or write the obvious. At least, this is how Rabinovitch explains the leaflets to the agent: They are empty because what they state is obvious. However, he, of course, has to talk to the agent, because these things are not obvious for the latter. The leaflets thus refute the possibility of representational silence in the first place. What that means, however, is that representation gets circumscribed by a more fundamental operation, that of refutation, so that even silence (the zero degree of representation) becomes a positive degree of refutation.

The power of refutation over representation has implications for understanding both *Ge-stell* and *Ge-stalt*, including the two spectrally interconnected and differentiated modern *Gestalts*, the "human being" and the Jew. As Lacoue-Labarthe argues, by tacitly excluding mimesis from representation, *Ge-stell* can at best introduce *being* that is open to the future, access to being vis-à-vis the open future.[24] The openness of the future, however, would still continue to support the suppression or elision of mimesis. Of course, the suppression of mimesis is much more familiar in the version of Plato's eternal (rather than temporized) being. However, per Lacoue-Labarthe's analysis above, the loss of mimesis is still there in Heidegger's futurist version of ontology. Still, and despite the difference between Plato and Heidegger, or between eternity and the temporization of being, the horizon of refutation exceeds the otherwise prevalent opposition between *Ge-stell* and mimesis. It does so because the latter two operate in and only in the realm of representation. What Rabinovitch accomplishes with his political action consists in refuting, and his political action should not be misunderstood as a happening in the realm of representation alone.[25] Rabinovitch's empty leaflets are what Schmitt would not have imagined: the representation of representation of a particular kind. The clean and wide-open sheets of paper represent without any mimetic representation at all. Not only is this act different from the zero degree of representation, but also and much more importantly, it is circumscribed by the radically different plane of refutation, which conditions both the primary and secondary representations that Schmitt discerned.[26]

Infallibles

Seen in these lights, the common denominator between Roman Catholicism and the Talmud in terms of the political form has to do with the infallibility principle. In the case of the church, it is the infallibility of the words of the pope *ex cathedra*. In the Talmud, it is the infallibility of the words of the authorities, say, in the Mishnah, an early third-century code of instruction for rabbinical courts, or of the post-Mishnaic masters (*amoraim*) named in the Talmud as opposed to the nameless rabbinic students who run discussions archived in records and compositions that, since the Middle Ages, have been called the Babylonian Talmud. In the case of the church, the infallibility principle is an axiom. In the Talmud, however, while the authorities of the past are still infallible by axiom, the memory of their words and deeds is infallible only when proven so. In the Talmud, one begins with a heuristic attempt to refute the accuracy of that memory. Furthermore, as already indicated, refutation serves not only as the vehicle of remembering, but also as the truth criterion of what is remembered, as well as a main mode of delivery, and thus of establishing the character of the nameless students, which they also ascribe to their teachers of earlier generations.

Of course, the prevalence of refutation and remembering in the Talmud does not cancel the importance of representation (including the representation of representation), but circumscribes the plane of representation. As a parenthetic example, perhaps this is why the Talmud recognizes the possibility of and opposition to the representation of representation—in the Talmud, a sage or other authority should not use his status as a scholar (the representation of representation) to gain advantage in a dispute about his private matters, for example, to defend himself against allegations in court.[27] More generally, in the Talmud, unlike the case of the church, ultimately, refutation controls representation, not the other way around.

The Talmudic form of refutation thus emerges as more than merely a rhetorical art or technique, for it informs a sagely way of existence, producing a distinct perspective on being, representation, and memory, matters that traditionally belong to the domain of "first philosophy." However, that does not make the form of Talmudic refutation a philosophical concept. Talmudic refutation does not quite lend itself to the confines of the philosophical theory of representation, let alone to Schmitt's "representation of representation." Instead, just as in the Talmud memory orients thinking to the open past (in contradistinction to Plato, for whom thinking orients memory toward eternal ideas and/or being), Talmudic refutations propel memory. Refutations produce at once the outcome of remembering (e.g., advancement in remembering the Mishnah), its delivery (e.g., the character of the sage and of the student of the sage), and its truth (only things that soundly refute other things can be true). Refutation both frames and helps judge all three of these elements. Talmudic refutation therefore expands beyond the realm of *idea* in Plato's sense, but, as I will momentarily explain, does not take us only and exclusively in the direction of *Ge-stalt*. This is certainly not to exclude representation (let alone the representation of representation) but to limit its power by the power of refutation, to which it now belongs. Talmudic refutation no longer turns on *ideas*.[28]

But What about Types?

The above analysis complicates Lacoue-Labarthe's assessment of the fictioning essence of reason. If modern reason must produce fictions, such as the human or the Jew or both in one, fictions that elide any mimetic representation, what kind of new fiction would the empty sheets of Rabinovitch's leaflets entail? What does the above analysis of the Talmudic form of refutation and of the refutation of a refutation mean in terms of the current moment of increasingly complex relationships between humans, Jews, and other "types" that modern rational action and thought must create?[29]

Due to the role of refutation, the notion of "the representation of representation" no longer suffices to grasp the scope of the "the political form" of the Talmud. Instead, that form has to do with the refutation of a refutation as memory, a form in which, because of the multiplicity of its truths, there is no longer an orientation to privileging being (either eternal as in Plato or temporized as in Heidegger) over its mirror of nonbeing, as well as over the being's real other, which is what only seems to be. However, and by the same token, this means that the form of the refutation of a refutation, of refutation and counterrefutation, exceeds the distinction between being and mimesis or between "typography" (as Lacoue-Labarthe collectively designates the historically changing forms of the "fictioning essence of reason") and mimetic representation.

If so, where does the new vantage point on Talmudic refutation lead us in thinking about the modern intertwining types of the Jew and the human and about the common production of fiction, or the fictioning essence of reason, that underlies them?

In thinking about that question, I have so far primarily directly related to Schmitt's earlier formulation of "political form" in his *Roman Catholic Church and Political Form*. We will now have to go beyond this earlier work to Schmitt's later thinking. As I have already briefly indicated, his concept "the representation of representation" continues to be at work in his later analyses of the political in terms of the sovereign, of the state of exception/emergency, and of the friend-enemy grouping.[30] In proclaiming the state of exception/emergency, the sovereign suspends (but does not cancel)[31] the law; she or he does so based on the authority that can only be the authority that represents its own representation. The same applies to the friend-enemy grouping; the sovereign assigns content to an a priori friend-enemy divide. In that sense, the political represents the representation of a friend-enemy grouping (in contradistinction from, as Schmitt has it, ethical good versus evil, ontological being versus seeming to be, the logically true versus the false, the aesthetically beautiful versus the ugly, or other binary groupings). Thus, Schmitt's sovereign is the one who represents representation by proclaiming the suspension of representations of the second order (the order of law, for example), thereby bringing forth the first order of representation, the representation of representation, as the foundation, indeed, the condition of possibility, of political action.

There is more. The core of the political in both the "Roman Catholic" version of "political form" and in Schmitt's broader sense of the political as the friend-enemy grouping is futuristic. The futurism of Schmitt's political thought follows the lines of Heidegger's futurism in its treatment of the intimate relationships between being and time, in which time is first and foremost the form of having a future and only secondarily a form engaging the past and the present. At stake in Schmitt's understanding of political action is one's existence and one's style of life (*conatus*, in Hobbes's terms), which can be at stake only if the figure of having a future is at work.

Needless to say, both in Heidegger and in Schmitt, the futurism of human existence artificially diminishes the importance of the past, reducing it to the fiction of a starting point and directing both thinking and memory to being (again, eternal for Plato, which leads to *ideas* and theory, or temporized for Heidegger, which leads to replacing theory by *critique* framed in terms of *Ge-stalt* as *Ge-stell*).[32]

Recognizing the limitations of Schmitt's futurism invites looking for a broader version of the political that might become an alternative to the political not only in Schmitt's sense, but also, perhaps, to the political as such. The status of that broader version of the political is to remain undecided, for now. However, as the form of Talmudic refutation suggests, to achieve that broader notion of the political is to reclaim the well-forgotten importance of the past. The forgetting of that importance has itself been well forgotten (to borrow Hayyim M. Luzzatto's language)[33] by and through recalling the past, either imaginary or "real," in the mode of "what was," as strictly distinct from what that "what was" is marshaled to refute, as a Talmudic reading of the past would require.

How, then, to renegotiate the understanding of the political form as that of refutation and counterrefutation? First, such a renegotiation involves a new reconsideration of the referentiality of representation as the core model of meaning. That implies that beyond its referential aspect, meaning must be understood as always already a refutation. To remember would therefore mean inventing and discovering what is being refuted in a given speech, text, or any other representation. Refutation becomes essential for understanding any representation.

Second, this concerns not only secondary representation (reference), but also primary representation (the representation of representation). If refutation circumscribes secondary representation, that would apply to primary representation as well. That means renegotiating the political as the refutation of a refutation, rather than the representation of representation. The first step on the way there consists in understanding the political in terms of expression, rather than representation alone.

Instead of the double of a representation and the represented (or even of *noema* and *noesis*), expression always exceeds its relationship to the expressed by turning on a third element, the difference between what is being expressed (but never gets to full expression), on the one hand, and what is indeed expressed, however different it might be, on the other, as Deleuze highlighted these fine distinctions in his rereading of Spinoza.[34] Complex as it is, this new dimension of expression takes us beyond the confines of representation. In these terms, instead of the representation of representation, the political is to be understood more broadly as the expression of expression. That means a political action is possible even if it does not represent, but only expresses.

However, inscribing representation in expression is necessary, but insufficient. It is necessary because it introduces the multiplicity (what is being expressed can never fully coincide with what is expressed)[35] from which the open past stems. It is insufficient, because the expression is yet to be rediscovered as refutation of what is not even being expressed.

Third, recollection needs to give way to remembering. The former implies a subject, either individual or collective, who recollects. The latter does not have to center on a subject. Approaching the new (or well-forgotten) form of the political that the Talmudic form of refutation (and in particular, the refutation of a refutation) exemplifies, would mean, as I have already indicated above and elaborated in greater detail elsewhere, a reconsideration of refutation as the fundamental figure of memory as opposed to figures of recollection. The latter as a form of memory assumes either the subject (in the Middle Ages) or at least the agent (in Augustine) of memory as a single and/or homogeneous agent or subject. In contrast to either individual or collective recollections, refuting, let alone counter-refuting, as a form of memory, can never entail a single subject or agent, again either individual or collective, because refuting must involve the position that is being refuted. In the case of Talmudic practices, that position must be strong enough to deserve refutation; it must not be obviously wrong, and thus, even if being refuted, it must have the power to endure. Such an experience therefore never involves a single agent or subject, or, speaking in modern terms, a single man and/or a nation's business. It is no longer the business of any version of homogeneity whatsoever.

Rabinovitch

In light of these observations, I would now like to come back to Rabinovitch. His story not only illustrates but also exceeds the models of the political advanced in Schmitt. The figure of Rabinovitch extends beyond the modern type or *Ge-stalt* as the foundation of human rational presence advanced in Lacoue-Labarthe, as well. Even if taken as a double specter of a human being and the Jew, Rabinovitch does not necessarily represent, but necessarily refutes. He therefore escapes these specters in which he would remain confined if the framework of fictioning reason in the opposition to mimesis continued to reign in the political action that he performs. The figures of refuting that he performs refute the oppositions of fictioning and mimesis and also reach places where the intertwining specters of the human and the Jew could not reach. Instead, he invokes the dimension of the political as an open past beyond the domains of either being or time. The Rabinovitch anecdote both illustrates and defies Schmitt's understanding of the political by reinscribing it into a broader view of the political form as refutation and counterrefutation. On the flip side of the same coin, the anecdote is also a counterexample to Lacoue-Labarthe's analysis of the elision of mimesis from "the fictioning essence of reason," from which stemmed the complex relationship between humans and Jews as mutually conditioning modern types.

Rabinovitch is neither distinctly Jewish, nor distinctly human. Instead, Rabinovitch is political.

This is because Rabinovitch is a genius of remembering: Memory controls thought and operates where there is neither a type or *Ge-stalt* of the human nor a type or *Ge-stalt* of the Jew, for, as the Talmudic form of the political exemplifies, remembering follows neither time nor being. A genius of remembering, Rabinovitch does not bid on the open future, which would be a national notion rooted in a subject (collective or individual). Instead, he turns to the open past, which he enacts with his empty leaflets.

As a result, there, on the Red Square, there is ultimately no type, and there is no story. Living in the open past, where invention (creating a new thing) and discovery (finding an old one) are the same, Rabinovitch no longer lives in a time container, either naturalist or futurist; instead, the remembering that he shows to the agent no longer coincides with the individual (and by extension collective) recollection of a past, either imagined or real. In this story, one therefore no longer exists in a futurist sense. Rabinovitch's story, then, one might summarize, has no hero at the center, because Rabinovitch does not represent properly. Instead, Rabinovitch refutes.

Whither Rabinovitch?

This inevitably preliminary sketch leads to the task of outlining the role of refutation and counterrefutation for understanding the political in the much broader scope of the traditions of philosophy, rhetoric, sophistry, and other lines of political thought. By way of both comparison and evocation, I might call that broader task "writing *Talmudic Elenchi*" (by counteranalogy with Aristotle's *Elenchi* or "Sophistical Refutations"), a phrase that connotes both the necessity and challenge to understand refutation and counterrefutation in these domains, traditions that have served as both foundations and components collectively contributing to what would otherwise be and has been a much more limited view of political form.

The first step toward *Talmudic Elenchi* as a way of thinking about the political form would be to outline, in broad strokes, differences between the refutation of a refutation, on the one hand, and negative dialectics, philosophical dialogue, and liberal disputation without decision, on the other. I take that preliminary outline as an indication of the direction this essay projects for the next steps in analysis.

Negative Dialectics, Dialogue, and Liberal Disputation without Decision

The refutation of a refutation differs from negative dialectics. A technical difference, which medieval Aristotelian commentators of the Talmud already noted, is that the second refutation, the counterrefutation, idiomatically termed by those commentators *terutz* or *peruk* (respectively: "excuse" or "dismantling,") has to be weaker than the first refutation. If *peruk* were to produce the full destruction of what it is to refute, the whole process of refuting would have led to nothing, and the process of Talmudic argumentation would have to start from ground zero. Instead, *peruk*, or the counterrefutation, builds atop of the first one. The result is a better memory, one that is both a more reliable and a more elaborate memory of the traditions, teachings, or accounts of law. The process of refuting and counterrefuting is thus heuristic. After the process of refuting and counterrefuting, the initial traditions are remembered better both in terms of neutralizing mistakes of mechanical transmission and in terms of the implications (or more precisely *inventions*) that the rabbinic traditions are understood to have had.

Needless to say, the result of refuting and counterrefuting is not Hegelian dialectics of *Aufhebung*, sublation, nor is it the Platonic clarification of confusion. The outcome of the refutation of a refutation, the building up of memory and remembering, is not a synthesis of contradictions negating and suspending each other. It is so not only because, like Aristotelian hermeneutics and rhetoric, the Talmudic refutations operate not with contradictions, but with contrarieties, but also, and more important, because the process does not have to take one direction only. Refutations of refutations can branch out and even go rhizomatic, starting, as they often do, not with a tradition at hand, but instead with another tradition not immediately obviously related to the tradition currently considered in discussion. Branches and rhizomes of the refutations of refutations introduce a register of refuting that enriches memory by building it up on refutations of refutations in more than one way, along the lines of more than one trajectory of analysis, something that the dialectics of cumulative *Aufhebung* cannot afford.

The refutation of a refutation is both similar to and different from the Platonic genre of dialogue. Despite seeming openness in terms of content, Platonic dialogues follow the path of irony to direct the audience to a formal end. The latter is known in advance: the victory of the philosopher of being over his deeply confused interlocutors, immersed, unbeknown to themselves, in the limbo of nonbeing, which also leads them into evil, mistake, and illusion. Parenthetically, in this construction, however, there is no room for sin, but only for mistakes. The former, if taken in a religious context, may be rationally ungraspable, yet it would still be correctable through the genre of confessing to a church official, who might not understand which of the thoughts or deeds of the subject were sinful, but who nevertheless removes the sin through the formal power of the confession. Plato, that is to say, would address only mistakes. The dialogue redeems the mistaken or confused only, not sinners, who even when redeemed, may never know what their sin might have been.

Platonic dialogues seem to be open-ended, but always lead from the confidence of knowing what and how things are to a realization that such confidence was anything but true. Similarly, the Talmudic lines of refutations and counterrefutations seem open-ended, but always take a very definitive direction, if not to being, then to memory. In both cases, there is a rigor of direction combined with an open-ended character in terms of the content. In Plato, that direction is from seeming to being and therefore from evil, equated with being trapped in appearances, to the good, equated with being. In Talmudic refutations of refutations, the direction is toward making sure the memory, and thus the authority, of the tradition at hand is reliable. However many lines of refuting and counterrefuting it takes, the direction remains the same, even if the end result is not as uniform as it may be in Plato. The latter always ends up with one and only one correct view of what the matter in question really is. The rigor of Talmudic discussion is limited to the formal direction it takes (improvement of memory as both the foundation for and the core of a just action), while having no limit in the number of ways traveling in that direction can pave. The direction of the Talmudic discussion is not toward establishing what is, or in terms of the forensic branch of the art of rhetoric, what was, but rather toward probing the reliability of the witness, both the witness in a court case and the witness of what were the teachings of the law of the earlier sages. That difference plays out in yet another way. Platonic dialectics strives for justice rooted in the certainty of knowing being. The Talmudic counterpart thereof strives for acting justly (thinking justly and remembering justly included), even if and precisely because that action is to be taken in the condition of radical uncertainty.[36]

By way of yet another difference, perhaps a more technical one, in Plato's dialogues, the characters with personal names, or even the characters developed enough to have some at least rudimentary flesh, blood, and other elements of a body image, stand (and more specifically also sit, walk, lie, and so on) always either onstage or offstage, or at least, as I have argued before, in the virtual space from which, even if the truth of their being or existence comes into question, they can still take the most active part in the onstage discussion about their existence. In contrast, as shown elsewhere, in the Talmudic discussions, the flesh-and-blood body images, the flesh-and-blood characters, are always offstage, in the past, while the here-and-now of the discussion remains unspecified, so that even the narrator conveying it has no words at all to pronounce, let alone a flesh-and-blood body image of "the author" to appear onstage. The narrator, if any, only lets the characters appear onstage and disappear from the stage.

Are the Talmudic lines of the refutation of a refutation "decisionist" in Schmitt's sense? Are they alternatively a version of what he criticizes as "liberal debate," with no end or decision ever attained? As per what is already exposed above, the line of the refutation of a refutation is not a spurious infinity, but is instead cumulative, and that cumulation differs from the dialectics of cumulative sublation (*Aufhebung*) as well. Instead of either a spurious infinity of negation or dialectical synthesis, after each completed step of refuting and counterrefuting, the memory of the past (and thus of oneself as a function of the past) advances a step forward, thus affording a just action, which after each step would be more precise than before. In contrast, "liberal disputation," as Schmitt sees it, reaches no decision because it is spurious and because, for him, it lacks political form and therefore has no political will to interrupt a spurious multiplicity of opinions in discussion.

The work of memory in this respect is similar to the work of the examination of a witness in a rabbinic court in the Talmud. The court examines claims of witnesses pertinent to a case. Similarly, the rabbinic academy examines witnesses who remember the traditions, teachings, and acts of the sages of the past, or even, for the lack of a better choice, remember the records of them. The attitude toward both kinds of witness is fundamentally the same: refuting and counterrefuting for the sake of verifying the reliability of the witness and/or for the sake of getting a more precise grasp of the testimony. For example, in court practice, that means attempting to verify the reliability (or unreliability) of a witness's claim, rather than attempting to establish what happened or deducing it under a given law. (This is why the rabbinic form of approaching a witness gives the lie to Kant's diagnosis of "Jewish Law" as positive as opposed to transcendental.) Yet even if the refutation of a refutation is decisive, it is intrinsically not closed, because it promotes uncertainty as a basis for a just action, rather than striving for certainty envisioned as determining what is/what was. The latter striving, the desire for certainty, claimed to be guaranteed by knowing what is, both drives the "liberal debate" and, at the same time and by the same token, due to the multiplicity of what-is claims, lets the debate come to no resolution.

In all practical terms, an action consisting of and based on the refutation of a refutation differs from what Schmitt would criticize as politically powerless and thus politically formless "liberal debate," exemplified by debate in Weimar, which goes on without any definite end and without any authority, leading therefore to no decision, to crisis, and to the emergence of a figure whose sole role is to decide, the political figure of the sovereign. The ability to make a decision, instead of either following rules and procedures in a bureaucracy or of calculating means is for Schmitt one of the outcomes of political form. The latter is distinctly different for him from bureaucratic, capitalist, or legal forms. The decision is therefore an act based on political form. Paradigmatic of political form are for Schmitt the medieval figures of the merchant, the king, the pope, and the knight. These figures, in his terms, represent representation, which for him is also the ground of sovereignty.

In the first approximation, the representation of representation may be interpreted as the personification of personification. Such an interpretation works, also, in the example of the king, and his two bodies.[37] The current king's body represents the king's body in general. The former dies; the latter lives on. The second body is represented, and the first represents that representation. Notably, that does not represent any kind of phantom body of a king as specter, which would be a possibility ruled out by medieval theology connecting, as it does, *corpus christi* (the church) with *corpus mysticum* (Eucharist) and eliding, by the force of that connection, the third term, *corpus historicum* (the Messiah out of the tomb, as it were) which, on Kathleen Biddick's account, becomes an unwelcome specter, a zombie of flesh and blood.

With no philosophical-political will for being (or, again, time), these forms can arrive at decisions the truth or falsity of which they cannot grasp, or else, trapped in a spurious infinity of discussion, they fail to arrive at any decision whatsoever, hoping to act instead on an agreement on what is, which is in practice never achievable without political will.

Still, either scenario of liberal debate is driven by ontology, for the debate revolves around being, including the impossibility of grasping it. By contrast, the line of refuting and counterrefuting is not grounded in any ontology. It, of course, may involve ontological claims about what is or what was, but only within the procedure of verifying the reliability (and in particular, the vulnerability) of the witness of laws, crimes, or matters of fact. As briefly pointed out, in the rabbinic court in the Talmud, there is no forensics of being. There instead is only the forensics of witnessing. What this means is that the line of the refutation of a refutation is not rooted in any kind of personification, let alone in the personification of personification. In fact, the role of the personal and in particular of the impersonal is downplayed in favor of the process of refuting and counterrefuting. That process provides no flesh-and-blood body image for anything Schmitt would call political power, because it is not oriented to being or toward persons, and also because for Schmitt, the political decision is needed when ontology cannot provide certainty as a basis for action.

In the line of action called the refutation of a refutation, however, uncertainty is the ground of a just decision and is cultivated, rather than overcome. There is a way to take a just action precisely because the situation is established in terms of a well-structured uncertainty. Such just action is based on prudent remembering, as distinct from either the ability or the inability to know what is, which still accompanies, as it must in Schmitt, the political will to decide.

So to conclude this brief prospectus for writing "*Talmudic Elenchi*" as a way of thinking about the political form, in sum, the refutation of a refutation that exhibits the fundamental aspects of political form in the Talmud is not a negative dialectics, because the refutation of a refutation has a cumulative effect; and not a dialectics of *Aufhebung*, because that cumulative effect branches out and even goes rhizomatic, remaining always open for continuation; and not quite a Platonic dialogue, because the orientation toward memory takes radical precedence over the orientation toward being; and not quite liberal disputation, because of the lack of concern with what is as a basis for decision-making; and not quite a personification of personification, either, because single individual figures or personae play no central role in the refuting and counterrefuting process in the Talmud. The line of the refutation of a refutation is therefore not Schmitt's representation of representation either.

Yet if it is not quite any of the above, then what is it? Answering that question amounts, if not to an explication, then to an exemplification of these claims of difference in order to renegotiate their implications for understanding a form that, unlike either bureaucracy or the capitalist rationality of means toward ends, can be the genuine opposite of Schmitt's vision of the political. Talmudic refutation as a tacit alternative to Schmitt's political form is what Rabinovitch and his empty pamphlets can help us discern and display.

NOTES

1. The title of the present essay reverberates with an article by Michael Weingrad, "Jews (in Theory): Representations of Judaism, Anti-Semitism, and the Holocaust in Postmodern French Thought," *Judaism: A Quarterly Journal of Jewish Life and Thought* 45, no. 1 (1996): 79–98. The parentheses in Weingrad's title playfully signal an answer he gives to the question of the role of the Jews in "postmodernist theory." The answer is that "representations of Judaism" in postmodern French theory are "disturbingly" far away from the practice of the "real" Jews. To that end, the author offers a critique of French postmodernist "theory" for reducing "Jews" to an abstract—that is, in accord with his usage, "theoretical"—essence, whereas, as he strongly argues, the core of postmodernist theory consists precisely in criticizing reductionism and essentialism. The present essay departs from Weingrad's line of inquiry by converting his answer to a question: Is there a necessity by which Jews must figure in theoretical thinking, in an either abstract-theoretical or real-practical way, and can this necessity be accounted for within the framework of a simple opposition of the theoretically-abstract versus real-concrete "Jews" that Weingrad is enacting? At stake are Jews as the necessity of political reason, a necessity that, as this essay suggests, shapes both "real" and "abstract" Jews alike and inseparably one from another. "In Theory" in the title of the present essay is therefore no longer an answer, but an indication of a problem. The parentheses thus must disappear, and the comma must replace them in the title.

2. Unlike Lyotard's *Heidegger and the "the jews"* (Minneapolis: University of Minnesota Press, 1990), to whom, as this essay highlights, Lacoue-Labarthe is responding in *Typography: Mimesis, Philosophy, Politics* (Stanford: Stanford University Press, 1989), in the text I write *Jews*, *Jew*, and *Jewish* with a capital "J" and without quotation marks in order to indicate the full-fledged reality of the Jew as a modern type translated into and de facto politically inscribed on the flesh, blood, and psyches of the people, whose genealogy goes back to biblical, Talmudic, and medieval Israel. That capitalized "J" and the erasure of the quotation marks from "Jews" is of course not a regression to what Lyotard suspends as a naturalist view of Jews. Rather, in the context of this essay, the erasure and capitalization only indicate the full-fledged reality of flesh, blood, and psyche of the modern Jews as what Lacoue-Labarthe helps understand as a type, in the technical sense as something neither natural nor figurative, as I elaborate in the essay. To express that technical sense of Jews as type means to avoid understandings insisting on the dichotomies between natural, biological, racist views of humans and thus of the Jews, on the one hand, and the "religious" view of Jews as a religious group, on the other. To indicate a departure from that dichotomy, I would, if I could, simultaneously both use and erase quotation marks when writing "Jew," "Jews," or "Jewish." Because that is not graphically feasible, I instead use Jew, Jews, and Jewish, thus indicating the excess, the (im)possibility or at least problematic character of these dichotomies between "natural" and "religious" in application to Jews and to things Jewish.

3. Philippe Lacoue-Labarthe, *Typography*, trans. Chris Fynsk (Stanford: Stanford University Press, 1989).

4. See Carl Schmitt, *Römischer Katholizismus und politische Form* (1925; Stuttgart: Klett-Cotta, 1984) and, in English translation, Carl Schmitt, *Roman Catholicism and Political Form*, trans. G. L. Ulmen (Westport, Conn.: Greenwood Press, 1996).

5. Schmitt, *Roman Catholicism and Political Form*, 32; translation amended, 19. For grasping the polemical tone of the argument, Ulmen's translation is double-edged sword: It creates more problems than it solves. In general usage "the idea" is different from the representation of it; "idea" intimates a content that preexists its representation. Yet Schmitt targets the "form." Even if there is some content, of course, the "external form" does not go away and is arguably more important and most certainly more invariable than any content, however circumstantial, fluent, and changing the form might be. The form therefore is all-important even beyond the "mocking" or more precisely, beyond the "epigrammatic." "Representing nothing other than the idea of representation" is, of course, precisely this: representing nothing else but representation, a representation of representation. Marginal,

and again "*epigrammatisch*" or "mocking," or, again more precisely "epigrammatic" as this definition of the political form is for Schmitt, it nevertheless affords him very strong, perhaps even the strongest grounds for differentiating political representation, which he supports, from techno-economical representation, which he dismisses as a distorted notion of representing.

6. Ibid. 7.

7. The decision on the exception in the face of perceived emergency that Schmitt described in his later work thus can generate any content as long as it generates *a* content. That content includes indicating who, or rather what, the hidden enemy is and who is a friend. This is why, after *Roman Catholicism*, Schmitt can say, "The specific political distinction to which political actions and motives can be reduced is that between friend and enemy" (Carl Schmitt, *The Concept of the Political*, trans. George Schwab [Chicago: University of Chicago Press, 1996], 26). Making such a decision follows the logic of immanence in the political form of the representation of representation, because the form relies on no external factor—neither on a group of "formed interests," as in representative government, nor on the figure of any particular leader, as in a dictatorship. Because the logic of political form does not depend on any external reference and/or content, it can produce any reference and/or content. That enables the representative of representation who is performing that form to make a decision, rather than to apply or create a rule. It also leads to an immanent legitimization that precedes, suspends, and supersedes any positive legality of the law as a set of rules.

8. The example of the pope will be of particular help below for a comparison and contrast with the provisional, albeit, in this case, not absolute assumption of infallibility with which the characters in the Talmud treat the words of the *tann'aim*, the reciters of the teachings of the earlier authorities, the sages of the Mishnah.

9. For example, the mathematical notion of a point is a fiction, at least in the sense that it can never be empirically real, and it is a necessary fiction without which geometry, that particular domain of reason, cannot operate.

10. Precisely because "specter" only exemplifies *Ge-stalt* in certain contexts, it is more important to note that a specter *is Ge-stalt*. In such contexts, I use these terms together or interchangeably.

11. Hegel is yet another thinker for whom *Gestalt* functions as a specter, this time of an "organic whole" in which members are not parts, but rather organs and in which therefore a member embraces or "reflects" the "whole" of the organism, so that, as with men and women, the organism proceeds through differing implementations of one and the same set of organs, which are developed in different degrees in individuals of different sexes.

12. One might apply here Rodolphe Gasché's notion of singular universal, a singular that serves as a universal. See Rodolphe Gasché, "Piercing the Horizon," *Journal of French Philosophy* 7, no. 2 (2007): 1–12.

13. As Jonathan Boyarin has suggested, this sounds remarkably reminiscent of Abraham Joshua Heschel's interpretation of the Chasidic thought of Menachem Mendel of Kotzk (1787–1859) See Abraham Joshua Heschel, *A Passion for Truth* (New York: Farrar, Straus and Giroux, 1973).

14. Haunting as these objects or subjects always are, specters lurk and lure in dispelling them. In contrast, concepts may work without ever presenting themselves as either object or subjects. They instead can inform thinking and action without ever thematically emerging there.

15. See Daniel Boyarin, *Carnal Israel: Reading Sex in Talmudic Culture* (Berkeley: University of California Press, 1993).

16. For the analysis and complication of that dynamic relationship in medieval Jewish, Christian, and Muslim identities see Steven F. Kruger, *The Spectral Jew: Conversion and Embodiment in Medieval Europe* (Minneapolis: University of Minnesota Press, 2006).

17. For much earlier, Hellenistic negotiations of the borders of humanity see, for example, Jonathan Boyarin, "The Universe of the Human," in *The Unconverted Self: Jews, Indians, and the Identity of Christian Europe* (Chicago: University of Chicago Press, 2009), 7–90. As Boyarin argues, the rhetoric of kinship (which in the context of this essay and in Lacoue-Labarthe's terms is distinct from the fictive productions of reason in the form of *Ge-stell*) remains heavily at work.

18. Павел Флоренский "Идеи и судьба христиан" (Письмо к В.В. Розанову 1913. Октябрь, 26. Ночь. 361–67: 363.) In: Розанов, В. В. Сахарна. Обонятельное и осязательное отношение евреев к крови. Москва "Республика" 1988: 363. Pavel Florensky, "The Idea and the Fate of Christians" (letter to V. V. Rozanov, 1913 October, 26. Night. 361–67,) in V. V. Rosanov, *Sacharna: The Sense of Smell and the Sense of Touch in How Jews Treat the Blood* (Moscow: Respublica, 1988). "Indeed, there is nothing to say. Is there anything at all you can do with Jewish advocates? And why do you think we will learn from them . . . something deeper than the art of advocacy? Noteworthy, *advocacy*, and 'Enlightenment' in general—is *their* invention. It was they who stirred the controversy around the Catholic Church. Humanism derives from the Kabbalah. More generally, Jews used to and will continue to keep secrets for themselves, and they used to and will continue to give out only the shells: a white tie, 'Russkie Vedomosti' newspaper, cheap charities, and our right to supply newborns for them. Jews have always turned to us, the Arians, with that side of theirs, to which we, due to our lack of religiosity, have always been *seducible*; and they then always took advantage

of such a situation. They taught us that all people (*lyudi*, 'men') are equal,—in order to take advantage of us (lit.: sit on our neck); they taught that all religions are superstitions and atavisms of the Middle Ages (which they by the way dislike so much precisely because of its integrity, because, then, one knew how to deal with them),—in order to take away our power—our faith; they taught 'autonomous' morality, in order for them to take already existing morality away and to substitute for it what is banal and vulgar. If they just wanted to make us Jewish, that would be only a half-trouble. Yet the problem is that they have perfectly understood and still understand the value of every religious principle, and ultimately, its power to unite people, thereby secretly keeping their own religious principle for themselves" (363, my translation).

19. In *The Origins of Totalitarianism* (1958), in the section "Between Pariah and Parvenu," Hannah Arendt shows a complex interplay between "mankind" as an always repressive attempt to reduce the plurality of humanity to a unity and "humanity," which is always pluralistic and inclusive of, as she still critically quotes Herder, a "new specimen of humanity," which is not exactly a specimen, but rather an insider who is an outsider and an outsider who is an insider and someone of whom it cannot always be certainly told who he was or who he is—in one simple word, a Jew. Arendt thus insists on her being treated as a Jew within humanity, rather than as a pure "human being" among other human beings, the members of humankind. Humanity, thus, for her, does not predicate "human being" as its component. Because she was persecuted as a Jew, she demands to be respected as a Jew, rather than as a "human being." That defines humanity as a way of treatment of the other in the public discourse, rather than as a definition of private beings united in a group, say, into a nation-state, bypassing the public political dimension that Schmitt, in this respect not totally unlike Arendt, also indicated in his critique of the modern capitalist nation-states. On these grounds, which are of course rather different from those of Florensky, Arendt arrives at the strikingly similar conclusion that treating a Jew and everybody else as a "human being" is politically impossible. Despite the fact that Florensky conceptually replaces "human being" with "religion" and Arendt with "humanity," both thinkers arrive at the similar conclusion that treating a Jew, and thus everybody else, as a "human being" is problematic, because it erases the political (Arendt) or the religious (Florensky) dimensions of the life of society.

20. Hannah Arendt and Ron H. Feldman. *The Jew as Pariah: Jewish Identity and Politics in the Modern Age* (New York: Grove Press, 1978).

21. This is confirmed not only and not primarily by the emptiness of the leaflets. Instead, whatever the content of his protest might be, the grounds on which he protests are that of a universal human being (a subject of rights, in

one dimension of the protest) fighting for the universal and for Jewish values at the same time.

22. Sergey Dolgopolski, "Rethinking the Implicit: Fragments of the Project on Aggada and Halakhah in Walter Benjamin," in *Words: Religious Language Matters*, ed. Ernst Van Den Hemmel and Asja Szafraniec (New York: Fordham University Press, 2016), 249–68.

23. I find Jacques Rancière's diagnosis of the impasses of the philosophy of the political heuristically helpful, particularly in this respect. See his *Disagreement: Politics and Philosophy* (Minneapolis: University of Minneapolis Press, 1999).

24. That argument also works with both Hermann Cohen's way of relating time with the open future (Hermann Cohen and Albert Görland, *Logik der reinen Erkenntnis* [Berlin: B. Cassirer, 1902], as well as with Martin Heidegger's way of relating time, the future, and being beginning from his *Sein und Zeit* in 1929.

25. Lyotard's "what" also belongs to the plane of representation alone. Lyotard's treatment of the affect in *Discourse, Figure* as the pure "what" without the "who," the "to whom," or the "about what" is still taking place within the level of representation: the zero degree thereof. This is important in the context of this essay because of the contrast of Lacoue-Labarthe's position to Lyotard's *Heidegger and the "jews."* This connection, however, would require a separate treatment.

26. Refutation therefore is not just a fourth dimension on the plane of signification, manifestation, and denotation, in Deleuze's terms in *The Logic of Sense* (Gilles Deleuze, Constantin V. Boundas, and Mark Lester, *The Logic of Sense* [London: Continuum, 2012]) but rather is an altogether different plane, a dimension that circumscribes the level of representation on which the first three occur. Yet again that is to be developed elsewhere.

27. See, for example, Babylonian Talmud, b. Quiddushin 70a.

28. I am, of course, borrowing Lacoue-Labarthe's terms here.

29. That extends to asking about *Ge-stell* in digital speeds (in the sense of the speed of switching the registers), if that switch is still a *Ge-stell*, and if this is still a *Ge-stalt*.

30. Kathleen Biddick's analysis discerns how these constructions of Schmitt's tacitly follow the logic of medieval Catholic interpretation of *corpus verum* as the absent body of Christ (absent from the tomb, that is), *corpus christi* as the church, the symbolic body of Christ, that is, and *corpus mysticum* as the mystical, rather than merely symbolic identification of the church with the body of Christ, so that the church now is both the representation of Christ (as *corpus christi*) and what that representation represents (the mystical body of the currently absent Christ, or *corpus mysticum*). That leads, as

Biddick argues, to the elision of the absent body (*corpus verum*) from the equation, replacing it with an imaginary Christ, a "zombie" that the church "represents" in the second order of representation in order to enable the representation of the first order, which is the representation of representation. See Kathleen Biddick, *Make and Let Die: Untimely Sovereignties* (Earth, Milky Way: Punctum Books, 2016).

31. The law, or any other second-order representation, cannot be fully canceled, because the first-order representation (the representation of representation) cannot work without the second, or as Lacoue-Labarthe would explain, the first order of representation could not work without "fictioning" the second order. It is therefore not important whether the second order of representation is active or only suspended.

32. For the purposes of this argument, I bracket the question of Heidegger's return to the pre-Socratic moment. His discernment of being in pre-Socratics is guided by understanding being through time, futurist as it generally remains for him.

33. For Hayyim Luzzatto, an effort to remember through an enactment threatens to forget the importance of remembering through intellectual engagement, even with things that might seem obvious otherwise. See his introduction to *Mesillat Yesharim* in Moshe Hayyim Luzzatto, and Abraham Shoshana, *Complete Mesillat Yesharim: Dialogue and Thematic Versions* (Cleveland: Ofeq Institute, 2010). Luzzatto's example of such forgetting through reenactment is a religious group that forgets the importance of fear of heaven or of divine love by constantly enacting these things in their rituals.

34. See Gilles Deleuze, *Expressionism in Philosophy: Spinoza* (New York: Zone Books, 1990).

35. As Deleuze argues in his reading of Spinoza, just as Spinoza's "substance" can be expressed only through an attribute, one at a time, but can never be reduced to any particular attribute, more generally, by the tripartitioning logic of the expression as distinct from the dual logic of representation, what is being expressed ("substance") is always more than what is actually expressed ("attribute") in any particular ("modus") of the expression.

36. I apply Chaya T. Halberstam's useful concept of "uncertainty," even if her work, in my mind, does not pay enough attention to the tradition of rhetoric in this respect. Chaya T. Halberstam, *Law and Truth in Biblical and Rabbinic Literature* (Bloomington: Indiana University Press, 2010).

37. Ernst H. Kantorowicz, *The King's Two Bodies: A Study in Medieval Political Theology* (Princeton: Princeton University Press, 1957).

CHAPTER 6

The Jewish *Animot*: Of Jews as Animals

Jay Geller

Eric Santner opens his 1997 essay "Freud, Žižek, and the Joys of Monotheism"[1] with

> a well-known Jewish joke about a zoology course at a distinguished university in which the students were requested to write a term paper on the subject of elephants. The French student writes a paper with the predictable title, "On the Sexual Habits of the Elephant"; the German student submits a teutonically comprehensive "Introduction to the Bibliographic Sources for the Study of the Elephant"; the American student submits a paper on the topic of "Breeding Bigger and Better Elephants"; and, finally, the Jewish student chooses as his theme—what else?—"The Elephant and the Jewish Question."

There are a number of variants of this old joke,[2] including this elaborate rendition that Jacques Derrida delivered at his March 2004 appearance at London Jewish Book Week:[3]

> There are three people isolated on an island: a German citizen, a French citizen and a Jew, totally alone on this island. They don't know when they will leave the island, and it is boring. One of them says,

> "Well, we should do something. We should do something, the three of us. Why don't we write something on the elephants?" There were a number of elephants on the island. "Everyone should write something on the elephants and then we could compare the styles and the national idioms," and so on and so forth. So the week after, the French one came, with a short, brilliant, witty essay on the sexual drive, or sexual appetite of the elephants; very short, bright and brilliant essay, very, very superficial but very brilliant. Three months, or three years after that, the German came with a heavy book on the . . . let's say a very positive scientific book on the comparison between two kinds of species, with a very scientific title, an endless title for a very positive scientific book on the elephants and the ecology of the elephants on the island. And the two of them asked the Jew, "Well, when will you give us your book?" "Wait, it's a very serious question. I need more time. I need more time." And they came back every year asking him for his book. Finally, after ten years, he came back with a book called, "The Elephant and the Jewish Question."

Derrida's take on the joke displays a number of fascinating particularities: It is set outside of academia; the motivation of the castaways is to relieve boredom rather than making a contribution to "knowledge"; the object of their doing is part of their everyday; their works are intended both as individual and as collective exercises—these works are to be shared with and analyzed by each of them; one explicit assumption of the proposed exercise is that each production will testify to the national identification of its producer; only the Jew is manifestly gendered, and "he" is the only one *not* characterized as a "citizen"; the only information we are given about the Jew's book, aside from the length of time between commission and completion, is its title, which is also the only title of the three that is explicitly stated; and only the Jew refers to the elephants in the categorical singular. While each of these singular aspects of Derrida's version opens upon questions that are worthy of further analysis,[4] this chapter principally attends to the last: the use of the categorical singular by which elephants and—at least implicitly—Jews are here typecast.

Santner's analysis of "the Jew" as the *Pointe* of his and, presumably, all of the joke variants focuses on the typecasting of Jews:[5]

> The Jewish national character trait stands out as something of an anomaly in the context of the list provided by the joke. For one could say that what, according to the joke, marks the Jew as a Jew, is a preoccupation with the dilemmas and difficulties of being marked as having a national character trait in the first place. The Jew is typed as the

> one for whom the very experience of being typed constitutes his type, for whom the phenomenon of types and stereotyping is, as it were, his typical problem. To be Jewish is to be that exceptional type in whom the principle of typing and stereotyping—the principle organizing the list of national types exhibited in the joke—is reflected into itself, makes its appearance as a particular element in the list.

"The Jew" is figured as the type of type: as the meta-type of particularity. To adopt the language of Andrew Benjamin: What is particular about "the Jew" is that "the Jew" figures the particular.[6] But Jews are not the only entities in the punch line of Derrida's variant that have been figured by their categoriality—albeit as a dependent rather than independent variable—so are elephants.

Derrida's elephants, or rather his "Elephant," caught Devorah Baum's attention. After commencing her article "Circumcision Anxiety" with the scene of Derrida regaling his audience with the joke and its, perhaps, real punch line—the comment with which he supplemented his telling, "That's my work"—she appends her own gloss to both:[7]

> The proverbial elephant signifies the presence of something—a kind of open secret—which can be referred to, if at all, only obliquely, indirectly, jokingly. As such, given the numerous references to Jews, Judaism and Jewishness throughout the Derridean corpus, there may be reason to doubt whether the elephant, if there is one in the room of deconstruction, ought really to be designated a Jewish elephant; unless, that is, the elephant's Jewishness alludes to something else—to an unspeakable trauma perhaps? Trauma, after all, has, like the elephant, often been characterized as a figure of necessary reticence.

The elephant in the room of which no one wishes to speak, however, is the elephant (i.e., a member of the family *Elephantidae* and the order *Proboscidea*). I do not, however, wish to speak for elephants; "speaking for the elephant" is part of the problem.[8] The elephant is "only an animal"—to borrow the telltale justification that Theodor Adorno isolates in *Minima Moralia* on the possibility of "pogroms" against "savages, blacks, Japanese." Before offering his warning, Adorno speculates about how the victims traditionally associated with pogroms have been perceived: "Perhaps the social schematism of perception in anti-Semites is such that they do not see Jews as human beings at all." This aphorism is titled "*Menschen sehen dich an*" (People are looking at you), by which Adorno is ironically playing on *Juden sehen Dich an* (Jews are looking at you), Nazi ideologue Johann von Leers's 1933 antisemitic natural-historical taxonomy of "the Jew" that included chapters on *Lügenjuden* (liar Jews), *Betrugsjuden* (swindler Jews), *Zersetzungsjuden* (subversive Jews), and so on.[9] Perhaps if one reads Derrida's punch line "The Elephant and the Jewish Question" from right to left it would metamorphose into "The Jew and the Elephant Question" and thereby allow us to hear echoes of Adorno and Horkheimer in the "Elements of Antisemitism":

> They who propagated individualism, abstract law, the concept of the person, have been debased to a species [*Spezies*]. They who were never allowed untroubled ownership of the civic right [*Bürgerrecht*] that should have granted them human dignity [*Qualität der Menschheit*] are again called "The Jews" [*sic*!; the German reads "*Der Jud*," i.e., "The Jew"] without distinction [*ohne Unterschied*]."[10]

This chapter examines some of the entanglements of the Jewish Question, of the Gentile/Jew divide, with the Elephant Question—or, rather, with what has come to be known as "the question of the animal," with the human/animal divide. After briefly discussing Derrida's articulation of the latter question and then how he and others have on occasion brought "the Jew" and "the Animal" together, I turn to two of Franz Kafka's (nonhuman) animal protagonists—Gregor Samsa and Red Peter[11]—whom he depicts negotiating the human/animal divide. That analysis explores how he drew upon figuration that had been employed to bestialize and dehumanize Jews to negotiate the Gentile/Jew divide by engaging, to appropriate Derrida's neologism, the Jewish *animot*.

Theory as/and Animalapropism

In a 1997 lecture, (later collected in) *The Animal That Therefore I Am*, Derrida initiates an analysis of the "question of the animal," the deployment of the figure of "the Animal" in the Western carnophallogocentric philosophic tradition, during which he also briefly invokes Adorno's concern with such questions. In *Animal* Derrida introduces *animot*, a homophonic play on the French plural of animal, *animaux*, and the French word for word, *mot*. Derrida's neologism ironically points to how nonhuman animals in that tradition are denied the capacity to speak and are all but inevitably referred to in the categorical singular of "the Animal."[12] As Derrida and others[13] have argued, this foreclosure of both the diversity of animal species (aside from the opposed human [animal] and [nonhuman] animal) and the singularity of the individual nonhuman animal has served several anthropocentric purposes, including the exclusive determinations of "the (hu)man," of the (human) subject, and of the universal (over and against the particular).

Similarly, antisemitic discourses deploy "the Jew" rather than "the Animal" and some conceptual category of human (animal) collectivity—not excluding "species"—to maintain and justify comparable foreclosures and serve comparable ends. At one point in *The Animal*, Derrida "return[s] for a moment to Adorno [on the] Kantian or idealist hatred of the animal, this zoophobia. . . . For an idealist system, he [i.e., Adorno] says, animals virtually play the same role as Jews did for a fascist system."[14] Derrida then cites Élisabeth de Fontenay, first, in order to present another Jewish-accented relation to the animal question:

> Those who evoke the *summa injuria* [an allusion to Nazi zoophilia and Hitler's vegetarianism] only in order to better make fun of pity for anonymous and mute suffering are out of luck, for it happens that some great Jewish writers and thinkers of this century were obsessed by the question of the animal: Kafka, Singer, Canetti, Horkheimer, Adorno.

And second, Derrida erects both Fontenay's observation that these individuals had insistently inscribed this question in their "interrogation of rationalist humanism and of the solid ground of its decisions" and her claim about the ethical grounds for this inscription—that "victims of historic catastrophes have in fact felt animals to be victims also, comparable up to a certain point to themselves and their kind"—as a double foil against which he can interrogate the relative absence of the animal question in "the Jewish thinker who, no doubt with justification, passes in this [twentieth] century for the most concerned with ethics and sanctity, Emmanuel Levinas."[15] In this and subsequent publications Derrida does not return, with one brief exception,[16] to analyze those "Jew"-inscribed sites in Fontenay's canon.

As Fontenay observes, there is indeed a critical tradition of analyses of the Jew *and* the Animal, in which, for example, both have been situated within virtually homological hierarchical oppositions within the dialectic of enlightenment (as Derrida situates Adorno); or both have functioned as figure, especially the figure of the particular, in philosophic discourses (A. Benjamin and, differently, Horkheimer and Adorno in *Dialectic of Enlightenment*); or the diverse but in any case deadly assaults suffered by Jews and animals have been analogized with one other, whether the emphasis is on shared suffering (Fontenay)[17] or on the "making killable"[18] of bare life by the modern anthropological machine of the biopolitical (Agamben). Unfortunately understanding the constellation of the Jew and the Animal in terms of mechanical solidarity[19] leaves little space for Jewish (or animal) agency aside from bearing witness to victimization or offering an alternative social epistemology (drawn from neither Jewish nor animal lifeworlds) such as that signaled by the title of Benjamin's analysis *Of Jews and Animals*. Benjamin develops his alternative by running the specificity of "the Jew" (and, separately, "the Animal") as a particular figure of the particular back through philosophy to subvert the authority it ascribes to the general and/or universal.[20] Yet what is clearer in Benjamin, especially in his incisive critique of Agamben's failure to address the specificity of the decision to mark the Jews as killable,[21] than in Horkheimer and Adorno is that the figuration of Jews as the "figure of the Jew" exceeds the at-handness, the happenstantial availability, of Jews. Horkheimer and Adorno still tend to situate the Jews within series of distant and proximate others, including women and children. In sum, for all representatives of this critical tradition it's a matter of

> here is how the Jew is deployed, there how the Animal, or
> here how the Jew like the Animal, or
> here how the Animal like the Jew,

but not how a particular Jew figured as a particular (nonhuman) animal acts and interacts—by which both Jews and (nonhuman) animals perform their particularity and, thereby, put in question the hierarchical oppositions in which they would be situated as mere instantiations of the categorical singular.

Animot *Tales*

These investigations do not explore the organic solidarity of Jews and (nonhuman) animals: of Jews *as* animals. For this we need to step out of theory qua theory and examine the Jewish *animot*, how in praxis the appropriation of particular animal-figures (e.g., apes, dogs, and pigs; lice, mice, and other assorted vermin) that have served to bestialize and dehumanize Jews helped a number[22] of Jewish-identified writers to think through their situation in modernity. Such an examination will allow us to think through the relationships between their praxes and their situations. The "as" signals neither a tradition of metaphors and similes nor a canon of allegories, fables, and parables. Rather these writers have produced prose, poetic, and dramatic narratives entailing characters who should be understood less as becoming-animal, the Deleuze and Guattarian escape from Oedipus,[23] than as performing animal, literalizing their societally figured identifications.[24] In these texts the actions of the nonhuman animal protagonists as well as their interactions with other nonhuman and/or human animals would subvert, render undecidable, the human/animal divide as it was being played out on actual Jewish bodies and in Jewish-Gentile relations in their authors' lived experience. Rather than leaving Jewish language to "the rumor about the Jews," as Adorno characterizes antisemitism in *Minima Moralia*'s "Second Harvest,"[25] these writers sought to enunciate the Jewish *animot* and, thereby, either to resist (and, if possible, neutralize) or, alas, to succumb to those bestial figurations that would marginalize their purported referents, the Jews, in or foreclose them from the polis.

The remainder of this chapter focuses on two of Franz Kafka's (nonhuman) animal protagonists: Gregor Samsa and Red Peter. Kafka identifies neither as Jewish. Indeed, the Samsa family's Christianity is several times signaled—father, mother, and sister cross themselves over Gregor's corpse—and Red Peter's possible religious affiliation is never broached. Then again, Max Brod, after concluding a series of snapshots of his best friend Kafka's protagonists with the "monstrous insect" of *The Metamorphosis*, asserted in Martin Buber's journal *Der Jude*, a year before "A Report to an Academy" would appear in the same venue: "Although the word 'Jew' [*Jude*] never appears in his works, they belong to the most Jewish documents of our time."[26] One does not have to accept Brod's hagiographic Judaization of Kafka's corpus—an absolutist position rendered problematic since Walter Benjamin's 1931 review of Brod's collection of selected shorter writings from Kafka's *Nachlass*, *Beim Bau der Chinesischen Mauer* (The Great Wall of China)[27]—in order to pursue how the absence of explicit Jewish reference does not preclude situating these stories and their animal protagonists within a constellation of Kafka's Jewish-related contexts and concerns.

Into what kind of nonhuman animal did the traveling salesman Gregor Samsa, having most uncharacteristically slept through his alarm, wake up to find himself metamorphosed? One can't rightly say. Kafka steadfastly refused every request to have Gregor visually represented.[28] His description in *The Metamorphosis* doesn't correspond exactly to any known species; hence the famous entomologist and novelist Vladimir Nabokov opened his Cornell class lecture on Kafka's novella by asserting that, faute de mieux, Gregor is a "big beetle." Nabokov readily dismisses the numerous commentators who refer to him as a cockroach: "A cockroach is an insect that is flat in shape with large legs, and Gregor is anything but flat: he is convex on both sides, belly and back, and his legs are small."[29] He also notes that when the charwoman calls him an "*alter Mistkäfer*," an old dung beetle (*M*, 127), she is merely using a familiar epithet; toddlers crawling underfoot were often tagged *Mistkäfer* by caregivers.[30] Moreover, a dung beetle, no matter how large, would not possess the mandibles necessary to open the door as Gregor's had. Finally, Kafka provides only one zoological denomination of the "huge brown mass [*riesigen braunen Fleck*]" (*M*, 119) that Gregor has become—"*Ungeziefer*" (vermin)—and its single mention is in the novella's opening sentence. Included under this rubric are any number of small pests that gnaw or bite, such as rodents, insects, and lice.[31] This "animal category," which Grimms' *Wörterbuch* speculates originally designated animals that were unfit for sacrifice, became pathogenically associated with allegedly dirty and disease-bearing creatures, especially after the 1880s when the epidemic threat of typhus (*Fleckfieber*) failed to succumb to the explanatory security of the newly hegemonic germ theory. Anxious eyes then turned a potentially exterminationist gaze at such possible sources of contamination—including at Jewish-identified discoverers of infecting agents, who were pictured by the antisemitic press as themselves the agents of infection.[32] Still Jews were not the only human (animal) group so labeled.

While the reader encounters Gregor's description, nonhumanoid part by nonhumanoid part, of his transformed body, it is only when he is heard speaking that he is first identified by other characters as "animal." After Gregor delivers an extensive litany of apologies, excuses, and self-accusations as to why he has yet to open the door to his room, he is met with the chief clerk's "That was an animal voice" (*Das war ein Tierstimme*; *M*, 98).[33] Worse, he later came to realize, "since what he said was not understood by the others it never struck any of them, not even his sister, that he could understand what they said, and so whenever his sister came into his room he had to content himself with hearing her utter only a sigh now and then" (*M*, 109). Gregor is placed outside the circle of human language speakers, but by his confinement to a room *within* the family apartment, he nevertheless remains defined in terms of his relationship to that human circle (*menschlichen Kreis*; *M*, 99), however nonspecifically: that is, as animal.[34]

For the question is not "What kind of animal is Gregor?" but "Is he exclusively inscribed within the human/animal opposition?" Throughout the story Kafka is ironizing the role of animal or vermin commonplaces. The company porter whom Gregor was supposed to meet at the rail station is characterized by him "as the creature [*Kreatur*] of the chief's, spineless and mindless [*ohne Rückgrat und Verstand*]" (*M*, 91). Later, after the metamorphosed Gregor first becomes visible to others by pushing himself through the opening [*Öffnung*] and into the living room, he remains unaware "that his words in all possibility, indeed in all likelihood, would again be unintelligible" (*M*, 102) and is eventually driven back in by his father, who, by contrast, is "making hissing noises like a savage" (*stieß Zischlaute aus, wie ein Wilder*; *M*, 104).[35] Months later, Gregor reverses his retreat from "his human past" (*M*, 116) and moves—for what will be his last time—from his "naked den" (*Höhle* or "lair"; *M*, 116) into the living room. Then, coated with the useless detritus of human life ("dust; fluff and hair and remnants of food"),[36] he advances "a little over the spotless floor" to listen to his sister's violin-playing and asks himself: "Was he an animal [*ein Tier*], that music had such an effect upon him" (*M*, 130). By invoking the proverbial connection of animals and music, Gregor utters his first and only self-association with the label "animal"; it is a paradoxical moment of the "animal" reasserting his humanness by questioning his humanness, and it proves climactic. It is at this moment of crossing from the animal outside (which, again, is necessarily encrypted in the Samsas' apartment) to the human inside that Gregor becomes neither human nor animal: for from the site of his eruption Gregor would witness a telling exchange over social interpellating names and pronouns[37] between Grete and their parents.

"It Is What It Is"?

Once the family had discovered his metamorphosis, only Grete ever addressed Gregor directly by name, and then only once: Accompanying her mother into Gregor's room, Grete cries out, "Du, Gregor" (*M*, 119), after her mother, catching sight of the "huge brown mass on the flowered wallpaper," begins to decompensate. A number of weeks later, however, when Grete last encounters Gregor alive, she declares: "I won't utter my brother's name in the presence of this creature [*Untier*], and so all I say is we must try to get rid of it [*es*]. We've tried to look after it [*es*] and to put up with it [*es*] as far as humanly possible [*das Menschenmögliche*]. . . . We must try to get rid of it [*es*]." Her father, at a loss, "half-questioningly" laments, "If he [*er*] could understand us . . . then perhaps we might come to some agreement with him [*ihm*]" (*M*, 133). Grete and her father are employing different pronouns to refer to this *Untier*, this "un-animal."

His sister cuts to the quick:

> It [*es*] must go. . . . You must try to get rid of the idea that it [*es*] is Gregor. The fact that we had believed it for so long was our trouble. But how can it be Gregor? If it [*es*] was Gregor, he [*er*] would have realized long ago that human beings [*Menschen*] can't live with such

> a creature [*einem solchen Tier*] and would have gone away on his own accord. (*M*, 134; translation altered)

Grete is explicitly making the distinction between the metamorphosed protagonist as an unnamed (and unnamable?) "it" versus a namable and addressable "he," who would recognize the distinction between human and animal.

She then continues with a litany of ascribed acts, intentions, and desires that render this unnamable "it," not as bare life but as an all-powerful threat: "As it is, this creature [*dieses Tier*] persecutes us." This *Tier* is not an animal, for if *it* were Gregor (that is, one who played according to the rules of the human/animal divide), *he* would sustain human/animal difference (whether by staying in his ascribed place as animal or, now, by doing the human thing and leaving the apartment); rather, *it* is the outlaw, the werewolf.[38] This is made clear by Grete's next statement and its accompanying affect: "'Just look, Father.' She shrieked all at once, 'he's [*er*] at it again!'" (*M*, 134). Grete here employs the masculine pronoun. The earlier distinction between Gregor and this *Untier*—between the human/animal opposition "Gregor" emblematizes and its abject—by which she had endeavored to restore order to the family, has collapsed. The narrator describes the effects and affects of her blurring of the distinction: "And in an access of panic [*Schrecken*] that was quite incomprehensible to Gregor she even quitted her mother, literally thrusting the chair from her as if she would rather sacrifice [*opfern*] her mother than stay so near to Gregor" (*M*, 134). Unable to make a sovereign decision in this state of emergency, she flees in terror. Gregor eventually manages to crawl back into his room where by morning's light he would die, and thereby, in death and in family memory, restored to "*er*"; Grete, observing his corpse, comments: "Just see how thin he [*er*] was. It's such a long time since he's [*er*] eaten anything" (*M*, 136).

The Metamorphosis betrays the operation of the human/animal opposition (and the other "Great Divides"). In line with one prominent school of interpretation, Kafka's protagonist, ultimately perceiving no way out of his ascribed place within it, submits to an order-restoring (or even an order-founding) sacrificial death of the animal.[39] Then again, perhaps Gregor's last defile, the emergence of this *Untier* that bears the "*Un*" trace of the *ungeheuren Ungeziefer*, the death of which cannot serve as a sacrifice, called attention to, bespoke, the nonnatural, constructed status of order-maintaining hierarchical distinctions and divides. Perhaps echoing the contrapuntal exchange of his sister's "Finally" (*Endlich*) as she locked him back in his den and his last words, the question "And what now?"

(*Und jetzt*; *M*, 135), Gregor's final eruptive performance may have opened the way for the Samsa family to kick out the boarders and, with the family on a "tram into the open country [*ins Freie*] outside the town" (*M*, 139) as the novella closes, to endeavor to find some form of self-determination.[40]

Performing Animals, Performative Jews

Supplementing this analysis of *The Metamorphosis* and its silenced protagonist with a discussion of Kafka's "A Report to an Academy" and its loquacious narrator will help clarify how his exploration of the human/animal opposition was imbricated in the relationships between Gentile and Jew. The eponymous report is presented by Red Peter, who is an ape or *Affe*. It recounts his life from capture on the Gold Coast by representatives of the Hagenbeck Zoo through acquisition of language to pursuit of a career on the variety stage.

Given the long association of Jews with apes in the Central European imaginary, let alone the story's appearance in *Der Jude*, it is not unreasonable to assume that Kafka realized that many of its readers would identify Red Peter as a Jew: This star of the variety stage can no longer be taken to be some incontinent, flea-ridden animal who thereby embodies (the oppressors' image of[41]) the ugly, filthy, smelling (East European) Jew; instead, he appears as the performing ape who enacts (the oppressors' image of[42]) the self-deluded, assimilating (Western) Jew. Yet beneath the mask of the report is an indictment of a dominant culture that both requires and denies Red Peter's—and the Jews'—move toward (Gentile) European bourgeois humanity. Red Peter concludes that the only "way out" (*Ausweg*; RA, 253) of the cage (of ascribed identity) is to imitate his tormentors. He begins to adopt their vices, such as spitting: first to entertain them—they cannot beat him when they are convulsed in laughter—and second to prove that he is one of them. He undergoes a rote catechism in humanity (and *goyische naches*)[43] by way of repeated mock drinking from a bottle of spirits. This practice culminates in a communion-like scene with his first swallow and first human word—the word that performs admission to the human community ("Hallo!"; RA, 257).[44] Here Red Peter even apes a conversion; he is, as it were, born again.

Kafka's protagonist realizes when he lands in Hamburg that to imitate the worst in his European Gentile captors is insufficient: That path leads only to the zoo, in other words, to a new cage. Red Peter does not yearn for freedom—recognizing that its pursuit would only lead to the greatest disillusionment (*Täuschung*)—rather he seeks only a "way out" (*Ausweg*—this word is repeated fourteen times in the story). So he opts for *Mimik*, the variety stage, and attaining the "cultural level of an average European" (RA, 258). The story itself—a report delivered to a scientific academy—is the ultimate mimetic act:[45] Although he is the object of the report, Red Peter is also its subject. He is reading in the guise of a race scientist.

Red Peter may have begun his report with the claim that "it is now nearly five years since I was an ape" (RA, 250), but in the end he remains to the implied scientific audience of the academy a talking ape—and to many readers, a European-aping Jew and a self-deluded one at that. At the story's conclusion, by constantly performing—by aping the "civilized"—Red Peter is able to survive: "I do not complain, but I'm not satisfied [*zufrieden*] either" (RA, 258; trans. adapted). Kafka may here be echoing the late-eighteenth-century, native-Yiddish-speaking Jewish philosopher Solomon Maimon, who taught himself German by reading Hebrew-letter transcriptions of German language science texts and who in his autobiography, a work read and recommended by Kafka,[46] gave an account of his reception by Berlin's educated elite:

> At first [Moses Mendelssohn's] friend regarded me as a speaking animal [*ein redendes Tier*], and entertained himself with me, as one is apt to do with a dog or a starling [*Star*] that has been taught to speak a few words. The odd mixture of the animal [*Mischung des Tiereschen*] in my manners, my expressions, and my whole outward behavior, with the rational in my thoughts, excited his imagination more than the subject of our conversation roused his understanding.

Then again, perhaps it is Red Peter's audience who is suffering from self-delusions. In the story of his development, Red Peter portrays those models of Gentile human behavior, whom he calls his "mentors" and "teachers" (RA, 250, 258), as the bestial tormentors they were. From the beginning of his report, Red Peter alerts Kafka's readers as well as his listeners:

> To put it plainly—your life as apes, gentlemen, insofar as something of that kind lies behind you, cannot be farther removed from you than mine is from me. Yet everyone on earth feels a tickling at the heels: the small chimpanzee and the great Achilles alike. (RA, 250)

For some readers, Red Peter has reversed the moral hierarchy of human and animal. The Europeans are the true brutes, the loud oppressors of silenced victims.[47] But would Kafka be seeking simply to change the referents of the hierarchical opposition (humans are beasts, and beasts human)? The distinction and its structural oppression would still remain.

Becoming a Minor Literature

Kafka's texts can generate, *inter alia*, an alternative reading consonant with his own prescription, written a year before *Metamorphosis*, for a literature that helps an ethnic minority like the Jews forge a national identity and a communal memory and that supports such a group "in the face of a hostile surrounding world." One trait of this "minor[ity] literature" is "the presentation of national faults in a manner that is very painful, to be sure, but also liberating and deserving of forgiveness."[48] Consequently, both Red Peter and Gregor Samsa can be viewed as attempts to historicize those faulty images—these animals are written in ink not in the genes—and can be seen as attempts to reappropriate the cudgels that have been used against Kafka and his fellow Jews. Kafka has not merely taken the reigning stereotypes of Jewish character and reproduced them *tout court*. He insinuates a tragic dimension to both. Each is a sympathetic figure. And while redemption is indefinitely deferred, there is at least hope for, as Red Peter puts it, "a way out" of the worst situations. The *Ausweg* is, however, left indeterminate.

More significant, while Gregor cannot come to speech, his defiling defile that climaxes *The Metamorphosis* generated an excess of language that may have disrupted the identifications by which he had been confined. "Report" tells a different animal story. It is not simply *about* an ape; it is told *by* an ape. By allowing him to speak and to recount his history, Kafka has created a character who, in part, makes himself in his storytelling. While Red Peter's inability to reconstruct his existence prior to his capture (as commissioned by the academy), to detail his simian origins and subsequent acquisition of language, may be more than an ironic commentary on the relationship between language and human/animal difference,[49] it may also be a ploy: His repudiation of the effort to reduce him to, to define him by, his purported origins and/or as a "talking animal." To return to his opening deflection of the request to corroborate the academy's assumption of his genealogical difference, specifically to the "tickling of the heels" shared by "small chimpanzee and the great Achilles alike" (RA, 250): The ape's supposed absence of a heel was held to be yet another signifier of the human break from the simian line of development. Hence the reference to Achilles' heel calls attention to how vulnerable the absolute line between human and ape—Gentile and Jew?—by which the human—the Gentile?—proclaims its difference and consequent superiority, is to erasure.

In sum, Kafka's creatures do not present the Jew as the dominant antisemitic society's "other," the monstrous animal-object constructed by Gentile, bourgeois fears, hatreds, and identification practices. Rather, Kafka presents individuals and groups whose identifications are shaped by their interpellation into such a society. Not only do Kafka's creatures indict a dominant culture that both requires and denies the Jews' move toward (Gentile) European bourgeois humanity. His work also grants insight into the complex forms, institutions, and practices of identification in Central European society since the advent of Emancipation as well as the attempts of Kafka and other Jewish-identified writers (from Heinrich Heine to Curt Siodmak) to undermine their authority by uncannily rendering, via the Jewish *animot*, the purported Jewish referent of those interpellating identifications indefinite: as both animal and human and neither; as both Jew and Gentile and neither.

NOTES

1. Eric L. Santner, "Freud, Žižek, and the Joys of Monotheism," *American Imago* 54, no. 2 (1997): 197.

2. It's so old that, according to the "Pillage Idiot," a midrash says that G-d told it to Moshe Rabbenu at Mount Sinai, http://pillageidiot.blogspot.com/2005/01/elephant-and-jewish-question.html (accessed May 2, 2013). Other examples include Joseph Frank, "His Jewish Problem," *New York Review of Books* 27, no. 19 (1980): 43; Chava Willig Levy, "The Kindle and the Jewish Question," June 23, 2009, http://www.ou.org/index.php/shabbat_shalom/article/55274 (accessed May 2, 2013); Rabbi Ethan Linden, "The Civil War and the Jewish Question," March 3, 2011, http://www.shirchadash.org/the-civil-war-and-the-jewish-question (accessed May 2, 2013).

3. See Devorah Baum, "Circumcision Anxiety," *Textual Practice* 27, no. 4 (2013): 695.

4. For example, the identification of the ethnic, national, and/or civil status of the three islanders raises such questions as: Is either "German" or "French" necessarily indicative of ethnicity? Or is either an indicator of nation-state belonging? What then is the "nationality" of "the Jew"? Is "the Jew" a citizen of any nation-state?

5. Santner, "Freud, Žižek," 197–98.

6. Andrew Benjamin, *Of Jews and Animals* (Edinburgh: Edinburgh University Press, 2011).

7. Baum, "Circumcision Anxiety," 695–96. Then again, Derrida is also probably alluding to the entanglement of the "numerous references . . . throughout the Derridean corpus" to animals and the "Question of the Animal" with those other "numerous references" as aspects of his persistent

intervening in the tacit workings (institutional, categorical, practical, etc.) and manifest effectings of *différance*.

8. Cf. Gayatri Chakravorty Spivak, "Can the Subaltern Speak?" in *Marxism and the Interpretation of Culture*, ed. C. Nelson and L. Grossberg (Urbana: University of Illinois Press, 1988), 271–313.

9. Theodor Adorno, *Minima Moralia: Reflections from Damaged Life*, trans. E. F. N. Jephcott (London: Verso, 1974), 105. Jephcott references the natural historian Paul Eipper's series of illustrated animal portraits, *Tiere sehen dich an* (Berlin: D. Reimer, 1928). The titles are similar; however, unlike Johann von Leers's *Juden sehen dich an* (Berlin: N. S. Druck und Verlag, 1933), its content bears no correlation whatsoever with Adorno's aphorism.

10. Max Horkheimer and Theodor W. Adorno, *Dialectic of Enlightenment: Philosophical Fragments*, ed. Gunzelin Schmid Noerr, trans. Edmund Jephcott (Stanford: Stanford University Press, 2002), 143–44.

11. From, respectively, *The Metamorphosis* and "A Report to an Academy." The translations are adapted from Franz Kafka, *The Complete Stories and Parables*, ed. Nahum N. Glatzer, trans. Willa Muir and Edwin Muir (New York: Quality Paperback Book Club, 1983), 89–139, 250–59. Page references in the text to *The Metamorphosis* will be indicated by *M* and to "A Report to an Academy" by RA.

12. Jacques Derrida, *The Animal That Therefore I Am*, ed. Marie-Louise Mallet, trans. David Wills (New York: Fordham University Press, 2008). Joanna Bourke, *What It Means to Be Human: Reflections from 1791 to the Present* (Berkeley: Counterpoint, 2011), provides a historical account of the diverse ways, in addition to the capacity for speech, "to demarcate the territory of the human from that of the non-human" (5) in and out of philosophic discourse.

13. See, inter alia, Giorgio Agamben, *The Open: Man and Animal*, trans. Kevin Attell (Stanford: Stanford University Press, 2004); A. Benjamin, *Of Jews*; Élisabeth de Fontenay, *Le silence des bêtes: La philosophie à l'épreuve de l'animalité* (Paris: Fayard, 1998); Tom Tyler, *Ciferae: A Bestiary in Five Fingers* (Minneapolis: University of Minnesota Press, 2012); Kari Weil, *Thinking Animals: Why Animal Studies Now?* (New York: Columbia University Press, 2012); Cary Wolfe, *Animal Rites: American Culture, the Discourse of Species, and Posthumanist Theory* (Chicago: University of Chicago Press, 2003).

14. Derrida, *Animal*, 102–3, is drawing upon a c. 1940 fragment that would be included in Adorno's *The Philosophy of Music: Fragments and Texts*, ed. Rolf Tiedemann, trans. Edmund Jephcott (Stanford: Stanford University Press, 1998), 80.

15. Derrida, *Animal*, 104–5; the passage is from Fontenay's "La raison du plus fort," in Plutarch, *Trois traités pour les animaux* (Paris: POL, 1992), 71.

16. The one exception is Derrida's acceptance speech for the 2001 Theodor W. Adorno Prize, published as "*Fichus*," in Derrida, *Paper Machine*, trans. Rachel Bowlby (Stanford: Stanford University Press, 2005), 164–81, in which he imagined a book "interpret[ing] the history, possibility, and the honor of this prize," the last chapter of which would be devoted to Adorno on animals. Derrida did not use the occasion to recognize Adorno's 1956 assertion that "philosophy is truly there to redeem what lies in the gaze of an animal" (cited by Eduardo Mendieta, "Animal Is to Kantianism as Jew Is to Fascism: Adorno's Bestiary," in *Critical Theory and Animal Liberation*, ed. John Sanbonmatsu [Lanham, Md.: Rowman & Littlefield, 2011], 151) as anticipating his own epiphany that, in part, launched philosophy's turn to the question of the animal: "Something that philosophy perhaps forgets, perhaps being this calculated forgetting itself—[the cat] can look at me. It has its point of view regarding me. The point of view of the absolute other, and nothing will have ever given me more food for thinking through the absolute alterity of the neighbor or of the next[-door] than these moments when I see myself seen naked under the gaze of a cat" (Derrida, *Animal*, 11). Derrida instead chose to illustrate his projected chapter with the reference to that 1940 Beethoven fragment (see n. 14 above and corresponding text) and an extract from one of the "Notes and Drafts" that Adorno and Horkheimer published as part of *Dialectic of Enlightenment*, "Man and Beast/Mensch und Tier" (203–12). Derrida repeated, verbatim from the earlier lecture (*Animal*, 103), his citation of Adorno's virtual homology of the hierarchical oppositions animals:idealism::Jews:fascism and Derrida's own gloss, including "Animals [would be] the Jews of idealists, who [would be] thus just virtual fascists" (181; curiously the translator of "*Fichus*" changes Derrida's future conditional to the indicative). It was also the only mention of Jews in Derrida's "TV Guide" (177) outline of his hypothetical opus.

17. Fontenay, *Le silence*, 13, pointedly decries in her "Avant-propos" any effort either to identify the industrial farming/slaughterhouse with Auschwitz (unlike Charles Patterson, *Eternal Treblinka: Our Treatment of Animals and the Holocaust* [New York: Lantern Books, 2002], or, less stridently, Boria Sax, *Animals in the Third Reich: Pets, Scapegoats and the Holocaust* [New York: Continuum, 2000]) or to correlate animal advocacy (such as vegetarianism, anti-vivisectionism, etc.) with misanthropy.

18. To adopt Donna J. Haraway's riffing on Derrida's discussion of animals and the logic of sacrifice in her *When Species Meet* (Minneapolis: University of Minnesota Press, 2008), esp. 77–85. Agamben and others fail to distinguish dehumanization from animalization—in animalization, the animal, courtesy of the opposition, is still in some instrumental relation with (and as determined by) the human; in dehumanization, the animal is animal insofar as

it is animate; it is only a threat to be eliminated; when eliminated it is referred to in thing language ("das Zeug"/"the thing" as the charwoman refers to the dead Gregor Samsa; or as Vilna survivor Motke Zaidl told Claude Lanzmann in *Shoah* [New York: Da Capo Press, 1995], 9: "The German even forbade us to use the words 'corpse' or 'victim.' The dead were blocks of wood, shit. . . . The Germans made us refer to the bodies as *Figuren*, that is, as puppets, as dolls, or as *Schmattes*, which means 'rags.'"). *Saujude* bestializes the Jew; the *Judenlaus* dehumanizes.

19. That is, extrapolating from Durkheim's sociological distinction between mechanical and organic solidarity, "mechanical solidarity" refers to the observation of resemblances between (the treatment of) Jews and animals rather than theorizing the possible interrelationship between the representations and identifications of Jews and animals that I characterize below as "organic solidarity."

20. Not unlike Horkheimer and Adorno's deployment of "idiosyncrasy" that follows their discussion of the Enlightenment abjection of nature and its projection onto the Jew in *Dialectic of Enlightenment* (147–53). See Jan Plug, "Idiosyncrasies: of Anti-Semitism," in *Languages without Soil: Adorno and Late Philosophical Modernity*, ed. Gerhard Richter (New York: Fordham University Press, 2010).

21. Cf. Dominick LaCapra, "Reopening the Question of the Human and the Animal," in *History and Its Limits: Human, Animal, Violence* (Ithaca: Cornell University Press, 2009); LaCapra also calls Agamben to task for not addressing the figuration of "the Jew" in Nazi discourse as a "powerful, world-historical, subversive force, a phobic, ritual containment," that is, a "scapegoat" (159–60).

22. Which is to say that by no means all appropriations of these animal-figures by Jewish-identified writers were deployed, consciously or unconsciously, in acts of resistance against their ascribed categorical identity. Often animal figures were employed by members of one Jewish-identified group to characterize, so as to distinguish themselves from, another Jewish-identified group—whether *Westjuden* speaking of *Ostjuden*, acculturated Jews speaking of traditional Jews, Zionists speaking of anti-Zionists. Moreover, a number of Jewish-identified individuals acted out their ambivalence or even hatred toward themselves and their situation by ascribing such debasing animal figurations to themselves.

23. See Gilles Deleuze and Félix Guattari, *Kafka: Toward a Minor Literature*, trans. Dana Polan (Minneapolis: University of Minnesota Press, 1986), 22: "intensities overrun by deterritorialized sound or words that are following their line of escape." Their failure to historicize and to particularize Kafka's animals, according to Haraway, *When Species Meet*, 27–30, extends to all

animals, whether the products of an author's pen or those who dwell either inside or outside livestock pens.

24. Also see Colleen Glenney Boggs, *Animalia Americana: Animal Representations and Biopolitical Subjectivity* (New York: Columbia University Press, 2013), and its analyses of animal representations where "the literal and the symbolic meet and unsettle the terrains of modern taxonomization" (189).

25. Adorno, *Minima Moralia*, 110.

26. Max Brod, "Unsere Literaten und die Gemeinschaft," *Der Jude* 1, no. 7 (1916): 464.

27. Walter Benjamin, "Franz Kafka: *Beim Bau der Chinesischen Mauer*," in *Selected Writings*, vol. 2: *1927–1934*, ed. Michael W. Jennings, Howard Eiland, and Gary Smith, trans. Rodney Livingstone (Cambridge, Mass.: Harvard University Press, 1999), 494–500; see also Benjamin's 1934 "Franz Kafka: On the Tenth Anniversary of His Death," trans. Harry Zohn, in *Selected Writings* 2:794–818; and his 1938 "Review of Brod's *Franz Kafka*," trans. Edmund Jephcott, in *Selected Writings*, vol. 3: *1935–1938*, ed. Michael W. Jennings and Howard Eiland (Cambridge, Mass.: Harvard University Press, 2002), 317–21.

28. In an October 25, 1915, letter to the publisher of *Der Verwandlung*, Kurt Wolff, Kafka pleaded "out of [his] deeper knowledge of the story": "It struck me that [Ottomar] Starke, as an illustrator, might want to draw the insect itself. Not that, please not that! . . . The insect itself cannot be depicted. It cannot even be shown from a distance" (*Letters to Friends, Family, and Editors*, trans. Richard Winston and Clara Winston [New York: Schocken Books, 1977], 114–15). The original cover art foregrounds a man in a bathrobe, pants, and slippers, standing up, his slightly bent face covered by his clutching hands (in horror?) and his back turned to double doors, one of which is partially open, that lead to a darkened interior.

29. www.vahidnab.com/kafka.htm (accessed May 2, 2013). Nabokov goes on to point out that the only thing Gregor has in common with cockroaches is that, as Kafka thrice mentions, he is brown. In an earlier story, "Wedding Preparations in the Country" (1906–9), Kafka's character Raban daydreams: "As I lie in bed I assume the shape of a big beetle [*eines großen Käfers*], a stag beetle [*Hirschkäfer*] or a cockchafer [*Maikäfer*], I think." Raban goes on to imagine "pressing my little legs [*Beinchen*] to my bulging belly [*gebauchten Leib*]" (in Kafka, *Complete*, 56). Only once in all of Kafka's extant writings (a mid-November 1920 letter to Milena Jesenska; http://homepage.univie.ac.at/werner.haas/1920/mi20-120.htm) does he refer to cockroaches (*Schaben*): He ironically analogizes them to those "heroic" Jews who would remain where they are so hated and so mortally vulnerable to violence, thereby

transfiguring the bestializing epithets he heard Czech antisemites scream at his fellow Prague Jews.

30. Similarly, when my brother was a young child he was fondly called a "little *Vonts*" (a little bedbug) by our aunt. In a March 20, 1913, note to Kafka, the publisher Kurt Wolff wrote: "Herr Franz Werfel has told me so much about your new novella—is it called "The Bedbug" [*Die Wanze*]?—that I would very much like to take a look at it. Would you send it to me?" (homepage.univie.ac.at/werner.haas/1913/kw13-011.htm). Wolff's publishing house would release *The Metamorphosis* two years later. Also note the diary entry for September 18, 1912, with its account of the stories about *Ungeziefer* and *Wanze* told by his coworker Hubalek (*The Diaries 1910–1913*, ed. Max Brod, trans. Joseph Kresh [New York: Schocken Books, 1948], 273).

31. Given that (1) the only description of Gregor that the narrator ascribes to the perception of someone besides Gregor, aside from the characterization of his voice (*M*, 98), is an amorphous one—"the huge brown mass" (*den riesigen braunen Fleck*)—that (2) Gregor is metamorphosed into a creature that transgresses taxonomic specificity (a point already suggested by the qualification of the *Ungeziefer* as "*ungeheuer*"—not simply as "gigantic," but monstrous, unnatural, misshapen)—and that (3), as noted above (n. 28), Kafka implored that no insect appear on the cover of his published text, Kafka has left open the possibility that Gregor's metamorphosis into an *Ungeziefer* was, empirically speaking, delusional (as Fernando Bermejo-Rubio has recently extensively [if, in my opinion, not convincingly] argued in a series of articles, including "Does Gregor Samsa Crawl over the Ceiling and Walls? Intra-narrative Fiction in Kafka's *Die Verwandlung*," *Monatshefte* 105, no. 2 [2013]: 254–90); nevertheless, Gregor's narrated thoughts, affects, and actions literally act out that identification.

32. See Paul Weindling, *Epidemics and Genocide in Eastern Europe, 1890–1945* (Oxford: Oxford University Press, 2000), and Markus Jansen, *Das Wissen vom Menschen: Franz Kafka und die Biopolitik* (Würzburg: Königshausen und Neumann, 2012). Characterizing Jews as *Ungeziefer* did not, however, first emerge in this period; Nicoline Hortzitz documents its use (along with many other bestializing epithets) in the early modern period (*Die Sprache der Judenfeindschaft in der frühen Neuzeit [1450–1700]* [Heidelberg: Winter Universitätsverlag, 2005]). Rainer Erb and Werner Bergmann, *Die Nachtseite der Judenemanzipation: Der Widerstand gegen die Integration der Juden in Deutschland 1780–1860* (Berlin: Metropol, 1989), chart the association of Jews with *Ungeziefer* since the late eighteenth century in Germany as well as cite (199) an 1841 analogization of Jews with *Käfern* by Karl Stöber in his story "Dörrenstein: Einige Blätter aus der Chronik dieses Dorfes." In

his massive monograph study *Kafkas "Verwandlung": Entstehung, Deutung, Wirkung* (Frankfurt/M: Stroemfeld, 2004), Hartmut Binder suggests that Danish writer J. V. Jensen's recently published short story "Ungeziefer" influenced Kafka's choice of "animal category."

33. The Muirs' translation reads "That was no human voice." Here and in several passages below I have altered their translation when it obscures the play of human/animal difference and have provided instead a more literal rendering.

34. Despite the chief clerk's conclusion and although his words qua individual semes did not appear to be understood by those on the other side of the locked door, Gregor felt that he had communicated to them that "something was wrong with him" and "felt himself drawn in once more into the human circle" (*den menschlichen Kreis*; *M*, 99).

35. In German "*Wild*" refers to game or wild animals; *der Wilder*/the savage like the nondomesticated animal occupies the space beyond the bounds of human community proper. In a later scene "Gregor hissed [*zischt*] loudly with rage because not one of them thought of shutting the door to spare him such a spectacle and so much noise" (*M*, 126).

36. After the boarders move in, "many things [that] could be dispensed with [and] that it was no use trying to sell but that should not be thrown away either . . . found their way into Gregor's room. The ash can likewise and the kitchen garbage can" (*M*, 128). In his "Notes on Kafka" (in *Can One Live after Auschwitz? A Philosophical Reader*, ed. Rolf Tiedemann [Stanford: Stanford University Press, 2003], 238), Theodor Adorno suggests that Kafka locates the possibility of hope amid the "nonexchangeable, useless" things, the *Ladenhüter* or "white elephants," that litter his narratives.

37. Kafka had already demonstrated earlier that year (1912), in his now-famous "Speech on the Yiddish Language [*Jargon*]," how the deployment of pronouns both indicates and puts in question assumed antipodal identifications when he offered: "For example the Yiddish [*Jargon'sche*] *mir seien* develops more naturally out of the Middle High German *sin* than does the New High German *wir sind* [we are]." Would not Kafka's *Jargon*phobic audience also have been unsettled by the use of the first person singular dative (*mir*) instead of the first person plural nominative (*wir*) as well as by the use of the first person plural subjunctive (*seien*) instead of the first person plural indicative (*sind*)? Kafka's chosen exemplar thereby attempted to unsettle the distinction from Yiddish-speaking Eastern Jews that his acculturated, self-satisfied Germanophone audience desired to maintain. See Vivian Liska's translation and analysis of Kafka's speech in *When Kafka Says We: Uncommon Communities in German-Jewish Literatures* (Bloomington: Indiana University Press, 2009), 26–33.

38. See Giorgio Agamben, *Homo Sacer: Sovereign Power and Bare Life*, trans. Daniel Heller-Roazen (Stanford: Stanford University Press, 1998), 105–8.

39. See, e.g., Bernd Witte, *Jüdische Tradition und literarische Moderne: Heine, Buber, Kafka, Benjamin* (Munich: Carl Hanser Verlag, 2007), 170–76. This sacrificial logic may have been signaled by the narrator's speculation that Grete in her terror may have been willing to sacrifice her mother in order to be free from Gregor as well as by the novella's framing: In place of the *verwandelt* body of Gregor lying on his back and barely lifting (*ein wenig hob*) his head that opens the novella is the young *aufgeblüht* body of his sister Grete as she springs herself up (*sich erhob*) at its end.

40. The phrasing appears to echo the title of Schnitzler's 1908 encyclopedic depiction of Viennese Jews, *Der Weg ins Freie*. Though no fan of Schnitzler, Kafka may have no less appropriated both Schnitzler's title and its ironic edge.

41. But not only the oppressors' since this stereotype was shared by, among others, a number of Western acculturated Jews. See Steven E. Aschheim, *Brothers and Strangers: The East European Jews in German and German Jewish Consciousness, 1800–1923* (Madison: University of Wisconsin Press, 1982).

42. But not only the oppressors' since this stereotype was shared by, among others, a number of Zionist-leaning Jews. See Iris Bruce, *Kafka and Cultural Zionism: Dates in Palestine* (Madison: University of Wisconsin Press, 2007), 130–37.

43. An assumption shared by physicians, social critics, and the general public was that Jews by nature lacked any predilection toward what was also a particular form of Gentile male display and point of pride: alcohol abuse and drunkenness. Jews were not assumed to be able to hold their liquor better than non-Jews; rather, they were seen as generally abstemious—especially in the company of Gentiles. See John M. Efron, *Defenders of the Race: Jewish Doctors and Race Science in Fin-de-siècle Europe* (New Haven: Yale University Press, 1994), 108–17.

44. See Gerhard Neumann, "Der Affe als Ethnologe: Kafkas Bericht über den Ursprung der Kultur und dessen kulturhistorischer Hintergrund," in *Für Alle und Keinen: Lektüre, Schrift und Leben bei Nietzsche und Kafka*, ed. Friedrich Balke, Joseph Vogl, and Benno Wagner (Zurich-Berlin: diaphanes, 2008), 94.

45. That is, an act of Darwinian mimesis, imitation as a form of adaptation in order to survive (as well as to subvert the anthropocentric teleology and triumphalism of Social Darwinism), rather than Aristotelian mimesis that results in a cathartic purification or freedom; see Paul Haacke, "Kafka's

Political Animals," *in Philosophy and Kafka*, ed. Brendan Moran and Carlo Salzani (Lanham, Md.: Lexington Books, 2013), 141–57; and Margot Norris, "Darwin, Nietzsche, Kafka, and the Problem of Mimesis," *MLN* 95, no. 5 (1980): 1232–53.

46. Kafka, letter to Felix Weltsch, beginning of December 1917 ("Report" was published in November 1917): "When you read Maimonides, you might want to supplement it with *Solomon Maimon's Autobiography* (edited by Fromer, published by Georg Müller), an excellent book in itself, and a harsh self-portrait of a man haplessly torn between East and West European Judaism. But it also summarizes the teachings of Maimonides, whose spiritual child he feels himself to be. But probably you know the book better than I do" (*Letters to Friends*, 173). The extract is from Solomon Maimon, *An Autobiography*, trans. J. Clark Murray (Urbana: University of Illinois Press, 2001), 216.

47. On the problematic reversal of the human/animal hierarchical opposition, see Boggs, *Animalia Americana*, 71. For Margot Norris, Red Peter's "report dramatizes that becoming human and civilized also requires the disavowal of the brutalities of the civilizing process. . . . The ape's animality is inscribed negatively in his talk, in its silences and omissions, in what he cannot or refuses to articulate rather than in what he actually says" ("Kafka's Hybrids: Thinking Animals and Mirrored Humans," in *Kafka's Creatures: Animals, Hybrids, and Other Fantastic Beings*, ed. Marc Lucht and Donna Yarri [Lanham, Md.: Rowman & Littlefield, 2010], 23).

48. Kafka, *Diaries 1910–1913*, 191, 192 (December 25. 1911).

49. See Agamben, *Open*, 33–38, on how historically the possession of language served as the principal diacritic between human and animal.

CHAPTER 7

The Off-Modern Turn: Modernist Humanism and Vernacular Cosmopolitanism in Shklovsky and Mandelshtam

Svetlana Boym

I would like to explore an alternative tradition of Jewish thought that Hannah Arendt called "passionate thinking," one that mediates between philosophy and experience, between judging and acting. In my investigation of the twentieth century's disasters and delusions I became fascinated with the thinkers and writers who in the most difficult circumstances of mid-twentieth-century Europe did not get history tragically wrong by aligning themselves with Stalinism or Nazism. These were lucid dissenters and fellow travelers who exercised an often improbable art of judging that didn't follow prescriptive routes and defied the logic of extremity. During the difficult time of the postrevolutionary transition in the late 1920s one of these figures, the critic and writer Victor Shklovsky, called for a "third way" of thinking that follows the zigzag movement of the knight in the game of chess and a double estrangement of theory and historical experience. His friend, the poet Osip Mandelshtam, echoed this notion, speaking of the "honest zigzags" of the creative journey that make one's work timely but not necessarily contemporary, in the sense of keeping some distance from the immediate political demands of the day.

Does this strategy have anything to do with Jewish self-identification? Echoing earlier twentieth-century writers, the Italian historian Carlo Ginzburg wrote that all his life he was fascinated by distance and estrangement. For him these constituted the most pronounced feature of the Jewish perspective.[1] The figures of distancing and estrangement are abundant in the works of German/Eastern-European/Russian-Jewish writers. Georg Simmel's stranger and adventurer, Walter Benjamin's flâneur and collector, Shklovsky's "strange man from a strange country," Hannah Arendt's pariah and "the girl from abroad" are a few of the best-known examples. In her essays of 1944 Hannah Arendt reflected on the pariah's and stranger's capacity for independent thinking and self-distancing, and at the same time she raised the question whether such contemplative freedom and the special intimacy of the pariah community might come at the expense of engagement with the world, *amor mundi*, and a concern for political rights.

I would argue that there is a different history of critical estrangement in the twentieth century that is not an estrangement *from* the world, but an estrangement *for* the world; not a form of "negative identity," but of responsible artistic and political engagement with complex politics and history.

This alternative "off-modern tradition" helps us rethink the implications of the "linguistic turn" in theory in the political and historical context and reconsider means and ends of critical thinking in the humanities beyond "the end of history" that seems to mark the twenty-first century. The off-modern writers tended to be not systematic but essayistic. They proceeded through parables, paradoxes, and "honest zigzags" rather than through Hegelian spirals, partaking in but not belonging to various theoretical movements, nor did they follow more familiar paradigms of Jewish idealism, Marxism, Zionism, or a quest for messianic redemption. We often lack frameworks and vocabulary to account for the "third-way" thinking, but it comes closest to thinking in freedom. Hannah Arendt believed that freedom is "our forgotten heritage" because it defies history that has been written by the victors.[2] Similarly passionate thinking is often a dissident thinking or free thinking that has escaped the history of theory in its postmodern version. It is not by chance that Shklovsky's invention of estrangement in response to the modern habituation involves the attitude toward surrounding objects, love, fear, and war: "Habituation devours things, clothes, furniture, one's wife and the fear of war."[3] Artistic estrangement can make one's wife more lovable and the fear of war more real. The specific unexplored zigzag of modern thought that I discuss here is this conjunction between the aesthetic practice of estrangement and confrontation with the fear and cruelty of modern warfare and later totalitarian politics.

Inspired by Shklovsky's conception of the knight's move, I developed the idea of the off-modern. Most of us have heard that postmodernism died quietly in its sleep some time in the zero decade of the twenty-first century. In my quest for redefinition of the modern project I want to get away from the endless "ends" of art and history and of the prepositions "post," "neo," "avant," and "trans" of the charismatic postcriticism that tries desperately to be "in."[4] There is another option: not to be out, but off. As in off-stage, off-key, off-beat, and occasionally, off-color. Off-modern involves exploration of the side alleys and lateral potentialities of the project of critical modernity. It brings into focus lateral and alternative modernities and alternative solidarities beyond the Western European and American systems of coordinates. *Off* in the off-modern comes from the prefix *of*, with an additional onomatopoeic "f"; it signifies both belonging to and estrangement from the project of critical modernity.

In my attempt to unearth the archaeology of "third-way" thinking and develop a new vocabulary, I will elaborate a series of oxymorons such as engaged estrangement, vernacular cosmopolitanism, uncanny worldliness, modernist humanism, brave fear—a series that affords what Freud called a "realistic assessment" of the historic dangers. My focus is the work of Victor Shklovsky and Osip Mandelshtam in the prism of the twenty-first-century conception of the "off-modern." Whereas the "linguistic turn" in literary and cultural theory followed Roman Jakobson's version of formalism that focused on binary oppositions and system building, Shklovsky's paradoxical theory of estrangement offers us another "turn" toward poetic and parabolic storytelling that brings together theory and history.

Modernist Humanism as a Double Estrangement

Victor Shklovsky's idea of vernacular cosmopolitanism emerges through the confrontation of his theory of estrangement and his experience in the military campaigns in Central Asia, Caucasus, Persia, and Turkey during World War I, as described in his autobiographical text "*The Sentimental Journey*" (1921–23). Best known for his paradoxical literary science, Shklovsky was also an experimental writer who described himself humorously as "a half-Jew and a role player."[5] This was not an artistic alibi for staying out of politics. On the contrary, the experience of the campaign, the encounter with many local and displaced people of Jewish and non-

Jewish extraction, and the firsthand knowledge of military and revolutionary violence transforms Shklovsky's theory of estrangement into an existential practice, a form of modernist humanism, and an unconventional civic dissent.

It is little known that the founder of the Formalist theory had an adventurous albeit brief political career and wrote some of his early theoretical texts on the fronts of World War I, in the revolutionary underground and in exile. His love for poetry and poetics was hardly academic. Severely wounded twice, with seventeen pieces of shrapnel in his body, Shklovsky recited the avant-garde poetry of Velimir Khlebnikov while being operated on in the military hospital, hoping perhaps that this could help him estrange or at least be distracted from the pain.

Shklovsky embraced the revolutionary spirit, but as one of his critics would later comment, he "confused the revolutions." Or perhaps, he got it right? While a supporter of the February Revolution of 1917, he did not initially embrace the events of October 1917 and the storming of the Winter Palace. Shklovsky joined the Socialist Revolutionary party, which won the majority at the Constitutional Assembly, the revolutionary parliament that convened right after the storming of the Winter Palace. It is a well-known but frequently forgotten fact that the Constitutional Assembly was brutally dispersed by the Bolsheviks, thus putting an end to the variety of left and social democratic politics in Russia. After voting against the dispersal of the Constitutional Assembly Shklovsky joined the anti-Bolshevik underground (together with the writer Maxim Gorky, the future classic Soviet Socialist realist writer).[6] This was his own version of "socialism with a human face," if one were to apply an anachronistic definition. Threatened with arrest and possible execution, Shklovsky crossed the Soviet border on the frozen Gulf of Finland and eventually found himself in Berlin. There he revived his original theory of artistic estrangement and transformed it into the conception of the "third way" and the "knight's move."

In Shklovsky's early essay "Art as Technique," "estrangement" suggests both distancing (dislocating, *dépaysement*) and making strange.[7] Estrangement brings forth a new beginning and a transformation of vision, echoing Hannah Arendt's definition of freedom as a miracle of infinite improbability. In Shklovsky's view, shifting perspectives and making things strange can become an antidote to the routinization and automatization of modern life that leads to mass apathy and disenchantment.

With hindsight we see that estrangement was not strictly speaking a mere technique or a set of stylistic techniques that define a structure of an autonomous artistic corpus. Rather, this is an artistic, and later political and existential, practice, a form of phenomenological experiment in living and thinking. It is not a foundation of a theoretical movement but a productive embarrassment of theory that can inspire free thinkers and artists. Thus the device of estrangement can both define and defy the autonomy of art. The technique of estrangement differs from scientific distance and objectification; estrangement does not seek to provide the "Archimedean point" from which to observe humanity. Estrangement lays bare the boundaries between art and life but never pretends to abolish or blur them. It does not allow for a seamless translation of life into art, nor for the wholesale aestheticization of politics. Art is meaningful only when it is not entirely in the service of real life or realpolitik, and when its strangeness and distinctiveness are preserved.

Shklovsky's understanding of estrangement is different from both Hegelian and Marxist notions of alienation.[8] Artistic estrangement is not to be cured by incorporation, synthesis, or belonging. In contrast to the Marxist notion of freedom that consists in overcoming alienation, Shklovskian estrangement is in itself a form of limited freedom endangered by all kinds of modern teleologies and utopian visions of the future.

In the postrevolutionary situation in the Soviet Union, when the world itself has been estranged by the state, Shklovsky proposes to practice double estrangement—mediating between conceptual and experimental practice. He proposes the figure of the knight in the game of chess to symbolize his non-Hegelian vision of cultural evolution.

Shklovsky's zigzag of freedom includes eccentric parallelism, paradoxes, and subversive parables that come from the Bible and world literature. The "knight's move," however, is not a figure of what Daniel Boyarin and Jonathan Boyarin called "diasporic evasion."[9] Far from being a compromise, the third-route thinking and the knight's move evade limited master-slave dialectics of the "dutiful pawns and single-minded kings," offering instead a "tortured road of the brave" to those who dare to think independently.

Here is how Shklovsky paraphrases Marx's and Lenin's formula familiar to all Soviet citizens that "social being determines individual consciousness": "Material being conditions consciousness but conscience remains unsettled."[10] This key formulation was made in Shklovsky's *Third Factory* (1926) in which the ideas of the improbable third-way thinking are explicitly put forth. The gap between conditioned consciousness and unsettled conscience exemplifies the work of double estrangement of theory and the historical circumstances of its production. This unsettled conscience will lead to the transformation of the arts of estrangement into the arts of judging and even dissent, opening up a space of moral reflection that defies the imperative of revolutionary violence.

Vernacular Cosmopolitanism and Critique of Revolutionary Violence

This gap is explored further in Shklovsky's unsentimental *Sentimental Journey* written by the "half-Jew and role player" who becomes interested in vernacular cosmopolitanism. *A Sentimental Journey* is an amazing multigenre text that recounts Shklovsky's many encounters with local people and records their tales of misfortune. Curiously, the pioneer of estrangement Shklovsky doesn't frame his travels through Persia and Turkey as a journey to the exotic East or to the land of the strange other. Rather unconventionally for a soldier of the Russian army, he declares: "My orientation was local. There was one feature in 'the East' that reconciled me to them, there was no antisemitism here."[11] Shklovsky contrasts that to what he calls a "transsensical [*zaumnyi*] antisemitism" of the Russian army, using a literary term to lay bare its irrationality. The literary term *zaumnyi* is used to estrange the common cultural forms of behavior and to defamiliarize what has become a form of habitual cruelty.

Shklovsky, like Babel, warned the locals about the pogroms against local Jews as well as other local people planned by the army and once even tried to stage a fake pogrom in order to avoid the real one. (No wonder his fellow soldiers considered him a brave man and a strange man.) The writer attributes this strangeness to his conflicting revolutionary and humanistic imperatives as well as to his half-Jewishness.[12] The son of a Jewish father and a half-German, half-Russian mother, Shklovsky plays with multiple identifications that allow him to engage with the many dislocated and uprooted people that he encounters on his way. Possibly it is the experience of the Russian army that made him identify himself with the Jews, since he was not promoted to become an officer because he was considered "a son of a Jew and therefore a Jew."

In any case, when it comes to Jewish identification, we see a comedy of errors on all fronts. Shklovsky relates that when the British conquered Jerusalem, a delegation of the Assyrians came to visit Shklovsky carrying as a gift some sugar and kishmish:

> Your people and my people would live together again. It is true we destroyed the Temple of Solomon a long time ago but we also restored it. They spoke that way because they considered themselves Assyrians and

> me, a Jew. In fact, they were mistaken: I am not quite a Jew and they are not the descendants of the Assyrians. They are Aramaic Jews.[13]

The irony of the mutual misrecognition resides in the fact that both sides see the other as more Jewish. And yet this encounter leads to deepened human connections. Recognition of estrangement does not preclude empathy, and this uncommon encounter shapes Shklovsky's perspective and expands his frame of references. Unlike his fellow soldiers, he is involved in constant conversation with the locals, sometimes enjoying their friendship or hospitality.

Shklovsky is fascinated by Jewish heteroglossia and by cultural plurality in general. He collects as much material as he can about the languages, habits, and political situation of local minorities, Jews and non-Jews, Kurds, Armenians, Georgian Jews who speak a "tatar dialect," but also more exotic ones: Assyrians, Aissors-Nestorians, Askers will figure in many of Shklovsky's autobiographical parables of his relationship with the Soviet power in which he identifies with those eccentric heretics.

Speaking as a half-Jew and a role player both in *A Sentimental Journey* and in his second autobiographical text, *Zoo, or Letters Not about Love*, Shklovsky offers us a series of political parables to understand the crucial problems of his time. The most pertinent example is Shklovsky's twentieth-century parable of the revolutionary Shibboleth that is his response both to structuralist linguistics and to the dilemmas of revolutionary violence. Shklovsky retells the famous biblical tale (originally, of course, about intertribal Israelite warfare) as one in which the aggressors are Philistines:

> The Jews set patrols at the crossing. On that occasion it was difficult to distinguish a Philistine from a Jew, both were in all likelihood, naked. The patrol would ask those coming through: Say the word "shibboleth."
>
> But the Philistines couldn't say "sh"; and they were killed.
>
> In Ukraine I ran into a Jewish boy. He couldn't look at corn without shaking. They told me the story. When they were murdering in Ukraine and needed to know if they were murdering a Jew they would ask them "say *kukuruza*." And the Jew would say: *kukuruzha*—And they killed him.[14]

This was not merely a binary phonemic difference between two sounds, as Saussurian structuralist linguistics would suggest, but also a matter of life and death. The teller of the parable speaks from the gap between consciousness and conscience. Shklovsky's parables prefigure Jacques Derrida's discussion of shibboleth in his essay about Paul Celan. Shibboleth (a Hebrew word that also exists in Judeo-Aramaic, Phoenician, and Syriac) functions as a password that demarcates a border-crossing. Shibboleth can become a "secret configuration of the places of memory."[15] Derrida doesn't dwell on the interesting case of intertextuality Celan's poem speaks about, "the estrangement of homeland—die fremde der Heimat," nor about Celan's "Petropolis of the unforgotten which was Tuscany for your heart." The addressee of Celan's poem is, in fact, none other than Osip Mandelshtam, whom he was translating at the time, making the poem itself into a configuration of Jewish cosmopolitan memory, and returning us as well to the biblical question of inter-"Israelite" mistrust and miscommunication.

Sentimental Journey abounds in descriptions of violence, presented in the most stark and unsentimental fashion. Violence is by no means excused or glorified as a part of the "necessary revolutionary sacrifice" for the sake of the future liberation of humanity. Nor are the numerous descriptions of dismembered bodies presented as examples of modernist aesthetic disfiguration or the "dehumanization of art."[16] In describing pillage, slaughter, pogroms, and the daily cruelty that he witnessed at the front, Shklovsky redirects his estrangement. It no longer "dehumanizes" in Ortega y Gasset's sense but rather makes real the "fear of war"[17] that has become so habitual for soldiers and for the ideologues of violence. Thus, the technique of estrangement lays bare the senseless dehumanization of war. It is as if only through estrangement could the revolutionary writer Shklovsky rediscover that after all he is a humanist. Reporting the practices of war Communism—the execution of poet Nikolai Gumilev and the death of poet Alexander Blok—Shklovsky appeals to the Soviet citizens:

> Citizens!
>
> Citizens, stop killing! Men are no longer afraid of death! There are already customs and techniques for telling a wife about the death of her husband.
>
> It changes nothing. It just makes everything harder.[18]

Similar address to the invisible "citizens" and a report on violence is found in Shklovsky's telegram to the military authorities about the pogrom of the Kurds:

> That night I sent the TASK a panicky telegram:
>
> "I have inspected Kurdistan units. In the name of the Revolution and Humanity, I demand the withdrawal of troops."

> This telegram didn't go over too well—apparently it seemed naïve and funny to demand the withdrawal of troops in the name of humanity. But I was right.[19]

Haunted by the brutal materiality of war, Shklovsky sticks to the "literature of facts" and resists the transformation of violence into metaphor or a mere means to a beautiful end: "I wrote [*A Sentimental Journey*] remembering the corpses that I saw myself."[20] Shklovsky's "sentimental journey" is hardly sentimental in any conventional way, but it is extremely sensitive; it does not try to domesticate the fear of war; it individualizes the dead and the wounded, humanizing them through art.

Shklovsky speaks about dehumanization explicitly in his insightful and generally sympathetic portrait of Maxim Gorky: "Gorky's bolshevism is ironic and free of any faith in human beings. . . . The anarchism of life, its subconscious, the fact that the tree knows better how to grow—these are the things he couldn't understand."[21] Shklovsky never accepts the instrumentalization of human beings and had a keen concern for the "crooked timbre of humanity" (to paraphrase Kant). Shklovsky's modernist humanism is paradoxical and is based not on the nineteenth-century conceptions reflected in many psychological novels, but rather on anarchic spontaneity that preserves the "mystery of individuality," to use Simmel's term. This runs parallel to the interest in what Shklovsky calls "local laws" and conventions of art that for him are a part of the memory of world culture. Shklovsky's war memoirs estrange the revolutionary teleology and political theology of Lenin and Carl Schmitt alike, offering an alternative way of reflecting on the modern experience without the sacrifice of human unpredictability, which brings Shklovsky close to the thought of Hannah Arendt and Georg Simmel.

Shklovsky wrote that the Soviet writer of the 1920s has two choices: to write for the desk drawer or to write on state demand. "There is no third alternative. Yet that is precisely the one that must be chosen. . . . Writers are not streetcars on the same circuit."[22] One of the central parallelisms that Shklovsky explores in *The Third Factory* is the unfreedom of the writer caught in the play of literary convention and the unfreedom of the writer working under the dictate of the state, specifically an authoritarian power. The two deaths of the author—one a playful self-constraint and the other the acceptance of the state telos—are not the same. Inner freedom and the space of the writer's creative exploration are shrinking in the context of public unfreedom. Shklovsky speaks about the secret passages in the walls of Parisian houses that are left for cats, an image that seems to refer to the shrunken literary public sphere in the 1920s. This is a forever shrinking space of freedom. The practice of aesthetic estrangement had become politically suspect already by the late 1920s; by 1930, it had turned into an intellectual crime. Later Shklovsky was accused of "cosmopolitanism" and "practicing the cosmopolitan discipline of comparative literature," the accusation that followed him even after he (halfheartedly) denounced formalism in 1930.

In the case of Shklovsky we can observe a transformation of estrangement from the world into estrangement for the world, a distinction that comes from the work of Hannah Arendt. Estrangement from the world has its origins in the Stoic concept of inner freedom, in the Christian conception of freedom and salvation, as well as in romantic subjectivity and introspection. It suggests a distancing from political and worldly affairs. In contrast, estrangement for the world is a way of seeing the world anew, a possibility of a new beginning that is fundamental for aesthetic experience, critical judgment, and political action. It is also an acknowledgment of the integral human plurality that we must recognize within us and within others. Like Shklovsky, Arendt uses an example of aesthetic practice to speak about public freedom; public or worldly freedom is a kind of art, but its model is not the plastic arts but the performing arts. Freedom for Arendt is akin to a performance on a public stage, that needs common language but also a degree of incalculability, luck, chance, hope, surprise, wonder. Importantly, Arendt's conception of the art of freedom is just as different from the notion of a total work of politics as is the Shklovskian art of estrangement. It entails a non-Wagnerian conception of aesthetic practice that focuses on the process and not on the product. It depends on individual ability to estrange from oneself and see the stranger in the other. In other words, freedom is a recognition of inner plurality within individuals that allows for action and co-creation and not only for external pluralism.

Osip Mandelshtam: Co-creation with Fear and the Ends of Theory

"We will remember in Lethe's cold waters/That earth for us has been worth a thousand heavens"—these words by Osip Mandelshtam are used by Hannah Arendt in her discussion of worldliness and gratitude toward being. Contrary to the poetic dictum that philosophy is about homecoming, there could be a different way of inhabiting the world and making a second home, not the home into which we were born but a home that we freely choose for ourselves.

Joseph Brodsky described Osip Mandelshtam as a "homeless poet," and yet he was at home in the republic of "world culture." Like Shklovsky, Mandelshtam had unconventional politics, more committed to civic courage and artistic freedom than to a particular political party and state ideology, which made him "nobody's contemporary," someone who was "out of pace" with his "brutal century." And yet it was Osip Mandelshtam who became one of the very few writers in the Soviet Union to write a satirical epigram on Stalin, for which he was severely persecuted and sent to the Gulag. Mandelshtam insisted that the poet has to always renew his beginnings and move in "honest zigzags," flirting with foreign speech and confronting the fear and the noise of time.[23]

Like Shklovsky, Mandelshtam worked in many genres, including essays on the theory of literature and culture, as well as on linguistics and science. He was in dialogue with the members of the OPOYaZ circle, Jakobson, Shklovsky, Tynianov, with Henri Bergson and his conceptions of memory and virtual reality of imagination, as well as with experimental linguists, followers of Marr and his eccentric ideas of hybridity and grafting in the Indo-European and non-Indo-European languages, as well as with experimental biologists and physicists.

Mandelshtam's semi-autobiographical novella *The Egyptian Stamp* (1928) takes place in the turbulent time between the February and October Revolutions. It offers us a striking combination of Mandelshtam's theory of the "end of the novel" and of the radical novelistic practice that is not always loyal to the theory. Its main protagonist, a Chaplinesque figure named Parnok, is said to be "connected to the dance of modernity" only by a tenuous "safety pin." He embodies Mandelshtam's notion of "lyrical hermaphroditism," a poetic dialogue between masculine and feminine.[24] Parnok is a character with little personal biography; instead, he is a walking bibliography, an amalgam of other failed heroes and heroines and avid readers, from Gogol's Akakii Akakievich to Madame Bovary and Don Quixote. His national origins are equally uncertain; he is one of the immigrants of the desolate city, and yet he tries to become the city's savior, a Don Quixote who opposes the violence of the lynch mob.

The narrator's own autobiographical ruminations run parallel to Parnok's, but sometimes those parallels meet as in non-Euclidean geometry: "It is *terrifying* to think that our life is a tale without a plot or hero, made up of emptiness and glass, out of the feverish babble of constant digressions, out of the Petersburg influenza delirium."[25]

Is this a description of a book of life or a modernist anti-novel? I notice that the Russian word for "terrifying" has actually nothing to do with terror, but rather with fear (*strashno*, from *strax*). This is neither terror nor sublime awe, and this kind of fear shouldn't be lost in translation since it is a key to Mandelshtam's evolving theory of prose and of the experience of Jewishness.

Mandelshtam declares that he will fearlessly speak about fear, both personal and historical. *The Egyptian Stamp* performs the end of biographical and historical genres by weaving together outtakes that contain his drafts, doodles, and lateral memories.

> I do not fear incoherencies and gaps
> I shear a paper with long scissors.
> I paste a ribbon as a fringe
> A manuscript is always a storm, worn by rags, torn by beaks.
> It's the first draft of a sonata.
> Scribbling (*marat'*) is better than writing.
> I do not fear seams or the yellowness of the glue.
> I am a tailor, I am an idler.
> I draw Marat in his stocking.
> I draw martins.[26]

In this metaliterary digression about fear, fearlessness, and a new literary form, the fear survives between the lines and doodles of the text, gradually acquiring form. Here the old-fashioned techniques of cutting and hemming used by the Petersburgian Jewish tailor and trickster Mervis merge with the new revolutionary technologies of cinematic montage to compose a modern fan of memory. The broad margins of Mandelshtam's text are filled with puns, allusions, and daydreams. There is no opposition here between the text and marginalia; their relationship is not dialectical, but diagonal. Here the manuscript itself resembles a storm (*buria*), but this is a creative storm orchestrated by the poet himself in which the radical hero of the French revolution and martins cohabit on the same page. Such a creative storm works like a homeopathic pill against the storm of history, which the writer is not always able to divert, but at least the bold creativity offers a placebo from existential fears.

The stormy creative form proceeds through syncretic associations, what the aesthetic psychologist Vygotsky called the "superordinary structures" characteristic of child's imagination. "Superordinary structures" in this understanding are the modes of thinking and creating that follow neither everyday nor scientific logic; they do not recognize barriers and hierarchies between different conceptual orders and move freely from one cognitive or sensory code into another.[27] Yet this is not quite the same as the surrealist chance encounter. Here the emphasis is not on the revelation of unconsciousness but on the connections between individual dreams and cultural forms. The texts are both dialogical and a little glossolalic, because dialogues here do not happen on the level of characters or individuals but at the atomic level of the word itself, which is already a hybrid, a graft, a memory of other roots, accents, intonations, the soft timbre of the ghost writers of the past.

At the end *The Egyptian Stamp* explicitly confronts the relationship between fear, Jewishness, and passionate thinking. In Mandelshtam's first autobiographical prose piece, *Noise of Time* (1923), he describes his family as "tongue tied"; they spoke many languages with the same embarrassing accent. Tongue-tiedness is not always an impediment for creativity; it can be the onset of the new tongue, the beginning of an unforeseen liberation at least in literature. Moses, the great biblical hero, had a speech impediment and was reluctant to take on the burden of history, to confront the tyrant and lead on the difficult road to liberation. In *The Egyptian Stamp* the tongue-tiedness becomes a part of the modernist texture that incorporates different forms of speech with syncopes and breaks.

One such revealing break comes at the end of the novella when the narrator moves from the third person to the first and recounts his own recurring childhood dream of escaping to the town Malinov (from "malina"—raspberry, an uncanny Raspberryville), possibly away from persecution or pogrom. The little Jewish boy finds himself fleeing in the wrong carriage with a Jewish family that's not his own, and he is desperately trying to tie his shoes, over and over again. If only he could tie them in a perfect bow, everything would turn out okay. But he can't; his family ties are broken, and he is tied up by fear.

> Fear takes me by the hand and leads me. A white cotton glove. A woman's glove without fingers. I love fear, I respect it. I almost said: "With fear I have no fear." Mathematicians should have built a tent for fear, for it is the coordinates of time and space, they participate in it like the rolled up felt in the nomad tent of the Kirkiz. Fear unharnesses (unties) the horses when one had to drive and sends us dreams with unnecessarily low ceilings.[28]

What happens here is both an estrangement and a poetic domestication of fear. Fear "unties" the horses and drives the narration. But this is no longer that terrifying emotion that would paralyze the boy, not even letting him tie his shoes. Fear is a part of the new system of coordinates; it is given space and time of its own and is respected, almost loved. Fear acquires its own nomadic architecture, which provisionally houses it without containing it fully. Such fear management produces a strange feeling of joy on the part of the narrator; there is almost a mutual attachment between him and fear. Fear is personified into a strange Muse of Jewish luck. She leads the narrator by the hand on the dangerous modern journey. The narrator is guided by fear in order not to be driven by it. Fear estranges the novelistic form that dehumanizes the individual and enables the final metamorphosis and the work of poetic judgment.

Mandelshtam's contemporary Sigmund Freud contributed to the understanding of fear and its role in the modern psyche. Freud distinguished between "real fear" (i.e., fear based on the realistic assessment of danger) and "neurotic fear," dividing the latter into two categories, fright and anxiety. Real fear has an "object" and actually mobilizes self-defense—a combination of reasonable fear and resistance, which can alert one to existing dangers and enable coping mechanisms. Fright is a sudden experience of danger without anticipation that can produce a traumatic response, and anxiety is a free-floating dread without a specific object. Modernist theories made much more of anxiety without object than of the experience of "real fear" that alerts to existing dangers.

In Mandelshtam's experimental autobiographical prose we observe a transformation of free-floating anxiety into the confrontation with "real fear." The nomadic architecture that the adult narrator creates to house his childhood fears allows him to lay bare some traumatic memories of escape from a pogrom that many Jewish children of his time might have shared. Such poetics of fear doesn't evolve into paranoia or suicide; quite the contrary. In Mandelshtam's tale coming to terms with fear saves the hero and possibly the narrator-writer from the fate of his literary predecessors, dreamers and obsessive readers of another time, Anna Karenina and Madam Bovary.

Let us examine this transformation step by step. Right after the discussion of the nightmarish road of fear, the last chapter of the novella moves to a general discussion of the railroad and its role in modern literature and theory:

> At the beck and call of my consciousness are two or three little words: "and there," "already," "suddenly"; they rush about from car to car on the dimly lighted Sevastopol train, halting at the platforms where two thundering frying pans hurl themselves at one another and crawl apart.
>
> The railroad has changed the whole course, the whole rhythm of our prose. It has delivered it over to the senseless muttering of the French

> moujik out of Anna Karenina. Railroad prose like the woman's purse of that ominous moujik is full of the coupler's tools, delicious particles grappling iron prepositions and belongs rather among things submitted in legal evidence; it is divorced from any concern with beauty and that which is beautifully rounded.[29]

We notice here obvious references to the ending of Tolstoy's novel *Anna Karenina*, only the perspective is radically different. We are not watching the road from the point of view of the suicidal heroine or desperate hero; psychological reflection gives way to reflection on the language and syntax of the prose itself. This is the moment where the novelistic dialogue doesn't happen on the level of the character but on the level of language itself. However, that's not merely the modernist gesture of dehumanization that Ortega y Gasset spoke about when he suggested that the center of gravity of the modern text is no longer the subject but the language itself. Neither is this the dramatization of the end of the novel as Mandelshtam saw it, representing the centrifugal force of modernity. Instead, I would argue that this is a radical case of "aesthetic therapy" where confrontation with fear and its double estrangement saves the hero and (possibly) the narrator from suicidal thoughts. This is the off-modern open-ending, not predetermined by an authorial moral universe and not guided by "the legal evidence" the way *Anna Karenina* was. The creation of the modernist literary architecture that encompasses fear allows the hero and the narrator to escape the suicidal outcome of nineteenth-century "railroad prose." This is a striking example of the modernist humanism that Mandelshtam elaborates in his theoretical essays.

At the end, Mandelshtam claims that "with fear I have no fear" and follows the same serpentine road of the brave that was chosen by Shklovsky. *The road of self-reflective fear wouldn't lead to any kind of redemption, reconciliation, feel-good palliative, or happy ending*. On this road Mandelshtam's perception of Jewishness undergoes radical transformation. He writes from the particular historical moment between revolution and historic terror, and the deroutinization of fear is a first step toward lucidity and independent thinking. It might be scary and even terrifying to think that our life is a novella without a plot and a hero, made of Petersburg influenza delirium. But by the end of the text we realize that this influenza delirium is contagious and healing at once; it provides fear and inspiration, poison and cure, like a Derridean pharmacon. The confrontation with fear is a part of the "honest zigzag" of his passionate thinking that Mandelshtam follows through the last decade of his life. This thinking involves a personal transformation, an explicit rethinking of Jewish belonging in "The Fourth Prose" and the later poems and a further civic engagement with his "beast of a century."[30]

Nostalgia for World Culture and the Storm of History

Mandelshtam offers us his most complete version of his ars poetica and a practice of modernist humanism in his essay "Conversation about Dante." His Dante is an experimental artist: Dante, the Dadaist who rhymes through different times and spaces. He is a temporal and spatial misfit, an exile and a citizen of the republic of letters who struggles with fear and anxiety that open into a new historical understanding:

> The inner anxiety and painful, troubled gaucheries which accompany each step of the diffident man, as if his upbringing were somehow insufficient, the man untutored in the ways of applying his inner experience or of objectifying it in etiquette, the tormented and downtrodden man—such are the qualities which both provide the poem with all its charm, with all its drama, and serve as its background source, its psychological foundation.[31]

This modern Dante is ill at ease in his time and a foreigner in his own land, almost like a wandering Jew. His untimely anxiety and tragic embarrassment are the human drives behind the *Divine Comedy*.[32] In Mandelshtam's story the central figure of the European culture comes out a little off; his embarrassing errors in etiquette in life and art made him a cultural survivor. What kind of form can the drama of tragic awkwardness and exile take? According to Mandelshtam, *Divina Commedia* is neither a total work nor even a unified formal corpus but a poetic laboratory for the future. At its core it is not "form creation" (*formoobrazovanie*) but "impulse creation" (*poryvoobrazovanie*), not the making of a new language but a dynamic grafting and hybridization, more estranging and vital than a neologism. This is a virtuoso performance with vectors directed toward the past and the future, like the mirroring spirals of the Tatlin Tower. Rather than looking at technology in a contemporary sense, Mandelshtam examines a variety of material practices that inspire Dante's metaphors, such as seafaring, navigating, and shipbuilding as well as mineralogy and meteorology. According to Mandelshtam, this material ars poetica both uses and estranges the techniques of other arts and probes the improbable. Such radical use of techniques of imagination allows a poet to prefigure quantum and the wave theories of light that will be discovered by the physicists some six hundred years later.

Mandelshtam focuses on mineralogy and meteorology to find the patterns of impulse-creation that offer unpredictable shapes that conventional logic doesn't accommodate—zigzags, serpentine lines, bifurcating lines in the stone, folds. Mandelshtam's off-modern exhibit number one is not a technological artifact but a simple stone caressed by the waves of the Black Sea and the poet's fluid imagination.

> I permit myself here a small autobiographical confession. Black Sea pebbles tossed up on shore by the rising tide helped me immensely when the conception of this conversation was taking shape. I openly consulted with chalcedony, carnelians, gypsum crystals, spar, quartz and so on. . . . Mineral rock is an impressionistic diary of weather accumulated by millions of natural disasters; however, it is not only of the past, it is of the future: It is an Aladdin's lamp penetrating the geological twilight of future ages . . .
>
> Having combined the uncombinable, Dante altered the structure of time or, perhaps, to the contrary, he was forced to a glossolalia of facts, to a synchronism of events, names and traditions severed by centuries, precisely because he had heard the overtones of time.[33]

The Koktebel stone, a forgotten found object from Mandelshtam's happier past, brings back the memories of creative wandering. The small Crimean town of Koktebel preserved a hybrid heritage of Khazars, Tatars, Greeks, Italians, Jews, Russians, Ukrainians, Armenians, and many others and at the turn of the century became a *patria chica* of cosmopolitan artists and poets, including Annensky, Voloshin, Tsvetaeva, and Akhmatova. This imaginary Koktebel souvenir now solidifies the fluid logic of the third way and a hybrid of meteorology and mineralogy. The trope of crystallization of the past for the sake of the future brings together Benjamin and Mandelshtam. Benjamin's "pearl diver" and Mandelshtam's sea stone-gatherer are half-brothers, only Mandelshtam is not pursuing "dialectics at a standstill" or crystallization of the past for the sake of the future. Rather, his focus is on the impulses and graftings of the creative process. The amateur mineralogy to which Mandelshtam devotes many pages in the "Conversation about Dante" provides alternative shapes of evolution, bifurcating veins in the nonprecious stones, curvatures, zigzags, palimpsests, and spirals without synthesis. These shapes point beyond the familiar paradigm of modern natural and political science and anticipate some of the thinking in Gilles Deleuze's "The Fold." World culture is imagined as a work in progress, constructed through impulses and unforeseen synchronicities and not through Hegelian dialectics or a museumification of the canon.

This palimpsest of free-willing zigzags also offers a temporary poetic remedy to the cruel irreversibility of time that lies at the heart of the human fear of mortality. At the same time it works in counterpoint to the linear progress and the forward march of history that in the 1930s was clearly not leading to a happy ending. The poet is filled with foreboding of an impending catastrophe, but he doesn't wish to succumb to its inevitability.

If we look for a single drive in Mandelshtam's corpus, we can find it not in the main body of the text but in outtake No. 13, which was published only in the 1990s in the complete edition of Mandelshtam's essay, together with its earlier versions. This fragment reads like a prophetic premonition of the poet's personal and historical anxieties:

> The foundation of the composition of all cantos of *Inferno* is the movement of the storm. It ripens as a meteorological phenomenon and all questions and answers revolve around it: beware, to be or not to be, will there be a storm.
>
> To be more precise it is about the movement of the storm, which passes us by, and definitely moves aside [*mimo, obiazatel'no storonoj*].[34]

Storona shares the root with estrangement *o-stranenie*. The storm passes "astray, "moves aside," laterally (*storonoj*). Perhaps, Mandelshtam didn't include this outtake because it could be read too "literally." At once too ominous and too optimistic, it reads like a political allegory particularly apt in the Stalinist Russia of the 1930s and an exercise in wishful thinking, of the dreams of conjectural history as changeable as the weather conditions. The impending storm hides in the *Divine Comedy*, like an anamorphose in baroque painting that is only visible from a certain lateral perspective. The storm, like a historic disaster, is not "written in [the] stone" of necessity; it can still go astray and spare the land. The logic here is quite different than Benjamin's more familiar description of the Angel of History. It is more lateral, impulsive, and conjectural. In other words, the theoretical knight's move becomes a figure of historic hope that didn't come true.

The off-modern thinking of history is not made of the "aha" moments of inevitable disasters intuited by the great thinkers, but of such lateral moves. The experimental theorist and practitioner of new arts, Dante the Dadaist, has many features of Mandelshtam and his various alter egos. In the outtake 13 we find the poet's last "knight's move" and a hope for a nonteleological history of the fragile world culture.

In conclusion, we can only begin to outline the off-modern turn in contemporary theory through the eccentric writings of several "Jewish" thinkers and writers. These writers didn't embrace the binary system of thinking and defied political theology and teleology. Their outlook is non- or almost anti-messianic. They look for "the third way," lateral moves, everyday genres in literature and life. They invite us to rethink the relationship between aesthetics and politics through the experience of freedom, dissent, and estrangement beyond the much misunderstood parallelism of Walter Benjamin in his opposition between aestheticizing politics (in Fascist Italy and Nazi Germany) and politicizing aesthetics (in the Soviet Union).[35] Aesthetics is not understood here as an analysis of autonomous works of art but as a form of knowledge that proceeds through a particular interplay of sense, imagination, and reason. In the center is not the model of aesthetic autonomy (or specificity of the media), but rather the practice of estrangement and radical perspectivism that informs imagination and judgment in the public world.

In other words, Shklovsky and Mandelshtam explore what Arendt calls public "worldliness"—this-worldly human culture and everyday life that is not regarded as an evil world of inauthentic appearances to be transcended and a longing for "world culture" (without much hope for the dream fulfillment). Aesthetically they practice double estrangement of contemporary theories and practices but believe in a literary public realm, an imaginary community of the republic of letters that can never be entirely politicized.

Worldliness is not the same as cosmopolitanism, but the two notions overlap. The history of discourse about the world involves conversation across national borders and offers what Kwame Anthony Appiah calls "the case for contamination."[36] There are many vernacular cosmopolitans coming from different localities that require us to recognize inner pluralities within oneself and one's culture, not only of external pluralisms of national, cultural, or religious identities.

Worldly modernist humanism here is often expressed "via negativa" and in a minor key; it works through rethinking scale (through antimonumentalism) and offsetting any attempt at a total work through experimental compositions, unfinalizable parables, and humor. Modernist humanism operates through the estrangement of cruelty, non-instrumentalization of the human being, and foregrounding of embarrassment and human erring that resist any kind of revolutionary teleology that justifies violence. The relationship between aesthetics and politics has to be reexamined through the experience of freedom, dissent, and estrangement. We have to return to the earlier original use of the word "aesthetics," not as an analysis of autonomous works of art but as a form of knowledge that proceeds through a particular interplay of sense, imagination, and reason. The focus here is not on the model of aesthetic autonomy (or specificity of the media), but rather the practice of estrangement and radical perspectivism that informs imagination and judgment. Looking back at twentieth-century history, Arendt proposed to estrange the immanency of disaster. To do so one has to "look for the unforeseeable and unpredictable," for "the more heavily the scales are weighted in favor of the disaster, the more miraculous will the deed done in freedom appear; for it is disaster, not salvation, that always happens automatically and therefore always must appear to be irresistible."[37]

NOTES

1. Carlo Ginzburg, *Wooden Eyes: Nine Reflections on Distance* (London: Verso, 2002).

2. Hannah Arendt, "What Is Freedom?" in *Between the Past and the Future* (New York: Viking, 1966).

3. Viktor Shklovsky, "Art as Technique" (1917), in *Four Formalist Essays*, ed. and trans. Lee T. Lemon and Marion J. Reis (Lincoln: University of Nebraska Press, 1965), 12.

4. Svetlana Boym, *Another Freedom: The Alternative History of an Idea* (Chicago: University of Chicago Press, 2010).

5. Shklovsky was a son of a Jewish father and a German / Latvian / Russian mother. He received no formal Jewish education, yet he appears remarkably knowledgeable about the Bible. Throughout his life Shklovsky speaks explicitly about different Jewish languages, uses biblical parables, discusses Jewish publishers and writers. Later in life he wrote about Russia's first Jews at the court of Peter the Great and contributed an account of Nazi atrocities against the Jews in Kislovodsk for Ehrenburg's *Black Book*. Shklovsky's contribution at 293ff.

6. For more on Shklovsky, see Richard Sheldon, "Victor Shklovsky and the Device of Ostensible Surrender," in Viktor Shklovsky, *Third Factory*, ed. and trans. Richard Sheldon (1926; Ann Arbor, Mich.: Ardis) 1977), vii; and A. P. Chudakov, "Dva pervykh desiatiletiia," in Viktor Shklovsky, *Gamburgskii schet. Stat'i—vospominaniia—esse (1914–1933)*, ed. Aleksandr Galushkin and Aleksandr Chudakov (Moscow: Sovetskii pisatel', 1990), 17.

7. *Stran* is the root of the Russian word for country, *strana*, and the word for strange, *strannyi*, its Latin and Slavic roots superimposing on one another, creating a wealth of poetic associations and false etymologies.

8. In his essays on the phenomenology of art, Hegel also speaks about freedom and alienation as well as art's particular role in mediating between different realms of existence. In a discussion of Dutch paintings, he calls art a "mockery" of reality, a form of irony. These ideas are close to those of the Formalists, yet Shklovsky by no means embraces the larger frame of the Hegelian system. In his later work, Shklovsky engages directly with Hegelian theories of literature. Speaking of Don Quixote, for example, Shklovsky (in *O teorii prozy* [1925; Moscow: Sovetskii pisatel', 1983] 370) observes that Hegel was not interested in "Don Quixote but in Don Quixotism," not paying attention to the particular strangeness of art. "In the words of Hegel there is no movement. Hegel had an impression that he sees from the hindsight of eternity everything, including the imperial police." The Brechtian *Verfremdungseffekt* can be read as a creative reinterpretation of Hegel.

9. Daniel Boyarin and Jonathan Boyarin, *Powers of Diaspora* (Minneapolis: University of Minnesota Press, 2002).

10. Shklovsky, *Third Factory*. This translation has been slightly modified; the original is "*Bytie opredeliaet soznanie, no sovest' ostaetsia neustroennoi.*" The slogan "material being conditions consciousness" has been attributed in the Soviet sources to Feuerbach, Hegel, Marx, and Lenin. Importantly, in Shklovsky's context, this slogan opened the 1924 declaration of a radical Constructivist group that declared that the writer had to serve the demands of the social and industrial revolution (LTsK [Literature section of Constructivists], "Tekhnicheskii Kodeks," quoted in T. M. Goriaeva, *Politicheskaia Tsenzura v SSSR* [Moscow: Rosspen, 2002], 123).

11. Viktor Shklovsky, "Sentimental'noe puteshestvie," in *Eshche nichego ne konchilos'* (1923; Moscow: Propaganda, 2002), 125. For English, see Viktor Shklovsky, *A Sentimental Journey: Memoirs, 1917–1922*, trans. Richard Sheldon (Ithaca: Cornell University Press, 1984). On "transsensical [zaumnyj] antisemitism," 81,

12. Shklovsky, *Sentimental Journey*, 195.

13. Ibid., 112. Exactly what Shklovsky intends by "Aramaic Jews" here is unclear.

14. Victor Shklovsky, *Zoo, or Letters Not about Love* (New York: Dalkie Archive), 45–46.

15. Jacques Derrida, *Shibboleth: pour Paul Celan* (Paris: Galilee, 1987).

16. It no longer "dehumanizes" but rather makes real the "fear of war." The term "dehumanization of art" was coined by the Spanish philosopher José Ortega y Gasset, who argued that in contrast to Renaissance art and the nineteenth-century novel, man is no longer at the center of modern art; the new art does not "imitate reality," but operates through inversion, by bringing to life a reality of its own and realizing poetic metaphors. Ortega y Gasset

wrote: "The weapon of poetry turns against the natural things and wounds or murders them" (José Ortega y Gasset, *The Dehumanization of Art*, trans. Helen Weyl (1925; Princeton, N.J.: Princeton University Press, 1968), 35.

17. Shklovsky, "Art as Technique," 12.

18. Shklovsky, *Sentimental Journey*, 238.

19. Ibid., 101.

20. Ibid., 60.

21. Shklovsky, "Sentimental'noe puteshestvie," 195–96.

22. Shklovsky, *Third Factory*, 47–49.

23. See Osip Mandelstam, "Fourth Prose," in *Mandelstam: The Complete Critical Prose and Letters*, ed. Jane Gary Harris, trans. Jane Gary Harris and Constance Link (Ann Arbor, Mich.: Ardis, 1979), 312–25.

24. Svetlana Boym, "Dialogue as Lyrical Hermaphroditism," *Slavic Review* 50, no. 1 (1991): 118–26.

25. Osip Mandelshtam, *The Egyptian Stamp*, in *The Noise of Time*, trans. and ed. Clarence Brown (New York: Penguin, 1993), 161. Translation is modified by Svetlana Boym.

26. Ibid., 149.

27. Charles Isenberg, *Substantial Proofs of Being: The Prose of Osip Mandelshtam* (Columbus, Ohio: Slavica Publishers, 1987), 168.

28. Mandelshtam, *Egyptian Stamp*, 162.

29. Ibid.

30. The poem is translated into English as "My Age," and begins in translation, "My Age, My Beast." http://www.poetryconnection.net/poets/Osip_Mandelstam/8104, accessed 11/8/2015.

31. Osip Mandelstam, "Conversation about Dante," in *Mandelstam: The Complete Critical Prose and Letters*, 406.

32. Mandelshtam first writes about the impulse-creation in his essay on the great Jewish actor Mikhoels, whose Jewish mask also resembles the theater of Greek antiquity and who performs through the "vibration in his thinking fingers, which are animated like articulated speech" (*Mandelstam: The Complete Critical Prose and Letters*, 261–62).

33. Mandelstam, "Conversation about Dante," 439. Most important, Mandelshtam is not interested in creating a museum of the past but in perpetuating a certain social architecture that for him constitutes a form of contemporary humanism, where contemporary is always a little out of step with the present moment to rhyme with the past and the future. In his visionary essay of 1922 "Humanism and the Present" (*Gumanizm i sovremennost'*) Mandelshtam does not think of humanism in terms of nineteenth-century psychology and biography-centered literary culture, but in broad Renaissance terms. His humanism is a form of social architecture that does not use human

beings as material for the authoritarian pyramids but exists for humans and in the human scale. Here Mandelshtam extends his temporal range from Assyria and Babylonia to the contemporary moment, challenging the use of the word "revolution" and putting it in service of humanism and never subscribing to the doctrine of necessary violence: "There are epochs which maintain that man is insignificant, that man is to be used like bricks or mortar, that man should be used for building things, not vice-versa—that things be built for man. . . . Nevertheless, there is also another form of social architecture whose scale and measure is man. It does not use man to build, it builds for man. Its grandeur is constructed not on the insignificance of individuality but on the highest form of expediency, in accord with its needs." Osip Mandelshtam, "Humanism and the Present," in *Mandelstam: The Complete Critical Prose and Letters*, 181.

34. Osip Mandelshtam, *Sobranie sochinenij*, ed. G. P. Struse and A. B. Filippova (Washington, D.C.: Mezhdunarodnoe Literaturnoe Sodruzhestovo, 1967–81), 4:103.

35. Benjamin's reflection is obviously more complex than alluded to here, and it changed from one essay to another. This issue is discussed in detail in Svetlana Boym, *Another Freedom*, chap. 5.

36. Kwame Anthony Appiah, *Cosmopolitanism: Ethics in the World of Strangers* (New York: W. W. Norton, 2006).

37. Arendt, "What Is Freedom?" 170.

CHAPTER 8

Old Testament Realism in the Writings of Erich Auerbach

James I. Porter

It is surprising how influential and even fashionable Erich Auerbach (1892–1957), the mild-mannered and understated German-Jewish intellectual from Berlin, has come to be in the world of high theory and among contemporary readers generally. His works are reprinted and newly translated every few years,[1] while books and special issues of journals devoted specifically to him keep appearing in the English-speaking and German worlds.[2] Moreover, his archives continue to yield a small flood of previously unpublished essays and correspondence that is slowly making its way into English, and in theoretically prominent journals at that.[3]

The shelf life of Auerbach's writings is indisputably impressive. Nonetheless, it is not the same Auerbach who has survived from one generation to the next, but rather an Auerbach whose identity changes with the vicissitudes of theory and criticism. Originally, Auerbach was recognized as a Romance philologist who followed in the footsteps of a long line of distinguished scholars from Weimar Germany (among these, Karl Vossler, Ernst Robert Curtius, and Leo Spitzer). Starting in the 1960s, Auerbach was claimed as a founder of modern comparative literature.[4] When critical theory ousted old-style comparativism, his credentials were updated, and he has since been celebrated as an exilic intellectual, a figure of secular criticism, and as a prophet of global literary studies or "world literature."[5] Most recently, a handful of scholars have sought to assimilate Auerbach to a newly revived interest in political theology.[6] None of these portraits is entirely convincing, and another approach is needed. With this in mind, I would like to begin developing a different portrait of Auerbach, one that more accurately reflects his cultural and historical location as a Jewish intellectual who had a significant stake in the ends of theory. My aim is not to enlist Auerbach's support for any particular contemporary theoretical approach. On the contrary, it is (at least in part) to demonstrate some of the ways in which Auerbach's thought and writing have been, and remain, particularly resistant to co-optation.

A self-confessed if nonobservant Jew who lived through the most turbulent decades of Germany's modern history,[7] Auerbach was a consummate student of the literary and cultural inheritances of the West in their comprehensive totality. Throughout his writings he strove to capture nothing less than the evolution of historical consciousness as it moves out of a universe filled with myths and religion into one that is saturated with history. This evolution was one he applauded, not least because it led to the difficult discovery of the human and social worlds in their concrete and palpable reality—in a word, one that Auerbach made entirely his own, the discovery of "realism." What he means by this term is less a genre or a style than it is an apprehension of the sensuous, earthly, and human world as the bearer of all the reality that matters. Christianity has a significant though not quite central place in this narrative: It occupies, we might say, the displaced center of the historical evolution that Auerbach relates. At the real center of his story stand the Jewish inheritances of Christianity and their later residues in the West, which is to say the contribution of the Jewish traditions to an evolving sense of historical consciousness that was registered in literature as a sense of human, this-worldly reality.

These two factors, historical consciousness and a sense of the real, are for Auerbach intertwined: Where the one is deficient, the other will be too. As a rule, the ancient (pagan and classical) tradition is marked by Auerbach as severely lacking in both.[8] Historical consciousness first appears in the Hebrew Bible.[9] It then matures within, but to a great extent in spite of, the Christian tradition. And it is eventually emancipated during the secular age—though it never fully emancipates itself from its Jewish origins. For all of these reasons, Auerbach's thought is irreducible to Romance philology in a narrow sense, to literary criticism or comparative literature in the modern sense, or to Christianizing eschatology in any sense. On the contrary, from start to finish Auerbach is practicing a kind of Jewish philology in the guise of Romance philology, that is, an inquiry into the specifically Jewish origins of Western historical consciousness. And because this philology is written largely in response to and against the prevailing ideologies of Weimar and Nazi Germany, Auerbach's project has a further, essential dimension: It is a politically and culturally *resistant* philology that is aimed at undoing contemporary paradigms. Auerbach developed this method at the precise moment when Judaism and Jewishness were most endangered. His method, it should be emphasized, is not a form of Jewish theology. In some sense it is entirely godless and secular. But it is defiantly and strategically Jewish in its response to efforts in Auerbach's midst to blot out the inheritance of Jewish thinking from the Western world.

To say this is not in any way to imply that Auerbach wishes to shore up and stabilize Jewish identity. On the contrary, his intention is to construct an image of the Jews as a way of destabilizing contemporary identity politics, and then to move on from there to more uncertain and less charted ways of rethinking (primarily) Jewish, Christian, and secular identities in the past and in the contemporary world. Thus, while Auerbach's philology is in one sense a form of cultural, ethical, and spiritual remembrance aimed against racial and religious forgetting, in another sense his philology has a sharply critical and at times destructive edge that puts him in the tradition of Spinoza and Nietzsche. That is why it is plausible to say that what Auerbach produced was a Jewishly inflected intellectual and spiritual history of the West from antiquity to the present—a true *Weltgeschichte*—arrived at by way of a Jewish or Judaizing philology.[10] Given the uncertain place, in this history, of Jewish identity for Jews and non-Jews alike, Auerbach can be said to be writing not just a history of the past, but a critical history of the present. "Jewish philology"—a term not used by Auerbach but one that fits his project well—signifies no more and no less than this.

Toward the end of his life Auerbach renamed his method "*Weltphilologie*," which is to say, a philology of the world and not just of the word. The name changes nothing, though it does put his project's largest contours into sharper relief. *Weltphilologie* is a philology that pertains first and foremost to the radically human world. Because Auerbach considers history to be secular (at least tendentially), vital, and concrete, which is to say both human and humane, his philology is in the end an *earthly, this-worldly philology*, a philology that takes as its ultimate object the human world as a whole, that is, the world as it is represented, experienced, and lived by human agents. This is the ultimate meaning of *dargestellte Wirklichkeit* ("represented reality") in the subtitle to his classic study from 1946,

Mimesis: The Representation of Reality in Western Literature. Mimesis is not limited to literary representation. It primarily captures the various ways in which the world is conceived, experienced, lived, written, and read, or, to borrow a phrase from *Mimesis*, the way in which "the material of the real world" comes to be "stylize[d]" (*M*, 538)—not so much as a product of language or literature, but rather as a product of the human mind.[11]

From the idea of reality (*Wirklichkeit*) comes one further key concept in Auerbach's theory: *realism*, which likewise has nothing to do with the conventional meanings of the term, literary or other.[12] Realism for Auerbach is a grasp of this experience of reality, be this phenomenological and felt or literary and conveyed through imitation (in which case literary realism is a representation and expression of phenomenological realism, though of equal validity): Realism "is [an] imitation of the sensory experience of life on earth—among the most essential characteristics of which would seem to be its possessing a history, its undergoing change and development" (*M*, 191, trans. slightly adapted).[13] Such realism is furthermore crucially *tragic*, not least because it is tinged by a sense of its own ineluctable contingency. Reality that has passed through the mind and the senses, and hence has been "stylized," is in a legitimate sense more real than reality. Realism conceived as designating either a degree of correspondence to some outer object or a literary genre or style is insufficiently robust to capture the meaning of realism for Auerbach, for whom the concept of realism tracks the violent registration and seizure, by human consciousness, of its own conditions. But more on this in a moment.

History, reality, life in its concrete and sensuous particularity, experience, realism—each of these elements runs through the ambitious cultural history that Auerbach pieces together through his reading of mostly major and sometimes minor texts, starting with the Old Testament and culminating in Dante's *Divine Comedy*, a work that, he claims, signals the onset of modernity, although Auerbach as it were reverse engineers this history: He arrived at his reading of the Old Testament in its fullest form only in 1942 when he was exiled in Istanbul, having first mapped out the decisive turning point of this history in his masterpiece on Dante from 1929 when he was a postdoctoral student in Berlin. As we shall see, the order of events here makes no difference to Auerbach's theory, because the underlying model is consistently in place from start to finish. But why, then, the recourse to religion in either its Jewish or Christian (and in the case of Dante, Roman Catholic) forms? To anticipate my argument, Auerbach locates the origins of historical consciousness where one least expects to find it—not in modernity when religion finally relaxed its grip on the West, but in the Old Testament itself, where history and historical consciousness were first discovered, and which provided the structure and framework for all subsequent expressions of historical thought and experience from early Christianity onward. Modernity discovers itself, one might say, in a return to Old Testament realism, but only "becomes" modern in its later expressions after Dante, be this in Boccaccio, Rabelais, Montaigne, Marcel Proust, or Virginia Woolf. In order to see how this progression unfolds, we will need to begin with *Mimesis* and work back to Dante, and then work forward again to *Mimesis*.

The Discovery of History and Tragic Realism in the Old Testament

The opening chapter of *Mimesis*, Auerbach's single most familiar piece of writing, is based on a provocative contrast between Homer and the Old Testament. His argument, quickly sketched, is that the Old Testament presents the intrusion of the divine in the form of a gap or abyss that rips through space and time, thanks to the plunging intervention of God's purpose from above. The intrusion of God into human reality might appear to render these two outer dimensions of human existence (space and time) momentarily insignificant. In fact, the exact opposite occurs. As Auerbach views things, God's sudden presence in the world does not de-realize the human coordinates of space and time; it *realizes* them for the first time, virtually *validating* them. Instead of creating a sense of the timeless and transcendental, it implants in human individuals a consciousness of time and of time's passing. By consciousness we should understand not a sense of time and place that is easily characterized, but rather the need and the desire to fill out the coordinates of these two dimensions in an intelligible fashion, and in this way to assign meaning to events. In a word, Yahweh brings a sense of history into the world. The paradoxical effect of the transcendent is, in the Jewish vision of things, a sense of historical reality. History is the specifically Jewish *response* to the illocality of the divine; it is its direct reflex.

We can trace this impact in two ways. First and most obviously, the events told in the Old Testament are taken by the Jews to be "real": They really did take place in the world, God really did intrude himself into human reality. Such are the claims of historical reality as they impose themselves as a true narrative, indeed as the "only" true reality, on the minds of later generations (*M*, 14–15, 19–20). But at another level, we can say that the intrusion of the vertical dimension of the divine *etches* a sense of historical reality *into* time—first, in the patterns that the events narrated in the Old Testament make on the characters they concern; second, in the impression of historical reality that these same stories make on Jewish readers who treat these events *as* historical; and finally, in the unbounded claims that the Old Testament as a whole makes on world history (*Weltgeschichte*), for its ultimate pretensions are to map out the historical nature of the world (*M*, 15–17, 23). But we should make clear what Auerbach is not claiming with this reading of Old Testament realism. He is not necessarily supporting a claim about the religious truth of the Jewish Old Testament. In fact, his claim is far more limited. It is that the ideology—Auerbach calls it the *Auffassungs- und Darstellungsweise*—that frames and supports this grasp of reality is itself decidedly historical. Thus, he writes that "the concept of God held by the Jews is less a cause than a *symptom* of their manner of comprehending and representing things [*ihrer Auffassungs- und Darstellungsweise*]" (8). The sentence is easily passed over, but it would be wrong to do so. Auerbach's chief object in this essay (and everywhere else) is not theology but the human activity that produces it. And his point about the Old Testament is that it is the product of a particular mode of construing the, so to speak, vertical and horizontal axes of human experience as both utterly imbricated and mutually inextricable. The intrusion of the divine vertical axis does not introduce a timeless and transcendental dimension into everyday reality. Nor does it point those whom it affects to another world beyond the present. On the contrary, it introduces historical depth *into* the everyday reality of an entire people. Another word for this same capacity is "*Wirklichkeitsauffassung*" ("grasp of reality," rendered by Trask as a way of "comprehending reality," 16).

The Binding of Isaac episode from Genesis 22 is adduced by Auerbach as the most emblematic instance of this process. It is also the most charged, both theologically and, for Auerbach writing in exile from Germany in the year 1942, ideologically.[14] Abraham's journey to Moriah is bereft of spatial and temporal coordinates twice over. First, as Auerbach puts it in a highly poetic and suggestive paraphrase, "the journey is like a silent progress through *the indeterminate and the contingent*, a holding of the breath, a process which has no present, which is inserted, like a blank duration, between what has passed and what lies ahead" (10; emphasis added). Second, Moriah exists nowhere except textually: The word, Auerbach speculates, may have been introduced into the text by a later redactor in order to put a name on a place that he did not know either because it never had any geographical reality or because the location was not given in the original (10). Whether or not Auerbach is correct, the direction of his reading is clear. Drained of all contours and all meaning, more enigmatic than real, and "indefinite and in *need* of interpretation" (11: *unbestimmt und deutungsbedürftig*; the English translation gives "undefined and call[ing] for interpretation"), time and space in the Old Testament exist for one purpose only: They serve as a staging point for endlessly receding layers of meaning (God's purpose, which remains obscure to the end).[15] Indeed, they *provoke* this search: "They positively *demand* the symbolic meaning which they later received" (10; emphasis added).[16] Later, but not earlier, because the Jewish way of reading responds to this demand in a completely different manner from the later, Christian approach to the Old Testament. The Jewish reading looks for historical and moral meaning, and it finds these intertwined and immanently located within the text, or rather immanently located in the world to which the text points. The Christian reading looks for symbolic meaning that is extrinsic to the text, and indeed to the historical world altogether. To return to the point about history made above, we can say that the puzzling manifestation of Yahweh in the Old Testament demands—cries out for—spatiotemporal location. The Jewish response to this demand, Auerbach claims, was to root reality in its spatial and temporal location and to give it a historical presence. The Christian response was an attempt to de-historicize and dislocate this reality all over again.

It is in this context that Auerbach's theory of *figura* must be understood.[17] For, if we follow out the logic of this last remark from *Mimesis*, we have to acknowledge that the later practice of Christian figural interpretation responds to the precise provocation of the Old Testament, that it is virtually called into existence *by* this indeterminacy of meaning that is embedded in the Jewish text, but also (and here Auerbach lets out an audible sigh) that it does so at the cost of overwhelming and finally dissolving the Old Testament's claims on reality (Marcion, who sought to exclude the Old Testament from the canon of holy scriptures in the second century, is only the most extreme case of this tendency).[18] The Old Testament is so darkly elusive, Auerbach writes, that it is "*in constant danger of losing its own reality*, as very soon happened when interpretation became so overgrown that the real disintegrated [*daß sich das Wirkliche zersetzte*]" (15; trans. adapted, emphasis added). Auerbach does not mince his words. With Paul, the Old Testament was "devalued":

> An adaptation of the [biblical] message to the preconceptions of a far wider audience, its detachment from the specific preconceptions of Judaism, became a necessity. . . . The Old Testament was devalued [*entwertet*] as the history of a people and as the law of the Jews, and it assumed the appearance of a series of "figures," that is, of prophetic

> announcements and anticipations of the coming of Jesus and all that was implied in this event. . . . The total content of the sacred writings was placed in an exegetical context that often removed the narrated events far from their sensuous foundations, as the reader or hearer was forced to turn his attention away from the sensuous event and towards its meaning. (*M*, 48; trans. adapted; cf. 16)

To claim that biblical background meanings "can *only* be recovered by a very particular act of interpretation," one that Auerbach "described as figural interpretation," is to get hold of the matter from the wrong end.[19] Figural readings do not "recover" biblical meaning; they foist meaning on what was never meant to be grasped. Indeed, figural reading is nothing other than a desperate response to this perplexity of the Jewish faith, and an inherently destructive one at that.[20] In Auerbach's view, figural reading is an act of *disfiguration* and *disvaluation*. Mimesis is *opposed* to the figural interpretation of reality, not identical with it.[21]

Paradoxically, in their superficial meaninglessness, their abstractness, and their virtual emptiness (God and his events display *Gestaltlosigkeit*, *Ortlosigkeit*, and *Einsamkeit* ["lack of form," "unlocatability," and "solitude/seclusion"]), the narratives of the Hebrew Bible create, in the minds of the faithful, a powerful sense of time, fate, and consciousness (8). They do this in two ways. First, the featurelessness of time and space gives rise to a desire to anchor events in historical reality, as in the case of Moriah, where this desire verges on compulsivity for the later commentators. Second, every individual moment and each person "from Adam to the prophets" "*embodies*"—renders palpably concrete and particular—the vertical relationship to God. The sensuous and palpable reality of this relationship merely intensifies the mystery that lies behind it: "God chose and formed these men to the end of embodying his essence and will" (17). The fact *that* mankind embodies God's essence and will may be certain, but the revelation *of* that essence and that will is not immediate: It only comes to light over time. Consequently, even as God scatters the clues to his purpose, "choice [*Auserwählung*] and formation [*Formung*] *do not coincide*, for the latter proceeds gradually, *historically*, during the earthly life of him upon whom the choice has fallen" (17; emphasis added). God's purpose is disclosed, to the extent that it is, only in space and time.

And so it happens that time, originally evacuated of meaning, transforms into its opposite: It becomes rich, significant, laden with purpose and scattered clues; it thickens with layers of inevitable meaning; it deepens. Time becomes more than merely a facet of present-tense experience;

it becomes *historical.* And the same is true of space. As these two conditions of human experience regain their original properties (so to speak), albeit now in a heightened form, they acquire a palpable sensuousness (a *Sinnlichkeit*) that can be felt in the narratives that relate events and in the events themselves ("the sensible material of life," 14; trans. adapted).[22] Grounded in an attentiveness to *what does not coincide*, aware of differences, of a meaning that reveals itself over time (for example in the distinctive biographies of evolving, incomparably unique individuals who are "touched" by time [18]—Auerbach calls this "the intensity of [a] personal history" that a reader feels [ibid.]), though never fully revealing anything (for history never comes to an end, at least not for historical creatures like us), and so too fraught with doubt and uncertainty, this heightened form of perception discovers meaning in the inner complexity and layered quality of events. This is what Auerbach means by the "depth" that the Old Testament displays at every turn.[23]

To become aware of these depths of meaning—to become aware of their "reality"—is to develop a historical consciousness. But to develop such a consciousness is not the same thing as attaining a complete and perfect sense of historical reality. Quite the contrary. To attain or have historical consciousness is to become painfully cognizant of the imperfect nature of the experience and meaning of time. As a result, historical perception is constitutively (Auerbach will soon add: "tragically") incomplete. Or rather, the perception that this kind of historical awareness teaches is one that will never be satisfied with simple and exhaustive explanations. History, in Auerbach's eyes, is not a record of easily digestible facts. It is the symptomatic record of writhing contradictions, as well as the slow and painful awareness of this fact.[24] To be aware of an event in time is to become aware of a reality that cannot be grasped intellectually but only passionately in the very desire to grasp it and to hold onto it.[25] It is to experience—to be visited by—a fundamental discrepancy between signs and meanings, and thus to experience reality in and as "oppressive tension" (*Spannung*).[26] This discrepancy is the source of the "tragic" in the Old Testament's realism (about which there will be more to say in a moment). But isn't this tension constituted only in relation to a meaning that descends from above? Yes, but not exactly, because divine truth remains forever concealed, lurking inaccessibly in the *surface* of human reality, which henceforth acquires a verticality all its own. Owing to this elusive concealment, interpretation is "required" and "demanded," but also never fully rewarded: it remains, precisely, an endless endeavor, as uncertain and contingent as "genuine" historical reality itself (*die echte Geschichte*, 20). Of course, one might argue, historical contingency exists in the Old Testament simply because of God's inscrutable purpose, which can intrude on earthly life at any time. In fact, Auerbach's point is the reverse: God's purpose is merely the Jews' way of discovering the rich if painful contingency of historical time.[27]

The definition of "historical" is undergoing extraordinary pressure in Auerbach's hands. History for Auerbach is not something given. Rather, it has to be teased out of circumstances as their evolved and significant product. To deduce history from events in this way is to develop an awareness that can be located only in the kinds of difficult antagonism that are brought to light in the Bible. And to do all this is to embark on the road toward historical consciousness in the West, and in the very form in which we currently experience history ourselves. The Jews invented history in this precise sense. *That* is their contribution to the West.

There ought to be nothing terribly controversial about any of this. After all, the text under inspection by Auerbach is not a mirror of reality; it is the re-creation of a reality, produced not by prophets and priests but by scholars and editors (he names the proto-historical Elohist as the author of the Abraham and Isaac episode [8] and the Yahwist for other episodes [11]). And these redactors "were not poets who created legends; they were writers of history whose notion of the structure of human life was schooled in history."[28] The view is one that he held on to right up to the very end of his life. The correction (insertion) of "Moriah" where no place-name was available is a case in point: The historical instinct seeks to locate divine meaning, despite its ineradicable uncertainties, in phenomenal time and place. Divinity thus serves as a catalyst to sense-making, but not as its telos. God, after all, is a *symptom* of the Jewish way of grasping reality. And for the same reasons, historical experience is for Auerbach anchored in the experience of conflict and antagonism: It is here that it touches the real. For it is "precisely the most extreme circumstances, in which we are immeasurably forsaken and in despair, or immeasurably joyous and exalted, [that] give us, *if we survive them*, a personal stamp which is recognized as the product of a rich existence, a rich development" (8), and that gives such events "a historical character." The sudden intrusion of the personal voice here ("we") points to Auerbach's own present circumstances, but also to his own cherished beliefs.

With this, Auerbach has grazed the core of his theory of mimesis as the representation of reality, what he generally calls "tragic realism." "Tragic realism" is misleadingly named. It does not designate either tragedy or realism as genres, and it is not even at bottom tragically colored. Rather, "tragic realism" is Auerbach's way of naming the troubling juncture between the surfaces of life and language, which one can both know and feel, and the plunging vertical aspect of some other dimension altogether, which one can only sense—although ultimately what one senses is the depth of these same surfaces, which makes them what they are and which defines the subject of this experience as the individual he or she is. It is at such moments that mimesis is achieved—the representation of the essential unity of a character with its fate in all of that unity's blinding reality and luminous "evidence," as revealed in a singular act of the self.[29] Anticipating Foucault by half a century, Auerbach calls such moments "problematizations" of the ordinary—though what he is designating is in fact the substratum of reality that underlies all ordinary experience, an element that is absolutely characteristic of the Old Testament narrative style and that stands in stark contrast to the epic style of Homer: "In the Old Testament stories, the sublime, the tragic, and problematic take shape precisely in the domestic and the commonplace: scenes [like these] are inconceivable in the Homeric style" (*M*, 22). They are this because they interrupt the surface narrative and its flow of events with a power that is harrowing, but which is unknown to Homer, whose sole purpose was "to make us forget our own reality for a few hours" (*M*, 15). Auerbach also recognizes, however, that much of the time such abrupt communications with the real do not occur at all: We live in reality but rarely commune with it. And that is most likely why, when such moments do occur, they warrant the name tragic—for they signal their own self-consuming fragility, and their own passing. Poets of the real have a knack for articulating these possibilities in a way that few others do.

Such moments may be rare, but they are also indelible. Their occurrence is marked in literature by a radical convergence of two kinds of style, which in the vocabulary of classical rhetoric are called the high and the low styles. This convergence of styles (*Stilmischung*) is not a blending of styles that are otherwise rigorously separated into high, middle, and low (a phenomenon known as *Stiltrennung* in German) as this is found in classical literature from Homer to Tacitus, but the shattering of style (the "violation of all style" [*M*, 185]) as a meaningful criterion of anything at all.[30] What particularly interests Auerbach is a radical projection, so to speak, of the vertical axis of meaning onto the horizontal axis of time, which is to say, he is interested in the way a dimension of depth suddenly opens up in the realm of the everyday. Such moments, when voiced in literature, are the expressions of a passionate subject who is firmly located in space and time here and now and who is communicating a powerful apprehension of this-worldly, and not other-worldly, reality. These moments are "tragic," he writes in an essay from 1933, because tragedy is what results whenever the "forces of individualism, historicism, and lyricism . . . r[i]se up against the past as with a common will to embrace the world in all its concrete immanence and to experience the world's spirit through its living body."[31] They are also sublime, not in the sense of a style (a sublime style), to which even Homer has access, but in the sense of a profound grasp of what lies, as it were, before one's feet. In classical aesthetics, as Auerbach understands this, sublimity is opposed to reality because it is a feature of the heroic and the ideal.[32] In Auerbach's preferred understanding of the sublime, sublimity is not opposed to reality and the real: It has nothing to do with idealization, except insofar as it points to the profound defection of all ideals.[33] On the contrary, it reveals what is most vitally real about reality.[34]

Auerbach's account of the historical realism of the Hebrew Bible is premised on this very same idea. The individuals narrated in the Old Testament take on the concrete features of personality they have precisely because "they are bearers of the divine will, and yet they are fallible, *subject to misfortune and humiliation* [*Erniedrigung*]—and in the midst of misfortune *and in their humiliation* their acts and words reveal the transcendent sublimity [*die Erhabenheit*] of God. Humiliation and elevation [*Erhöhung*] go far deeper and higher than in Homer, and they belong basically together" (18; emphasis added). Humiliation and elevation belong together because they obey the principle of *Stilmischung*, or the confounding of stylistic categories that occurs whenever an overwhelming confrontation with historical reality is had.[35] We should beware of reducing Auerbach's biblical analysis to a simple analysis of style. His theory of style is, quite the contrary, a theory of reality (and historicity) as experienced.[36] And it is the Old Testament—and *not* the Christian Gospels, as is widely believed[37]—that marks the foundational moment in the discovery of these features of human, worldly, and earthly reality, and their concomitant principles of *Stilmischung* and tragic realism. (The odd excurses in chapter 1 on Goethe and Schiller's theory of the tragic, and on the "retarding" versus the "tragic procedure," which lead to the contrast between Homer and the Hebrew Bible, can be explained in no other way.[38]) Once Auerbach has put his finger on this radical convergence of styles in the Old Testament, he can rightly claim to have simultaneously located "the sublime, tragic, and problematic," which "take shape precisely in the domestic and commonplace" (*M*, 22). These features will reexhibit themselves in all subsequent literary history outside of the classical paradigm, and in all subsequent communications with the (historical, significant, and ethical) real—including, above all, in the Christian traditions of the West, where the same processes gather momentum.[39] Demonstrating this acceleration and intensification of factors that first appear in the Jewish tradition was the motive that lay behind Auerbach's writings on Dante, to which we may now turn.

Dante

In 1929 Auerbach published his landmark work, *Dante as Poet of the Earthly World* (*Dante als Dichter der irdischen Welt*).[40] The book's thesis, and its main provocation, is that Christianity in fact intensified the sensibility for, and attachment to, earthly existence, a fact that Christianity's core if legendary "myth" (11–12, 19)—"the story [or "history," *Geschichte*] of Christ on earth" (19)—both advertises and embodies symptomatically.[41] Hence the tragic realism that is distinctive of Dante's poem, and that also mirrors the tragic realism of the Christian faith, but which also reflects its "historical core" (11), identifiable in its two key elements: Christ's Incarnation ("the appearance of Christ as a concrete event, as a central fact of world history" [16; trans. adapted]) and his Passion (the suffering that this event produces). Significantly *not* the focus of Auerbach's attention in this theory are two further aspects of Christology: Resurrection and Ascension. These are not acts of concretion and they have no historical "evidence" in the two senses of discernible proof and, of equal importance, empirical validity. Auerbach's account has something of a manifesto about it.[42]

Auerbach is distilling a mixture of inherited views. To the problem of the historicity of Christ, treated in several studies by Auerbach's teacher Ernst Troeltsch,[43] Auerbach adds the crucial twist of existential agony. Christianity for Auerbach is essentially defined by a series of difficult traits, some of which are already familiar from the Hebrew Bible: doubt, dissonance, and torment (12); constant restlessness, irresolvable tension (*Spannung*) (13); and despair (13). Auerbach does not restrict these traits to believers alone; even "Christ himself lived in continuous conflict (*Spannung*)!" (14). Christianity shows itself to be the incarnation less of Spirit than of conflicting aspirations. These aspirations and passions are fully on display in the individual biographies that make up the substance of the *Divine Comedy*, each of which is endowed with as much concrete reality, development, and historicity as any individual from the Old Testament: They are thickly described. As in the Old Testament personalities, so too here: Their characters and actions reveal their fates. The conflicts and even the reality remain structurally the same (the European world continues to "think with" the Jewish Bible),[44] but Dante's naturalism renders the dilemmas all the more wrenching, rooted as they are in the sensuous particular of each given human reality, but also given the condition of urgency that is imposed on every individual by the prospect of sin and salvation. The result is an intensification, not transcendence, of the original dilemmas of the Old Testament. After all, "uncertainty"—or "insecurity" (*Unsicherheit*)—"in the earthly world is a Christian motif," Auerbach would observe in 1932.[45] The focus, in Dante, falls entirely on

> the narrow cleft [*Spalt*] of earthly human history, the span [*Spanne*] of man's life on earth, in which the great and dramatic decision [of a person's destiny] must fall. . . . The cleft is truly open, the span of life is short, uncertain, and decisive for all eternity; it is the magnificent and terrible gift of potential freedom which creates the urgent, restless, no less human than Christian-European atmosphere of the irretrievable, fleeting moment that must be made the most of. (*D*, 132; trans. adapted, emphasis added)[46]

As Auerbach says about the Old Testament, "doctrine and promise [*Lehre und Verheißung*] are incarnate [*inkarniert sich*] in [the narrative's stories] and inseparable from them" (*M*, 15). Auerbach speaks of promise, not of actualization. And the same holds for his analysis of Dante.

Dante's achievement was to capture this unsettled frame of mind through the compelling mimetic character that he gave to his souls, who were caught in the meshes not of redemption but of history. "Man requires a temporal process, history or destiny, in order to fulfill himself" (*D*, 85). The attachment to the world of the here and now is made stronger, not weaker, by this requirement. In Auerbach's view, Dante made two significant innovations over his predecessors, and these were linked: He "discovered" the individual living person while simultaneously "plac[ing] him in the realm of history, *which is his true* [*wirkliche*] *home*"; and he achieved a novel "vision of reality" (*D*, 178; my trans.). In contrast to the aestheticizing reading promoted by contemporary Dantists like Karl Vossler, Dante's vision was for Auerbach an agent of profound cultural change. The logic of his poetry led not to an embrace of transcendence but to "something new," an unprecedented sense of historical immediacy and a rich capacity for grasping human experience in its most vital if vulnerable aspects. As a result, Dante was realizing a potential within the Christian theological worldview that led to the dissolution of that worldview altogether. In Dante, "the indestructibility of the whole historical and individual man turns against [the divine] order . . . and obscures it. The image of man eclipses the image of God. Dante's work realized the Christian-figural essence of man, and destroyed it in the very process of realizing it." So Auerbach in *Mimesis* (202), reiterating a claim from his *Dante* book, where we read how in Dante and in his aftermath "history as such—the life of the human being as this is given and in its earthly character—underwent a vitalization and acquired a new value." Almost immediately, "the historical realm becomes a fully earthly and autonomous entity, and from there the fecundating stream of sensuous and historical evidence spills forth over Europe—to all appearances utterly removed from its eschatological origins, and yet secretly connected to these by the bonds that hold man fast to his concrete and historical destiny" (*D*, 178; my translation). This "secret" connection is no more the sign of a "secret theology" than are the bonds that link Christian and post-Christian realism to the Jewish Old Testament.

Contemporary reviewers like Vossler objected to this radical reading by the young Auerbach, and for all the right reasons.[47] On the one hand, Auerbach was using Dante to illustrate the inexorable movement of history toward secular humanism, a movement whose seeds he located in the very devotional poetry of Dante. On the other hand, he was painting a rather unflattering portrait of the anxiety-ridden Christian mind. Finally, he was underscoring how Christ's messianic project crucially *failed*. In Auerbach's words, Christianity was "a movement which by its very nature could not remain fully spiritual" and was "never fully actualized . . . in the world"—"all that was a lamentable failure" (*D*, 12, 13; trans. adapted; cf. *M*, 76: "such attempts were bound to founder"). This was the essence of the tragic realism of the Christian faith. De-Christianization (*Entchristung/Entchristlichung*) was endemic to Christianity from its beginnings.[48] And yet it was by means of its own internal paradoxes, or rather paroxysms, that Christianity helped propel the world forward into time and history. Christianity is for Auerbach a vanishing mediator.

Dante's poem is a conjuration not of Christian triumph, but of this very paradox:

> Certainly [the personalities in the *Divine Comedy*] are all set fast in God's order, certainly a great Christian poet has the right to preserve earthly humanity in the beyond, to preserve the figure [i.e., the historical reality of the person] in its fulfillment [in the afterlife] and to perfect the one and the other to the best of his capabilities.

This is, however, not what Dante did:

> But Dante's great art carries the matter so far that *the effect becomes earthly*, and the listener is *all too occupied by the figure in the fulfillment.*

> The beyond becomes a stage [*Theater*] for human beings and human passions. . . . We experience an emotion which is concerned with human beings and not directly with the divine order in which they have found their fulfillment. . . . The result is a direct experience of *life which overwhelms everything else. . . . The image of man eclipses the image of god.* ("Farinata and Cavalcante," *M*, 201–2; emphasis added)

By imparting *too much reality* to the individuals depicted, the figure "destroys" the divine order on which Dante's representation is initially, but not finally, premised (ibid.). The irony here is that in its representational effects, the figure destroys the process of figuration itself. The figural mechanism of the poem, premised on fulfillment, is broken: "The figure *surpasses* fulfillment," thereby negating not only the fulfillment but also the very concept of the figure (*M*, 200; emphasis added).[49]

One reason why Auerbach's figural reading of Dante is so often misunderstood is that his highlighting of the destructive character of figural reading is never appreciated for what it is, namely as an act of intellectual revenge by Auerbach on the attempt to drain the Old Testament of its reality and historical validity. He builds an irony into the very theory that he goes on to explicate. Historical reality cannot be erased, he claims, because this reality is the very premise that figural reading requires in order to validate its self-fulfilled meanings. The entire edifice of Christianity is built on this same paradoxical logic (the earthly character of the world is needed in order for the world qua earthly to be eliminated). But, Auerbach counters, not so fast: Just as you can erase a mark but not the act of erasing itself, so too figural reading cannot annul its proof texts. Figural reading turns out to be a frustrated and self-canceling rather than a self-fulfilling effort. History triumphs in the end. In a word, Dante's inexhaustible thirst for realism short-circuits the theological foundations of the poem and returns the poem to its origins in history, life, and human reality. What is more, in rendering reality in this way, Dante is reenacting the Old Testament logic that governs the mimesis of reality.[50]

As in the case of the Old Testament, God turns out to be but a "symptom"—now of the *Christian* poet's *Auffassungs- und Darstellungsweise*, which is likewise geared toward human historical reality, though the poet arrives at realism through a much altered filter now, one that passes through Christian eschatology and certain theological assumptions (such as Thomism). And while one might imagine that the individual characters and their passions undergo an equivalent transmutation in Dante's poem, Auerbach indicates nothing of the sort. On the contrary, their sufferings are filled with earthly longing, civic history, worldly political power, pride, and aspirations, paternal nostalgia for abandoned offspring, or simply love of life and "the sweetness of light" (*M*, 192)—this is the truculent "*vivo*" of the dead (*M*, 179).[51] Strikingly absent from their sufferings are all signs of Christian theological anxiety, even if the poem effectively reproduces the divided loyalties of the Christian believer in the very act of turning our focus away from the Beyond. Hence the "almost painfully immediate impression of the earthly reality of human beings" that the poem gives (199). This is genuine earthly passion ("preserved in full force"), however much it may represent a theological conflict of interests in a medieval reader's heart. The afterlife is thus converted into a proscenium (*Schauplatz*) on which to stage the this-worldly reality of emphatically "human beings and human passions" that touches "all earthly things" (201; 200), not only in the *Inferno*, but throughout the entirety of the poem.[52] In serving this purpose, the eschatological Beyond becomes the equivalent of a device or pretext, "a means of heightening the effect of [the characters'] completely earthly emotions" (200). And readers, drawn into a passionate identification with these recognizable earthly figures, soon forget the divine machinery that acts as their "setting," as the figures, charged with "actual historical events and phenomena" (197), become "independent" (or "autonomous," "*selbstständig*") of their otherworldly realization and capable of realization in themselves (202).[53] *Figurae* are de-figured by becoming, once more, the individual figures that they always were.

And yet if Christianity vanished in the wake of its mediations, the structures that brought it into being did not. These remain in place in Dante, who has inherited the Judeo-Christian traditions of realism (as Auerbach consistently labels these, as if to remind readers of the first half of their hyphenation) and has adapted them to his own circumstances. One such alignment is noted early on in "Farinata and Cavalcante," in an analysis of Dante's abrupt and dramatic scene changes, for instance when Farinata, introduced for the first time, makes his presence known by interrupting Dante and Vergil with a sudden intrusion: "O Tosco, che per la città del foco / vivo ten vai" ("O Tuscan who goes through the city of fire alive," *Inferno* 10.22–23), or when Cavalcante suddenly intrudes in turn on Farinata's conversation, introduced by "Allor surse" ("Then it befell," ibid., 52), thus "cut[ting] in two [*in zwei Teile gespalten*]"[54] a scene that has already been cut in two by an interruption (178), or when a shade suddenly looms into view in *Purgatory*: "—e l'ombra tutta in sé romita / surse ver' lui" ("—and that spirit, who had been so absorbed in himself, rose up [and ran] towards him," 6.72–73), and so on. Abrupt and emotional, such interruptions "rise from the depths" of the moment (178). They herald the "overpowering . . . irruption of a different realm" (the voice of a shade animated by *life*: "*vivo*," 179). They intensify the transitions from one scene to the next, punctuating the narrative flow like caesuras ("this abruptly interruptive and sudden 'then,' . . . *et ecce*," 180; trans. adapted). And they create jagged suspense ("the sudden breaking in of something dimly foreboded," ibid.). But above all, what these scenes signify is not the intrusion of a living voice from the Beyond, but the intrusion of a live presence, and indeed of Life itself, *into* the Beyond. It is the very intactness of the Beyond that is being interrupted. And at each of these moments the reader is likewise being interpellated by the poem in all his or her vital substance. The "overpowering . . . . irruption of a different realm" is nothing other than the irruption of Life into Death. And what it "forebodes" is the undoing of eschatological teleology.

To say that all of these effects stand in stark contrast to the devices of Homeric epic is to risk stating the obvious. But Auerbach takes that risk. In Homer, as Auerbach reads him, scenes are juxtaposed along a single plane through parataxis, creating successive foreground moments without any background (contrastive) illumination. These pass from one moment to the next smoothly, almost blithely: They are "connected together without lacunae" in "a continuous rhythmic succession of phenomena," each staged in "a local and temporal present which is absolute" (*M*, 11, 6–7). Such is the case with the narrative sequence that is triggered by the mention of Odysseus's scar, which Auerbach brings back to mind here in the chapter on Farinata and Cavalcante, only to label the Homeric sequence incomparable to Dante's: "Nor is this comparable with what we found in . . . Homer. . . . [T]here is no question of any parataxis in Dante's style" (178). By the same token, Dante's narrative sequences, lurching from one interruption to the next, recall nothing so much as the Old Testament narrative. The Old Testament, for its part, has none of the traits that are salient in Homer but all of the traits that are salient in Dante: ruptures on the surface intimating troubles and "unplumbed depths" below (8).

Nevertheless, while Auerbach's alignments are crystal clear, his arguments for them are less so. For one thing, Homer is typically understood to have composed his poems in a paratactic style.[55] Is Auerbach claiming the opposite and picturing Homer as a hypotactic poet after all, as his text sometimes suggests?[56] For another, what aligns Dante with the Bible is precisely the use he makes of interruption by means of "paratactic forms" (181), which also happens to characterize "the Biblical form of parataxis" (71): It is likely, if not certain, "that Dante introduced the linguistic maneuver of this abruptly interrupting [adverb] into the elevated style and that it was a Biblical echo for him" (181; cf. 185, 201; see below on "the Biblical *et ecce*"). How can Auerbach insist, then, that Dante's realism is biblical and yet not paratactic, as he does on page 178 of *Mimesis*, and as he repeats three pages later?[57]

The answer, I believe, is that Auerbach's logic is operating with a more complex theory of parataxis than is ordinarily assumed. He in fact recognizes *two* kinds of parataxis, or rather two ways of "exploiting the possibilities" of the same literary device (117). The one is inert, "flat," and superficial (as exemplified by Homer, later epic, the *chansons de geste*, and Boccaccio; 114–15, 117, 214), the other is dynamic, dramatic (a symptom of inner psychological conflict), and sublime (as exemplified by the Bible, Augustine, and in later Christian texts, including *The Song of Roland* and Dante; 70–71, 75, 100–1, 105, 109–10, 180–81, etc.). The former obeys the principle of *Stiltrennung* (stylistic homogeneity in the low register, here expressed through parataxis), the latter that of *Stilmischung* (the violation of stylistic purity through abrupt incursions of the low register into the high register, of biblical parataxis into classical, Latinate hypotaxis, and of tragedy into epic; 185). Once Auerbach's statement about Dante's use of parataxis is inserted into this larger context and rephrased, the thought becomes perfectly comprehensible: "There is no question of any *flat* parataxis in Dante's style," only an interruption of classical hypotaxis by biblical parataxis, exactly as is the case with Augustine (70). There would be more to say about Auerbach's complex approach to parataxis, but this is not the place to develop it.[58]

The resemblances between Dante and the Bible are explicitly drawn by Auerbach. *Allor surse* is a perfectly ordinary expression found in everyday life that is being put to extraordinary use in order to create "harsh" dramatic tension in an elevated style. The effect, Auerbach claims, is unprecedented in medieval literature. The closest analogue he can point to is found in the language of the Old Testament. And the example he gives turns out to be none other than the Binding of Isaac episode. There, a narrative rupture is marked by the parallel expression in the Latin translation with which Dante would have been familiar, "the Biblical *et ecce*": "When Abraham takes the knife to sacrifice his son Isaac, we read: *Et ecce Angelus Domini de caelo clamavit, dicens, Abraham, Abraham* [And the angel of the Lord called unto him out of heaven, and said, Abraham, Abraham: and he said, Here am I]" (180). The correspondence, Auerbach says, is "perfect": *et ecce* is the closest "equivalent" in Latin of *allor surse*, which "gives the full force" of the vernacular phrase; Dante's own phrase "corresponds perfectly with the elevated style of the Bible," which is to say, with the tragic realism that was first put to literary use in the Old Testament. Both moments mark an irruption of life in the midst of death. And so it happens that we are suddenly transported back, as if by a theoretical rupture of Auerbach's own making, to the opening chapter of *Mimesis* with its initial set of contrasts: Homer and the Bible. And once again, it is the Jewish Old Testament that proves its superiority. There, developments keep "emerging from the depths of the people of Israel-Judah" (*M*, 21–22), thanks not least to the "overpowering . . . irruption of a different realm" into daily life and the discovery of a sublime dimension in the ordinary circumstances of life. Dante's narrative logic, itself predicated on ruptures that emerge from glaring contrasts, produces "a mixture of sublimity and triviality," the latter reflecting the "humble realism" of earthly existence in its everyday manifestations, the former reflecting the otherworldly setting in which the characters find themselves (184). The characters address both Dante and the reader with a disarming immediacy, as if they just happened to be meeting on the street: "All these quotations, detached from their context, could well be imagined in any ordinary conversation on the familiar level of style" (ibid.). The resulting clash of styles, themes, and registers is "monstrous" when "measured by the standards of antiquity" (ibid.). But in every other respect, the effect is tragically real and incomparably moving—and heavy with equally "monstrous" implications for the Christian worldview. This is Auerbach's practice of "*in*comparative literature" at its best.[59]

The Old Testament in Modernity

In Dante, then, the Jewish Old Testament lives on: He has fully absorbed its structures and what Auerbach considers to be its most lasting lessons. That is why Auerbach includes them in his projects and aligns them in the way that he does. In both the Old Testament and the *Divine Comedy* we find the "overpowering . . . irruption of a different realm" and "the sudden breaking in of something dimly foreboded." But what sets these two texts apart is the source of this irruption. In the Old Testament, the interruption of daily life comes from God and his divine realm intruding itself onto earthly existence: "the sublime influence of God . . . reaches so deeply into the everyday that the two realms of the sublime and the everyday are not only actually unseparated but basically inseparable" (*M*, 22–23). In Dante, the interruption comes not from God, but from a human voice that is filled with earthly reality and that suddenly makes itself heard in the Beyond: The world of the here and now intrudes itself, strangely, onto the afterlife.

Both kinds of interruption are momentous. They create a powerful sense of depth and of "verticality" in the respective worlds that each text envisions. But there are inevitable differences. There is a "painful immediacy" to Dante's human subjects that strikes a jarring note in their otherworldly setting; they represent something like a resurgence of the real in the irreality of the Beyond. God's presence in the Old Testament, in contrast, produces a sense of remoteness, of unlocatability, and of hyperreality in a realm, that of the world we inhabit, whose chief characteristics are the opposite of each of these things (our world occupies the realm of the near, of the here and now, and of everyday reality with a lower case "r").

And yet despite the differences that set apart the biblical and the Dantean worlds, the final upshot of each kind of intrusion is in Auerbach's analysis remarkably similar: In both cases, the resurgence of the real, whatever its source, validates everyday, earthly, and historical reality. The Old Testament inaugurates historical consciousness, which in Auerbach's view means that it opens up the possibility of a sense, however enigmatic, of the particularities of life lived in all its richness and in its abyssal depths of yet unplumbed purpose and meaning. The meaning of existence is not something exterior to existence: It is generated in and by existence, or as he puts this in *Mimesis*, it involves an "order and interpretation of life *which arise from life itself*" (549; emphasis added). This is the notion, familiar from Vico, that history is man-made, as is its significance, with the all-important qualification that the act of interpretation is never final and never finished: The world remains a work in progress; it is not teleological. On the contrary, the world is the place where history is discovered for the first time, and where reflection on this possibility enters into the work of comprehending what this means in repeated acts of contact with the real and in a never-ending process of world-making. These moments of recognition, of what Auerbach calls "tragic realism" and "historical consciousness," can only ever be fleeting and provisional. They are what lie behind the notion that the everyday world contains unfathomable depths ("variations in the depths of everyday life," *M*, 33).

The Old Testament is the early pole in which these two forms of awareness arise. Dante is a later revision of the same structures of knowledge and feeling ("Dante's work was the first ["since classical antiquity"] to lay open the panorama of the common and multiplex world of human reality," etc. [*M*, 220]). But in fact, *every* work singled out for analysis by Auerbach, apart from Homer, reflects these things, which are fundamental even to our secular world today—namely, problems of meaning, action, and what might be termed the ethics of the real. And as it turns out, the project of

Mimesis was foreseen already in 1929 (I quoted only a fragment of this moving statement above):

> With the discovery of individual destiny, modern mimesis discovered the person. *It . . . placed him in the realm of history, which is his true home. . . . The immanent realism and historicism that are found in the eschatology of the Divine Comedy flowed back onto actual history* and filled it with the lifeblood of authentic truth. . . . Radiating out from here, *history as such—the life of the human being as this is given and in its earthly character*—underwent a vitalization and acquired a new value. . . . With Petrarch and Boccaccio the historical realm becomes a fully earthly and autonomous [*selbständigen*] entity, and from there the fecundating stream of sensuous and historical evidence spills forth over Europe—to all appearances utterly removed from its eschatological origins, *and yet secretly connected to these by the bonds that hold man fast to his concrete and historical destiny*. . . . Out of this situation there arose a whole new world of possibilities for genuine mimesis, but also grave dangers. To set these forth lies beyond the scope of this book. (*Dante als Dichter*, 217–18, corresponding to *D*, 178–79; my translation; emphasis added)

Mimesis takes over where the Dante book leaves off, or rather it completes the argument that is implicit in the earlier work and traces it back to its Jewish origins: Realism and historicism lie at the root of a secularization process that religion brings to *fruition* rather than hinders. And if these secular developments remain "secretly connected" to their eschatological origins, that is because the secular process reflects not a "secularization *of* eschatology," but a "secularization *by* eschatology," as Hans Blumenberg would later say (possibly with Auerbach in mind). These residual ties are not a sign of any lingering attachment to theology.[60] On the contrary, for Auerbach eschatology accelerates the pace of historical consciousness in the West. The conceptual structures of the past, including those of eschatology, are never erased, nor do they remain locked outside of time. Rather, they are folded productively back into history, generating a heightened sense of human time and its insuperability.

If Auerbach is right, then the same structures of thought that inhabit the Jewish Old Testament should have remained indelibly in place into his own day.[61] That this is in fact what he contends can be easily shown. It is, in fact, the ultimate theory that lies behind *Mimesis*, which makes the whole of that work into a study of the ineradicable *persistence* of a Jewish modality of thought—Old Testament realism—throughout the whole of Western literature, a survival that, Auerbach claims, is more significant than that of the Greek and Roman classical traditions that originate in Homer: "But the [Hebrew] Bible is written history; it was read or listened to by the vast majority of Christians. It shaped their view of history, their ethical and esthetic conceptions."[62] This is a highly provocative thesis, though it has not completely registered among Auerbach's readers.[63] Validating the lessons learned from the Old Testament and Dante, Auerbach concluded *Mimesis* with a chapter on Woolf and Proust that explored the continuities that ran from both of these historical predecessors right down to his immediate present in the modern and modernist era. We may conclude our own study of Auerbach with a brief look at this aspect of his argument, which will give us a good insight into the way in which the structural coherences that ran through both predecessors like genetic code were, in Auerbach's mind, carried forward into his immediate present.

Chapter 20 of *Mimesis* ("The Brown Stocking") is an object lesson in the way Old Testament thought has been translated into modern stream-of-consciousness fiction, as exemplified by Marcel Proust's "great novel" (*M*, 536) and, especially, Virginia Woolf's *To the Lighthouse*. All the elements of the first chapter are in play here again. The setting is informed by an utterly common, everyday occurrence: Mrs. Ramsay knitting, thinking and reflecting, measuring a stocking. Interrupting these simple actions are intrusions from without that are so sudden and jarring that they seem to be entering into the present from another plane of time and reality altogether, and in a valid sense they do—stray bits of conversation or judgments, fragments of a telephone call, typically expressed in free indirect discourse, as a stream of consciousness, or as private interior monologues and recollections. "Most of these elements are inner processes, that is, movements within the consciousness of individual personages," Auerbach says (529), although their source is not always obvious or marked. The narrative runs on between these "intervals," which it, in fact, exists to enable. Auerbach singles out one of these interruptions that appears to intrude on the narrative from outside its boundaries: "Never did anybody look so sad." And by an act of critical alchemy he elevates the phrase into an emblem of the whole that it colors. The comment "is not an objective statement" (532). "Who is speaking?" Auerbach asks. "Who is looking at Mrs. Ramsay here? . . . Who is expressing these doubtful obscure suppositions—about the tear which—perhaps—forms and falls in the dark, about the water swaying this way and that, receiving it, and then returning to rest?" (531).

The statement, and the voice, register a kind of "shock," and they appear to issue from "a realm beyond reality" (532):

> And in the ensuing passage the speakers no longer seem to be human beings at all but spirits between heaven and earth, nameless spirits capable of penetrating the depths of the human soul, capable too of knowing something about it, but not of attaining clarity as to what is going on there, with the result that what they report has a doubtful ring, . . . [one that is] "questioning and wondering." (532; trans. slightly adapted)

Whether Auerbach is justified in transforming Woolf's novel into this otherworldly dialogue is beside the point—unless by "otherworldly" we understand, as I believe we should, something like an alien-seeming quality that inheres in this-worldly reality itself, one that becomes available to us only in fleeting moments and then proves to be most characteristic *of* reality. What Auerbach has done, in fact, is to reread the novel through the filter of his own theory of tragic realism—a trait that, it turns out, is utterly characteristic of modern writers, for example, Proust, who "work[s] . . . consistently within the realm of the tragic and problematic" (27). But most immediately, Auerbach has created out of Woolf's modernist setting a retrograde scenario that returns us to the Binding of Isaac scene that was described in the opening chapter of *Mimesis*. Like Abraham and the readers of Genesis 22, "No one is certain of anything here: it is all mere supposition," an "enigma" that no one "can solve." What is this enigma? It is the source of Mrs. Ramsay's sadness (like a shadow that flickers, partially "hidden behind her radiant beauty"), and the source of the knowledge of it to which we are made privy without ever learning the true import of this information—we have at best a partial knowledge of the problem. Everything suddenly takes on a penumbra of obscurity. We are "transported . . . to an undefinable scene beyond the realm of reality" (532). Somewhere in the past, a telephone conversation is had, "evidently with reference to a journey they are planning to make together" (532). One is reminded of the journey to Mt. Moriah. "The time is not stated" (533). "The paragraph . . . has a concretely earthly but not clearly identified scene" (533), much like the location of the scenes from Genesis ("time and place are undefined and call for interpretation," 11). The voice over the phone has the same aura as that of Yahweh summoning Abraham. The "problem" that Mrs. Ramsay has become and everything surrounding her is radically "insoluble," "heavy with unsolved mystery" (533). In order to make sense of it all, we have to plunge deeper "into the depths of time" (534), but this only deepens the enigma without ever relieving us of the pressure to comprehend it. "These are the characteristic and distinctively new features of the technique: a chance occasion releasing processes of consciousness" that "winnows and stylizes the material of the real world" (538). The form of the narration is unquestionably new. But is the structure of the problem that is being presented new?

As the allusions to the Old Testament above suggest, there is much that is reminiscent of the earlier analysis in *Mimesis*. And as if to prove the point, Auerbach goes on to rewind, so to speak, the tape and to replay his contrastive analysis of Homer and the Jewish Bible. The scar scene is explicitly recalled in the sequel ("the passage on the tear," reflections from without about Mrs. Ramsay, and the telephone call form "an excursus of the same type as the story of the origin of Odysseus' scar," 538). And taking the place of the Old Testament, and specifically the binding scene and its true meaning, is the story of Mrs. Ramsay's enigmatic personality. The same contrasts are at work. And the same critical results obtain: The superficiality of Homer is foregrounded; there is nothing really in common between the style of narration in Woolf and that in Homer—not for the obvious reasons of genre differences or the remoteness in time and culture that separates the two poles, but because Woolf's is "different *in structure*" (538; emphasis added).

By the same token, despite the superficial differences with the Old Testament, we can safely state that the narratives of Woolf and the Bible are the *same* in structure, as are their representations of reality. Both open onto "the depths of time" and "of consciousness." Both turn on an unsolved enigma. Both are "attempts to fathom a more genuine, a deeper, and indeed a more real reality" (540), one that is "more real than any experienced present" (541) because it represents, in Auerbach's critical idiom, the irruption of reality into the everyday (there is not even a whiff of eschatological yearning here).[64] Both are examples of "the layered structure of a consciousness engaged in recollection" (a further trait Woolf shares with Proust, 542). And both involve a sense of reality's layered temporal and delayed, even enigmatic, quality—the ingredients of not only of individual or artistic, but of genuine historical consciousness, in other words (547). "Never satisfied" doubts swirl around such moments: They are frustrated by the search for the "order [that] is ultimately hidden behind so much apparent arbitrariness" (544). The contingency of phenomena conceals a "more" and a "beyond." But the real source of the enigma is the fact that nothing is actually hidden: The "other" reality is in fact embedded in the reality of this reality, the reality of the everyday and of "life" (548; cf. 537). Following the clues to the beyond within, "one comes upon the order and the interpretation of life which arise from life itself," the "subject matter" of which "is our own self" (549). And so *Mimesis* comes full circle, back to its Old Testament origins, back to the search for meaning, for a self, and for an answer. The very search for these things turns out to be the common thread of Auerbach's study, and indeed of all his writings. Theory for Auerbach is never an end in itself: It verges on a kind of exhortative ethics of the real—which is why Auerbach remains the towering intellectual that he is, and a challenging model for theory in the present.[65]

NOTES

1. Erich Auerbach's *Scenes from the Drama of European Literature* (1959) was reprinted in 1973 by a trade reprint publisher and then again in 1984 in the Minnesota Theory and History of Literature series. The German edition of *Mimesis* (1946) was reprinted in 2001. The English translation (1953) was reprinted, with a new introduction by Edward Said, in 2003 and in 2013. A German reprint of *Dante* (1929) appeared in 1969 and again in 2001. The English translation (1961) was reprinted as a New York Review Book in 2007. *Literary Language and Its Public in Late Latin Antiquity and in the Middle Ages* (1965) was reissued in 1993. Further essays by Auerbach appeared in English for the first time in James I. Porter, ed., *Time, History, and Literature: Selected Essays of Erich Auerbach*, trans. Jane O. Newman (Princeton: Princeton University Press, 2014; rpt. 2016).

2. The most recent German collection of essays on Auerbach appeared in 2007 (Karlheinz Barck and Martin Treml, eds., *Erich Auerbach: Geschichte und Aktualität eines europäischen Philologen* [Berlin: Kulterverlag Kadmos, 2007]).

3. Erich Auerbach, "Walter Benjamin and Erich Auerbach: Fragments of a Correspondence," ed. Karlheinz Barck, trans. Anthony Reynolds, *Diacritics* 22, no. 3/4 (1992): 81–83; Martin Elsky, Martin Vialon, and Robert Stein, "Scholarship in Times of Extremes: Letters of Erich Auerbach (1933–46), on the Fiftieth Anniversary of His Death," *Proceedings of the Modern Language Association* 122, no. 3 (2007): 742–62. A new and more complete edition of Auerbach's correspondence is promised by Martin Vialon.

4. Harry Levin, "Two *Romanisten* in America: Spitzer and Auerbach," in *The Intellectual Migration: Europe and America, 1930–1960*, ed. Donald Fleming and Bernard Bailyn (Cambridge, Mass.: Belknap Press of Harvard University Press, 1969), 463–84.

5. Edward W. Said, "Introduction: Secular Criticism," in Edward W. Said, *The World, the Text, and the Critic* (Cambridge, Mass.: Harvard University Press, 1983), 1–30; Aamir R. Mufti, ed., *Critical Secularism*, special issue of *boundary 2: an international journal of literature and* culture, 31, no. 2 (2004); Emily Apter, "Global *Translatio*: The 'Invention' of Comparative Literature,

Istanbul, 1933," *Critical Inquiry* 29, no. 2 (2003): 253–81, e.g., 258: "Early comp lit was always and already globalized."

6. Matthias Bormuth, "Krise des Historismus und provisorische Existenz: Hannah Arendt, Erich Auerbach und Walter Benjamin," in *Hannah Arendt: Verborgene Tradition—Unzeitgemäße Aktualität?* ed. Stefanie Rosenmüller and Robert Furlong (Berlin: Akademie, 2007), 145–165; Jane O. Newman, "Force and Justice: Auerbach's Pascal," in *Political Theology and Early Modernity*, ed. Graham Hammill and Julia Reinhard Lupton (Chicago: University of Chicago Press, 2012), 159–180; Emily Apter, *Against World Literature: On the Politics of Untranslatability* (London: Verso, 2013), claiming Auerbach as an advocate of a resacralized "secret theology," the program of which was "to reconcile worldly 'reality' with messianic eschatology" (197, 202). For what is in effect a counterreading, see Victoria Kahn, *The Future of Illusion: Political Theology and Early Modern Texts* (Chicago: University of Chicago Press, 2014): "In Auerbach's interpretation . . . the *Commedia* performs an immanent critique of Dante's theology," and it ultimately functions "as an allegory of the production of secular literature" (78–79; the reference is to the "Farinata and Cavalcante" chapter of *Mimesis*). I regret not having known about Kahn's study when I published my introduction to *Time, History, and Literature*, where the identical argument is made. The net benefit of this alternative approach will correspond in part to what Apter nicely identifies as Auerbach's "ethical realism" (*Against World Literature*, 201), once we remove the trappings of "eschatology" and the "prophetic."

7. James I. Porter, "Erich Auerbach and the Judaizing of Philology," *Critical Inquiry* 35, no. 1 (2008): 115–47.

8. "The implication is that these things mark the limits not only of the realism of [classical] antiquity but of its historical consciousness as well" (Erich Auerbach, *Mimesis: The Representation of Reality in Western Literature*, trans. Willard R. Trask, introduction by Edward W. Said (Princeton: Princeton University Press, 2003), henceforth abbreviated as "*M*"; here, p. 33). By "these things" Auerbach intends the lack of appreciation for "everyday life" and its "historical background," as well as the shelving, and spurning, of all such considerations as too insignificant to register in literature except under the rubric of the depreciated "low style" (ibid.). Tacitus and Thucydides, both of whom are named by Auerbach in this chapter from *Mimesis* ("*Fortunata*"), are in this respect no more advanced or advantaged than Homer. Auerbach was well aware of how harsh his judgment about classical literature appeared to his colleagues; see his "Epilegomena to *Mimesis*" (*M*, 559).

9. Auerbach uses the phrase "Old Testament" (*Altes Testament*), following the conventions of his time, though he deliberately marks this document as "Jewish" (especially in *Mimesis*; see Porter, "Erich Auerbach and the Judaizing of Philology"), where today Jewish and religious studies favor

"Hebrew Bible." In what follows I will for the most part adopt Auerbach's phrasing in order to be consistent with his usage.

10. See Porter, Introduction to *Time, History, and Literature*, ix–xlv. The present essay represents a development of some of the arguments put forward there and in "Erich Auerbach and the Judaizing of Philology." Said locates a similar mix of Jewishness founded in "pride and defiance" but not in religious belief in Sigmund Freud (Edward W. Said, *Freud and the Non-European*, introduction by Christopher Bollas, response by Jacqueline Rose [London: Verso. 2003], 31). "Jewish philology" (my coinage) is a particularly apt counterpart to what Nietzsche exposes under the rubric of "Christian philology" (*die Philologie des Christenthums*) in *Daybreak* §84, namely the extravagant attempts by Christian theologians, from the time of early Christianity into his own day, to de-Judaize the Old Testament.

11. Auerbach's view here is influenced by Vico's theory of human *poiesis*, which is in no way restricted to poetry, because it refers to "le modificazioni della nostra medesima mente umana [the modifications of our own human mind]" (a formula that is quoted like a refrain in Auerbach's various essays on Vico; see, for example, Porter, ed., *Time, History, and Literature*, 31n19, 32, 40, 53).

12. Cf. Eric Downing, *Double Exposures: Repetition and Realism in Nineteenth-Century German Fiction* (Stanford: Stanford University Press, 2000) for a trenchant critique of conventional views of realism in literature.

13. References to the German original are to Erich Auerbach, *Mimesis: Dargestellte Wirklichkeit in der abendländischen Literatur*, 3rd ed. (Bern: A. Francke, 1964).

14. See *M*, 73, for the reminder that Isaac's binding was standardly taken by Christian apologists to prefigure the Crucifixion. The episode from the Bible was so disturbing to contemporary German apologists that it had to be banished from the classroom—unless the Old Testament could be banished altogether. See Porter, "Erich Auerbach and the Judaizing of Philology," 122–23, and id., "Disfigurations: Erich Auerbach's Theory of *Figura*," *Critical Inquiry* 44, no. 1 (2017): 80–113.

15. "God gives his command in direct discourse, but he leaves his motives and his purpose unexpressed" (*M*, 11).

16. In contrast to Homer, the Old Testament's meanings, like the psychological states that it also describes, are of a *hintergründigen oder sogar abgründigen Charakters*: their "depth of background is veritably abysmal" (*M*, 12).

17. Auerbach, "*Figura*" (1938), in *Time, History, and Literature*, ed. Porter, 65–113.

18. On Auerbach and Marcionism, see Porter, "Erich Auerbach and the Judaizing of Philology," 125, and Porter, "Disfigurations," 86–87 and 104–5.

19. Edward Said, introduction to Auerbach, *Mimesis*, xii; emphasis added. Similarly, David Dawson, *Christian Figural Reading and the Fashioning of Identity* (Berkeley: University of California Press, 2002): "Auerbach argues that ancient Christian figural readers . . . preserved the historicity of biblical figures"; cf. 110: "the Jewish character of the text endured, preserved through figural reading." Dawson further states that figural reading for Auerbach does not "*inevitably* dissolve the sensible character of [the] figure," and with that its validity (91; emphasis added). Both claims are wrong. Simply to create a "figure" out of an Old Testament narrative element is to hypostasize and devalue that element. It is inherently destructive of the proof text: "The old Law [the Old Testament] is suspended and replaced [viz., superseded] (*aufgehoben und abgelöst*)," and is deemed "pointless, even harmful," etc. (Auerbach, "*Figura*," 94).

20. Destructive not only of Jewish reality (*M*, 116, 119), but of the Christian idea of reality as well (see below in the text).

21. Thus, it cannot be that "Auerbach writes the history of *mimesis* as a story of the development of a specific kind of *figuration*" that runs "from the time of the Evangelists" onward (Hayden White, "Auerbach's Literary History: Figural Causation and Modern Historicism," in *Literary History and the Challenge of Philology: The Legacy of Erich Auerbach*, ed. Seth Lerer (Stanford: Stanford University Press, 1996), 132; cf. 137). On the contrary, at the core of Auerbach's project lies the phenomenon of *tragic realism* ("What we are tracing [in our study] is the combination of the everyday with tragic seriousness," *M*, 282), which originates in the Hebrew Bible and finally undoes and overcomes Christian figuralism. See further Porter, "Disfigurations."

22. Cf. *M*, 443–44 for a good statement of the connection between historicity and the depths of inner forces that work themselves out in "a more concrete and a more profound sense." Auerbach's gaze is always alert to the demands that attachment to this world makes on human subjects, who in a very real sense cannot help but historicize—make concrete, anchor, and value—their own experiences in the act of living them.

23. Thus, to state that "Abraham himself is wholly abstracted from the real world" (Apter, *Against World Literature*, 200) is to misgauge Auerbach's reading of this episode. It is also to impose, probably unwittingly, an unfortunate Hegelian reading on Auerbach. See Hegel's early antisemitic tract, "The Spirit of Christianity and Its Fate" (1798–1800), in Georg Wilhelm Friedrich Hegel, *Early Theological Writings*, trans. T. M. Knox and Richard Kroner (Chicago: University of Chicago Press, 1948), §1 ("The Spirit of Judaism"), 182–205). In this work, Hegel criticizes the Jews for having, precisely, only an abstract and alienated relation to reality and to God, a claim that Auerbach emphatically rejects. Hegel seizes on Abraham as the founding

figure of Judaism and its history. So does Auerbach, but in a completely different spirit.

24. Cf. *M*, 19–20, on the intrinsic complexity of history and its representation, which contrasts with the simplicity of legend and propaganda.

25. Cf. *M*, 11: "overwhelming suspense" (see n. 38 below) and 14: "The Biblical narrator, the Elohist, had to believe in the objective truth of the story of Abraham's sacrifice. . . . He had to believe in it passionately."

26. In contrast, Homer's poems are innocent of any kind of "anxious striving [*das gespannte Streben*] toward a goal" (*M*, 5; trans. adapted).

27. Contingency in this case is the product of an interruption within, not outside of, historical time. Cf. Taubes's thesis from the late 1940s: "Israel is the restless element in world history, the leavening that *first actually produces history*" (Jacob Taubes, *Occidental Eschatology*, trans. David Ratmoko [Stanford: Stanford University Press, 2009], 16; quoted in Apter, *Against World Literature*, 200). But the similarities end there. Taubes's view is resolutely eschatological and redemptive. Recent scholarship that presses Auerbach in the direction of eschatological thinking, however secularized, is misleading for the same reasons. For an attempt to de-Judaize Auerbach and to read him as a "Christian humanist" who privileged "Christian realism," see Malachi Haim Hacohen, "Typology and the Holocaust: Erich Auerbach and Judeo-Christian Europe," *Religions* 3 (2012): 556–87, http://www.mdpi.com/2077-1444/3/3/600 (accessed July 15, 2013). The reading proposed by Hacohen was already foreseen and refuted by Helmut Kuhn, "Literaturgeschichte als Geschichtsphilosophie," *Philosophische Rundschau* 11, no. 3/4 (1964): 222–48.

28. This last statement appears in every German edition of *Mimesis* (23), but for whatever reason it was omitted from the English translation by Trask, along with a few more lines of the original German text. The omission may be owing to an oversight by Trask, or it may be that in the English version Auerbach decided not to enter more deeply into the motivations of the redactors (as he does in the sequel of the German). It is unlikely, however, that Auerbach had second thoughts about his assumptions concerning the biblical redactors' being historians (he accepts their role on page 20: "the same [men] who edited the older legends"). These assumptions have been standard in biblical criticism at least since Spinoza's *Political-Theological Treatise*, which presumes that the Old Testament is a redaction by historians of a much later age (Spinoza, *Theological-Political Treatise*, ed. Jonathan Israel (Cambridge: Cambridge University Press, 2007), e.g., 127, 130–31). In fact, Spinoza (and prior to him Ibn Ezra, the medieval Jewish biblical scholar from Spain) notes the very same problem as Auerbach does and understands it in the very same way: "'Mount Moriah': That is, [as named] by the historian, not by Abraham," etc. (263; cf. 120 on Ibn Ezra). The same general view reigns today (see

John Van Seters, *Prologue to History: The Yahwist as Historian in Genesis*, 1st ed. [Louisville, Ky.: Westminster/John Knox Press, 1992]). It is worth noting that where Spinoza and modern biblical criticism take the contradictions in the Old Testament to be proof of the inexact transmission of the biblical materials, Auerbach takes these contradictions to be proof of the Hebrew Bible's historicity, or at least of its sense of the real: "The contradictions and crossing of motives both in individuals and in the general action have become so concrete that it is impossible to doubt the historicity of the information conveyed." That is "because the confused, contradictory multiplicity of events, the psychological and factual cross-purposes," are what "*true history* reveals" (*M*, 20; emphasis added; cf. ibid., 19: "a situation so *complicated—that is to say, so real and historical!*"). For a closely similar view of the birth of history by way of the Bible, see Yosef Hayim Yerushalmi, *Zakhor: Jewish History and Jewish Memory*, foreword by Harold Bloom (1982; Seattle: University of Washington Press, 1989), chap. 1, esp. 8 ("It was ancient Israel that first assigned a decisive significance to history and thus forged a new world-view whose essential premises were eventually appropriated by Christianity and Islam"), and 12–15. But Auerbach is not satisfied with a positive notion of "history," let alone with that of "universal history," unless these things are accompanied by a sense of realism and anchored in human experience. See Robert Alter, "Literature," in *Reading Genesis: Ten Methods*, ed. R. Hendel (Cambridge: Cambridge University Press, 2010), 17: The Hebrew Bible depicts "the tangled contradictions [and "complexities"] of living out a life through the cumulative vicissitudes of experience, [that is,] the quirky stuff of human nature itself, through which we are bidden to work out, however imperfectly, God's design on earth." Alter calls this kind of insight "existential realism," and he connects it directly to chapter 1 of *Mimesis* (ibid., 16–17). Similarly, Ron Hendel, *The Book of Genesis: A Biography* (Princeton: Princeton University Press), 229–41.

29. Erich Auerbach, *Dante: Poet of the Secular World*, trans. Ralph Manheim (Chicago: University of Chicago Press, 1961); "Montaigne the Writer," in *Time, History, and Literature*, ed. Porter, 207: "It is luminously obvious in his writing" ["Es strahlt von Evidenz"]. One might wonder how Rabelais makes it into *Mimesis*, Auerbach notes, because the calls of "deep feeling and high tragedy" barely register in his poetry, or so it seems. And yet this would be a misprision. For Auerbach, tragic seriousness does not form a contrast with comic, even obscene, joviality: These are manifestations of one and the same operation, namely that of an uninhibited "discovery" of life's teeming "possibilities" (*M*, 284). Rabelais's further qualifications for being deemed a tragic realist include his bold "un-Christian" temperament, his naturalism and "hyperrealism," and his capacity to transform the everyday into "polyphonic"

lyrical poetry (*M*, 276, 283). All of these qualities give us a better index of tragic realism than the nomenclature suggests.

30. See *M*, 187: "nowhere does mingling of styles come so close to violation of all style as in Dante." Auerbach is overstating the novelty of this violation. But his work is full of such overstatements, which need to be carefully weighed against one another. The Old Testament violation of styles is just as radical as Dante's, who merely reenacts the biblical model, albeit now in a postclassical setting. See *M*, 110 and text below. Auerbach may have borrowed the term "*Stiltrennung*" from his mentor, Karl Vossler, *Die göttliche Komödie*. 2 vols. (Heidelberg: C. Winter, 1907–8), 2:195, who also knows its contrast, "*Stilmischung*" (ibid., 234). In adopting the terms and transforming their meaning Auerbach makes them his own.

31. Erich Auerbach, "Romanticism and Realism," in *Time, History, and Literature*, ed. Porter, 149; trans. adapted.

32. "From the rule of the separation of styles which was later almost universally accepted and which specified that the realistic depiction of daily life was incompatible with the sublime" (*M*, 22). Homer is "closer" to this "rule" than is the Old Testament (ibid.). For a more expansive reading of the sublime traditions of Greece and Rome, see James I. Porter, *The Sublime in Antiquity* (Cambridge: Cambridge University Press, 2016).

33. See "Romanticism and Realism," 152: Balzac, the Romantic realist par excellence, "had no success in representing any actual freedom or true ideality" (trans. adapted); his actual object was "life" itself, which knows neither of these in any pure form. Such was "the modern European spirit's discovery . . . that reality itself is in a state of perpetual becoming, and that there is nothing but life [*Lebendiges*] all around us" (154). Idealization, by contrast, "takes us very far from the imitation of reality" (*M*, 136). Not for nothing is "the tragic and problematic" a virtual hendiadys for Auerbach (*M*, 22, 27, 72, 343, 354, 443, 481).

34. Auerbach at times signals this heightened sense of reality with the word *überwirklich*, as in his essay on Rabelais in *Mimesis* (e.g., *M*, 276, 284, rendered as "super-real" by Trask) and with *echte* or *wahre Wirklichkeit* ("genuine" or "true reality") in "Romanticism and Realism." Auerbach's chapter title says it all: "The World in Pantagruel's Mouth." (For a recent appreciation, see Timothy Hampton, "'Comment a nom': Humanism and Literary Knowledge in Auerbach and Rabelais," *Representations* 119, no. 1 [2002]: 37–59.) A similar point is to be found in Žižek, in a discussion of love: "'Sublime' is the magic *combination* of the two dimensions, when the sublime dimension transpires through the utmost common details of everyday shared life—the 'sublime' moment of the love life occurs when the magic dimension transpires even in common everyday acts like washing the dishes or cleaning the apartment. (In this precise sense, sublimation is to be opposed to idealization)" (Slavoj Žižek,

On Belief [London: Routledge, 2001], 41). The same principle applies to God's incarnation in Christ, which reflects a radical intrusion of the sublime into the realm of the ordinary (Žižek, ibid., 89), as Auerbach well knew (see his book on Dante). But here the resemblances stop. Auerbach adds historicizing dimensions, a tragicomic sense of surfeit, and a recuperation of Jewish sensibilities to the purely formal inversion that Žižek's theory seeks to explain along rather Hegelian lines. Thus, where Žižek posits a Christian reversal of Jewish sublimation, resulting in "the descendence [*sic*] of the sublime Beyond to the everyday level" (89–90), Auerbach has already accounted for this "descent" in his reading of the Jewish Bible, where it is first found and fully exploited, thus nullifying Christian triumphalism and supersessionism.

35. The point is made explicit a few pages later: "With the more profound historicity and the more profound social activity of the Old Testament text, there is connected yet another important distinction from Homer: namely, that *a different conception of the elevated style and of the sublime is to be found here*" (22). That conception is the one just described, and which involves simultaneous lowering (humiliation) and elevation (sublimity). See further "Romanticism and Realism," 146: "Realism . . . thoroughly and radically shattered the barriers that separated the styles." The violent mingling (viz., shattering) of styles just *is* what realism is and does.

36. Thus, like any writer, Dante "stylizes the material of the real world" in the way that he grasps it, rather than by means of his language (*M*, 538). Similarly, Rabelais and Montaigne celebrated "as much a style of life as a literary style" (*M*, 281). But there is nothing aestheticizing about this view of Auerbach's.

37. Cf. Terry Eagleton, "Pork Chops and Pineapples: The Realism of Erich Auerbach," review of Erich Auerbach, *Mimesis: The Representation of Reality in Western Literature*, 2003), *London Review of Books* 25, no. 20 (2003): 19: "Behind this realist mingling of styles lies the influence of Christianity. It is in the Christian gospel . . . that the affinity between . . . 'sublimitas' and 'humilitas' is first established"; and see Said's introduction to Auerbach, *Mimesis*, xvi: "Christianity shatters the classical balance between high and low styles, just as Jesus' life destroys the separation between the sublime and the everyday. What is set in motion, as a result, is the search for a new literary pact between writer and reader, a new synthesis or mingling between style and interpretation that will be adequate to the disturbing volatility of worldly events in the much grander setting opened up by Christ's historical presence." Auerbach couldn't be any clearer than he already is: "The conceptual pair *Stiltrennung-Stilmischung* is one of the themes of my books, and it has the selfsame meaning throughout all twenty chapters, from Genesis to Virginia Woolf" (*M*, 563; my translation).

38. "But here, in the story of Abraham's sacrifice, the overwhelming suspense [which is the mark of the tragic, not of epic] is present; what Schiller makes the goal of the tragic poet [namely, the intense concentration of the viewer, his or her utter involvement, in the face of a heart-stopping, existential crisis of a protagonist] is effected in this Biblical narrative" (*M*, 11; trans. mine).

39. What Auerbach is describing is less a shift in the conception of styles than a contrast between nonclassical and classical attitudes toward reality and its representation on the one hand and the changing dynamics of "realism" in literary expression on the other.

40. Erich Auerbach, *Dante als Dichter der irdischen Welt* (Berlin: W. de Gruyter, 1929). References are to the English translation, cited in n. 29 above (henceforth abbreviated as "*D*"), which renders "*irdisch*" with "secular," a much paler equivalent.

41. This is not well appreciated, but Auerbach is clear about the point. The historical core of Christianity is inflected with mythical touches—the "fantastical procession" of Christ to the temple, "and then the apotheosis, grounded in the visions of few men, possibly only a single man, a fisherman from the lake of Gennesaret." And yet, for all its power, this "mythologization and dogmatization" was unable to penetrate more than partway into the conception of Christ; it was blocked from full penetration by the countervailing elements of "dubiety, inconcinnity, and tormenting perplexity," which "perpetually erupt out of," and hence cast a dark shadow of uncertainty on, "the underlying events" (*D*, 11–12; my translation; Manheim's translation does not capture the forcefulness of the original). Myth eventually wins in the end: "The story of Christ became the formative myth of the peoples" in the era of European Christendom (*D*, 19; my translation).

42. Blumenberg makes an identical point (see n. 61 below). On this omission by Auerbach, see my introduction to *Time, History, and Literature*, xix–xxiii, xxxv. The omission is also noticed by Dawson, *Christian Figural Reading*, 98, though he offers a different explanation for it.

43. E.g., Ernst Troeltsch, *Die Bedeutung der Geschichtlichkeit Jesu für den Glauben* [*The Significance of the Historicity of Jesus for the Christian Faith*] (Tübingen: J. C. B. Mohr, 1911) and id., *Die Absolutheit des Christentums und die Religionsgeschichte* [*The Absolute Nature of Christianity and the History of Religion*], 2nd rev. ed. (Tübingen: Mohr, 1912).

44. Cf. *M*, 16: "Thus while, on the one hand, the reality of the Old Testament presents itself as complete truth with a claim to sole authority, on the other hand that very claim forces it to a constant interpretative change in its own content; *for millennia it undergoes an incessant and active development with the life of man in Europe*" (emphasis added).

45. Erich Auerbach, "On Rousseau's Place in History," in *Time, History, and Literature*, ed. Porter, 249.

46. *Spalt* and *Spanne* are closely related terms for Auerbach. Cf. *D*, 23: "The inner cleavage [*Spaltung*] of the soul . . . striving to master the torment of passion." *Spanne* recalls *Spannung* (tormenting tension within).

47. See Karl Vossler, *Deutsche Literaturzeitung* 50, no. 2 (1929): 69–72, esp. 70: If Auerbach were right, then "everything to do with the Beyond would be only so much glitter and glaze," useful for giving reality "a shining, ordered, and enduring look," but nothing more. Having made Auerbach out to be an aesthete, and having even labeled him a follower of the "neo-pagan" George circle (which Auerbach decidedly was not), Vossler declares that Auerbach's assumptions, which reduce Dante to being "only [*nur*] a poet of the earthly world" (72) and which "[have] no use for anything transcendental" (71), are "fundamentally false" (70). Auerbach would agree with the diagnosis but not the verdict. The criticisms of Hermann Gmelin, who reviewed *Dante als Dichter* in the journal *Die neueren Sprachen* in 1929 (vol. 27: 510–15), were in the same vein as Vossler's: "That is all historical mumbo-jumbo *à la* Hegel" (514).

48. Erich Auerbach, *Das französische Publikum des 17. Jahrhunderts* (Munich: Max Hueber Verlag, 1933), 46, 49, 52 (cf. 53: "*Entweltlichung*," "unworlding," viz., emptying the world of significance); "On Rousseau's Place in History," 247, 250.

49. A character's figural function dissolves along with its surpassing. Thus, Vergil is a figure—but of what? Merely of "the prophet-poet as leader-guide" in the other world (Auerbach, "*Figura*," 108). It is only logical that the figural function, once it recovers the full freight of reality that it always already had, should fade away once its historical reality (or founding antagonism and perplexity) is returned to it in the poem. Hence, "the historical Vergil already embodied the fullness of earthly perfection that destined him" to his figural role for Dante (ibid.). The net gain is zero.

50. *Pace* Dawson, *Christian Figural Reading*, a typical view. Albert Russell Ascoli ("Auerbach fra gli Epicurei: Dal canto X dell'*Inferno* alla vi gornata del *Decameron*," *Moderna: Semestrale di teoria e critica della letteratura* 11, no. 1–2 [2009]: 135–52), grasps well "Auerbach's thesis about the valorization of the natural world and of its realistic representations in the text of Dante," but then rejects it on the grounds that the *Commedia* refutes this very possibility (140). Perhaps it does. But in question here is not the correctness of Auerbach's reading but its place in the framework of time, history, and literature that he is developing. Auerbach's thesis about Dante and Christianity may be controversial, but no more so than his readings of Homer and the Old Testament, which I believe are designed to contest contemporary political ideologies and to put forward a more humane ethics of attitude and action.

51. Cf. Farinata's "love of life on earth" and his "belief in the autonomous greatness [*freie Größe*] of the human mind" (*M*, 177).

52. "What we have in mind is not restricted to Hell nor, on the other hand, to Dante's admiration or sympathy [for the individuals located there]. . . . All through the poem there are instances in which the effect of the earthly figure and its earthly destiny *surpasses or is subserved by* the effect produced by its eternal situation" (*M*, 200; emphasis added). "It is with the same power that Dante treats all earthly things of which he laid hold" (*M*, 200).

53. "What actually moves us is not that God has damned them [scil., Farinata and Cavalcante], but that the one is unbroken and the other mourns so heart-rendingly for his son and the sweetness of the light" (*M*, 200). "We experience an emotion which is concerned with human beings and not directly with the divine order in which they have found their fulfillment" (*M*, 201). Cf. 193.

54. See n. 46 above on this term.

55. See James A. Notopoulos, "Parataxis in Homer: A New Approach to Homeric Literary Criticism," *Transactions and Proceedings of the American Philological Association* 80 (1949): 1–23. As Egbert J. Bakker notes (*Pointing at the Past: From Formula to Performance in Homeric Poetics* [Washington, D.C.: Center for Hellenic Studies, 2005], chap. 4), Auerbach's position is strikingly close to Notopoulos's. But it is also far subtler.

56. Though the terms "parataxis" and "hypotaxis" do not appear in chapter 1 of *Mimesis*, they are plainly at work there, for instance on page 6: "To the word scar (v. 393) there is first attached a relative clause ('which once long ago a boar . . .'), which enlarges into a voluminous syntactical parenthesis; into this an independent sentence unexpectedly intrudes (v. 396: 'A god himself gave him . . .'), which quietly disentangles itself from syntactical subordination, until, with verse 399, an equally free syntactical treatment of the new content begins a new present which continues unchallenged until, with verse 467 ('The old woman now touched it . . .'), the scene which had been broken off is resumed." Note how hypotaxis serves to introduce a paratactic construction or scene, which then takes control of the narration. See *M*, 106–9 and n. 58 below.

57. *M*, 181–82: "However abruptly the events may succeed one another, we cannot call this a paratactic construction of style" (trans. adapted). Note that Auerbach is extending the idea of grammatical parataxis to include *narrative* syntax and "style."

58. I leave aside the further complication that hypotaxis also plays a role in Homer, as in *M*, 6: "Particles which express logical and grammatical connections are [never] lacking or out of place" within each epic episode. The result is a careful delimitation of each scene that can never be breached or disturbed (Auerbach uses the expression "*grenzen* [*sich*] *gegeneinander ab*"). "A continu-

ous and ever flexible connection [*Verbindung*]" of "uniformly illuminated phenomena" characterizes each of the episodes (6–7), which are strung together without perceptible gaps. But the overall effect is to retard the through-line, not to advance it or to give it dramatic tension or promote suspense (5): each present moment lives for itself alone, as only befits the conditions of oral composition and performance in Homeric epic, which is geared to entertainment (15). In other words, in Auerbach's Homer flat parataxis is the dominant ("predominant," 70, 241); hypotaxis is subordinated to it, subserving its functions, in particular the exclusion of dramatic interruption. In the biblical line of succession, as Auerbach reads this, dramatic parataxis operates in a dynamic, even antagonistic, interplay with hypotaxis, sometimes predominantly (70, 106), sometimes by providing a sharp climax (71, 182), but always by interrupting the narrative through-line. In the Bible itself, hypotactic connection is less supplied than it is intimated by divine vertical meaning (17 ["*ein Moment der* gedachten *vertikalen Verbindung*"])—a veritable subordination (cf. 15: "subordinated")! But note that this kind of hypotaxis is neither positively given nor "uniformly illuminated." Rather, it is *produced*, in language and for the reader, *by parataxis*, that is, by the way parataxis presents itself as a violent interruption. Interruption of what? Of something whose nature is never fully stated (hence, "*gedacht*," "thought" or "imagined"). Conversely, Homeric parataxis has its own peculiar but essential relationship to hypotaxis, as witnessed in n. 56 above. If this is correct, then we would have to say that neither parataxis nor hypotaxis ever exists in a pure form; they are both found only in paired relations, the literary effects of which map onto the two-sided history of realism that Auerbach's theory charts (23). Needless to say, this history envisages two corresponding uses of hypotaxis as well. With this knowledge, it should be possible to redescribe Auerbach's project according to the different and ever-evolving relations between parataxis and hypotaxis. Thanks to Vicky Kahn for asking a good question, which turned out to be devilishly difficult, and which prompted this brief excursus.

59. See Porter, "Erich Auerbach and the Judaizing of Philology," 120.

60. Hans Blumenberg, *The Legitimacy of the Modern Age*, trans. Robert M. Wallace (Cambridge, Mass.: MIT Press, 1983), esp. pt. 1, chap. 4 ("Secularization by Eschatology"), esp. 44 on the way Christianity "historicized" itself and in this way proved to be an essential factor in the general process of the production of the world *as* world (*Verweltlichung*, translated here as "secularization" and parenthetically glossed as "becoming worldly," 37). So close are the views of Blumenberg and Auerbach, one has to wonder if Auerbach is not in fact a silent partner in dialogue with Blumenberg. One clue that he may be is found in Blumenberg's discussion of "aesthetic realism," which is said to be realized in the Christian topos of Incarnation (ibid., 46). Blumenberg may

actually be critiquing Auerbach in this instance, but if so he has failed to see how their positions are in fact closer than he assumes. He also suggests what may be an overlooked source for Auerbach's thinking on this point: Franz Overbeck (ibid., 45). No doubt this line of thinking reaches back even further into the nineteenth century; see next note.

61. See Blumenberg's apposite discussion of Jean Paul, for whom "poetry as incarnation" means "not only the elevation from the natural to the realm of the ideal but also the constant exhibition of how the ideal cannot be realized," an ambivalence that is "deposited in the products of linguistic secularization" (Blumenberg, *Legitimacy of the Modern Age*, 109). And see Jean Paul (in his *Vorschule der Ästhetik* from 1804): "Poetry, like everything divine in man, is chained to time and place and must always become a carpenter's son and a Jew" (1.5, §22, quoted by Blumenberg, ibid.).

62. Erich Auerbach, *Literary Language and Its Public in Late Latin Antiquity and in the Middle Ages*, trans. Ralph Manheim with a new foreword by Jan Ziolkowski (Princeton: Princeton University Press, 1993 [German original edition, 1958]), 52.

63. His first reviewers were the most acutely aware of this thesis, and they objected to it. "Epilegomena to *Mimesis*" (translated in Auerbach, *Mimesis*, 559–74) is Auerbach's attempt to clarify his position against these objections.

64. Cf. Auerbach, "Romanticism and Realism," 147, where Auerbach's concern is the nineteenth-century realist novel, which participates in the same paradigm as we have been exploring in this chapter: "Here, everydayness does not merely interrupt tragedy. Rather, it is the very home of the tragic itself."

65. Thanks to the editors of this volume for helpful comments on earlier drafts, to fellow participants and audience members for feedback at the time of the original presentation of this essay, and to Bob Alter, Ron Hendel, and Vicky Kahn for feedback on the final version.

CHAPTER 9

Buber versus Scholem and the Figure of the Hasidic Jew: A Literary Debate between Two Political Theologies

Hannan Hever

I

In 1941, Gershom Scholem gave a lecture series in New York, which was later published as his famous book *Major Trends in Jewish Mysticism*.[1] He concluded the series with a lecture on Hasidism, the Jewish pietistic mystical movement that arose in opposition to the rabbinic establishment and swept Jewish communities through Poland, Galicia, and Ukraine from the second half of the eighteenth century onward. Scholem's historical assessment of the movement is arguably embodied in a tale he tells his audience, a Hasidic tale he heard from S. Y. Agnon, who two and a half decades later would be awarded the Nobel Prize in literature. The tale begins with the Ba'al Shem Tov, who was perceived as the founder of Hasidism, who, whenever he had a difficult task before him, would go to a certain place in the woods, light a fire, and meditate in prayer—and whatever he set out to perform would be done. It then goes on to relate how the next generations gradually lost the knowledge: first of how to light the fire, then of meditational prayer, and finally of the specific place in the woods—remaining with only one, but no less successful, mode of achieving a difficult task: the simple telling of the tale. "One can say," Scholem posited, "that this small and profound tale symbolizes the decline of a great movement."[2]

In the early 1960s, Scholem assumed the same position in his famous dispute with Martin Buber, in which he criticized Buber's modernist rendition of Hasidism. In effect, it was the Hasidic legend that stood at the heart of their disagreement. Scholem castigated Buber for ignoring the movement's corpus of teachings and for presenting Hasidism solely through the prism of its later tales, which were composed and written fifty years after the movement's constituting tales, and which Scholem considered the less prominent part of the movement's legacy.[3] In other words, Scholem chose to highlight in Agnon's tale the decline from the focused actual deed of the founder of Hasidism to the mere spoken tale, even though Agnon speaks clearly to the fact that "the latter [the tale] was as important as the former three," that is, going into the woods, lighting the fire, and praying. Scholem rejected the possible opposite interpretive conclusion—that of the theurgic importance of the tale, which, after all, achieved the very same actual result.

Buber, in contrast, praised Hasidic storytelling as a genre in and of itself. He did it first in 1906, when he published a selection of Rabbi Nachman of Braslav's tales in German, then through the publication in Germany in the 1908 of collections of Hasidic tales, *The Legend of the Ba'al Shem*, and finally with the Hasidic novel *Gog and Magog* and the anthology of Hasidic tales *Or HaGanuz* (A Hidden Light), which he compiled in 1924. Scholem, who, indeed, never denied the importance of the Hasidic tale, criticized Buber for his sole interest in storytelling over other types of Hasidic teachings and commentaries. It seems, moreover, that Scholem accused Buber of creating new versions of these tales, unfaithful to the originals.[4]

My aim in this essay is to read the Buber-Scholem controversy from a literary and political point of view. This may be better understood using Rivka Schatz Uffenheimer's claim that "one can state the essence of Buber's great vision of Hasidism as closing the chasm between God and the world."[5] This kind of closing the chasm has a significant political meaning. First of all we should take into account that debate followed the severe contradiction between Buber's opposition to establishing the State of Israel as an exclusively Jewish state and Scholem's support of the idea of an exclusive Jewish sovereignty. Buber held the anarchistic belief in the dialogical interaction between the Hasidim in their religious Eda (congregation, *Gemeinschaft*), ruled by the Tzadik (righteous man), as its sovereign. In contrast, Scholem supported the mainstream Zionist idea of establishing a Jewish state. As I'll describe later, this political opposition between two friends developed into a harsh political conflict between two kinds of political theology narratives. The debate between the two models of sovereignty—the anarchistic Jewish Eda versus the sovereign Jewish state—was transformed into a confrontation between opposite interpretations of the Hasidic tale narrative and its political implications.

In this context, it is important to note that Scholem clearly distinguishes between the scholar of philology and objective historian, on the one hand, and Buber's approach, on the other: between, that is, the *Wissenschaft des Judentums*, with which Scholem, most likely, affiliated himself, and Buber's combination of "facts and quotations as suit his purpose, which is to present Hasidism as a spiritual phenomenon and not as a historical one," of which Scholem accused Buber.[6] For all his criticism of nineteenth-century Judaic studies' apologetics, Scholem certainly saw himself as belonging to this discipline, which put a premium on comprehending historical phenomena in their historical contexts.[7] Buber, in contradistinction, is an intuitive artist-scholar[8] who adheres to the Nietzschean maxim of serving history only to the extent that it serves life.[9]

Nevertheless, it seems that although Buber's approach is phenomenological and Scholem's is historical, the two are not mutually exclusive, as Moshe Idel has contended. Both Scholem and Buber, in fact, "considered Jewish mysticism as a possible bridge between Jewish tradition and Jewry in the present."[10] A more apt description of this dispute would therefore be as one between two interpretive discourses: Buber, acting as a creative artist who has "not made use of a filter; [I] became a filter";[11] and Scholem, who similarly constrained himself, but within the conceptual framework of the philologist historian. The main issue is, as Laurence Silberstein puts it, "While Scholem related to Hasidism as a system of theological concepts, Buber viewed it as a way of life."[12]

In "Buber's Activity in the Field of Hasidism" (1949) Scholem charts the evolution of Buber's engagement with Hasidism. Scholem contends that Buber moved from rewriting Hasidic texts freely and artistically to a more "humble and less pretentious" treatment in which he bases all on the "holy anecdote" while disregarding the Hasidic teachings.[13] From a literary point of view, it becomes clear that the debate is over the evaluation of the role played by Hasidic literature in the history of modern Jewish literature. For Scholem, at the center of the modern Hebrew canon stand S. Y. Agnon and H. N. Bialik as classical Hebrew authors who bridged the gap between Jewish past and future.[14] The Hasidic tale as transmitted to us belongs to the past and has little significance in this canon. In contrast, Buber endeavors to incorporate Hasidic literature into the canon of modern Jewish literature. They also differ in their views of the tradition of the Hasidic tale: Whereas Buber reproduced and adapted these tales for a contemporary readership by translating, editing, and anthologizing them, Scholem emphasized the importance of the original texts of the Hasidic tale. Scholem, always careful to frame the dispute within the boundaries set by the academic historical discourse, demanded that judgment be limited to the original texts and to the real, concrete historical-chronological development of the Hasidic movement. He blamed Buber for ignoring the status and influence of the Hasidic teachings and for preoccupying himself with obsolete tales of bygone days with little significance for the canon of modern Jewish literature. Buber's response, however, does not merely state the opposite: He readily acknowledges that he is no historian and that his interests lie in the here and now. The neo-Romantic approach of his adaptations, he contends, aims precisely at enabling the Hasidic tale to continue and function in the very present as an actual and a concrete component of modern Jewish literature and culture.

This, then, accounts for the centrality of the Hasidic tale in Buber's thought. He acknowledges that Scholem's claim that the narrative is a later phenomenon in Hasidism is correct but dismisses his negative assessment that the tale manifests a falloff from the "driving force" of Hasidism. Buber, indeed, professes to have no interest whatsoever in the history of mysticism.[15] He praises the legends of the Hasidic tales, much like the Sufi and Zen Buddhist's tales (a comparison Scholem opposes),[16] as being at "the center of their religious-historical development." The tale is a special kind of mysticism: "The kind to which I point here is the one whose essence development can be seen most clearly in the mode of lived realization, and thus in that of the event."[17] Over and against Scholem's proclamation that his position is nontheoretical, Buber explicitly chooses an epistemological position. So, for example, he claims that the language of the Hasidic tales is not fiction: "It is foolish to protest that the legend does not convey to us the reality of Hasidic life. Naturally, the legend is no chronicle, but it is truer than the chronicle for those who know how to read it."[18]

That Buber never concealed his—sometimes dramatic—intervention-by-adaptation suggests that the appearance of the debate as a solely academic one is misleading. It reveals this emotionally charged dispute, which some consider to be one of the most important debates in Jewish studies in the twentieth century, as a sharp political struggle, which feeds on Buber's decision to print the Hasidic tale in a new form.

My central point is that through the discussion of literature, Buber and Scholem negotiate the central political question that has been troubling

Jews since the eighteenth century, namely, that of Jewish sovereignty. It is the question of what modern Jews are and how they could become sovereign agents, in charge of their fate, while belonging to a people that lacks national sovereignty and which exists as a liminal political subject. It is further the question of how modern Jews can negotiate their presence as Jews, especially in the European public sphere, which was and still is, essentially, a Christian sphere. Ultimately, the Scholem-Buber dispute addresses the open and visible conflict modern Jews face as they endeavor in their encounter with Europe to reconcile the universalistic aspiration for emancipation and the particular loyalty to their Jewish identity.

I wish to claim that the dispute between Scholem and Buber about the correct mode of reproduction of the Hasidic tale, as well as the debate whether Buber's rendition of Hasidism indeed represents historic Hasidism is, in fact, a political confrontation between two divergent conceptions of the essence of Jewish sovereignty. The debate is over the desired political identity of the modern Jewish subject, whom the neo-Romantic Buber casts in the figure of the Hasid.[19] It is based on the understanding that the Jewish aspiration to citizenship, inasmuch as it entails the participation in modern sovereignty by Jews *as Jews*, cannot be separated from its theological foundation. On one crucial level, though, this theopolitical debate did not pit two diametrically opposed views:[20] Scholem and Buber both claimed that political theology is a national theology, that is, Zionism. Both believed that Zionism offers modern Jews a territorial alternative of self-emancipation from European colonialism.[21] But still, there was a big difference between their Zionist perspectives. Unlike Buber, who continued to believe that the best solution to the Jewish-Arab question would be to establish a binational state based on shared sovereignty, Scholem, who had maintained such a political position, changed his mind and became a supporter of the Jewish sovereignty of the Jewish state.

We can rephrase, then, the Buber-Scholem debate as one between two opposed readings of the role of the Hasidic tale in Zionist literature. Scholem believed these tales to be part of history, memory traces that allow the historian to reconstruct the past. Buber, for his part, believed in the actual, immediate role the Hasidic tale has in reviving the Jewish people and in presenting it with a political and social model for a modern Jewish community. Hence also the opposing meanings extracted from Agnon's tale: Whereas for Scholem the tale relates to past occurrences and tradition and charts the decline of Hasidism, Buber underscores that the tale "was as important as the former three" acts. As Buber would have it, the actual, material telling of the tale, itself a reconstruction of a set of articulations, performs a political act that constitutes the present-day "us," to which Agnon refers in the tale as "all that remained with *us* today from all this."

2

For Buber, the figure of the Hasidic Jew, whether in the guise of what he called "the simple man" or that of the Tzadik, the leader of the Hasidic congregation who mediates between believers and the Lord, lives a life of responsibility. The ultimate expression of this responsibility is the commitment to interpret the world anew in each and every moment: "In the place of esoterically regulated mediations has stepped the unprescribable endowing of each action with a strength of intention arising ever again from the moment."[22] Responsibility as manifested in the act of interpretation ties Buber to the figure of the Hasid that he lionizes.[23]

Scholem stresses this point in his critique of Buber. Buber, according to Scholem, opines that the responsibility of a Hasidic person is immeasurably more important than the dogmatic formulas of the religion, with its ossified institutions.[24] Scholem then lambastes Buber for replacing "the ideal of the Kabbalist, who knows supreme knowledge and is privy to the secrets of the mysteries of God, with the ideal of the simple man." Yet immediately after contending that the simple man is not the paragon of Hasidism, Scholem admits that, "Hasidism tirelessly reiterates . . . the mutual link between the holistic man, the man of spirituality . . . and simple men, men of materialism."[25]

For Buber, the responsible connection of the Hasid to the Hasidic sacred congregation is a real connection to the immanently sacred concrete reality. The Hasidic attachment to the sacred concrete reality has created a political movement that was based on the political theology of the Tzadik as the master of the Hasidic Eda.

Indeed, Buber asserts that the term "Goy Kadosh" ("Holy Nation"), the term used in the covenant between God and his people (Exodus 19:6), already states the theopolitical bodily commitment to God[26] that is expressed in the sanctification of the concrete and the corporeal in Hasidism. In this respect Hasidism is a suitable foundation for Buber's political theology, which is based on the biblical sovereignty of God in the Kingdom of Heaven. Paul Mendes-Flohr reads this as criticism of political messianism in favor of the elevation of the daily and the concrete, which he detects in the anti-apocalypse in *Gog and Magog*, Buber's Hasidic novel. Buber, who confronted the eschatological Sabbatean messianism, saw in Hasidism redemption through daily moral force and in that he was party to Scholem's assertion that messianism has been neutralized in Hasidism.[27]

But in contrast to Buber's divine sovereignty Scholem represents the notion of the sovereignty of the Jewish human being. Here one must note how Zionism tied itself to Schmittian theology from 1942 on. After the Reichstag Fire on February 27, 1933, Germany initiated a Jewish state of emergency by declaration of the Nazi sovereign; it was a state of exception that subjected Jews, the mentally ill and challenged, homosexuals, and Roma to the Schmittian apparatus, which excluded them from the protection of the law and marked them as enemies of the state. The Zionist response to the Nazi state of emergency as proclaimed in the Biltmore Program on May 11, 1942, was, consequently, articulated in Schmittian terms: The plan amounted to the constitution of a sovereign of the future Jewish state, declared a state of emergency, and proclaimed the obligation to protect its Jewish subjects.

The Biltmore Program became the central Zionist tenet, when the delegates of the American Zionists gathered at the Biltmore Hotel in New York. The aim of the Biltmore Program was to reformulate the Zionist policy in light of the urgent need to open the doors of Palestine to Jewish refugees escaping from Nazi terror. Following the false assumption that Palestine was deserted, the plan demonstrated that the Jewish people "have made the waste places to bear fruit and the desert to blossom." But in contrast to this assertion about a deserted Palestine the conference reaffirmed the Zionist position "expressing the readiness and the desire of the Jewish people for full cooperation with their Arab neighbors." The next paragraph of the plan points to the Balfour Declaration, which stated that the Jewish people were "to found there a Jewish Commonwealth." Using the Hobbesian term "Commonwealth," the text of the plan reaffirmed the Zionist's goal to build "the country, including the development of its unoccupied and uncultivated lands; and that Palestine be established as a Jewish Commonwealth integrated in the structure of the New democratic world."[28] Six years later the formulation of Zionism's aim was even more explicit: "We Hereby Proclaim the establishment of the Jewish State in Palestine."[29]

The Biltmore Program declared that the goal of the Zionist movement was the foundation of a Jewish State: a unique, exclusive Jewish territorial sovereignty that would exclude every non-Jewish inhabitant in Palestine from owning equal rights. This was exactly the content of Buber's reaction to the Biltmore Program in his article "Dialogue on Biltmore Program"

(1944). Buber's main thesis in this dialogue was that uneven citizens' rights in the Jewish state would result in uneven economies: "If two nations live in the same state and one of them rules the other, and if the ruling nation's productivity is manifestly greater, if their skill and activity in the world economy is manifestly greater, the other nation will naturally be reduced to the status of second-class citizens in the state's economy, one way or another."[30]

Scholem took upon himself the burden of national responsibility for the very existence of the State of Israel,[31] and adopted a point of view, that is, for all intents and purposes, similar to the model of sovereignty offered by Carl Schmitt. According to Schmitt, the "sovereign is he who decided on the exception,"[32] and who, in that state of emergency, acts without regard to the ordinary constraints of the law in order to preserve the state: "The exception in jurisprudence is analogous to the miracle in theology. Only by being aware of this analogy can we appreciate the manner in which philosophical ideas of the state developed in the last centuries."[33] In contrast to Buber's concept of God sovereignty for Schmitt the sovereign is a flesh-and-blood ruler whose power is analogous to God's; his authority is divinely sanctioned, and he is, in fact, an earthly substitute for transcendental authority.

As Christoph Schmidt, who highlights the parallels between Scholem and Schmitt, claims: "Scholem's political theology successfully ties theology to modern Jewish politics by the re-revelation of a religious hero: the heretic Shabtai—people like Shabtai Zvi, Bruchia Ruso, and Yaacov Frank—enables theology and the modern at one and the same time since he arises out of an internal Jewish process of secularization which can lead to a politico-historical redemption in a Jewish State."[34]

It is no surprise, then, that in contrast to Scholem, Buber opposed the political realization of the religious national vision in the figure of a single national sovereign.[35] He founded his opposition to the Biltmore Program on the claim that if "the purpose of the Jewish state is to grant one people the rule of the land there will be no other course than to turn the others into second-rate citizens within the state."[36] Thus, claims by the two rivals and many of their commentators notwithstanding, we find here an intra-Zionist dispute between two Zionist thinkers, who present two opposing Zionist political theologies. On one side is Scholem's political theology, according to which, similarly to Schmitt's political theology, the sovereign is he who declares a state of emergency and whose deed is analogous to a divine miracle—God at the foundation of the Jewish nation-state under Jewish sovereignty.[37] This is the reason why Ernst Simon, Buber's friend and student, stated that the critical source of their controversy (about Hasidism and about Zionist politics) was the very fact of the establishing the State of Israel.[38]

This is the place to emphasize that the main statement in the article that Scholem's political theology was a Schmittian political theology is a result of speculation. Besides Ernst Simon's comment on the opposed opinions of Scholem and Buber regarding the establishing of the State of Israel we have no document or historical fact that can prove that Scholem was Schmittian. Nevertheless, my argument that Scholem was Schmittian is based on analyzing Scholem's support for the political and the theological implications of the very act of the establishing the State of Israel. The main part of the argument is that the State of Israel was established as a Jewish state as a reaction to the Jewish state of exception that took place after the Holocaust and the eruption of the 1948 war. This is the reason why we can assume that Scholem's opinion was not so far from the famous Ben-Gurion formula that portrayed the establishing of the State of Israel as a messianic redemptive event that was caused by the apocalypse of the Holocaust.[39]

An intriguing example of the ambivalent and even supportive perspective Scholem had toward David Ben-Gurion is revealed in his participation in the meeting of Ben-Gurion with a group of Israeli intellectuals in 1961. The agenda of the meeting was the intellectuals' public protest against what they described as a nondemocratic political involvement of Ben-Gurion in the very hot and emotional political debate that then took place in Israel and which was titled "The Affair" ("Ha-Parasha").

The main issue in this controversy was the big question of who really gave the order in 1954 to a Jewish Egyptian underground to sabotage (the saboteurs were caught) American and British facilities in Egypt, which act served Israeli interests. Ben-Gurion refused to accept the conclusion of the government committee that relieved Pinchas Lavon, who served then as the defense minister. He insisted that the only conclusion he would accept as legitimate was that of a juridical committee, and he threatened to resign if his demand was not met. A group of Israeli intellectuals (Scholem included) met with Ben-Gurion after having published a protest proclamation accusing Ben-Gurion of violating the basic rules of democracy. The meeting was stormy, and Scholem was one of the main speakers. But what was amazing was that Scholem's political response to Ben-Gurion was an embarrassing mix of political criticism and many efforts to keep Ben-Gurion's political authority beyond any political controversy, sometimes even with a kind of flattery. But the most embarrassing part of the meeting was when as a response to Scholem's remark that he would love to accept

Ben-Gurion's offer to meet again with the group, he got a cold answer that was directed personally at Scholem: "I feel far from your life work." Scholem's response was (I guess without irony): "Thank you; you gave us the opportunity to talk to you."[40]

But Buber opposed the common Schmittian Jewish interpretation of the 1948 war and came up with the idea that "'history is not a sequence of the conquests of power and actions of power, but the context of responsibilities of power in time.' Buber criticizes Schmitt for defining political history in which 'there is no reconciliation, no mediation, no adequate expiation' of foes."[41] The following brings me to the completion of my argument by pointing out that the controversy between Scholem's and Buber's political theologies can supply a good explanation for the reason for their opposed perspectives about the Hasidic tale.

Buber held an anti-Schmittian belief regarding the Schmittian sovereign; Buber favored a theocratic sovereignty, in which God is the sovereign, and there is no mediator between God and the people. Buber developed his concept of political theology in his 1932 book *Kingship of God*. In this book Buber portrays the people of Israel as led in their holy land by God their ally, much like the flock of believers who follow the Hasidic Tzadik. In no way, shape, or form are the people a sovereign state, but rather a community of believers, led by the Tzadik, the charismatic Hasidic leader, a community that has merited the grace of God as their sovereign.[42] Buber bases his notion of the earthly leader on the biblical judge, who is a temporary leader, with no dynasty. His prime example is Gideon, whose famous response to the people's request that he rule over them Buber quotes: "I will not rule over you myself, nor shall my son rule over you; the Lord alone shall rule over you" (Judges 8:23). The nationality of the people is not exaggerated, but rather, as Buber says, the text recognizes the transnational accountability of the nation:[43]

> If the affinity between the people of Israel and the land of Israel should be understood within the category of holiness, then the meaning of the covenant between the people of Israel and their God, from which stems the affinity of the People and the land of Israel as a holy land, should be read as a clear theopolitical category. . . . Zionism is actually a movement dedicated to realizing the theopolitical covenant between the people of Israel and their God, which centers on the reformation of the worldly kingdom by the heavenly one.[44]

In the prophecy of First Isaiah Buber finds what he calls the "theopolitical hour," a time that demands a concrete political category of a messianic king in the Kingship of Heaven, which is ruled by God.[45] The political conclusion that Buber deduced from his own political theology was to repudiate the concept of a "Jewish state" and to propose a binational Jewish-Arab state. Buber objected to exclusive Jewish sovereignty and to any political decision-making that would be rooted in the Jewish majority.[46] He perceived the imminent nationality, established in the sovereign Jewish state, as excessive and based on distancing from the other and on cohesion derived from a sense of common threat that would inevitably breed militarism.[47]

Buber expressed his refraining from the political theology of the hegemonic Zionism when, from his actual Zionist interest in Hasidism, he wrote, "Our historical reentry into our land took place through a false gateway."[48] As early as 1944, in his reply to Baruch Kurzweil's critique of his Hasidic novel *Gog and Magog*, Buber distinguished himself from the hegemonic Zionist political theology: "What brought the book into being, after twenty years, was undoubtedly an objective factor, the current war, the international crisis, the terrible forces and false messianism at home and abroad."[49]

In contrast to Buber, who found in Hasidism a vital source for a binational and nonexclusive Jewish political theology, the young Scholem wrote in his "Zionist Esoteric" (private manuscript from August 2, 1918) that "it is impossible to renew Hasidism. The Zionist cannot be a Hasid."[50] But despite his early statement against using Hasidism as a spiritual source for Zionism, later, in 1932, with the publication of Buber's *Kingship of God*, Scholem sent Buber an enthusiastic letter in which he identified with the political theology of the book and stressed how vital it was to the very understanding of Judaism:

> As for your presentation of, and formulations about, theocracy and anarchy, I have read them with the utmost interest, since I have come to the same conclusion in my own studies. . . . The significance of this connection for *every* stratum of Jewish reality is incalculable, and I deem myself fortunate to have found confirmation of your testimony of this in such a prominent place.[51]

These were also the times when they both espoused, as Paul Mendes-Flohr describes it, the binational position put forward by the Jewish political group Brit Shalom in opposition to the positioning of an exclusively Jewish state as the final goal of Zionism.[52] Scholem, who was known for his anarchistic stance and also as a follower of Ahad-Haam,[53] objected to any and all kinds of state rule, and had never claimed that the State of Israel or, for that matter, any other political entity, could provide a clear solution to "the Jewish question."[54] But all this went through a dramatic change after the Holocaust and the establishment of the State of Israel in 1948.[55] Scholem then seemed to embrace the State of Israel as an attempt for Jewish intervention in history. We can assume that in the State of Israel, Scholem saw approvingly the intention to encounter the Jewish problem, an attempt that demands taking responsibility and even paying a price.[56]

Buber, in contrast, rejected the sovereignty of the Jewish state, and resentfully resigned himself to its establishment. Buber's opinion about the Jewish using power in the 1948 war can be deduced from his idea that

> God sanctifies the world through a call for taking the responsibility of holding power, and not for granting some degree or other of its possession. Power is not possessed, on this view; it is received. The materially power*ful* live on borrowed time; the power*less* shall return. . . . In the view from below [in opposition to Schmitt's enforced power from above], power rightly deployed not only makes for survival, but also enables the creature to aim for salvation.[57]

Buber insists that the 1948 war should not be interpreted only as a war for the survival of the *Yeshuv* but also as a spiritual event that has a lot to do with taking responsibility. According to Buber the Jews should take responsibility for the Nakba, and that this kind of use of power should take into account that "the powerless shall return." This is the reason for the striking fact "that Buber could not begin to imagine the destruction of European Jewry without recognizing the plight of the Arabs in Palestine."[58]

But after the State of Israel became a fait accompli Buber, who still resisted the idea of Jewish sovereignty,[59] continued relentlessly to demand publicly that the State of Israel enact its spiritual, faithful dimension of the Prophetic vision. Buber's famous confrontation with David Ben-Gurion can reveal his political perspective regarding the new State of Israel. This can be summarized by Buber's belief that the political theology dimension of the State of Israel should be based as an alternative to Carl Schmitt's definition of the political. Instead of the friend-foe formula of the political, "in Buber's thesis of *I and thou*, we may see that just as one cannot live without I-It (although lives without I-Thou relations remain I-Thou incomplete), so too the political state is necessary but not sufficient."[60]

Scholem presents a dual position. On the one hand, he opposes the kind of state established by David Ben-Gurion,[61] a state based on the Schmittian political theology[62] of a sharp, clear-cut distinction between friend and foe.[63] He censured, in other words, the kind of sovereignty that would turn

Arabs into the enemy. On the other hand, traumatically shocked by the Holocaust and overcome by the realization of a state of emergency, he also endorses Jewish sovereignty in the form of the State of Israel as a response to this state of emergency. This is the reason why, despite their political disagreements Scholem found himself, regarding the issue of political messianism, on the same page with David Ben-Gurion.

The year 1948 was for Scholem a political turning point, according to Simon's testimony; Simon was a friend of both Scholem and of Buber. It is well known that the 1948 war created a violent and implacable dichotomy between a friend and a foe as a direct result of the war as a state of emergency. There is no evidence that in contrast to Buber[64] Scholem ever spoke up either against war crimes, the Nakba, the expulsion of hundreds of thousands of Palestinians during the 1948 war, or the military government that governed the life of the Palestinians who possessed Israeli citizenship. Buber never accepted the Schmittian Ben-Gurion's statism (*Mamlachtiut*) and even confronted Ben-Gurion regarding this matter.

Scholem's reaction to Buber's Hasidic political theology is thus articulated within the framework of a discourse that is already framed by a sovereign Jewish state, constituted on theological foundations. Indeed, the fact that Scholem and Buber's heated dispute erupted in the aftermath of the Holocaust is crucial for the full understanding of its importance in modern Jewish history. I do not wish to claim in any way or manner that the debate over Hasidism, which I have framed here as a debate over the very essence of modern Jewish sovereignty, is simply and clearly a debate between the Schmittian Scholem and the anti-Schmittian Buber. Rather, my claim is that the concrete political reality of the time—namely, the declaration of a Jewish state of emergency and the establishment of Jewish sovereignty by the Zionist movement in response to the Holocaust—informed their discussion of Hasidism and set into motion the conceptual and political Schmittian apparatus within Jewish discourse. I agree with Noam Zadoff, who portrays Scholem's attitude toward Zionism as a despairing determinism that adheres to the Zionism of "no choice." Zadoff writes that as early as his immigration to Palestine in 1923 Scholem lost faith in the future of political Zionism as a real revolution in the spiritual and cultural life of the Jewish people. After the 1929 riots, he disengaged himself from political involvement, and his despair became obviously deeper after the huge catastrophe of the Holocaust.[65] I would suggest however that, notwithstanding Scholem's declared intentions, Zionist political discourse in the aftermath of the Holocaust still shaped his substantive political position.

Whereas Schmitt developed his political theology as an alternative to the weak liberal governance in the Weimar Republic, this same political theology helped Scholem respond to the state of emergency that annulled any and every law that might have protected Jews in Europe. The political theologian that he was, Scholem did not exclude the possibility of a theological basis of Jewish sovereignty. Unlike Buber, who did not believe the State of Israel could have religious significance, Scholem refused to rule out this possibility in advance, and even added that a secular Israel would contain a religious dynamic.[66] This reveals Scholem's ambivalence regarding Zionism's messianic politics. On the one hand, as is written above, as early as in 1929, he vehemently negated its legitimacy.[67] On the other hand, he argued that Zionism is saturated with theological meaning, and he especially claimed that the significance of the religious dimension of the State of Israel, which is in fact the messianic materialization of Zionism, remains an open-ended question.[68] So, although, in 1929 he resisted the concept of the Zionist movement and denied the right of Zionism to use religious language for political purposes, it seems that after the Holocaust, he found himself in a Schmittian political situation. Buber glorified the theocratic Hasidic congregation of dialogue, against Schmitt's political theology, and by so doing blurred, at such a critical time in Jewish history, the political necessity to respond to the Jewish state of emergency. Buber contented himself (for example, in *Gog and Magog*) with the critique of Nazism's false secular messianism,[69] and its sanctification of the state. He had, therefore, a complicated stance toward the founding of a Jewish state. Instead of focusing on its function as a Zionist response to the Jewish state of emergency, he was bothered by the danger that it would become a kind of a fetish and lead to a violent sovereignty. But indeed, "It is striking how Buber's critique of the overwhelming power asserted by Nazism, which threatened the demise of Europe, was translated into a critique of that asserted by Jewish nationalism, which increasingly challenged the viability of success for Jews living in the settlement [*Yishuv*] of Palestine."[70]

Buber's enthusiastic adoption of Hasidic theopolitics clouds the fact that, as Nitzan Lebovic shows, during the Holocaust Buber in fact changed his position. In the chapter "The Theopolitical Hour" in his book *The Torah of the Prophets* Buber adopted to a certain extent Schmittian terminology; and when he studied the translation of theological terms into the field of the profane, he even highlighted the need to clearly define the enemy and accepted the Schmittian stance, which defines the political as a contradiction between friend and foe.[71] Yet later, in 1953, in the article "The Validity and Limitation of Political Principle" he attacked harshly Schmitt's concept of the political.[72] Yet later, in 1964, Buber's reaction to the issue of the sovereignty of the Jewish state was formulated, on the contrary, in accordance with his anti-state political theology. In a conversation with second-generation members of kibbutzim Buber was asked whether one can draw from the Holocaust the lesson that a Jewish state is needed as a protection of the Jews. His answer, that the state has only sentimental, not factual, value, should not surprise those who are familiar with his political theology. The protection of the Jews by the state will never change Jewish history. We need a state, said Buber, not for the [dangerous] time of exception, but only for the real national development of body and soul.[73]

A crucial development in Buber's thought about Jewish sovereignty can be found in the way he dealt with the ethics of the state's practices of governance. He was critical of the establishment of the State of Israel, and then to the Schmittian totality of the political theology of the Israeli "statism" (*Mamlachtiut*), which was coined and implanted by David Ben-Gurion. Their famous confrontation took place in 1949 during the meeting of Ben-Gurion with Israeli writers, where he declared "The building of the State is above everything."[74] Despite Ben-Gurion's angry response to Buber's involvement in the discussion, Buber spoke about the necessity of a spiritual quality; he said that immigration should be selective and that the State of Israel should not be built on pragmatic purposes. From a political perspective Buber accepted the idea of mass immigration to the State of Israel as a reasonable move, but from the pioneering and the human points of view he doubted its value. Instead, he proposed the idea that the State of Israel should be committed to the realization of spiritual nationalism, which, according to his famous belief should be based on a dialogue between individuals.[75] As an alternative to the political theology of Ben-Gurion's statism, Buber, after the Jewish state had become a historical fact (despite his earlier resistance to its establishment), proposed what he called "the line of demarcation":

> A thorny business this is; but without it one cannot serve God in the [political] party, one cannot render Him in the sphere of political organization what is His, God's. What is at stake here is shown most clearly when the nature of the proposed means contradicts the nature of the goal. Here, too, one is obliged not to proceed on principle, but only to advance ever again in the responsibility of the line of demarcation and to answer for it; not in order to keep one's soul clean of blood—that would be a vain and wretched enterprise—but in order to guard against means being chosen that will lead away from the cherished goal

> to another goal essentially similar to those means; for the end never sanctifies the means, but the means can certainly thwart the end.[76]

Indeed, the updated political aim Buber formulated after the establishment of the State of Israel was based on a resistance to Ben-Gurion's secularism. Instead, Buber promoted a kind of theocracy in which God wants the people all over the world to acknowledge his kingdom. "God's demand of the people of Israel is that they subordinate all their public life in his kingdom. They should implement justice and truth in their relationships as a nation inside and outside itself. These values will be realized in the Israeli way of life, particularly in his way of life as a member in the society and as a citizen of the state."[77]

3

In contrast to the Schmittian sovereign, who reigns by the force of the analogy between him and God, Buber offers theocracy: the immediate rule of God. For Schmitt, the meaning of human sovereignty can be understood through his well-known assertion about the theological foundations of the concepts of the modern state:

> All significant concepts of the modern theory of the state are secularized theological concepts not only because of their historical development—in which they were transferred from theology to the theory of the state, whereby, for example, the omnipotent God became the omnipotent lawgiver—but also because of their systematic structure, the recognition of which is necessary for a sociological consideration of these concepts.[78]

This secularizing theological concept is the exact move the literary critic Baruch Kurzweil ascribed to Scholem.[79] In contrast, Buber's political doctrine of Hasidism replaces the human sovereign with "the principle of the responsibility of man for God's fate in the world"[80] This tenet, which stems from the theurgic philosophy of the Kabbalah, decentralizes one's role in support of God's sovereignty. The most prominent expression of Buber's model of sovereignty appears in his discussion of the prophet, who is the bearer of the divine word in the broadest sense of the term; the prophet is not only the "'bearer of the word in the vertical plan,' and, in fact, not merely from above to below, the bringer of a divine message, but [the prophet is] also from below to above."[81] Buber's concept of a decentralized, diverse, divine sovereignty seems to be a critique of the Schmittian notion of the sovereign (similar to the opposition arising from Foucault's critique of Schmitt in *Society Must Be Defended*). In the words of Paul Kahn: "That diversity could itself become a principle of unity—in both theory and politics—is not an idea that Schmitt could imagine."[82]

Buber harshly condemned Schmitt's concept of state sovereignty as early as 1936, in his article "The Question to the Single One." According to his opposition to Schmitt's definition of the concept of the political as an opposition between a friend and a foe, Buber asks Schmitt's fascist supporters whether the *option* of physical killing, of which Schmitt approved as part of the political is not, in fact, the *intention* of physical killing, thus pointing out that for Schmitt the political entails the destruction of one by the other and is none other than the result of God's veiled judgment.[83]

This political stance of Buber was criticized by Scholem, who displaced it to an attack on Buber's doctrine about relations between Kabbalah and Hasidism. Although Scholem agreed with Buber that, by revealing the Kabbalistic sparks that were emitted, according to Isaac Luria (the ARI), by the great cosmic rupture in the divinity, the figure of the Hasid holds an intimate relationship with that realm. But, still, Buber's political doctrine of Hasidism is different from Scholem's unified transcendental political theology. More specifically, Scholem takes issue with what he terms Buber's "existential" interpretation, in which existential dialogism precedes spiritual mystical unification between the I and God. Instead, Scholem offers what he characterizes as a platonic explanation, whereby Hasidism is "the law of fulfillment of the 'here and now.'"[84]

In so doing, Scholem understates the interests of his own research, which is, as Steven Kepnes has shown, an interpretation, and as David Biale has shown, a theological and dialectical historiographical position.[85] Scholem's interpretation of the writings of the Hasidim is dialectical:

> They do not teach us to enjoy life as it is; rather do they advise—nay, enjoin—man extract, I may even say distill, the perpetual life of God out of life as it is. This extracting must be an act of abstraction. It is not the fleeting Here and Now that is to be enjoyed, but the everlasting unity and presence of transcendence. . . . For in the very act of making the hidden life shine through, we destroy the Here and Now, instead of—as Buber wishes—realizing it in its full concreteness. . . . Moreover, the Hasidic conception of the ultimate realization of the concrete contains an essential element of *destruction* which I fail to notice in Buber's analysis.[86]

For Scholem, the Hasidic conception of the ultimate realization of the concrete contains an essential element of apocalyptic destruction. Scholem's interpretation emphasizes the violent apocalyptic confrontation between the host and full concreteness. In effect Scholem's analysis of this concreteness becomes similar to a Schmittian arena of violent war where the Hasid is willing to sacrifice himself by fighting against himself. But this sacrifice, which contains a messianic dimension, is an integral part of fighting and destroying Buber's concreteness as an enemy. As a matter of fact, Scholem accuses Buber of distorting the self-destruction of the Hasidic observer as well as the destruction of the object of his observation, because it did not fit in with the existentialist figure of the Hasid who bridges what Buber called "living in God" and "living in the world."[87]

4

The attachment of Hasidism to the concrete was for Buber the material basis for the constitution of the Hasidic congregation. This is exactly the "us" Agnon raises in his tale: a community based on faith and on God's rule. Above all, according to Buber, "What impels the narrator is an inner compulsion whose nature is about the Hasidic life, the blood-warm Hasidic connection of leadership and community [Eda]."[88] For Buber, the desired political regime is a theocracy, and the Hasidic tale relates the actions that constitute it. The political theology that Buber articulates is one of the collective consciousness of the Hasidic congregation. Since Buber claims that the central Jewish political theology tenet, according to Hasidism, is that "God and man do not divide the government of the world between them; man's effecting is enclosed in God's effecting and is still real effect,"[89] we can say that the very act of telling the Hasidic tale is an actual participation in the redemptive process. Buber thus places the Hasidic tale as the foundation of the Hasidic congregation, a modern political theology embodiment of the theocracy of "theo-political idea of a factual divine domination."[90] The profound Hasidic realization of an immanent divinity present everywhere is similar to the realization that what happened at Mount Sinai was "a royal pronouncement from above as an acclamation of royalty from below"[91] and coexists with it. Consequently, the Hasidic Eda is unlike the flock of Jesus' followers who, by saying "Give therefore to the emperor the things that are the emperor's, and to God the things that are God's" (Matthew 22:21), differentiates between divine sovereignty and secular flesh-and-blood sovereignty. Buber thus provides a political interpretation of Hasidism's divine ontology; and as a theocratic anarchist, who rejects the secular rule of the state and its laws and, in general, all forms of human rule, his interpretation insists that the sovereign cannot be a king of flesh and blood.[92]

Every kind of sovereignty is based on a narrative, and each one has its own way to tell and interpret its narrative. This is the reason why the question of sovereignty was the driving force in Scholem and Buber's debate. Buber's anarchist political theology is anchored in the Hasidic tale as a narrative that contributes to the cohesion of the small Eda. This is based on Hasidic narratives praising the Tzadik for his miraculous deeds that confirm his sovereignty, which relies directly on God. In contradiction to this stance, Scholem's concept of sovereignty is based on a narrative that tells how the authority of the sovereign is grounded in a Zionist political theology. This narrative portrays how the Jewish citizens of the Jewish state live their apparently secular life according to their religious identity.

The difference between Scholem's and Buber's perspectives regarding the sovereignty extracted from the Hasidic tale can be clarified through Agnon's tale that Scholem recites. The tale focuses on a series of material acts that establish a tradition which is then handed down through the generations, until it reaches the current stage, that of the material act of telling the tale. The very reproduction of the narrative is a material, political act, which touches on holiness. This act establishes an interpretive community of narrator and listeners and readers, of communication, where the narrator's strength resides in his hold over the state of affairs, his total control of the information and its dissemination. He directs the form of the text. He determines the themes and the strategies of their deliverance. Yet there is a great difference between the interpretive community created by the Hasidic tale, as Buber understands it, and the community created by the Hasidic tale as Scholem would have it.

According to Buber the interpretive community that has been established by the Hasidic tale is based on the figure of the Hasidic Jew, regardless of whether he is what Buber termed "a 'simple' man,"[93] or a saintly leader of a community, who presides over his followers' devotion to God and lives a life of responsibility.

5

Buber's understanding of the act of storytelling involves an explicit and even defiantly radical adaptation of Hasidic tales, which he chooses from a variety of sources according to his needs. Buber himself wrote about his adaptation of the Hasidic tale as transformation of a linguistically and structurally unrefined and unpolished tale to a crystallized and harmonious anecdote. He readily acknowledges his radical and in some cases even aggressive intervention in the original texts in order to create a new aesthetic object:

> After excluding the spurious products in which we frequently cannot find a shred of the original motifs, we still have an enormous mass of largely unformed material: either—and at best!—brief notes with no attempt to shape the event referred to, or—far oftener, unfortunately—crude and confused attempts to give it the form of a tale. In this second category of notes either too much is said or too little, and there is hardly ever a clear thread of narrative to follow. For the most part they constitute neither true art nor true folk-tale, but a kind of setting down, the rapturous setting down of stupendous occurrences.
>
> One like myself, whose purpose it is to picture the Zaddikim and their lives from extant written (and some oral) material, must, above all, to do justice simultaneously to legend and to truth, supply the missing links in the narrative. In the course of this long piece of work I found it most expedient to begin by giving up the available form (or rather the formlessness) of the notes with their meagerness or excessive detail, their obscurities and digressions, to reconstruct the events in question with the utmost accuracy (wherever possible, with the aid of variants and other relevant material), and to relate them as coherently as I could in a form suited to the subject matter. Then, however, I went back to the notes and incorporated in my final version whatever felicitous turn of phrase they contained. On the other hand, I considered it neither permissible nor desirable to expand the tales or to render them more colorful and diverse, a method the brothers Grimm, for instance, employed when they wrote down the stories they had by word of mouth from people. Only in those few cases where the notes at hand were quite fragmentary did I compose a connected whole by fusing what I had with other fragments, and filling the gaps with related material.[94]

Buber, then, not only rationalizes his editorial interventions in the service of his theopolitical ideas, but also endows them with an outstanding aesthetic splendor. Like Walter Benjamin's "redemptive destruction" theory of quotation, Buber does not act in order to conserve the reading experience of the Hasidic tale, but on the contrary: he takes the original apart, severs it aggressively from its original context, and produces out of it a messianic aspect,[95] which allows the deployment of the ancient Hasidic tale for actual political needs.

For Walter Benjamin, one does not portray the past in order to know it "as it was," but rather to catch memory as it flashes in a dangerous moment. In Benjamin's words the idea "establishes a conception of the present as now-time shot through with splinters of messianic time."[96] As Giorgio Agamben puts it in his discussion of Benjamin's philosophy of history: "By destroying the transmissibility of the past, aesthetics recuperated it negatively and makes intransmissibility a value in itself in the image of aesthetic beauty, in this way opening for man a space between past and future in which he can found his action and his knowledge."[97] It looks like this is what Benjamin meant when he wrote about the actual relevancy of the art of the storyteller who "takes what he tells from experience—his own or that he reported by others. And he in turn makes it the experience of those who are listening to the tale."[98] Buber likewise transforms the tale into an active agent of the national community, as the far-reaching adaptation of the original tale transforms it into a living reality, active and actual. In his adaptations of the Hasidic tale Buber basically invented a new figure of the Hasid that fit his actual political and spiritual interests. For this purpose, he severed the figure of the Eastern European Jew from his fading and destructed context and transferred him to the Jewish context of Western Europe and later of the Land of Israel. Steven Aschheim articulates this when he writes of Buber that "the emphasis on the legendary made it possible to dissociate the living Ostjude from the Hasid of legends."[99]

Buber's treatment of the Hasidic tale, however, contradicts itself. On the one hand, Buber tries to harmonize the new tale by using the quotations he pulls out violently from the original Hasidic text. On the other hand, he insists that according to his dialogical doctrine there is no solipsistic mysticism in Hasidism which involves, as Scholem explains, the destruction of the self, but only ethical and collectivistic expression of religiosity.[100]

In other words, it is the literary distortion and perversion, which Scholem condemns so vehemently, that lays the road to the truth. For it allows the modern reader—first the post-assimilatory Jewish reader from the beginning of the twentieth century, and later also the Hebrew reader in Palestine and in the State of Israel—to realize through formal aesthetic design the dialogue with the text in concrete, contemporary circumstances. This perspective is visible in Buber's remarks on Agnon as a modernist storyteller who is captured in "confused life" and confronts it as he who "conquers the disarray, even if there's no other more muddled in the entire world, until it stands in his tale like an actual existence."[101]

A no less important issue is the function of the Hasidic tale as a sacrament. Buber, who opposed the Schmittian secularization of the theological, regarded Hasidism as a political model that did not succumb to secularization. One can define the act of telling the Hasidic tale itself as a ritual that, in line with Hasidism, ties "life in God" together with "life in the world,"[102] that is, as a kind of a sacrament. He explicitly embraces the sentiment of the Reformation and announces his intention to unveil the truth behind the sacraments. Over and against what he saw as ossified Jewish rituals and laws, he set myth, tales that conceive every sensual happening as absolute divine happening.[103] Buber's mythical Judaism thus resisted what he saw as the stagnation of the official religion.[104]

Buber, who defines the Jewish myth as a tale that sees and describes a sensual occurrence as divine and absolute, finds this story in the Hasidic tale. According to Buber the practice of telling a Hasidic tale has a theurgic power.[105] But from a political point of view, it is clear that the very act of telling the Hasidic tale creates a community or congregation that can be perceived as constituting a theocratic sovereignty.

Buber's conception of reading clearly shows the influence of Protestant theology on his thought. In his analysis, the reader of the Hasidic tale does not occupy an inferior position vis-à-vis the authority of the sacred text, a position that would turn reading in effect into a sacrament. Rather, the reader is in dialogue with the text: He or she listens to its voice and implements in his or her reading the principles of Protestant philology, as Buber did himself in his and Rosenzweig's translation of the Bible. The reader should thus aspire to penetrate the *sola scriptura* (scripture alone) of the text, that is, its primal literal foundation, so as to put forward a personal and individualistic interpretation founded on immediate contact—without the intervention of the church—with the sacred text and by this with God, without intervention. Buber follows here his teacher Georg Simmel, who made the distinction between religion and (Protestant) religiosity.[106] Buber, in line with Protestant theology, underscores the importance of revelation and the presence of the voice of God. By this he opposed the catholic reading of the holy text, which fetishes the text itself and ultimately forgets or even dismisses the presence of the divine voice altogether. Still, Buber's literal reading that underscores the here and now differs from the resistance to the allegorical use of the original texts of Protestant philology.[107] Indeed, as the Bible for Buber is a dialogue between man and God,[108] so does the Hasidic tale realize a dialogic situation. Here, however, one should remember that Buber is not only the interpreter of the Hasidic tale, but also its creator. Translating the Bible into German, Buber and Rosenzweig, too, created a new text, which actualized a dialogue between man and God. In his handling of the Hasidic tale, on the other hand, Buber, under the influence of his Protestant conceptualization of the personal, immediate reading of the sacred text, went so far as to actualize the idea of literal reading, exempted from institutional mediators, and set himself and his very body as its sole filter.

6

It seems that Buber's Protestant condemnation of the sacrament led Scholem to charge him with ignoring the magical core of the pietistic movement and, consequently, with obfuscating the principles that inform the structure of Hasidic society. On his part, Buber never denies ignoring the Kabbalistic gnosis of Hasidism and justifies this by the necessity to select the elements most appropriate to rejuvenate the vitality of Hasidism.[109] For him, gnosis means hubris: gaining knowledge of God by ignoring the significance of faith and devotion. More than that, gnosis destroys prayer and real dialogue with God.[110] According to Scholem, however, one cannot distinguish how much of Buber's existentialist anti-Gnostic philosophy derives from Hasidism and how much of his interpretation of Hasidism derives from his philosophy.[111] In opposition to the theoretical and philosophical bent he ascribes to Buber, Scholem presents his own stance as nontheoretical. He claims that Buber's central interpretation of Hasidism shifts with the philosophical transformation between his book of *Daniel* (1913) and *I and Thou* (1923). It is a shift from mysticism to religious existentialism, and thus severed the earlier linkage to Hasidism. Whereas in his early writing, Buber linked Hasidism to Kabbalah, he later regarded Gnosticism in the Kabbalah negatively as separating the mystic from his Lord.[112] He rejected the ontological essence of evil[113] and the Gnostic claim to transform God's mystery to concrete knowledge,[114] with divine duality at its core.[115] Instead, he turned to the figure of the Ba'al Shem Tov, founder of Hasidism, as one who established affinity with God as an ideological "Thou."[116] Nevertheless, even though Scholem claims Buber wrong in ignoring the Kabbalistic source of Hasidism, he agrees with him that Kabbalistic Gnosis is not a creative foundation of Hasidism.[117]

Scholem was quick to point out that Buber accepted his view that Lurianic Kabbalah, the cornerstone of Hasidism, was a Gnostic thought model, but censured him for ignoring the Gnostic element, which, according to

Scholem, continued to undergird the Hasidic movement.[118] Within this framework, Scholem and Buber each chose a different period to identify with the movement's spiritual vitality.

On this point, Rivka Schatz Uffenheimer differs from Scholem. Whereas Schatz argues that, unlike Scholem, Buber is indifferent to the concrete, it seems that Scholem and Buber agreed that the relation to the concrete returns to its old form, but diverged over the route. Scholem proposes a dialectic path that involves connecting to the concrete, its nullification, and then its rehabilitation, whereas Buber rejected the negation entailed in Scholem's dialectic for a direct connection to the concrete through the sanctification of the deed.[119]

Rhetorically speaking, the *Aufhebung* of Scholem's dialectics pits Scholem's symbol against Buber's allegory. Unlike the symbol, which suppresses by the *Aufhebung* the act of mediation between the signifier and signified ("The Here and Now of created being is not identical with what shines through it once it has become transparent"[120]), Buber raises the banner of what he called the sacrament of Hasidism, in which the divine and the human do not merge (as in the symbol of Scholem), but rather interconnect.[121] In response to Schatz's claim that he closes "the rift between God and world," he accordingly emphasizes the presence of mediation: "It is not closed but bridged over, and certainly with the paradoxical instruction to man that he never again set foot on the invisible bridge and thereby make it real."[122]

Dealing with Spinoza as a predate of Hasidism Buber relates him to the Baroque,[123] which is known for its allegorical artistic style. On top of it, as recorded in 1959 in the diary of the philosopher S. H. Bergmann, Buber's friend, Buber told him "that he is moving farther and farther away from the symbol."[124] It is important to emphasize that Buber talked about a temporal process. And so, similar to the relation between Scholem's and Buber's above-mentioned views, the allegory is not the polar opposite of the symbol. The difference between symbol and allegory, as Paul de Man has demonstrated, lies in the temporal realm. Whereas the symbol is an immediate, momentary link between the signifier and signified, in allegory, they are left at a temporal distance from each other.[125] Scholem romantically views the symbol as expressing the ineffable and thus as constituting what he described as "a fleeting moment."[126] Conversely, Buber's allegory involves a nonsymbolic and nontheosophical connection with the here and now. As Buber puts it, it is not "that the moment becomes a mystical timeless now, rather it is filled with time: the fullness of time announces itself—not as a happening in the soul, but as a bodily happening in the world, out of the concrete meeting between God and man."[127] Buber's neo-Hasidism is based on an allegorical representation that opens up a temporal gap between signifier and signified. The signifier is read as an experience here and now, and so the gap between present and past is emphasized. In other words, the neo-Hasidic representation distorts and undermines the symbolic immediacy of the connection between past and present. In order to create the actual experience of the new and modern figure of the Hasid, the allegorical adaptation of the Hasidic tale orchestrates a distancing gesture that opens a gap with the past.[128]

7

The epitome of Scholem's objection to traditional Jewish messianism is his renowned claim that Zionism swept the Jews back onto the stage of history.[129] But, he also emphasized the movement's indecision as to whether it is a continuation of Judaism or rebellion against it. Although Scholem took issue with Zionism's attempts to nationalize Hasidism, his stance actually gave voice to Zionism's deep ambivalence toward messianism.[130] As a cultural Zionist who, by supporting the establishment of the State of Israel, became a political Zionist, Scholem interpreted Hasidism in a symbolic fashion that pointed to an element of redemption.[131] In doing this, he joined the Zionist mission of constituting a Jewish Schmittian sovereignty. His decision in favor of sovereignty is evident in his interpretive decision to adopt the symbol, which replaces the signified and creates an autonomous signification whose meaning is entirely self-contained in its own sovereignty. The fact that the symbol also tells a story of redemption makes the symbol a theopolitical figure whose articulation provides the narrator with the authority of a Schmittian sovereign.

Insisting on God as the only rightful sovereign, Buber, in contrast, formulates a national allegorical stance that rejects the notion of Jewish Schmittian sovereignty.[132] He indeed nationalizes Hasidism and considers it a messianic vision that would come to fruition in the Land of Israel.[133] In fact, Buber believes that if Hasidism were to join forces with Zionism, it would save the latter from following the negative path of other nationalist movements.[134] In the spirit of Hannah Arendt's claim that a Jewish nation-state would ipso facto exclude, persecute, and banish non-Jews from its midst, Buber opposes the mononational state as the embodiment of the national-religious vision.[135] As he wrote again and again, since one cannot separate Jewish religion from Jewish nationalism,[136] the Jewish national state will, by definition, exclude other religious minorities. Instead, as is well known, Buber, who harshly attacked the Biltmore Program with its unitary exclusive Jewish sovereignty, proposed an alternative concept of theological sovereignty which is based on shared sovereignty, namely, a binational entity.

The Jewish state is based on the symbol that creates transcendence for members of the nation, rendering them partners in an abstract community, whose goal is to connect with the concrete in order to transform it into an abstract. Allegory, in contrast, preserves the gap between the palpable and abstract, even thematizes and temporalizes it. For this reason allegory is not part of the symbolic narrative of messianic redemption in a Jewish state. Rather, as Walter Benjamin puts it, "In allegory the observer is confronted with the *facies hippocratica* [the dying's face] of history as a petrified, primordial landscape."[137]

Benjamin's view is indeed at the background of Buber's response to Scholem, which appeared in his 1963 article "Interpreting Hasidism." In this essay, Buber presents his entire Hasidism project as an effort to chart an "essentially different way of restoring a great buried heritage of faith to the light [by] recaptur[ing] a sense of the power that once gave it the capacity to take hold of and vitalize the life of diverse classes of people."[138] Buber's entire undertaking, then, is an allegorical expression of the destruction and the decline of the nation, which he sets out to revive.

8

Scholem and Buber radically disagreed about the historical significance of the Kabbalah, Sabbateanism, and Hasidism, and consequently developed two radically divergent versions of Jewish nationalism. Scholem viewed the Kabbalah and later Sabbateanism as levers for a messianic change in history and as precursors and forerunners of Zionism; he saw Hasidism, in contradistinction, as a conservative force, whose focus is the individual. Buber, on the contrary, rejected the Gnosticism of the Kabbalah and Sabbateanism, and deemed Hasidism a catalyst for national revival. Spurning the political Jewish sovereignty that derives from Scholem's messianic outlook,[139] Buber championed an anarchist-socialist-religious vision of a model society, a theocracy of devotional communities in the spirit of Hasidism, whose members aspire to a life of dialogue among themselves and with God. He felt that Ben-Gurion's messianic political Zionism[140] ran its course with the establishment of the state and the ensuing War of 1948, the triumph of which he viewed as the downfall of Zionism.[141] In its stead, he proposed an alternative messianic Zionism, which would find a community in which God shall reign.[142]

Opposed to Buber's religious anarchism Scholem believes that the tenets of the Hasidic ethos are not personally mystical, but flow from the wisdom of Israel, to which Hasidism bestowed a popular hue.[143] In his answer, Buber agrees with Scholem that Hasidism had become an ethos, but he reiterates his religious anarchism, and grounds the innovative lifestyle of the Hasidic community in his I-thou dialogue philosophy, which promises a dialogic unification among members of the Hasidic congregation as well as with God.

9

All this brings us back to the question of responsibility. In distinguishing between Kabbalah and Hasidism, Buber writes: "What Hasidism strives for as regards the Kabbalah is the deschematization of the mystery. The old-new principle that it represented is, restored in purified form, that of the cosmic-metacosmic power and responsibility of man."[144] For Scholem, Buber himself has to acknowledge his own responsibility for harnessing Hasidism to his spiritual needs. In this context, Buber's concept of responsibility appears to Scholem to be lacking, for it pulls out the Hasid from the world of the Jewish law and transplants him in the world of the form of the deed and its aesthetics, thereby eliding the content of the deeds.[145] This criticism, typical of the reception of Buber's Hasidic tales by Western European Jews in the early twentieth century[146] makes clear the reasons why Scholem belittles the importance of the Hasidic tale as the representative text of Hasidism.

Assuming responsibility, as Derrida argues in *The Gift of Death*, is an aporetic act, as the act that traps Abraham in the Binding of Isaac between answering the divine call and his obligations to his family, the perpetuation of which was promised to him by God.[147] For Buber, though, one is responsible to God to perform a worthy political deed, which is simultaneously a religious deed that sanctifies existence.

This issue of responsibility arises from Buber's theoretical discussion. From a literary point of view, Buber's theoretical position is revealed in his discussion of Sufi and Zen texts and testimonies. On the Zen texts Buber writes:

> There developed a class of literature altogether peculiar to Zen, the "Koan"—a word that is customarily translated as "example" but is more exactly understood as "demonstration." It takes the form of a concise report of meetings framed by introductory "hints," "elucidations,"

> poetically elevating "songs," and other forms. In the course of the "demonstration," a basic problem is stated, whether directly or not, that proves to be insoluble in speech. No sentence of the teaching is equal to this paradox, whose solution is found to lie in some essential attitude of the human person that breaks up all conceptualization.[148]

In other words, the tale is a pinnacle of theoretical activity, for reading it responsibly entails realizing the aporia that characterizes Buber's phrasing of the Hasidic anecdote. Buber claimed, however, that more than in Zen and Sufi fiction, in Hasidism, "the didactic character of the legendary anecdote"—trapped in an aporia between the oral tale and its written version—comes to the fore.[149] Buber contends that oral speech, "put forth as an indivisible part of the personal occurrence," must be saved "from the danger of translation in 'objective' concepts." Paradoxically, the solution is writing down the text; telling, after all, may "enable, over the course of the transmission of the tale, the penetration of elements that are not part of the original, and from the moment we realize this danger," he writes, "there immediately arises the desire to record it in writing so as to prevent any further corruption." Buber thus affirms that "the delay in putting it into writing, the delay in compiling, and even the delay in publishing the anthologies of mystical fables do not substantiate the claim that they should be considered a dubious source."[150] Thus, Buber, who aspires to give linguistic expression to the prelinguistic experience of revelation in the spirit of his *Erlebnismystik*, shows what David Biale describes as the "linguistic skepticism" of one who is well aware of the paradox that this aspiration entails.[151] Notwithstanding Buber's statement regarding the inevitable, transhistorical truth of the Hasidic tale, a position that brought him to belittle "secondary literary elaborations, which betray themselves as such at the first glance,"[152] he himself put a lot of effort in to adapt and anthologize Hasidic tales. It seems, then, that Buber's project of adaptation and anthologizing is based on aporia, on the assumption, that is, that the only way to retrieve the authentic tale is by its distortion. This paradox may also help us comprehend the theopolitical act of the Hasidic tale according to Buber: the simultaneous commitment to Zionism and to the Land of Israel and the repudiation of the Jewish sovereignty established there in consequence of the Holocaust.

10

Buber's theorization, namely his focus on the linguistic indetermination of the Hasidic tale, jeopardizes the glorious intellectual edifice he painstakingly erects. The political act that emanates from Buber's theorization as a translator of the Hebrew Bible and of Hasidic tales indeed entails a formidable risk that verges on the destruction of the stability of the political text. The linguistic indetermination of the reproduction of the Hasidic tale is an indetermination of its political meaning. In contrast to the total and fixed Schmittian concept of the political, which was based on a clear-cut dichotomy between friend and enemy, Buber offered the politics of dialogue. The danger of such politics comes from its potential to blur and by this to cover and to conceal power relationships of oppression and even of persecution. Buber confronts this political danger by the "line of demarcation between the lesser evil we are compelled to do (to the Arabs) so that we can exist, and the extended good we are commanded to perform in order to live the kind of life we strive for" as Jews in the holy Land of Israel, in contrast to any other land.[153] Buber does not perceive the Jewish settlement of the Land of Israel as immoral, but he does warn against the immoral way by which it was achieved and condemns it.[154] The theory which renders the conditions of political action difficult also constrains national aspiration to social rather than political existence. Buber's attempt to establish his treatment of Hasidism on the dialogue between I and Thou reaches its theoretical limits here.

The reading of the complexities spawned by the Buber-Scholem debate requires that we distance ourselves from what has become a prevailing view in Jewish studies, namely "the resistance to theory" approach. As Paul de Man puts it, it is the "resistance to the use of language about language."[155] This is the reason why it is important to pay attention to the theoretical difficulty presented by the dialogue. In their introduction to the *Theory after "Theory,"* Jane Elliot and Derek Attridge clearly address that difficulty, in their discussion of Eva Cherniavsky's contribution "The Canny Subaltern." Elliot and Attridge see in this essay an example of how "theory after theory redirect[s] our attention to the theoretical insights that . . . we forget at our political and intellectual peril." Studying the inner contradiction in Spivak's iconic critique of the status of the subaltern in postcolonial theories, "Cherniavsky suggests that [she] manifest a shift towards an attempt to learn from the subaltern that overlooks, without resolving, the problem Spivak originally pointed out: our inability to learn anything from the subaltern that we have not first imputed to her." This "still does not render subaltern agency legible within the spaces of the political."[156] Cherniavsky further writes:

> I am suggesting that what is irreducible to Subaltern Studies . . . is not the subaltern alterity, but rather the incommensurability between the terms of the investigator's analytic and the subaltern as "object" of investigation. . . . The statement "the subaltern cannot speak" is a report on the condition of the intellectual. The intellectual's privilege is her loss.[157]

I believe that these dangers may also lead to the opposite conclusion. The danger in theorization only illustrates the enormity of the responsibility that the political agent who is practicing theory needs to assume. This responsibility is taken by what Buber sees as a decisive personal decision to translate, to tell, or to write the Hasidic tale as a paradoxical act of telling. According to Buber, such a decision should be made by every act of reproducing a Hasidic tale and as a model for such decisions we should follow the Hasidic Tzadik. This is the reason that for the last word we can go to Buber's booklet *The Way of Man according to the Teaching of Hasidism*; Buber quotes the Tzadik Rabbi Zusya of Hanipol who said on his dying bed: "In the world to come I shall not be asked: 'Why were you not Moses?' I shall be asked: 'Why were you not Zusya?'"[158]

NOTES

1. Gershom Scholem, *Major Trends in Jewish Mysticism* (New York: Schocken Books, 1974).
2. Ibid., 22.
3. Gershom Scholem, "Martin Buber's Hasidism: A Critique," *Commentary* 32 (1961): 308.
4. Ibid., 306, 309.
5. Rivka Schatz Uffenheimer, "Man's Relation to God and World in Buber's Rendering of the Hasidic Teaching," in *The Philosophy of Martin Buber*, ed. A. Schilpp and M. Friedman (LaSalle, Ill.: Open Court, 1967; London: Cambridge University Press, 1967), 403–34.
6. Ibid., 306.
7. David Biale, *Gershom Scholem, Kabbalah Counter-History* (Cambridge, Mass.: Harvard University Press, 1979), 168.
8. Gershom Scholem, "Al Peulato Shel Martin Buber Bisde ha'hasidut," in *Ha'shalav Ha'akharon: Mekhkerei Ha'kHasidut Shel Gershom Scholem*, ed. David Asaf and Esther Libes (1948; Jerusalem: Am Oved & Magnes, 2008), 325.

9. Laurence J. Silberstein, *Martin Buber's Social and Religious Thought: Alienation and the Quest for Meaning* (New York: New York University Press), 57.

10. Moshe Idel, *Old Worlds, New Mirrors* (Philadelphia: University of Pennsylvania Press, 2010), 206.

11. Martin Buber, "Interpreting Hasidism," *Commentary* 36, no. 3 (1963), 221.

12. Laurence J. Silberstein, "Modes of Discourse in Modern Judaism: The Buber-Scholem Debate Reconsidered," *Soundings* 71, no. 4 (1988), 661.

13. Scholem, "Al Pe'ulato," 326.

14. Noam Zadoff, *Miberlin Leyerushalaim Ubehazara: Gershom Shalom Bein Israel Vegermania* (Jerusalem: Carmel, 2015), 48, 51.

15. Gershom Scholem, "Od He'ara Le'inyan Buber Ve'ha'kHasidut," in *Ha'shalav Ha'akharon: Mekhkerei Ha'kHasidut Shel Gershom Scholem*, ed. David Asaf and Esther Libes (1964; Jerusalem: Am Oved & Magnes, 2008), 354.

16. Ibid., 355.

17. Buber, "Interpreting Hasidism," 219.

18. Martin Buber, *The Origin and Meaning of Hasidism*, trans. M. Friedman (New York: Harper & Row, 1966), 27.

19. Christoph Schmidt, "Ha'teologia Ha'politit Shel Gershom Shalom," *Theoria Ubikoret*, no. 6 (1995): 153.

20. Idel, *Old Worlds, New Mirrors*, 206.

21. Amir Mufti, *Enlightenment in Colony: The Jewish Question and the Crisis of Postcolonial Culture* (Princeton: Princeton University Press, 2007). For an impressive (but different) discussion of Buber's political theology see Samuel Hayim Brody, "The Pathless Hour: Messianism, Anarchism, Zionism, and Martin Buber's Theopolitics Reconstructed," PhD diss., University of Chicago, 2013.

22. Scholem, "Martin Buber's Hasidism," 307–8.

23. Martin Buber, *Tikva Le'sha'a Zu: Sugiyot Me'inyaney Ha'ru'akh Ve'hametzi'ut* (Tel Aviv: Am Oved, 1992), 112.

24. Scholem, "Martin Buber's Hasidism," 315.

25. Ibid., 311.

26. Martin Buber, *Moses: The Revelation and the Covenant* (Amherst, N.Y.: Humanity Books, 1998),105–6.

27. Paul Mendes-Flohr, "The Kingdom of God: Martin Buber's Critique of Messianic Politics," *Behemoth*, no. 2 (2008): 29, 35.

28. "The Biltmore Program: Towards a Jewish State (May 11, 1942)," in *The Israel-Arab Reader*, ed. Walter Laquer and Barry Rubin (London: Penguin Books, 2008), 55–57.

29. "State of Israel: Proclamation of Independence (May 14, 1948)," in

The Israel-Arab Reader, ed. Walter Laquer and Barry Rubin (London: Penguin Books, 2008), 82.

30. Martin Buber, "Dialogue on Biltmore Program," in *A Land of Two Peoples: Martin Buber on Jews and Arabs*, ed. Paul Mendes-Flohr (Chicago: University of Chicago Press, 2005), 162.

31. Gershom Scholem, *Retzifut U'mered: Gershom Scholem Be'omer U've'si'akh* (Tel Aviv: Am Oved, 1994), 27.

32. Carl Schmitt, *Political Theology*, trans. George Schwab (Chicago: University of Chicago Press, 2005), 5.

33. Ibid., 36.

34. Christoph Schmidt, "Ha'teologia Ha'politit Shel Gershom Shalom," *Theoria Ubikoret* 6 (Spring 1995): 153.

35. Shalom Ratzabi, "Ha'medina Ha'yhudit Be'hagutu Ha'politit Shel Buber (1942–1965)." In *Atzma'ut: 50 Ha'shanim Ha'rishonot*, ed. Anita Shapira (Jerusalem: Merkaz Zalman Shazar, 1998), 195–200.

36. Martin Buber, *Israel and the World: Essays in a Time of Crisis* (Syracuse, N.Y.: Syracuse University Press, 1997), 146.

37. Schmitt, *Political Theology*.

38. Ernst Simon, *Yeadim, Zmatim, Netivim, Haguto Shel Mordechai M. Buber* (Tel Aviv: Sifriat Poalim, 1985), 326.

39. David Ohana, *Meshichiut Umamlachiut: Ben Gurion Veha'intelectualim Bein Hazon Medini Leteologia Politit* (Sde Boker: Hamerkaz Lemoreshet Ben-Gurion, 2003), 57–60.

40. Ibid., 151–201.

41. Gregory Kaplan, "Power and Israel in Martin Buber's Critique of Carl Schmitt's Political Theology," in *Judaism, Liberalism, and Political Theology*, ed. Randi Rashkover and Martin Kavka (Bloomington: Indiana University Press, 2014), 167.

42. Martin Buber, *Kingship of God* (New York: Humanity Books, 1990).

43. Ernst Simon, *Kav Ha'tikhum* (Giv'at Khaviva: Ha'merkaz Le'limudim Arvyim, 1973), 45.

44. Shalom Ratzabi, *Anarkhizm Be'tziyon: Bein Martin Buber Le'Aharon David Gordon* (Tel Aviv: Am Oved, 2011), 166, 179.

45. Martin Buber, *Torat Ha'nevyim* (Jerusalem, Tel Aviv: Mosad Bialik, Dvir, 1975), 141.

46. Simon, *Kav Ha'tikhum*, 31, 27.

47. Ronen Shamir and Dan Avnon, "Martin Buber Ve'hasotzyologya Ha'yisre'elit," *Te'orya U'vikoret* 12–13 (Winter 1999): 51.

48. Buber, *Interpreting Hasidism*, 255.

49. Buber, *Tikva Le'sha'a Zu*, 139.

50. Scholem, *Retzifut U'mered*, 14.

51. Martin Buber "Gershom Scholem to Martin Buber, Parma, June 29, 1932," in *The Letters of Martin Buber*, ed. Nahum N. Glatzer and Paul Mendes-Flohr, trans. Richard Winston, Clara Winston, and Harry Zohn (Syracuse, N.Y.: Syracuse University Press, 1991), 386–87.

52. Mendes-Flohr, "Kingdom of God," 33.

53. Noam Zadoff, *Miberlin Leyerushalaim Ubehazara: Gershom Shalom Bein Israel Vegermania* (Jerusalem: Carmel, 2015), 96.

54. Scholem, *Retzifut U'mered*, 29.

55. In his autobiography Scholem wrote about his Zionism before the First World War: "I should say that the reason I embraced Zionism was not that the establishment of a Jewish state (which I defended in discussions) as the main goal of the movement seemed urgent and utterly convincing to me. For me as for many others, this aspect of the movement played only a secondary role, or none at all, until Hitler's destruction of the Jews." Gershom Scholem, *From Berlin to Jerusalem* (Philadelphia: Paul Dry Books, 2012), 54.

56. Ibid.

57. Kaplan, "Power and Israel in Martin Buber's Critique," 156.

58. Gershom Scholem, *From Berlin to Jerusalem* (Philadelphia: Paul Dry Books, 2012), 172.

59. Paul Mendes-Flohr, introduction to *Martin Buber: The Land of Two Peoples*, ed. Paul Mendes-Flohr (Chicago: University of Chicago Press, 2005), 16. Martin Buber, "Zionism and 'Zionism': May 1948," ibid., 223.

60. Scholem, *From Berlin to Jerusalem*, 158.

61. Zadoff, *Miberlin I Leyerushalaim Ubehazara*, 342.

62. About the debate and the theopolitical meaning of the expression "Zur Israel" ("God" in Hebrew), in the "Declaration of Independence" of the Israeli State, see David Ohana, *Meshichiut Umamlachiut: Ben Gurion Veha'intelectualim Bein Hazon Medini Leteologia Politit* (Sde Boker: Hamerkaz Lemoreshet Ben-Gurion, 2003), 3.

63. For a harsh attack on the political theology of the State of Israel and its prime minister David Ben-Gurion see Yeshayahu Leibowitz, "The Religious Significance of the State of Israel," in *Judaism, Human Values, and the Jewish State* (Cambridge, Mass.: Harvard University Press), 214–20.

64. Martin Buber, "Memorandum on the Military Government," 283–88, "Letter to Ben-Gurion on the Arab Refugees," 294–95, "Ben-Gurion and Israel's Arabs" 296–97, "We Must Grant the Arabs Truly Equal Rights" 297–99, in *Martin Buber: The Land of Two Peoples*, ed. Paul Mendes-Flohr (Chicago: University of Chicago Press, 2005).

65. Zadoff, *Miberlin Leyerushalaim Ubehazara*, 176–77.

66. Scholem, *Retzifut U'mered*, 40, 42.

67. Gershom Scholem, "Psychoza Shel Pahad (Mihtav Lamaerechet)

[*Davar*, November 24, 1929]," in *Od Davar: Pirkei Morasha U'Tekhiya* (Tel Aviv: Am Oved, 1989), 88–89.

68. Scholem, *Retzifut U'mered*, 40, 42.

69. Ohana, *Meshichiut Umamlachiut*, 257–58.

70. Kaplan, "Power and Israel in Martin Buber's Critique," 169.

71. Nitzan Lebovic, "The Jerusalem School: The Theopolitical Hour," *New German Critique* 105 (Fall 2008): 101.

72. In refusing the radical contradiction between those included within the community and those violently excluded from it, Buber rejected the concept of the political as friend versus foe, basic to Schmittian sovereignty: "Already at the beginning of our historical period we saw teachers of the law appear who, obedient to this trait of times, defined the concept of the political so everything disposed itself within it according to the criterion 'friend-enemy,' in which the concept of enemy includes 'the possibility of physical killing'" (Martin Buber, "The Validity and Limitation of the Political Principle," in *Pointing the Way* (New York: Humanity Books, 1999), 216.

73. Avraham Shapira, "Pegishat Buber im bney hador hasheni shel hakibutz," *Kan Veachshav* (Jerusalem: Merkaz Martin Buber Shel Ha'universita Ha'Ivrit, 1982), 49.

74. Ohana, *Meshichiut Umamlachiut*, 117.

75. Ibid., 72–77, 125.

76. Buber, "Validity and Limitation of the Political Principle," 218.

77. Martin Buber, "About Uniqueness and Zion" (1961), in Ohana, *Meshichiut Umamlachiut*, 270, 273.

78. Schmitt, *Political Theology*, 36.

79. Ohana, *Meshichiut Umamlachiut*, 356.

80. Buber, *Origin and Meaning*, 117.

81. Ibid., 155.

82. Paul Kahn, *Political Theology: Four New Chapters on the Concept of Sovereignty* (New York: Columbia University Press, 2012), 92.

83. Martin Buber, "The Question of the Single One," in *Between Man and Man* (New York: Macmillan, 1978), 73–74.

84. Scholem, "Martin Buber's Hasidism," 313.

85. Steven Kepnes, *The Text as Thou: Martin Buber's Dialogical Hermeneutics and Narrative Theology* (Bloomington: Indiana University Press, 1992). On page 39 he writes: "They use different methods: *verstehen* and *erklaren*." See also David Biale, *Gershom Scholem: Kabbalah Counter-History* (Cambridge Mass.: Harvard University Press, 1979), 169.

86. Scholem, "Martin Buber's Hasidism," 312–13.

87. Buber, *Origin and Meaning*, 99. Rivka Schatz Uffenheimer expanded Scholem's criticism of Buber. She referred to the destruction of the Hasid-

ism's object of the mystical unification as accompanied by its indifference to the objects in the world. She states that "Hasidism never attempted to blur this basic dualism: world and God were always in its eyes, two opposed sides." She, however, immediately explains that "Hasidism did not in fact attempt to overcome the division between 'life in God' and 'life in the world,' . . . . Life in the world was transformed into life in God not because it was itself sanctified, thanks to some intrinsic 'potentiality for sanctification'; but because Hasidism developed an indifference to the concrete and raised its eyes to the meaning of existence and not to existence itself, to the element that establishes and maintains it and not its outer garments" (Schatz Uffenheimer, "Man's Relation to God," 410.

88. Buber, *Origin and Meaning*, 28.

89. Ibid., 105.

90. Buber, *Moses*, 106.

91. Ibid., 107.

92. Buber, *Kingship of God*, 136. See Zev Harvey, "Anarchism Veteokrathia Bemishnato Shel Buber," in *Philosophia Israelit*, ed. Asa Kasher and Moshe Halamish (Tel Aviv: Papyrus, 1983), 9–19.

93. Scholem, "Martin Buber's Hasidism," 308.

94. Martin Buber, *Tales of the Hasidim: The Early Masters* (New York: Schocken Books, 1961), vii–viii.

95. Vivian Liska, "The Legacy of Walter Benjamin's Messianism, Giorgio Agamben and Other Contenders," in *A Companion to the Works of Walter Benjamin*, ed. Rolf Goebel (Rochester, N.Y.: Camden House, 2009), 198.

96. Walter Benjamin, "On the Concept of History," in *Walter Benjamin, Selected Writings*, vol. 4, *1938–1940*, trans. Edmund Jephcott and others (Cambridge Mass.: Belknap Press of Harvard University Press, 2003), 397.

97. Giorgio Agamben, "The Melancholy Angel," in *The Man without Content*, trans. Georgia Albert (Stanford: Stanford University Press, 1994), 110.

98. Walter Benjamin, "The Storyteller, Observations on the Work of Nikolai Leskov," in *Walter Benjamin, Selected Writings*, vol. 3, *1935–1938*, trans. Edmund Jephcott, Howard Eilan, and others (Cambridge, Mass.: Belknap Press of Harvard University Press, 2002), 146.

99. Steven Aschheim, "From Rationalism to Myth: Martin Buber and the Reception of Hasidism," in *Brothers and Strangers* (Madison: University of Wisconsin Press, 1982), 127.

100. Paul Mendes-Flohr, *From Mysticism to Dialogue: Martin Buber's Transformation of German Social Thought* (Detroit: Wayne State University Press, 1989), 74–75.

101. Martin Buber, "Ha'mesaper Besha Zo," in *Tikva Le'sha'a Zu: Sugiyot Me'inyaney Ha'ru'akh Ve'hametzi'ut* (Tel Aviv: Am Oved, 1992), 172. In a

striking example analyzed by Ran HaCohen, Buber softened the ethnic opposition in the Hasidic tale by eliding from his adaptation of the story insulting names and attributes of non-Jews (Ran HaCohen, "The Hay Wagon Moves to the West: On Martin's Buber's Adaptation of Hasidic Legends," *Modern Judaism* 28, no. 1 [2008]: 7). Buber presented by this his commitment to his criticism on Schmitt's definition on the concept of the political. See Buber, "Validity and Limitation of the Political Principle," 216.

102. Buber, *Origin and Meaning*, 99.

103. Buber, *Kingship of God*, 63.

104. Indeed, like the Protestants, he perceived Jesus as a man of flesh and blood rather than the Lord of the church. Some Protestants accordingly portrayed Buber's Hasidism (with the Tzadik and the praise of corporeality) as a kind of Christianity. See Aschheim, "From Rationalism to Myth," 134; Karl Erich Grozinger, "Parshanuto Shel Martin Buber Letoldot Am Israel Kenisayon Lemodernizatzia Shel Hayahadut O: I-Ha'hvan Ha'kfula," in *'Habistoria Ha'germanit-Yehudit Shyarashnu', Germanim Tzeirim Kotvim Historia Yehudit* (Jerusalem: Leo Beck Inst., Magnes, 2004), 44–45, 48.

105. Martin Buber, "Hamythos Hayehudi," *Teuda Veyeud*, vol. 1 (Jerusalem: Hasifria Ha'zionit, 1963), 85–88.

106. Paul Mendes-Flohr, *Divided Passions: Jewish Intellectuals and the Experience of Modernity* (Detroit: Wayne State University Press, 1991), 188–89.

107. James Turner, *Philology: The Forgotten Origins of the Modern Humanities* (Princeton: Princeton University Press, 2014), 45–47.

108. Martin Buber, "Ha'dusiah Bein Ha'eloim Ladam Bamikra," *Teuda Veyeud*, vol. 1 (Jerusalem: Hasifria Ha'zionit, 1963), 244–52.

109. Buber, "Interpreting Hasidism," 219.

110. Guy G. Stroumsa, "Presence, Not Gnosis: Buber as a Historian of Religion," in *Martin Buber: A Contemporary Perspective*, ed. Paul Mendes-Flohr (Syracuse, N.Y.: Syracuse University Press, 2002; Jerusalem: Israeli Academy of Sciences and Humanities, 2002), 41.

111. Scholem, "Martin Buber's Hasidism," 327.

112. Rivka Schatz [Uffenheimer], "Perush Ha'kHasidut Ke'vituy La'hashkafa Ha'ide'alistit Shel Gershom Scholem," Gershom Scholem: Al Ha'ish U'fo'alo (Devarim Sh'ne'emru Be'you Ha'shloshim Le'histalkuto) (Jerusalem: Ha'akademya Ha'le'umit Le'mada'im, Magnes, 1983), 53.

113. Buber, *Origin and Meaning*, 100.

114. Ron Margolin, *Mikdash Adam: Ha'hafnama Ha'datit Ve'itzuv Khayey Ha'dat Be'reishit Ha'kHasidut* (Jerusalem: Magnes, 2005),15.

115. Buber, *Origin and Meaning*, 179.

116. Scholem, "Martin Buber's Hasidism," 307. Compare with Buber, *Origin and Meaning*, 91.

117. Scholem, "Martin Buber's Hasidism," 307.

118. Ibid.

119. Ibid., 313; Buber, "*Interpreting Hasidism*," 224; Buber, *Origin and Meaning*, 125.

120. Scholem, "Martin Buber's Hasidism," 314.

121. Buber, *Origin and Meaning*, 116.

122. Martin Buber, "Replies to My Critics," in *Philosophy of Martin Buber*, eds. A. Schilpp and M. Friedman (LaSalle, Ill.: Open Court, 1967; London: Cambridge University Press, 1967), 736.

123. Buber, *Origin and Meaning*, 95.

124. Buber, *Tikva Le'sha'a Zu*, 147–48.

125. Paul de Man, *Blindness and Insight* (Minneapolis: University of Minnesota Press, 1983), 187–208.

126. Scholem, *Major Trends*, 27.

127. Buber, *Origin and Meaning*, 106–7.

128. Ibid., 125.

129. Scholem, *Retzifut U'mered*, 31.

130. Ibid., 12.

131. Susan A. Handelman, *Fragments of Redemption: Jewish Thought and Literary Theory in Benjamin, Scholem, and Levinas* (Bloomington: Indiana University Press, 1991), 109.

132. Martin Buber, "And If Not Now, When?" in *A Land of Two Peoples: Martin Buber on Jews and Arabs*, ed. Paul Mendes-Flohr (Chicago: University of Chicago Press, 2005), 103.

133. Buber, *Origin and Meaning*, 206.

134. Ibid., 218.

135. Hannah Arendt, "Zionism Reconsidered," in *The Jewish Writings*, ed. Jerome Kohn and H. Feldman (New York: Schocken Books, 2007), 343.

136. "Israel is a people like no other, for it is the only people in the world which, from its earliest beginnings, has been both a nation and a religious community" (Martin Buber, "Hebrew Humanism," in *Israel and the World* [1941; Syracuse, N.Y.: Syracuse University Press, 1984], 248).

137. Walter Benjamin, *The Origin of German Tragic Drama*, trans. John Osborn (London: Verso, 1985), 166.

138. Buber, "Interpreting Hasidism," 218.

139. Simon, *Kav Ha'tikhum*, 22.

140. Ohana, *Meshichiut Umamlachiut*, 353.

141. Ratzabi, *Ha'medina Ha'yhudit*, 205.

142. . Buber, *Tikva Le'sha'a Zu*, 14.

143. Scholem, Martin Buber's Hasidism," 315.

144. Buber, *Origin and Meaning*, 124.

145. Schatz [Uffenheimer], "Perush Ha'kHasidut Ke'vituy La'hashkafa Ha'ide'alistit Shel Gershom Scholem," 55.

146. Zachary Braiterman, *The Shape of Revelation* (Stanford: Stanford University Press, 2007), 102–5.

147. Jacques Derrida, *The Gift of Death*, trans. David Wills (Chicago: University of Chicago Press, 1995).

148. Ibid., 220.

149. Buber, "Interpreting Hasidism," 220.

150. Martin Buber, Kama He'arot Le'te'oria Shel Ha'kHasidut." In *Ha'shalav Ha'akharon: Mekhkerei Ha'kHasidut Shel Gershom Sholem*, ed. David Asaf and Esther Libes (1963; Jerusalem: Am Oved & Magnes, 2008), 353.

151. Biale, *Kabbalah: Counter-History*, 85, 93; see also Ratzabi, *Anarkhizm Be'tziyon*, 153. Buber also broached in his work the living divine voice that is not to be heard in the Bible.

152. Buber, *Origin and Meaning*, 28.

153. Simon, *Kav Ha'tikhum*, 6, 15.

154. Buber, *Tikva Le'sha'a Zu*, 43.

155. Paul de Man, *The Resistance of Theory* (Minneapolis: University of Minnesota Press, 1997), 12.

156. Jane Elliot and Derek Attridge, "Introduction: Theory's Nine Lives," in *Theory after "Theory,"* ed. J. Elliot and D. Attridge (New York: Routledge, 2011), 9.

157. Eva Cherniavsky, "The Canny Subaltern," in *Theory after "Theory,"* ed. J. Elliot and D. Attridge (New York: Routledge, 2011), 157.

158. Martin Buber, *The Way of Man according to the Teaching of Hasidism* (New York: Citadel Press, 1996), 17.

CHAPTER 10

Against the "Attack on Linking": Rearticulating the "Jewish Intellectual" for Today

Martin Land

From the Margins

A theorist begins to speak. Her language is strange and the tone odd. We identify fragments of scholarly apparatus, but the mode of inquiry does not follow expected paths. What do we make of this intervention? Are we witnessing critical originality or transgression of well-policed scholarly boundaries? Perhaps imperceptibly we find ourselves interrogating the conditions of visibility for theory itself: How do we understand the figure of the theorist? So long as critical theory operates as a questioning of received sociocultural constructions, these queries, in their multiple reflexivities, will likely remain open. We may, however, provisionally suggest that the closure of critical theory as a formal canon of works produced by a recognized cohort of historical thinkers following authorized methods of inquiry in familiar rhetorics would be seen by many as an unfortunate end of theory. The voice that speaks from outside consensus—the other, the minor, the marginal—has been a concern of critical theory in its social and literary settings, and although otherness itself has been recognized as an unstable category, theory continues its struggle to hear that voice and make sense of it.

Although theory is attentive to the particular and historically contingent, it opposes the dissolution of explanation into disciplinary factions whose formalistic methodologies preclude shared insight, a priori. Theory blends modes of thought and inquiry originating in philosophy, social science, art and literature, treating their common object of study as a potential site of human emancipation from domination by social forces encoded in collective narrative. In this emphasis, critical theory distinguishes itself from "traditional" theories, in some sense, theories aimed precisely at constructing "narrative tradition," operating by accretion to erect self-reinforcing structures of technique and interpretation that conflate base and superstructure into opaque ideologies of nature. The distinction, then, is not one of subject matter but of intent, and approaches found useful in many fields of human understanding may be translated into a mode of inquiry appropriate to critical theory. Just as theory has turned to minor perspectives as a source of estrangement and inspiring subject matter, it has looked beyond those scholarly perspectives it found relevant in 1930s Frankfurt to complicate its approach to interpretation. Perhaps even a mode of theorizing as seemingly remote from the humanities as physics might open new directions for social critique.[1] Just such an intervention (not to say incursion) seems apposite at a moment when dominant ideology, encoded in the semantics of "technology," "energy" and "digital," functions to obscure the act of choice in erecting a particular political-economic superstructure on a base of scientific capability, rendering an image of seamless inevitability.[2] Despite much resistance to theory and announcements from various quarters that theory has come to an end (or equivalently, that we have evolved into a posttheoretical society), the goals of critical theory enumerated eighty years ago remain pointedly vital.

Approaching the humanities as a physicist in the face of the historic ontologizing of the professions suggests a reenactment of certain misapprehensions facing Jewish intellectuals entering the post-Enlightenment European academy: Scientists come from the *other* side of campus and may therefore be presumed to lack formal socialization into the traditions of critical theory, much as Jews coming from the putative ghetto were presumed to lack civility.[3] As a physicist, I bring with me the baggage of a very old but rather different heritage of critical thinking. On the one hand, my grasp of the language of the humanities acquires a linguistic turn, tending toward the semantic rather than flowing organically from the idiosyncratic meanings that evolve naturally within a community of practice.

On the other hand, an interpretation well posed within physical theory (as a narrative structure) may not be immediately recognizable as coherent inquiry to all readers. The awkward constructions will be conspicuous, as often occurs when language is acquired in a midlife migration. So in some sense, I speak from the margins and have reason to be concerned that the foreignness of my approach may color it as intrusively critical or even stereotypically pushy.[4] As a Jewish intellectual transgressing the boundaries of polite academic society, the suggestive intersectionality in this experience of otherness inevitably provokes a heightened interest in the functioning of marginality in the early twenty-first century, in particular the historical and contemporary forms of marginality experienced by Jews. In approaching these questions, I hope to make a compelling case for consideration of certain perspectives on relationality and marginality that have been usefully applied in physics and systems engineering, as well as sociology and psychoanalysis. These perspectives, blended into the critical impulse, are intended to open new interpretive schemes with which to revisit issues that may have been considered settled and closed, exposing social and political dynamics not yet fully explored.

Foreignness can be a mutual relationship, but marginalization suggests some asymmetry of power, whether facing the "tyranny" of the small group or hegemonic empire. Concern with one's own foreignness operates as an internalized marginality, a not unreasonable apprehension that as an outsider one's ideas will be judged for their form rather than their content, or worse, for one's perceived identity. And since the imperative—ethical and otherwise—to offer hospitality and recognition exists in dynamic tension with our habit of preferring the familiar and conventional, we need look no farther than our internal motivations to find evidence for the phenomenon of resistance to the other. In the functioning of a group, this tension reveals itself as a dichotomy between openness to the margins and preservation of homogeneity, each inclination supported with assertions of social benefit.

On the one hand, marginality is often regarded as a source of creativity. Even when not reflecting broader experience, authenticity, critical outlook, or access to previously unavailable cultural wisdom, a minor perspective may be valued precisely for its freshness, as when a child asks innocently why grown-ups fight.[5] The marginal as a source of freshness became a theme in literary theory through the aesthetic imperatives of the Russian Formalists. As described by Boris Tomashevsky (in the manner of his time and gender), young Russian poets around 1916 sought "to discover virile sources of inspiration, to create a 'palpable' art opposed to the effeminate poetry of the symbolists and their cult of the approximate."[6] Emphasizing technique, the formalists advocated writing that does not simply elicit automatic recognition of the familiar, but produces a new and vivid perception of its content. "Understanding a work of art depends on making the act of its creation alive again."[7] In describing his method, Viktor Shklovsky wrote that "by 'estranging' objects and complicating form, the device of art makes perception long and 'laborious,'" reviving the experience of first encounter.[8] Through the disruptions of war and revolution, the formalists also discovered a ready-made estrangement on the literary and geographical margins of Imperial Russia.[9] As formalists observed the sources of artistic evolution, "Attention was no longer confined to great writers; it extended to secondary writers, to minor genres, to mass movements."[10] For the recently "discovered" outsider, this association with creativity may seem encouraging.

On the other hand, creativity implies changes in outlook that must inevitably destabilize perceptions of stasis and familiar notions of identity, provoking an anxiety that conflates resistance to change with fear of an "outsider," who may be seen as a recent newcomer despite having long been physically present. Unsurprisingly, such concerns with homogeneity have become increasingly urgent in connection with migration, especially in demands for homogeneity of language, neighborhood "demographics," and public display of religious symbols.[11] In a revealing association, a search in *Le Monde* for the controversy surrounding regulation of the *hijab* led to an article titled "Comment le 'hoodie' est devenu symbole d'injustice," concerning the demonization of hooded sweatshirts following the killing of Trayvon Martin.[12] But an underlying ambivalence may also be revealed when a contemporary term such as *diversity* is used to soften older stereotypes about the artistic, athletic, culinary, or managerial skills of one or another minority. We may grant good intentions when SUNY Stony Brook writes on its website, "Capitalizing on diversity is seen as contributing to organizational goals such as profit, productivity, and morale, rather than just avoiding lawsuits or meeting legal requirements,"[13] and yet be reminded of Archie Bunker announcing, "I'm gonna go into town and get me a good Jew lawyer."[14]

Facing this dichotomy, awareness of one's own foreignness becomes a strategic concern in the creative process. In the essay "What Is Minor Literature?" Gilles Deleuze and Félix Guattari take this awareness as their starting point and identify three characteristics of writing produced under its influence: "The language is affected by a strong co-efficient of deterritorialization"; "every individual matter is immediately plugged into the political"; and "what the solitary writer says already constitutes a communal action."[15] How can a writer bear such weight? In his introduction to their essay, Robert Brinkley reminds us that behind this question is "a desire *not* to be interpreted," to escape the reading that reductively fragments the work into the atomic constituents of the dominant social code in order to reassemble the pieces as an instance of majoritarian reality.[16] To affirm a minority perspective, minor literature deploys a set of strategies designed to evade—one might even say confound—dominant interpretation. In doing so, minority writing does not merely introduce the majority to a consciousness already familiar at the margins, but produces an inherently nonconforming literature. Although the existence of a minority may undermine dominant narratives simply by presenting a counterexample to majority expectations, minor literature is often described as particularly subversive because it must find innovative means of expression in order to speak at all.[17] Modernism celebrates these innovations for their contribution to literature and has developed an extensive discourse on difference and marginality, recognizing in these themes a means for the literate majority to similarly shield itself from the hazards of reductive interpretation.

But in light of this discourse, modernism has also been criticized for limiting its attention to a particularly accessible subset of the marginal. A basic criterion for Deleuze and Guattari is that "a minor literature is not the literature of a minor language but the literature a minority makes in a major language."[18] Chana Kronfeld and others have described that approach as reproducing a certain hierarchy, "consolidating a Euro-American modernist canon from what was once a marginal literary trend and erasing unprivileged formations of marginality."[19] In her view, this consolidation not only produces a highly restricted notion of modernism, but ultimately recapitulates the process of reductive interpretation that minor writers work hard to evade. In response, Kronfeld seeks to reopen the relationship of modernism and minor writers, examining the ways that modern Yiddish and Hebrew literature exhibit and evade dominant interpretation.

These tensions find a closely related expression in "traditional" social science, where "the sociological study of intellectual innovation has long been polarized between romantic notions of the creative marginal intellectual and competing accounts stressing the benefits of national, organizational and network centrality in the production of knowledge."[20] Although ostensibly seeking to identify the conditions that enable intellectuals to efficiently manufacture creative ideas, these studies may ultimately reveal more about how innovation from the margins is received at the center, accounting for studies polarized to align with the dichotomy between openness to novelty and reliance on mechanisms that enforce homogeneity and stasis. Although innovation (as understood in the contemporary marketplace) need not imply actual change, this polarity acquires a temporal dimension under historical forces, so that the creativity of the marginal intellectual is variously deprecated or appreciated at different times, relative to routine knowledge production consistent with conventional norms. This model, also visible in Kronfeld's remarks on the elevation of a canon of marginal writing, overlaps somewhat with Kuhn's characterization of scientific revolution: a "paradigm shift" that establishes critical ideas previously considered marginal as the new "normal science," a set of conventions for the centralized organization of subsequent work by accretion of results that support, rather than criticize, the paradigm.[21]

In the same years that Russian Formalists discovered marginality as a source of creativity, American scholars invoked Jewish marginality to explain the disproportionate representation of Jewish intellectuals in the discourse of European and American social theory. Though Thorstein Veblen receives relatively little attention today, he was a highly influential critic of the culture of capitalism, known for developing the notion of conspicuous consumption. In a 1919 paper titled "The Intellectual Pre-eminence of Jews in Modern Europe," Veblen exemplifies how appreciation of the marginal may recapitulate reductive interpretation, offering a (rather fantastic) critical theory of Jews as practitioners of critical theory.[22] The sociologist Lewis Coser described the circumstances of publication:

> The editor of a leading Jewish magazine approached Veblen and asked him to write a paper discussing whether Jewish intellectual productivity would be increased if the Jews were given a land of their own and Jewish intellectuals were released from the taboos and restrictions that impeded them in the gentile world. Veblen accepted, and delivered his essay on "The Intellectual Pre-eminence of the Jews," in which he argued that the intellectual achievement of the Jews was due to their marginal status and persecuted role in an alien world, and that their springs of creativity would dry up should they become a people like any other in their own homeland. Needless to say, the essay was not published by the editor who had commissioned it. It appeared instead in *The Political Science Quarterly* of Columbia University.[23]

Although the discomfited editor most probably did object to the critique of the Zionist idea (and at just the moment that the Western powers were deciding how to dissect the Ottoman Empire), he may have been concerned about a number of Veblen's formulations, which do not precisely conform to Coser's description. Not quite suggesting that Jews had been impeded by a history of persecution and exclusion, Veblen acknowledges only the hardships of dispersion, writing that "this people have achieved great things while living under conditions of great adversity, scattered piecemeal among the gentiles of Europe" (Veblen, "Intellectual Pre-eminence of Jews," 34). He turns Coser's description of the marginal Jewish intellectual on its head, attributing Zionism to the Jews' "spirit of stubborn clannishness which has never been the least among the traits of this people" (34) and finding within it "a dominant bias of isolation and inbreeding" (33). Hinting at feelings of rejection, Veblen predicts that Zionist isolationism will be a "loss to Christendom at large" (42). The tone of regret here at the implicit Jewish marginalization of European culture may be associated with a traditional view of the Jews as those who rejected Jesus as messiah. In this scheme, Zionism appears as a regression to earlier habits, following a relatively brief but highly productive period in which Jews abandoned their introversion and began to participate in the intellectual work of gentile Europe. This participation, in Veblen's view, is necessarily disjoint from the accumulated wisdom of prior Jewish scholarship. He writes that the Jews'

> home-bred achievements of the ancient time, before the Diaspora, are among the secure cultural monuments of mankind; but these achievements of the Jewish ancients neither touch the frontiers of modern science nor do they fall in the lines of modern scholarship. So also the later achievements of the Jewish scholars and savants, in so far as their intellectual enterprise has gone forward on what may be called distinctively Jewish lines, within the confines of their own community and by the leading of their own home-bred interest, untouched by that peculiar drift of inquiry that characterises the speculations of the modern gentile world,—this learning of the later generations of home-bred Jewish scholars is also reputed to have run into lucubrations that have no significance for contemporary science or scholarship at large. (Veblen, "Intellectual Pre-eminence of Jews," 38)

Moreover, Jewish intellectual creativity should not be seen as Europeans capitalizing on diversity, because "this intellectual pre-eminence of the Jews has come into bearing within the gentile community" (37), and "its bearers have been men immersed in this gentile culture in which they have played their part of guidance and incitement, not bearers of a compelling message from afar or proselyters of enlightenment conjuring with a ready formula worked out in the ghetto and carried over into the gentile community for its mental regeneration" (37). Rather,

> it appears to be only when the gifted Jew escapes from the cultural environment created and fed by the particular genius of his own people, only when he falls into the alien lines of gentile inquiry and becomes a naturalised, though hyphenate, citizen in the gentile republic of learning, that he comes into his own as a creative leader in the world's intellectual enterprise. It is by loss of allegiance, or at the best by force of a divided allegiance to the people of his origin, that he finds himself in the vanguard of modern inquiry. (Veblen, "Intellectual Pre-eminence of Jews," 38)

In other words, naturalization brings more than mere citizenship, as

> the young Jew who is at all gifted with a taste for knowledge will unavoidably go afield into that domain of learning where the gentile interests dominate and the gentile orientation gives the outcome. There is nowhere else to go on this quest. He comes forthwith to realise that the scheme of traditions and conventional verities handed down within the pale of his own people are matters of habit handed down by tradition, that they have only such force as belongs to matters of habit and convention, and that they lose their binding force so soon as the habitually accepted outlook is given up or seriously deranged. (40)

Finally, the inexorable logic of the dialectic exposes itself, when

> the young Jew finds his own heritage of usage and outlook untenable; but this does not mean that he therefore will take over and inwardly assimilate the traditions of usage and outlook which the gentile world has to offer; or at the most he does not uncritically take over all the intellectual prepossessions that are always standing over among the substantial citizens of the republic of learning. The idols of his own tribe have crumbled in decay and no longer cumber the ground, but that release does not induce him to set up a new line of idols borrowed from an alien tribe to do the same disservice. . . . In short, he is a skeptic by force of circumstances over which he has no control. (41)

We may leave aside his flawed presentation of Jewish history and learning, including a long digression into racial theories of Jewish specificity, which he discounts as pertinent explanation, but not as potentially reasonable science. Veblen's paper is often cited as a pioneering modernist statement of the role of marginality in intellectual creativity, but his argument differs in important ways from what one expects to find in a contemporary account (although some of his claims about the necessary "escape" from Jewish heritage into modernity retain a remarkable currency in certain quarters in Israel). His is not the view of "traditional social science" (or perhaps, following Kuhn, "normal social science") seeing creativity flourishing at the margins, where diverse perspectives combine and self-organize into a multidimensional picture of society, away from the parallax distortions induced by conventional paradigms emanating from centers of power. Neither does it recognize the struggle for self-expression discussed by Deleuze and Guattari; it elaborately exemplifies the kind of reductive interpretation—surprisingly grotesque by contemporary codes—that minor literature seeks to evade. The essay does reflect the bubbling optimism in early modernism about the possibility of achieving complete "scientific objectivity" while studying ourselves (which is, of course, also a difficult question for "hard science"). Veblen sees modern intellectuals as detached skeptics alienated from tradition and received wisdom, and ascribes to Jews the privilege of more readily relinquishing their untenable heritage and thereby achieving the purity of the tabula rasa. As befalls the proletariat, in Veblen's description, the intellectual's devotion to science "has stripped him of every trace of national character. Law, morality, religion, are to him so many bourgeois prejudices, behind which lurk in ambush just as many bourgeois interests," and from the ashes of a human being arises a social critic.[24] And yet Veblen's essay remains important for a number of significant reasons, involving the many obnoxious claims that somehow retain currency to this day and a few crucial insights that have been lost over time. This importance becomes evident in various contemporary responses to Veblen made in "normal social science."

Veblen's account diverges significantly, of course, from the experience of difference for the hyphenate citizen compelled to negotiate two dissimilar cultural worlds. I can trace my own position as a social critic at least as far back as age five, suffering the minor indignity of being forced by my kindergarten teacher to sit on Santa's lap and tell him what I want for Christmas—hearing the other boys, I quickly learned that I must ask for a gun. In neglecting memory of nonrecognition, persecution, and exclusion as possible sources for a critical temperament among Jewish intellectuals, and shifting focus to a hypothetical decision by Jews to emerge from self-imposed "clannishness," Veblen's discussion suggests a certain anxiety at directly confronting the newly naturalized citizen, associated with what psychoanalyst Melanie Klein called projective identification.[25] Freud described projection as a defense mechanism in which we refuse to acknowledge some feeling we find unacceptable in ourselves and ascribe the feeling to another person. This familiar mechanism is seen, for example, in the accusation, "You thought I was paranoid the first time you saw me, didn't you!"[26] Klein observed that in some cases the listener, the object of projection, introjects the projection, that is, comes to identify with the feelings we project and experiences them as his or her own. In particular, Klein theorized that an infant, unable to control his or her mother, projects anger onto her, regarding the mother as hostile. But because the nurturing mother wishes to protect the infant from his or her own rage, she accepts the projected feelings, experiencing the anger as her own in order to safely isolate and contain it for the infant, until the infant is mature enough to acknowledge and defuse it in an adult fashion. In light of Klein's interpretive scheme, we may suggest that in ascribing to the Jews an isolationism and rejection of Europe, perhaps Veblen's gentile community, unable to contain its own displeasure, either toward Jews or possibly toward Europe itself, projected it onto the Jewish intellectual who symmetrically accepted the role of critic. Ironically, by safely containing this displeasure at a historical moment when Europe moved from celebration of its achievements to mourning its collapse into total war, it may have been easier for Europe to accept Jews as critics of European culture than as fawning assimilationists. To the degree that projective identification was present in European perception of Jews, in this case and in others associated with the construction of the Jew as figure, then this mechanism becomes useful in understanding reflexivity in the operation of Jewish marginality.

Today, "normal social science" largely rejects Veblen's interpretation, but in doing so, unsurprisingly minimizes the relevance of marginalization in conditioning social consciousness. The historian David Hollinger has written:

> Relatively little of the Jewish preeminence in science and scholarship can be explained by the Veblen thesis that their marginality fostered in Jews a greater capacity for detachment. Veblen ignored the cultural circumstances of communal Jewry, including literacy, and failed to deal at all with the Jews' economic position. . . . The question of the intellectual preeminence of Jews . . . should be studied in relation to other cases of Jewish over-representation, including the world of finance and the leadership of the Bolshevik Revolution.[27]

Following Hollinger, the sociologist Paul Burstein reviews common explanations for the economic and educational success of American Jews, which taken together, point primarily to the conceptual difficulty in defining success and distinguishing cause from consequence. Regarding marginality, Burstein notes that "Jews are sometimes described as investing more than other people in education because historic fears of being forced to emigrate lead them to invest in resources that are portable (such as knowledge of medicine) rather than in resources that could be expropriated or might have to be abandoned (such as land)."[28] Presumably one could add rugs, diamonds, and cameras to this list of portable assets. Nevertheless, he reports that American Jews enjoy "higher rates of return on education than non-Jews," meaning greater professional success than others with comparable education, and Burstein concludes that "so far, there seems to be no evidence that marginality affects Jews' education or labor market outcomes in the United States" (Burstein, "Jewish Educational and Economic Success," 217). Of course, this determination relies on a questionable reduction of marginality to episodes of overt antisemitic persecution, which unsurprisingly has had little influence on Jews' economic decisions in North America during the past half-century. Despite Veblen's misinterpretations and failure to consider the effects of economic and violent oppression, his essay had the virtue of allowing for experience of marginalization in relation to otherness and cultural difference alone. This aspect of Veblen's discussion will not seem especially inventive to critical theory, but it is worth noting that its absence in "normal social science" is an act of historical erasure.

Swapping cause and consequence, Burstein notes that Jewish educational achievement is also frequently ascribed to a rabbinic tradition emphasizing literacy, education, the method of yeshiva study, and facility with text analysis. But in social science, education cannot be taken as both a dependent and an independent variable, an outcome brought about by social factors such as marginality and a particularistic cultural value that coincidently produces economic success beyond its expected market value. Seeking to relegate marginality to a European past not directly experienced by most American Jews, "normal social science" constructs a picture of economic success and social equality ("privilege" in a certain American discourse). In the manner of "normal science," Burstein reframes cultural difference as "social capital," the "ability to secure benefits through membership in networks and other social structures," arguing that this view provides "a framework for showing how Jewish religious beliefs and practices, and the organizations created to sustain them, help Jews acquire skills and resources useful in the pursuit of secular education and economic success" (Burstein, "Jewish Educational and Economic Success," 215). While this direction implicitly poses a central role for the system of relationships within Jewish communities, and is thus consistent with traditional Jewish understandings of social and economic health, the resulting paradigm leaves little space to interrogate the experience of cultural difference and the potentially asymmetric perceptions of those differences between majority and minority.

It is worth noting how far these answers, and the conceptual framework in which they are offered, have wandered from our original questions about Jews and critical theory. Veblen saw marginality not as a key to social and economic success, but as a perspective to be transformed into effective critique of the social and economic system in which those notions of success are defined. His view is particularly significant because while Veblen is claimed by sociology, he was trained as an economist.[29] So here is the dynamic of paradigm shift in a nutshell. A century ago European Jews were regarded as a marginal group and yet (or perhaps consequently) became successful in the *skeptical trades*—science and criticism. But today sociologists investigate American Jews as a group associated with disproportionate economic and social success (especially within science and criticism), and this success is itself taken as evidence that Jews do not experience marginalization. So on the one hand, it seems that the older theory cannot account for more recent observations and must be replaced by a new explanatory paradigm. On the other hand, much in the current interpretation seems driven more by a preference for a particular paradigm than by evidence. Unlike the view in critical theory, much "normal social science" now values disproportionate economic success, and the very lack of proportion is taken to be an important measure of success. Intellectual endeavors are similarly monetized and evaluated in largely pecuniary terms, and there is less interest in Jewish Bolsheviks than in Jewish financiers. In this paradigm, the Jewish Question has been definitively answered by a narrative in which the global expansion of capitalism and its rational decision-making apparatus have freed the Jewish genius to reach its natural level (notwithstanding a few bumps in the decades immediately following the appearance of Veblen's 1919 paper). Certainly, marginality as measured by economic repression cannot provide an explanation of Jewish economic success or Jewish intellectual contributions largely seen as developing within, rather than against, the "normal" social conventions of a society that now rarely calls itself gentile (even when some insist it is essentially Christian). Perhaps this is an example of "capitalizing on diversity" for "goals such as profit, productivity, and morale," and one must admit that it feels preferable to the older trope, "those people are good with money."

To this paradigm we may add the conventional view that Jews were historically marginalized as Europe's prêt-à-porter Other, an experience that would not be repeated in America or contemporary Europe because these societies have found more convenient Others to marginalize. Although this view is uncontroversial as regards violence, segregation, and discrimination, it can be argued that certain misapprehensions and misreadings of the Jews as historical, sociological, and literary figuration have continued, largely unabated. Leaving aside the notably awkward conjuration of the Jew in recent philosophical discourse on universalism and particularism, an issue of less parochial concern is the mismatch between Euro-American notions of religion, nationality, and law, and forms of identity historically meaningful in Jewish communities. Beyond the occasional multicultural glitch (as when kindergarten meets Santa Claus), this issue continues to have practical consequences for Israel nearly seventy years after its founding, as the failure of "normal social science" to produce a semantics that adequately expresses Jewish communal expectations confounds attempts to define, to the satisfaction of a significant majority of Israelis, the desirable role of the state in regard to Jewish tradition, identity, personal status, and law, or the relationship of modern notions of citizenship and democracy to traditional Jewish experience of belonging.[30] By extension, this malfunction influences Israelis' view of their place as a modern state in the Middle East, and the associated impulse to interpret inevitable criticism of a fifty-year military occupation (or liberation, in another perspective) as expressions of unreconstructed anti-Semitism. This experience of otherness need not be linked to immediate persecution, but can derive from speaking in conceptual terms that cannot quite articulate one's concerns. We may approach this statement as following the path of Deleuze and Guattari from the garden of literary theory into the wilderness of social policy.

A different sort of question lurks beneath the sociological studies of Jewish success, one possibly inaccessible to sociological method: To what extent have Jews adapted inherited cultural baggage with the conscious intention of enhancing "labor market outcomes," and to what extent have Jews simply lived in a cultural environment partly influenced by tradition, finding that the wider society rewards them in certain endeavors and frustrates them in others? There is no definitive answer to this question, and it is the question, not the answer, that is important. As a means to evade the current round of reductive interpretation and to undermine its claim to generality, this unanswered question opens just enough space to insist that as individuals, communities, and a people, Jews are not reducible to simplistic categories—sociological, neurological, or genetic. In light of this rhetorical maneuver, I find it useful to identify a Jewish critical outlook with our noted tendency to answer questions with questions.

And why shouldn't I?

Coincidentally, or perhaps not so, theory can similarly be said to prefer the certainty of questions to the hazardous ambiguity of answers, and reliably poses new questions whenever loss of discomfort with accepted questions might suggest the emergence of a new "common sense." But although it may surprise academics, not everyone appreciates questions, especially the ripples of open-ended questioning, associated with critical theory and Talmud that demands "the unsettling of anything that might have been taken for granted: What is meaning?"[31] Such explorations may indeed feel unsettling, and this mode of theory has not been met with universal approval, even in the academy. But leaving aside scholarly disagreement over what might be a worthwhile mode of inquiry, we turn to a political question. In the world—both intellectual and political—that critical theory helped build, some degree of tolerance for questioning is necessary to achieve a corresponding degree of tolerance for otherness at the centers of power. The road opened by modernists in search of estrangement at the margins is by now well-traveled back from the margins to the center, accompanied by a partial willingness in the liberal democracies to complicate notions of "common sense" and indulge the questioning of comfortable certainties inherent in difference and otherness. But the current state of affairs in much of the world reveals a resistance to even this partial willingness, and a reassertion of majoritarian certainties. How can critical theory act in defense of its goal of human emancipation? How do we proceed to compare resistance to critical theory with resistance to the "normal theory" of mainstream science? What rhetoric is appropriate for this task?

Resistance to theory as a broad deprecation of critical thought and skeptical consideration of evidence has been a prominent and widely discussed social phenomenon for some time. In cases related to the ongoing crises of the early twenty-first century, hostility to rigorous thinking and engagement with intersubjectively available (empirical) observation goes so far as to undermine even "normal science," in areas such as human-induced climate change, the operation of systemic racism and sexism, the nonefficacy of torture, and the failure of economic austerity, to name just a few. It has become fashionable to view this hostility as a "populist" rejection from below of "elitist" ideas imposed from above. But we must ask whether this interpretation explains the observed phenomena, or is the interpretation itself perhaps another instance of just what it purports to explain? That this ostensible populism is theorized and disseminated from centers of hegemony by political and economic figures who wield power while characterizing themselves as society's truly marginalized casualties, suggests that examining the consequences of this attack on theory might aid in identifying the goals of its authors. As commonly observed by advocates of continued reliance on, at minimum, the logic of "normal theory," the denigration of accepted scholarly work in a range of areas operates through a set of alternative pseudo-theories whose causality and consistency can be maintained only in a fantasy world. This alternative is not merely inadequate theory proceeding from shaky foundations by way of specious reasoning to reach questionable conclusions. Pseudo-theory crudely simulates the narrative structure of argumentation, but its foundations, its "reasoning," and its conclusions share the status of a priori assumption, linked by little more than shared vocabulary. And yet these pseudo-theories are directed toward actionable conclusions that serve the political-economic interests of their proponents, leading many to conclude that cynical self-interest—rather than cognitive difficulties or principled adherence to an alternative pseudo-logic—is the key to interpreting these dreamlike constructs.

Hostility to theory ("normal" and critical alike) may thus be construed as empire striking back, seeking to recover power and ideological territory lost long ago, first to Enlightenment rationalism, then to modernism and all that has followed. The counterattack implicit in pseudo-theory is now central to "public discourse" in much of the developed world, seamlessly integrating assertion of hegemony from above with a perverse (one might even say, creepy) receptivity from below. As such, these questions must have significant consequences for Jews, among other Others. We may provisionally take for granted that power, whether in the sense of C. Wright Mills or Michel Foucault, will tend to assert itself by one means or another, and instead interrogate the unexpected receptivity to the manner in which it claims authority. One early explanation for resistance to theory is subsumed in assorted declarations of the "death of irony."[32] According to this narrative, the world has entered a period of unprecedented insecurity as our social, political, economic, technological, and physical environment becomes frighteningly complex.[33] As a result, we require an "age of sincerity" in which ideas are judged primarily by their effectiveness in preserving our sense of safety, diverting attention from real systemic complexity and its attendant risks. This understandable desire to shield comforting certainties against challenge and criticism can easily become an antagonism to the questioning viewpoint and hostility to theory.

Whether or not one identifies a hidden hand guiding the latest capitalism and newest world order, the complexity of contemporary politics, economics, and technology is indeed alarming, because a fundamental lesson of systems theory, whether in cybernetics, group psychology, or resistance to empire, is that complex systems possess an inherent potential for unpredictable and uncontrollable behavior. As elaborated by Klein, lack of control can cause frustration, often inducing fear and rage, which in turn may be projected onto others, further destabilizing the system. Here certain modes of interpretation borrowed from outside philosophy and social science are suggestive.

In engineering systems theory, complexity is operationally defined as a demonstrable characteristic associated with nonlinearity (akin to reflexivity), and complex systems are not merely complicated. For example, the planetary weather system can be described by just seven concise and relatively simple equations that describe necessary relationships among changes in various physical quantities such as temperature, wind speed, pressure, and so on. Under simplifying assumptions these equations can be linearized and, despite being complicated, produce deterministic solutions that adequately model mild day-to-day variations in weather. In most cases, this allows meteorologists to extrapolate a few days forward, predicting the weather from current atmospheric conditions. But under general conditions, those simple equations, taken together, describe a nonlinear dynamics whose full range of outcomes can also include unstable and unpredictably chaotic behavior. From these features we learn that extreme weather conditions are all too likely and that long-term prediction (let alone, control) is generally impossible (the so-called "butterfly effect"). In confronting our options in the face of this situation, Klein's mechanism of projection is a suggestive metaphor: We may either emulate the mature mother, accepting the existential reality of complexity in nature and preparing pragmatically for extreme climate scenarios, or emulate her frustrated infant by projecting destructive storms onto same-sex marriage.

The infantile approach resists theory by substituting pseudo-theory formulated in a rhetoric of oversimplification, superficially opening its material to questioning, but closing off exploration by promoting authority as an antidote to critical discourse. Oversimplification can be cute, as when children overregularize grammar, saying *I goed* instead of *I went*, in an attempt to forcibly reduce the inherent complexity of natural language. Traditional theory-building may also require some oversimplification as a provisional first step, as when Isaac Newton's initial theory of gravity treated planets as point-like objects, or when eighteenth-century economists modeled humans as ideal rational actors pursuing material self-interest with access to complete information. Behavioral economics, while continuing to view rationality through the lens of pecuniary gain, takes notice of the many oversimplifying and misleading heuristics we use in everyday decision-making leading to biases, fallacies, and economically "irrational" choices.[34] Taking this a step further, we may understand some "irrational" behavior as pointedly goal-oriented, by allowing that nonpecuniary considerations such as avoidance of fear and shame may be legitimate goals. In this sense, the characterization of climate change denial as simply "irrational" is itself an oversimplification that offers no way forward.

But preserving a sense of safety and making ourselves physically safe are not identical goals, and the theoretical movement from theory to pseudo-theory is significant. The point of Einstein's dictum, "Theory should be made as simple as possible, but not simpler," is that *over*-simplification in reasoned discourse replaces explanatory argument with a muddle of incoherent assertions that admit no effective course of action.[35] Whereas reductionism can be understood as an inadequate formulation within a conventional theoretical framework, the far more severe adoption of simplistic pseudo-theory as a mode of inquiry and an approach to choice becomes an act of disempowerment. As Orwell described this act, "The whole aim of Newspeak is to narrow the range of thought. In the end we shall make thoughtcrime literally impossible, because there will be no words in which to express it."[36] It seems that having just that goal in mind, power elites construct oversimplified narratives designed to advance their objectives, make their privately perceived self-interests appear to be supported by reason, and establish terms of discourse that must be laboriously deconstructed before clear thinking may proceed. A pseudo-theory may be judged successful when it produces a vocabulary, a frame story, and a set of neatly fitting pseudo-arguments that together displace reasoned discourse. Ideally, pseudo-theory should provide a narrative so comfortable and seamless—but intellectually ineffective as explanation—that consideration of alternatives becomes a task too dauntingly complex for nonspecialists to endeavor. An example is the success of oversimplification as a key element in constructing the "war on terror"—even in choosing its name—and the years that passed before this construct was seriously questioned outside progressive intellectual circles. In a meticulously staged simulacrum of reasoned discourse and evaluation of evidence by impartial world bodies, a systems approach was successfully applied to the problem of how best to market "national security" as means of disrupting systematic thought and stampeding Euro-American majorities into a schizoid pseudo-logic of "for us" and "against us." Rather than see this construction as born of cognitive failure, we must notice its success as conscious strategy, albeit in pursuit of goals different from those explicitly stated.

A basic technique in pseudo-theory borrows the canonical list of logical fallacies used to educate philosophers and lawyers, but for the purpose of producing recipes for rhetorical deception. A common example is a syllogism whose major premise is taken as axiomatic, despite being contradicted by the conclusion, such as the insistence that because free markets solve all problems, poverty and inequality simply *cannot be* problems.[37] Another is the false analogy that riffs on a common phrase to invoke a rule outside its proper domain, such as the justification of growth-inhibiting economic austerity with the assertion that because a family budget must be balanced, so must a government budget. Akin to the false analogy is the false dichotomy, as in the assertion that because poor, white Americans are exploited in the marketplace they cannot simultaneously participate in systemic racism. It goes without saying that this segregation of individuals and entire communities into immutable binary categories, "white hats" and "black hats," or in more traditional language, saints and sinners, is primarily harmful to the most vulnerable and marginalized members of society. But in another false dichotomy, the contention that no group can both have been persecuted and persecute others, may lead one to imagine that either Israel's occupation of Palestine has been entirely without untoward incident or Jews must never have suffered persecution. As this particular pseudo-binary takes hold, perception of Jews as perpetrators of violence and not also its historical victims appears to be gaining force, perhaps encouraged by the sociological claims that as a group Jews enjoy significant economic and social privilege. When simplistic pseudo-theory has previously dominated public discourse, the social-political-economic status of Jews has often suffered precipitously.

These examples of pseudo-theory are not merely inadequate reasoning; they come to teach. Pseudo-theory valorizes oversimplification as an approach to reasoning, whose rules of discourse can be studied and formalized:

1. Address every problem by reduction to a single unitizing origin while resisting engagement with the process of explanation.
2. Associate the preferred conclusion with familiar and comforting "certainties" labeled as common sense.
3. Invoke false analogies, blur important distinctions and avoid serious consideration of complexity and its causes.
4. Deny respect to notions of causality and proceed by agglomeration of disjointed "truths."
5. Remain indifferent to confounding evidence and self-contradiction.

6. Respond to criticism by accusing critics of having aggressively initiated the problem itself, just by having raised the question.

These rules can be recognized in their worst moments of application in fascist propaganda of the 1930s, but even a partial catalog of recent examples, from sources too familiar to dwell on, is beyond the scope of this essay.[38] The crises we face in the twenty-first century are serious, and are to a large degree the product of a global society equipped with the power of theory in its broadest social-technological-ideological sense. The question remains, why are so many apparently willing to accept a response based in oversimplification and lacking the ability to explain or provide effective solutions?[39] To address this question seems a basic impulse for critical theory, and perhaps an opportunity to further iterate the critical impulse.

Bion's Epistemological Approach

Returning to the "death of irony" theme, perhaps the choice to feel safe, when physical safety seems an impossibly ambitious goal, should be approached compassionately as a familiar emotional defense. It may provide comfort, in the form of *self-delusion*, against a generalized xenophobia experienced by many who feel themselves disappearing into an entirely foreign present populated by unfamiliar peoples, technologies, and political-economic arrangements. If this is so, then the appeal of pseudo-theory lives in the relationship between politics and individual psychology. Freud understood delusion to express a withdrawal from the *reality principle*, and indeed much liberal critique, from Jon Stewart to Richard Dawkins, characterizes certain conservative views as the product of "wingnuts" subscribing to fantasies originating randomly within their own minds.[40] But just as there is nothing random or undirected in these political views, even psychotic delusion can be seen to express meanings worth exploring. A useful approach is found in the work of Wilfred Bion, a psychoanalytic follower of Freud and Klein, who studied psychosis as a constructed reality.[41] Although Bion is not generally associated with critical theory, his underlying approach is not unfamiliar, and may be described as reading the psychosis as text.[42] Bion saw delusion as perception disrupted, with the detailed and specific goal of protecting the mind from painful knowledge. He argued that whatever the cause of psychosis, delusion should be understood as its methodology rather than its goal, and studied as a problem in epistemology. Therefore, his observations are not limited to psychosis, but are applicable to a wider class of phenomena involving disrupted knowing, and in particular, his conclusions can provide a systematic account of oversimplification as process.[43]

Freud described conscious thought as a web of relations among impressions formed by the objects of our experience, including words. For Bion, these relations and connections, which he called *links*, do not arise in an automatic or straightforward manner, but are constructed, subject to a complex inner dynamics. To think is to willingly internalize perceived links among external objects, making them part of our inner world, and to externalize internal links, seeing a correspondence between our inner recognition of the world and the objects among us. Knowledge is not merely an impression stored in our brain, but first and foremost a willingness to acknowledge a link between objects, and thus enter into an emotional relationship between ourselves and the observed link. In the language of critical theory, the act of knowing suggests an offer of hospitality to a matrix of links we experience among object-impressions, and may be seen as a prerequisite for political forms of ethical behavior dependent on recognition. Refusing to perceive a link in human relations becomes an act of denial and a failure to acknowledge the other, with predictable ethical and political consequences.[44]

Where Freud sees psychosis as disengagement, Bion sees engagement, but with a disorganized awareness of the links among objects, informed by a strategy of obfuscation. Rather than dismiss delusion as "just nuts," Bion described a means to subject it to close reading. In his view the opposite of knowing is "not just ignorance but the active avoidance of knowledge, or even the wish to destroy the capacity for it," leading finally to hatred of reality.[45] "Maximum severance from reality" is achieved by "launching destructive attacks on the link, whatever it is, that connects sense impressions with consciousness" (Bion, "Differentiation of the Psychotic from the Non-Psychotic Personalities," 267). The goal in these attacks is not to prevent links from forming, but to influence their formation, projecting unacceptable impulses onto the very apparatus of our perception, which introjects these impulses and so acts to "protect" us by rearranging perceived objects into delusions that appear to us as direct engagement with reality. Recognizable features of the external object and the aspect of personality projected onto it are blended into the delusion.

Bion summarized his clinical research on disrupted knowing in four principal consequences to the attack on linking. Applied to mundane, everyday self-delusion, his summary parallels and illuminates the rules of discourse for pseudo-theory:

Integration: Attacking the links between objects subverts the development of an integrated personality, which in turn, inhibits the ability to develop a holistic picture of the world. Space, time, and relationships all appear split, disjointed, episodic, asynchronous, fragmented, chaotic, and schizoid. And with no integrated self, I cannot contradict myself, and outright contradiction causes my claims no harm. Thus, as reported by Konstanty Gebert, a certain Polish blogger found no difficulty in denying that the Holocaust occurred and then immediately blaming its occurrence on the Jews themselves.[46] Despite the tendency to attribute these phenomena to the "disruptive" character of digital technologies and the solipsistic replacements for journalism these technologies have enabled, it is the attack on linking evident in certain uses of new media that ultimately expresses its significance. As pseudo-theory, such attacks may be mounted purposefully through seemingly incoherent and chaotic statements of policy. These "zigzags" both encourage supporters with comforting messages (however contradictory) while provoking others to a heightened anxiety designed to render appealing countervailing comforts, such as the notion that once elected a candidate must inevitably respect the dignity of office, cooperate with recognized experts and articulate consistent policies.

Articulation: The attack on links impairs the capacity to articulate and synthesize, so that the mind can fuse impressions into a jumble of slogans, but not a coherent program. Hence, nothing in experience is amenable to rigorous theory and all explanations are by nature ad hoc. Causal reasoning, by whatever system of ordering observed links into a calculus of logical implication, becomes impossible leaving unconscious fears as the primary basis for associating external events. Real-world distinctions are blurred and important categories rearranged to defy rather than enhance comprehension, so that in Bion's words, we move "not in a world of dreams, but in a world of objects which are ordinarily the furniture of dreams" (Bion, "Differentiation of the Psychotic from the Non-Psychotic Personalities," 268). Dreams to some and "alternative facts" to others. In this context, the difference between hearing demonic voices urging acts of violence and hearing the voice of heaven urging one to seek political office becomes one of degree, not etiology.

Problem resolution: Freud understood psychoanalysis (and by extension, all problem solving) in analogy to archaeology, involving the stages of uncovering, deconstruction, and reframing of issues, and then resolution of conflict. But in Bion's view, the attack on curiosity and refusal to learn produce a flexible delusion with an infinitely adaptive capacity for regeneration. In his words, "We are confronted not . . . with a static situation that permits leisurely study, but with a catastrophe that remains at one and the same moment actively vital and yet incapable of resolution into quiescence" (Bion, "Attacks on Linking," 310). Freed from recognition of links and the restrictions they impose on perception and thought, the delusion is able to absorb any criticism and reorganize itself to continue the task of resisting unwanted knowledge. This capacity for regeneration may help explain how repeated predictions of the imminent collapse of capitalism have led to disappointment. Bion's description of a resilient catastrophe endlessly re-creating itself can also be read as an evocative portrayal of Palestine/Israel over the past century, especially the creativity of Israeli governments in formulating a succession of "generous offers" to Palestine while accelerating displacement of Palestinians in Israel and the West Bank, and expanding intrusions into Palestinian areas by Jewish settlers. The attack on linking necessarily subverts the grasp of causation, so that consequences are not seen to follow from particular choices and actions, and problems cannot be formulated in terms of cause and effect, let alone addressed or solved.

Paranoia: Seeking to avoid causal understanding, problems are projected outward, typically onto objects chosen to symbolize the distress and especially onto anyone attempting to articulate the problems clearly. The object of projection becomes an *idée fixe* serving as the unitizing origin for all difficulties. Simplistic slogans, such as, "they hate our freedom" or "they will never accept us here" or "take back our country," are sufficient to "explain" the perception that the other treats us so poorly, despite our generosity toward them. Criticism of pseudo-theory is co-opted and redeployed so that in Bion's words, "The patient appears to have no problems except those posed by the existence of analyst and patient" (Bion, "Attacks on Linking," 311). The very act of posing questions is seen as an alliance with the object of fear, and in consequence the "media is to blame" and civil rights activists are condemned as promoting racism. In just this way, successive Israeli governments have declared themselves to be innocent of wrongdoing and nevertheless threatened by anti-Semites posing nonexistent problems in order to de-legitimize the state.

In common neurosis as in psychosis, fear and desperation can lead us to unconsciously, but still intentionally, attack certain links in order to resist uncomfortable knowledge and enter states of denial.[47] Where politics and individual psychology meet, pseudo-theory may originate as power asserting itself from above, and receptivity from below may be seen as a compliant introjection, an attack on linking that we design to protect ourselves from two simultaneous dangers: frightful knowledge of threats to our real physical safety, and the terrifying awareness that to acknowledge the link may place us outside the dominant collective narrative and expose us to marginalization. The result may become a broad hostility to theory and the way of life it embodies, from literary theory questioning the nature of meaning to climate theory questioning the meaning of nature.

Acknowledging the Links

Broadly understood, theory is not merely a pleasant way to make a living but, at this stage of industrialization, has become basic to human experience, necessary for human survival and as articulated by the Frankfurt School, a means of human emancipation. The resistance to theory, from above, as a means to exercise power and disarm subversion, or from below as a comforting defense against frightening knowledge, diminishes our ability to find significance in our lives and impairs agency in the face of complex material dangers. Perhaps the most prominent irony to survive its prematurely announced death is that these dangers are themselves the product of powerful but flawed theories, from the silent everyday construction of "common sense" to the explicitly and elaborate interweaving of scientific capability and social design we routinely accept as "new technology." Simplistic pseudo-theory may thus be viewed as a technology for silencing criticism. Where censorship is a clumsy tool that often works perversely to solidify opposition, pseudo-theory can be deployed as a precise instrument whose operation is nearly invisible.[48]

Pseudo-theory now routinely creates strategic difficulties for practitioners of theory, even targeting "normal science" as represented by climate scientists at NASA and the Pentagon, who must devote considerable time to refuting simplistic objections to their work. While pseudo-theory designates various fields of knowledge, especially in the humanities, as "unnecessary" in a competitive, technology-based global economy, its operation in the social-political-economic system can reduce those disciplines to disadvantageous career choices. Even within the public ecstasy surrounding STEM disciplines, the emphasis on "technology" (a blend of policy choices designed to enhance political-economic power through the automation of social control) belies a denigration of pure science and mathematics as humanistic endeavors.

In what sense might these general concerns be considered "bad for the Jews," to conjure a trope whose multilayered signification was familiar to earlier generations? The question is not meant to suggest that Jews face a particular repeat of past experience with discrimination, exclusion, expulsion, violence, and worse, especially at the present moment, when other Euro-American minorities are indeed subject to such abuse. It is rather that when conditions are generally bad, they will be bad for Jews in typically Jewish ways.[49] When oversimplification becomes a dominant ideology, as has often occurred in tandem with past episodes of anti-Semitism, it can place certain habits of Jewish life into conflict with wider demands for conformity and expressions of loyalty. The traditional modes of Jewish learning and thought that Veblen deemed to "have no significance for contemporary science or scholarship," depend on commitment to open-ended questioning, articulation of ever-finer distinctions, and restrictive conditions for the acceptance of received authority over reasoned argument. But even in the modern social context, provisional attempts to formulate a sense of Jewish identity chafe against the ill-fitting language of "normal social science." Jewish collectivities can be said to embody a minor literature, confounding reductive interpretation, and disrupting conventional categories of religion, race, people, nation, culture, language, politics, citizenship, and especially loyalty. In this sense, the distinct but parallel assertions, respectively embodied in the political assumptions of America and Israel, that the marginal position of Jews has been finally ameliorated seem simplistic at best, although acknowledgment of this link may conflict with other impulses. It is a telling irony that many who firmly embrace one or both of those assertions also seem most willing to detect unrepentant anti-Semitism in much legitimate criticism. Telling, because Bion's symptomology appears in full bloom: the confounding of integrated self-perception and articulation of causality, along with paranoia and the resistance to problem resolution.

In light of these developments, might critical theory extend beyond interpretation to praxis, an imperative both for theory[50] and in Jewish tradition?[51] It seems unlikely that focused disputation will significantly influence the ideologically motivated producers of pseudo-theory or those most vulnerable to its messages, increasingly bold in voicing ideas that had once seemed permanently discredited by events in the twentieth century. But invoking a public health metaphor, we might imagine an intervention intended to slow the spread of this particular disorder by ameliorating the conditions in which it festers. Perhaps a more direct engagement by public intellectuals would stimulate a wider public awareness of the ways that pseudo-theory underlies a range of systemic disruptions of democratic society, too often misrepresented as isolated improprieties produced by one or another incompetent individual.[52] Clarifying such links serves to destabilize the widely held misconstruction that these disruptions are "crazy" or "ignorant" or "dumb," words that imply a strategic ineffectiveness contradicted by everyday evidence (if we choose to acknowledge this subsequent link). Most important, such analysis directly confronts the advocacy of ideological oversimplification as a mode of inquiry and a method for decision-making, implicitly making the case for critical theory in the public sphere. It must be admitted that such an intervention is not entirely original—it was articulated eighty years ago by the Frankfurt School.

NOTES

1. Although this suggestion may bring to mind the Sokal affair, this essay will not invoke any particular physical theory as authority. These borrowings from scientific modes of thought may be judged for their usefulness in the current context.

2. A precedent for this approach can be found in Jonathan Boyarin and Martin Land, *Time and Human Language Now* (Chicago: Prickly Paradigm Press, 2008).

3. J. M. Cuddihy, *The Ordeal of Civility: Freud, Marx, Lévi-Strauss, and the Jewish Struggle with Modernity* (New York: Basic Books, 1980

4. Norbert Elias, an early Jewish associate of the Frankfurt School, may be a case in point. Trained in philosophy, Elias became dissatisfied with its treatment of social issues and turned to sociology, where his work on the development of European manners and norms of civility met initially (for its first thirty years) with only partial success. Jason Hughes ("Norbert Elias and the Habits of Good Sociology," *Human Figurations* 2 [2013], and available online at http://hdl.handle.net/2027/spo.11217607.0002.107) explains "the somewhat mixed reception of Elias's work as, in part, understandable in terms of Elias's transgression of a dominant code of 'sociological etiquette.'"

5. I am grateful to Janet Baumgold for a discussion of this point.

6. Boris Tomashevsky, "The New School of Literary History in Russia," *PMLA* 19 (2004): 124, http://www.jstor.org/stable/1261491. The author should not be confused with the great star of Yiddish theater, Boris Thomashefsky.

7. Ibid., 128.

8. Viktor Shklovsky, *Theory of Prose* (Champaign, Ill.: Dalkey Archive Press, 2016), 6.

9. Anne Dwyer, " Revivifying Russia: Literature, Theory, and Empire in Viktor Shklovskii's Civil War Writings," *Slavonica* 15, no. 1 (2009): 11–31. Shklovsky's father was Jewish, and Dwyer discusses the development of his ideas on estrangement and the marginal in part during a visit with Yiddish-speaking relatives east of the Urals.

10. Tomashevsky, "New School of Literary History in Russia," 129.

11. See, for example, "Rubio Introduces Immigration Amendment Ensuring English Proficiency Will Be Requirement for Permanent Residency," http://www.rubio.senate.gov/public/index.cfm/2013/6/rubio-introduces-immigration-amendment-ensuring-english-proficiency-will-be-requirement-for-permanent-residency. Or Kashti, "Private Israeli College Forbids Teachers from Speaking Arabic to Students," *Haaretz*, July 24, 2013, http://www.haaretz.com/news/national/.premium-1.537770. Laissez Passer, "Marketing 'No-Blacks' Apartment Buildings in Tel Aviv," *972 Magazine*, July 22, 2013, http://972mag.com/marketing-no-blacks-apartment-buildings-in-tel-aviv/76202/. Dahlia Scheindlin, "Demonizing and Conflating Arabs and Ultra-Orthodox," *972 Magazine*, August 29, 2013, http://972mag.com/demonizing-and-conflating-arabs-and-ultra-orthodox/78143/. Lahav Harkov, "Rabbis: 'Don't Rent to Foreign Workers,'" *Jerusalem Post*, July 8, 2010, http://www.jpost.com/Local-Israel/Tel-Aviv-And-Center/Rabbis-Dont-rent-to-foreign-workers.

12. Raphaelle Elkrief, "Comment le 'hoodie' est devenu symbole d'injustice," *Le Monde*, March 29, 2012, http://www.lemonde.fr/style/article/2012/03/29/comment-le-hoodie-est-devenu-symbole-d-injustice_1677014_1575563.html.

13. Stony Brook University, Office of Diversity and Affirmative Action, Difference between Diversity and Affirmative Action, http://www.stonybrook.edu/diversity/aboutus/difference.html.

14. "All in the Family: Edith the Judge (#2.22)" (1972), quoted at http://www.imdb.com/title/tt0509854/.

15. Gilles Deleuze, Félix Guattari, and Robert Brinkley, "What Is a Minor Literature?" *Mississippi Review* 11, no. 3 (1983): 16–17.

16. Ibid., 13.

17. This innovation may also be a strategy to avoid ostracism and political repression. See, for example, Leo Strauss, *Persecution and the Art of Writing* (Chicago: University of Chicago Press, 1952).

18. Deleuze, Guattari, and Brinkley, "What Is a Minor Literature?" 16.

19. Chana Kronfeld, *On the Margins of Modernism: Decentering Literary Dynamics* (Berkeley: University of California Press, 1996), 3. http://ark.cdlib.org/ark:/13030/ft1p30044r/.

20. Neil McLaughlin, "Optimal Marginality: Innovation and Orthodoxy in Fromm's Revision of Psychoanalysis," *Sociological Quarterly* 42, no. 2 (2001): 271–88.

21. Thomas S. Kuhn, *The Structure of Scientific Revolutions* (Chicago: University of Chicago Press, 1970). It may be noted that Kuhn, a Jewish physicist claimed by philosophy by virtue of his writing rather than his formal aca-

demic training, invoked a traditional Jewish mode of thought in understanding scientific thought as relative to a socially defined linguistic/conceptual context (paradigm). In *Einstein and the Generations of Science* (New York: Basic Books, 1974), Lewis Feuer describes changes in scientific outlook as generational shifts, which may be compared to the Talmudic idea that commentary and argumentation must be reformulated by each generation in its own trace of significances.

22. Thorstein Veblen, "The Intellectual Pre-eminence of Jews in Modern Europe," *Political Science Quarterly* 34, no. 1 (1919): 33–42.

23. Lewis A. Coser, *Masters of Sociological Thought: Ideas in Historical and Social Context* (New York: Harcourt, Brace, Jovanovich, 1977), 263–74. See also Jonah Lehrer, "The Reason Why Jews Became Intellectuals," *Jewish Chronicle Online*, February 10, 2011, http://www.thejc.com/comment-and-debate/comment/44936/the-reason-why-jews-became-intellectuals.

24. Karl Marx and Frederick Engels, "Manifesto of the Communist Party," chap. 1, February 1848, http://www.marxists.org/archive/marx/works/1848/communist-manifesto/ch01.htm.

25. Melanie Klein, "Early Stages of the Oedipus Conflict," in *Contributions to Psycho-Analysis* (London: Hogarth Press, 1973).

26. A joke circulating at the New School for Social Research circa 1969. Personal communication.

27. David A. Hollinger, "Why Are Jews Preeminent in Science and Scholarship? The Veblen Thesis Reconsidered," *Aleph: Historical Studies in Science and Judaism* 2, no. 1 (2002): 145.

28. Paul Burstein, "Jewish Educational and Economic Success in the United States: A Search for Explanations," *Sociological Perspectives* 50, no. 2 (2007): 217.

29. I am grateful to Chana Kronfeld for this observation.

30. See, for example, Martin Land and Jonathan Boyarin, "The State between Race and Religion," in *Race and Political Theology*, ed. Vincent Lloyd (Stanford: Stanford University Press, 2012), and references therein.

31. "Theory is often a pugnacious critique of common-sense notions, and further, an attempt to show that what we take for granted as 'common sense' is in fact a historical construction, a particular theory that has come to seem so natural to us that we don't even see it as a theory. . . . As a critique of common sense and exploration of alternative conceptions, theory involves a questioning of the most basic premisses or assumptions of literary study, the unsettling of anything that might have been taken for granted: What is meaning?" Jonathan Culler, *Literary Theory: A Very Short Introduction* (Oxford: Oxford University Press, 2011), 4–5.

32. Nietzsche identified the key to a differential diagnosis of this resistance in writing, "Objection, evasion, joyous distrust, and love of irony are

signs of health; everything absolute belongs to pathology." Friedrich Nietzsche, *Beyond Good and Evil* (1886), Project Gutenberg EBook, http://www.gutenberg.org/files/4363/4363-h/4363-h.htm.

33. Our dependence on a high level of sociotechnical organization, for better or worse, cannot be overemphasized. A significant disruption in the systems that distribute energy, fertilizer, food, and other resources will not simply diminish the social capacity to support current population levels; the resulting social disruptions could quickly degenerate into wars of mass extinction. Although it is commonplace to attribute this insecurity to the globalization of business and its allied "war on terror," the 1997 report of the President's Commission on Critical Infrastructure Protection found that among the most serious threats to U.S. security are short-sighted cost-cutting measures, especially elimination of jobs associated with routine maintenance. The report was removed from the State Department website shortly after the inauguration of George W. Bush, and is now circulated by the Federation of American Scientists, among others. See *The Report of the President's Commission on Critical Infrastructure Protection* (1997), http://www.fas.org/sgp/library/pccip.pdf.

34. S. Mullainathan and R. H. Thaler, "Behavioral Economics," in *International Encyclopedia of the Social & Behavioral Sciences* (2001): 1094–1100.

35. A paraphrase of his statement that "it can scarcely be denied that the supreme goal of all theory is to make the irreducible basic elements as simple and as few as possible without having to surrender the adequate representation of a single datum of experience." Albert Einstein, "On the Method of Theoretical Physics," Herbert Spencer Lecture, delivered at Oxford (June 10, 1933), *Philosophy of Science* 1, no. 2 (1934): 165.

36. George Orwell, *Nineteen Eighty-Four* (London: Penguin Books, 1949), 55

37. Paul Krugman, "A War on the Poor," N*ew York Times*, October 31, 2013. http://www.nytimes.com/2013/11/01/opinion/krugman-a-war-on-the-poor.html. Daniel Little, "Why a War on Poor People?" October 8, 2013, http://understandingsociety.blogspot.co.il/2013/10/why-war-on-poor-people.html.

38. For a detailed discussion of similar rules for fascist discourse see Umberto Eco, "Ur-Fascism," *New York Review of Books*, June 22, 1995. http://www.nybooks.com/articles/1995/06/22/ur-fascism.

39. This question was also raised in J. Boyarin and M. C. Land, "A Moment of Danger, A Taste of Death," *Cardozo Law Review* 26, no. 3 (2005): 1119–38.

40. *The Daily Show with Jon Stewart* (Mad Cow Productions, Comedy Central). Richard Dawkins, *The God Delusion* (London: Bantam Books, 2006).

41. Wilfred Bion, "Differentiation of the Psychotic from the Non-Psychotic Personalities," *International Journal of Psycho-Analysis* 38, no. 3–4 (1957): 266–75. See also Wilfred Bion, "Attacks on Linking," *International Journal of Psycho-Analysis* 40, no. 1 (1959): 308–15.

42. Bion himself was something of an outsider, raised in colonial India, educated in England, seeing combat in World War I and serving in the medical corps during World War II, where he treated "combat fatigue" (as PTSD was called at the time). One of the few prominent pioneers of psychoanalysis who was not Jewish, Bion was exposed to the field's Jewish influences, training under Melanie Klein, and joining with Hanna Segal and Herbert Rosenfeld to form the nucleus of her research group. In *Kabbalah and Psychoanalysis* (London: Karnac Books, 2012), Michael Eigen quotes Bion as remarking that he uses "Kabbalah as the framework for psychoanalysis," referring to certain notions of being and nonbeing. This approach touches on a number of the issues raised in this volume. For example, in *Clinical Seminars and Other Works* (London: Karnac Books, 1994), Bion discusses a medical student wracked with anxiety before an exam. The patient describes himself as being Jewish, because people tell him he is, but insists that he is not observant and does not feel like a Jew. Bion asks, "How does he know that he doesn't feel like a Jew? What does a Jew feel like?" One could sharpen this question and ask who determined for the patient that observance is essential to feeling like a Jew. Bion suggests that the student, having decided not to feel like a Jew, may be compared to a book with pages torn out, achieving an ability "not to be," and he thus faces his exam unable to know what he knows. In Bion's words, "To not know your breed involves a repudiation of breeding."

43. For an application of Bion's ideas in a different direction, see the work of Tel Aviv artist Michal Heiman, http://www.michalheiman.com/.

44. Sigmund Freud, "Formulations Regarding the Two Principles in Mental Functioning," in *Papers on Metapsychology; Papers on Applied Psycho-Analysis*, vol. 4 *of Collected Papers*, 5 vols. (London: Hogarth and Institute of Psycho-Analysis, 1971), 16. See also Sigmund Freud, *The Ego and the Id* (London: The International Psycho-Analytical Library, 1962), 19–33.

45. Michael Parsons, *The Dove That Returns, the Dove That Vanishes* (London, 2000), 48.

46. Konstanty Gebert, "A Theory about Jews: Contemporary Antisemitic Conceptualizations in Poland," Jews and the Ends of Theory: A Conference, Duke/UNC, April 30–May 1, 2013.

47. Stanley Cohen, *States of Denial: Knowing about Atrocities and Suffering* (Cambridge: Polity Press, 2001).

48. As befits the metaphorical "free market of ideas," explicit censorship is replaced with a flood of "ideas" that compete with serious critique in

much the way that fast food franchises and big box stores compete with local artisans by offering low-cost, low-quality products manufactured with little concern for public health. Continuing the metaphor, low-quality ideas are mass-produced in a production technique comparable to the knock-off of cheap digital electronics. The technology of manufacture, formalized as rules for grammar of simplistic discourse, is far more sophisticated than the end products.

49. My grandmother recalled that as a child in Medzhybizh, when World War I spilled over into the Russian Revolution and Civil War, she would ask her mother what will happen to them. Her mother always answered, "What will happen to the Jews will happen to us."

50. "The philosophers have only interpreted the world, in various ways; the point is to change it." Karl Marx, "Theses on Feuerbach" (Moscow: Progress Publishers, 1969).

51. "You are not obligated to complete the work, but neither are you free to desist from it." Pirkei Avot (Ethics of the Fathers), 2:21.

52. An example of such engagement is New York University English professor Feisal G. Mohamed's *New York Times* op-ed assessing Donald Trump's acceptance speech at the Republican National Convention, showing its similarity to the ideas of Carl Schmitt and contrasting those ideas with the thinking of Hannah Arendt. Feisal G. Mohamed, "Arendt, Schmitt and Trump's Politics of 'Nation,'" *New York Times*, July 22, 2016, http://www.nytimes.com/2016/07/23/opinion/trumps-perilous-nation.html.

CHAPTER 11

Recovering Futurity: Theorizing the End and the End of Theory

Elliot R. Wolfson

> It is the distinguishing characteristic of human existence that it is not realized through its mere being, that it "confronts" its possibilities in a very specific way, that it must first seize these possibilities and, in this seizing, live in the shadow of the question concerning its "to what end." . . . Even when bracketing any thought of purpose, one can still speak of a "to what end," namely when the "to what end" of existence is grounded in its own being. . . . Nor can the meaning of philosophizing, with regard to the original understanding of philosophizing, be conceived as the realization of a purpose transcendent to it. All genuine philosophizing has found its meaning in itself and grasped it through itself.
>
> —HERBERT MARCUSE, "On Concrete Philosophy"

I begin my reflections on the unveiling of the apocalyptic unveiling with a quote from Hans-Jost Frey that touches on the intricate nexus between language and the possibility of theorizing the beginning or the end:

> What, having begun, cannot begin, cannot end. The end would be the chance to begin, which the text endlessly misses by going on. Just as the beginning lies before as well as behind, so does the end lie behind as well as before. Because the end cannot be said, saying can have no end. Where the text ends it is unfinished, because although its end has come it is still unsaid, and when the text says it, it has not yet come to an end, since it is still in the middle of saying that it has. Writing, which must always already have begun in order to be able to say that it has, must always continue in order to be able to say that it is ending. It always ends too early or too late, and therefore does not end at all, for it misses its own end.[1]

Frey has deftly articulated the paradox that pertains to both the beginning and the end. To begin, the beginning must have already begun, otherwise it would not be the beginning, but, if this is so, then there is no beginning that is not prior to beginning. However, that which cannot begin cannot end. To be always beginning, therefore, is to be never-ending. Similarly, to end, the ending must have already ended, otherwise it would not be the ending, but, if this is so, then there is no ending that is not posterior to ending. Time is lived experientially in the moment wedged between the beginning that cannot begin and the ending that cannot end. In every moment, there is a beginning of the end and an ending of the beginning, and hence each moment is identical but distinctive, nay, identical because distinctive.

Time's Linear Circle and Reiteration of the Inimitable

We begin from the premise that the beginning never ends, but only that which ends everlastingly never ends. Utilizing a distinction made by Edward Said, we can say that the point of departure is inaccessible because it is not a transitive property determined by an anticipated end or expected continuity; it is rather a radical and intransitive starting point that has no object other than its own constant clarification and critical undoing.[2] The beginning is thus "*making* or *producing difference*; but—and here is the great fascination in the subject—difference which is the result of combining the already-familiar with the fertile novelty of human work in language."[3] By his own admission, Said's conception is indebted to the circular movement of the Husserlian phenomenological reduction whereby the search for the absolute beginning leads to its own undermining inasmuch as the beginning can show itself sensuously only as the beginning intended in the constitution of the intuitive object that "attains original givenness in and with the *form of a temporal duration*, rendering an encompassing and objective unity possible."[4] Even in its immanent essence as an absolute givenness, the beginning is always noetically at a distance from being the beginning of the beginning of being.[5]

The logic of this argument can be adduced further from Husserl's remark in the lectures on the consciousness of internal time from 1905, "But this *question of origin* is directed towards the *primitive* formations of time-consciousness, in which the primitive differences of the temporal become constituted intuitively and properly as the original sources of all the evidences relating to time."[6] Phenomenological—in contradistinction to psychological—apperception is not concerned with the empirical genesis whence the intuitions of objective space and objective time arise but only in the immanent sense and descriptive content of the experiences (*Erlebnisse*) bracketed from the natural standpoint and the ensuing epistemological inquiry into the presumed existence or nonexistence transcendent to consciousness. As Husserl boldly states,

> We do not fit experiences into any reality. We are concerned with reality only insofar as it is reality meant, objectivated, intuited, or conceptually thought. With respect to the problem of time, this means that we are interested in the *experiences* of time. . . . We seek to bring *the a priori of time* to *clarity* by exploring the *consciousness of time*, by bringing its essential constitution to light, and by exhibiting the apprehension-contents and act-characters that pertain—perhaps specifically—to time and to which the *a priori* temporal laws essentially belong.[7]

The origin, then, is not an objective time that can be calculated instrumentally by the ego in the world of physical things and psychic subjects,[8] but rather as the interior time of the eidetic experiences accessible phenomenologically and not psychologically.[9] When construed from this vantage point, the origin of time can never be something that originates in time, and thus the essence of the *arche* is inessentially *an-archic*. Husserl himself, it is worth recalling, defined philosophy more generally—although obviously the standpoint of phenomenology is privileged—as "a science of true beginnings, or origins, of *rizōmata pantōn*."[10] But the true beginning is the beginning that cannot begin. The constant quest for origin, which is the watchword of phenomenology as the science of pure phenomena, to go back to the things themselves (*zur Sache selbst*), is perforce a retreat to the domain where the very question of origin is interrogated as the origin of the question. At the beginning stands the impasse of the beginning. In lieu of a unitary point whence all things originate, we find a fold, duplicity, contravention, the doubling of infringement that marks the way of the beginning in the beginning of the way.

A similar account, albeit betraying the influence of both Husserl and Merleau-Ponty, is offered by John Sallis:

> Radical philosophy is a peculiar *return to beginnings*, a turning towards what already determines it. It is a circling which sets out from the beginnings so as to return to them, which it can do only if in its circling it never really leaves them. . . . Radical philosophy, as return to beginnings, is thus simultaneously a turning towards its own beginnings, towards those beginnings with which the return to beginnings is initiated.[11]

I would only add that this return is a return to the beginning where one has never been because the very notion of beginning, as Sallis himself wrote elsewhere, is always a "redoubling—which is to say no beginning at all."[12] The beginning bears the paradox of existing only "after the fact"; that is, its state of having "always already been the beginning" implies that it continuously begins and therefore can never begin.[13] In Derridean parlance, the commencement is permanently second, an echo, a trace, the "originary iterability."[14] Only that which is different can be duplicated, since what recurs is the same difference that is indifferently the same.

Perhaps more efficaciously than any other twentieth-century philosopher, Heidegger has expressed the intonation of time—or, to be more meticulous, what he calls the "primordial temporality" (*ursprünglichen Zeitlichkeit*) experienced in the ecstatic unity of past, present, and future, as opposed to the vulgar understanding (*vulgären Verständnis*) of time as the ceaseless succession of nows (*Jetzt-folge*)—as the concurrence of the heterogeneity of the homogeneous and the homogeneity of the heterogeneous. This confluence is expressed as well in spatial terms as "*the primordial 'outside itself' in and for itself* [das ursprüngliche "Außer-sich" an und für sich selbst]."[15] That time is extrinsic to itself in the manner of being intrinsic to itself suggests that the temporal flow consists of the return of the same in which the same is the replication of difference.[16] Following this notion of time, thinking itself is best characterized by a circular movement (*Kreisbewegung*) by which one is restored to where one has previously not been. In contrast to the path of philosophy, the pedestrian understanding "can only perceive and grasp what lies straight in front of it: it thus wishes to advance in a straight line, moving from the nearest point on to the next one, and so on. This is called progress [*Fortschritt*]."[17]

When viewed from this perspective, even the circular movement is treated in a linear fashion as a "straightforward progression" (*Geradeausgehen*), culminating in reverting to the starting point and coming to a standstill. Inasmuch as progress is the criterion that engulfs the ordinary understanding, the circular motion, which seemingly gets one nowhere but to the place whence one set out, is objectionable. However, a proper comprehension of the "essential feature of the circular movement of philosophy does not lie in running around the periphery and returning to the point of departure [*Ausgangsstelle*]. It lies in that view of the center that this circular course [*Kreisgang*] alone can provide. The center, that is, the middle and ground, reveals itself as such only in and for the movement that circles it."[18] The linearity of ordinary thinking is linked to the certainty of progress, but the circularity of philosophical thought is bound up with ambiguity (*Zweideutigkeit*) that is not eliminated or leveled by means of the synthetic exoneration of the conflict between thesis and antithesis according to the Hegelian dialectic.[19] To move at the *center of philosophizing* is to move in the greatest possible propinquity to the *ambiguity of philosophizing* because this move is always a retracing of one's steps to the beginning of the question that calls into question the question of the beginning.[20] The discourse to displace the closed circular movement—and the inferred assumption that the future truth is already determined by the past—must partake of that movement. For Heidegger, the task, as Derrida well understood, is not to escape from this hermeneutic circulation, as vicious as it might seem, but to engage it by going around it.[21] This is implied in the Heideggerian emphasis on resoluteness (*Entschlossenheit*) and authenticity (*Eigentlichkeit*):

> The experience of the circular closure does not close anything; it suffers neither lack nor negativity. Affirmative experience without voluntarism, without a compulsion to transgression: not to transgress the law of circle and *pas de cercle* but *trust in them*. Of this trust would thought consist. The desire to accede, by this faithful repetition of the circle, to the not-yet-crossed, is not absent. The desire for a new step, albeit a backward one (*Schritt zurück*), *ties and unties* this procedure [*démarche*]. Tie without tie, get across [*franchir*] the circle without getting free [*s'affranchir*] of its law. *Pas sans pas* [step without step/step without not/ not without step/ not without not].[22]

With regard to the temporal paradox of the law of the circle—the future signaling the return to where one has never been, the fourfold connotation of the idiomatic expression *pas sans pas*—there is continuity between the so-called earlier and later Heidegger.[23] To cite one relevant passage from *Sein und Zeit*: The three temporal modes are said to commingle around the notion that only the "*being that, as futural* [zukünftiges], *is equiprimordially having-been* [gleichursprünglich gewesend], *can hand down to itself its inherited possibility* [ererbte Möglichkeit], *take over its own thrownness* [Geworfenheit] *and be in the Moment for 'its time'* [augenblicklich sein für "seine Zeit"]. *Only authentic temporality* [eigentliche Zeitlichkeit] *that is at the same time finite makes something like fate* [Schicksal], *that is, authentic historicity* [eigentliche Geschichtlichkeit], *possible*."[24]

In some measure, Heidegger's early thought bears affinity to Husserl's description of the "eidetic laws of compossibility"—the "rules that govern simultaneous or successive existence and possible existence together"—anchored in the motivation of the transcendental sphere, as opposed to causation, structured as the "universal *unity-form of the flux*," that is, the "*formal regularity pertaining to a universal genesis*, which is such that past, present, and future, become unitarily constituted over and over again, in a certain noetic-noematic formal structure of flowing modes of givenness."[25] The ego transcendentally constitutes itself for itself in the unity of its history, and in that constitution are contained the constitutions of all the objectivities, whether ideal or real, transcendent or immanent, that exist for that concrete and monadic ego. Heidegger translated Husserl's insight into his own conceptual and terminological register: The authentic temporality of *Dasein*—the finitude that makes possible the destiny of our historicity—is distinguished by the resoluteness of claiming the present moment as the realization of the future recuperating the past. In that respect, the resoluteness "becomes the *repetition* [Wiederholung] of a possibility of existence that has been handed down."[26] That the repetition is deemed a "handing down" (*Überlieferung*) does imply that *Dasein* can relapse to the possibilities of where it has been, but this does not mean that there is an exact duplication of the past.

> The authentic repetition of a possibility of existence that has been . . . is grounded existentially in anticipatory resoluteness [*vorlaufenden*]; for in resoluteness the choice is first chosen that makes one free for the struggle over what is to follow [*kämpfende Nachfolge*] and fidelity [*Treue*] to what can be repeated. The handing down of a possibility that has been in repeating it, does not, however, disclose the *Dasein* that has been there in order to actualize it again. The repetition of what is possible neither brings back "what is past," nor does it bind the "present" back to what is "outdated." Arising from a resolute self-projection, repetition is not convinced by "something past," in just letting it come back as what was once real. Rather, repetition *responds* to the possibility of existence that has been-there. But responding [*Erwiderung*] to this possibility in a resolution is at the same time, *as a response belonging to the Moment*, the *renunciation* [Widerruf] of that which is working itself out in the today as "past." Repetition neither abandons itself to the past nor does it aim at progress. In the Moment, authentic existence is indifferent to both of these alternatives.[27]

The resolve to live momentarily (*augenblicklich*), to be responsive to the moment, depends on repetition, but an indispensable component of that repetition is renunciation of the past. Authentic existence entails being in the moment that is forged neither by retroaction nor by prolepsis but by repeating what is unrivaled with regard to the truth of what was once real. To leap to where one is no more is to retreat to where one is yet to be.[28] In the lecture course "Vom Wesen der Wahrheit: Zu Platons Höhlengleichnis und Theätet," offered in the winter semester 1931–32 at the University of Freiburg, Heidegger writes:

> For in *genuine* historical reflection we take just that distance from the present which allows us room to leap out [*hinauszuspringen*] beyond our own present, i.e. to treat it just as every present as present deserves to be treated, namely as something to be *overcome* [überwunden]. Genuine historical return is the decisive beginning of authentic *futurity* [Zukünftigkeit]. . . . In the end it is *historical* return which brings us into what is actually happening *today*. In the end it is also only a self-evident and therefore doubtful everyday opinion which takes history as something "past."[29]

Striking a similar note, Heidegger writes in a notebook entry from autumn 1932: "What truly remains in history is the unique [*Einzige*]—*un*repeatable [Un*wiederholbare*]—at once necessary; what can be '*repeated*' in the extrinsic sense [*äußeren Sinne*]—does not *abide*—instead, it vacillates and has no unassailable necessity. It is altogether something else to repeat what is unique [*das Einzige wiederholen*]—i.e., to carry out a proper necessity—and not just calculate [*ausrechnen*]."[30] Contra intuitively, uniqueness is not antithetical to repetition. Indeed, Heidegger insists that the mandate is to *repeat what is unique*. How does one repeat what is unique such that what is repeated remains in the status of being unique? As he put it in a second passage from the notebooks written at a later date, for the common understanding of the masses the notion of sameness (*das Selbe*) is set in opposition to what is novel, but "creative individuals" are committed to the "mystery" (*Geheimnis*) of sameness "in its ever-originary essentiality" (*immer ursprünglichen Wesentlichkeit*).[31] In a third passage, Heidegger opines that the assumption that what is most common is the universal and its universalization arises "from the incapacity to experience the ever-incomparably unique in the same [*das jeweils Unvergleichbare Einzige im Selben*] and to maintain it in its mystery."[32] A similar idea is expressed in the observation in the *Beiträge zur Philosophie (Vom Ereignis)*, composed between 1936 and 1938, that every essential occurrence of the essence of being "is determined out of what is essential in the sense of the original-unique [*Ursprünglich-Einzigen*]."[33] The upheaval in thinking that Heidegger sought to spearhead rests on this hermeneutical foundation: As opposed to the conservative wish to preserve *what was begun in the wake of the beginning*, the more revolutionary and genuine relation to the beginning demands acting and thinking *from the perspective of the future*, since the beginning is always a recurrence of difference and hence requires the "renunciation of the crutches and evasions of the habitual and the usual."[34]

In much the same cadence, Heidegger writes in another section from the *Beiträge* that the wish to traverse the course of the question of being (*Seinsfrage*), in the hope of retrieving the lineage of antiquity, can be fulfilled if one comprehends that the matter of repetition means "to *let* the *same*, the uniqueness of being, become a plight *again* and *thereby out of a more original truth*. 'Again' means here precisely 'altogether otherwise' ["*Wieder*" *besagt hier gerade*: *ganz anders*]."[35] *Prima facie*, one would not expect the concept of "the same" to be glossed as "the uniqueness of beyng" (*die Einzigkeit des Seyns*), since sameness, by definition, is demonstratively opposed to uniqueness. However, in Heideggerian terms, there is no opposition, for to attend to the same, which he contrasts with the identical, one must heed that which is recurrently different. This hermeneutical assumption furnishes the rationale for the pattern of time that posits the "same" as unique and the "again" as altogether otherwise. In *Einführung in die Metaphysik*, Heidegger writes that to "stand with Being" means "nothing less than to *repeat and retrieve* [wieder-holen] the inception [*Anfang*] of our historical-spiritual *Dasein*, in order to transform it into the other inception."[36] The repetition of the novel is the basis for the phenomenological nexus that Heidegger establishes between time (*Zeit*), eternity (*Ewigkeit*), and the moment (*Augenblick*): "The eternal is not the incessant [*das Fort-währende*]; it is instead that which can withdraw [*entziehen*] in a moment so as to recur [*wiederzukehren*] later. What can recur: not as the *identical* [*das* Gleiche] but as the newly transforming [*Verwandelnde*], the one and the unique [*Eine-Einzige*], i.e., beyng, such that it is not immediately recognized, in this manifestation, as the same [*das Selbe*]!"[37] Conspicuously suggestive of Nietzsche's doctrine of the eternal recurrence of the same, Heidegger insists that eternity is not set in opposition to time; it is rather that which withdraws each moment to recur. What recurs is not the identical but the same, that is, the unique being that is always—originarily—different.

In his exposition of Trakl's poem "*An einen Frühverstorbenen*," Heidegger notes that the premature death of the child Elis, which symbolizes the "stranger called to go under,"[38] reveals the wisdom about time fully expressed in the last line, "Golden eye of the beginning, dark patience of the end" (*Goldenes Auge des Anbeginns, dunkle Geduld des Endes*):

> Here, the end is not the sequel and fading echo of the beginning. The end—being the end of the decaying kind—precedes the beginning of the unborn kind. But the beginning, the earlier earliness, has already

> overtaken the end. That earliness preserves the original nature—a nature so far still veiled [*verhüllte*]—of time. This nature will go on being impenetrable to the dominant mode of thinking as long as the Aristotelian concept of time, still standard everywhere, retains its currency. According to this concept, time—whether conceived mechanically or dynamically or in terms of atomic decay—is the dimension of the quantitative or qualitative calculation of duration as a sequential progression.[39]

Already in *Sein und Zeit*, as we saw above, Heidegger contrasts the primordial temporality and the vulgar understanding of time. The latter coheres with the Aristotelian perspective insofar as time is viewed as the succession of interchangeable now-points. As long as this perspective prevails, the true nature of time is veiled. The deeper phenomenology of time rejects the calculative approach, and hence we can reverse the timeline: The end precedes the beginning, and yet the beginning overtakes the end. The time swerve is open at both termini, and hence the end cannot be ascertained from the beginning nor the beginning from the end; the reversibility of the circular linearity implies not closure but an ever-changing fluctuation, an indeterminacy that destabilizes the model of an irreversible succession proceeding unidirectionally from start to finish.

Endlessly Speaking of the End of Speaking

From the beginning, then, we can discern the end, albeit from an inverse perspective. That is, the end can only be imagined as the terminus that can never be terminated. In that respect, the unending end—the end that has no ending to being the end—is the mystery that marks the horizon of our delineating the limit of language. As Frey insightfully remarked, *Because the end cannot be said, saying can have no end.* This subtle insight underscores the complex intertwining of the apophatic and the kataphatic: There is no end to speaking precisely because the end cannot be spoken. The paradox is especially pertinent in the written text. We cannot speak of textual closure—a book may be sealed but the text remains open—because even at the conclusion the text is unfinished and what has been said therein remains unsaid. To speak of the unsaid does not mean to speak about the silence of not speaking but rather to speak of what is still to be spoken. Just as there is no way to speak of the beginning that has not already begun and therefore cannot end, so there is no way to speak of the end that has not already ended and therefore cannot begin. Language, therefore, can begin and end, but it cannot either terminate speaking of the beginning or commence speaking of the end. From the inability to control the discourse about beginning and end, it is impossible, as Frey observed, to imagine a sense of a whole, and beginning and end are reduced to arbitrary markers.[40]

In traditional Jewish theorizing about time, the sign of the end that has commanded much attention through the generations is the eschaton, the omega that complements the alpha of creation. I do not think it would be unreasonable to consider eschatology as a form of speculating about mortality writ large, moving from the ontic-existential anxiety of the individual with the looming certainty of death to the ontological-historical trepidation of the larger human community with either the impending uncertainty of the ecological demise of the planet or the possibility of mass destruction even greater than we have witnessed heretofore. The apocalyptic secret orients one to the decisive interval in time, the future, the breaking point of the limit, the end close at hand that persists as what is always most distant. Ingrained in the texture of Jewish apocalyptic is the structure of secrecy as the mystery of the future, which originates in the past, revealed in the present as not being present. What is yet to be, accordingly, reverts to what has already been, but what has already been issues from what is yet to be. Apocalyptic hope—the hope that renews itself sporadically as the hope that is deferred perpetually—stems from this linear circularity, the infinite negativity of time, the impossible possibility that makes it always possible that the future that is coming threatens not to be the future for which one has hoped. The paradoxical nature of time thus entails that what recurs is what has never been. The delay of the end's materialization is precisely what secures the potency of its constant instantiation. The continual stay of the moment, the not yet that is resolutely yet not at hand, is what eternalizes the temporal and temporalizes the eternal. The exposure of the secret of the end as the end of the secret—sometimes expressed as the unveiling of the truth without any garment, the seeing of the face without any mask—in the present bridges the rupture between past and future by imparting hope in the return of what is not to come, the quintessential event of the nonevent.

Contrary to the commonplace understanding, the apocalypse is not about the end of the old world or the beginning of a new world but rather about the end of the end and the beginning of the beginning. As David Leahy put it,

> We are dealing not with beginning now of the world, not with the creation of the world, but with the beginning of the beginning now of the

> world, not merely with the beginning, but with the beginning of the beginning. We are dealing not with the final now of the world, not with the end of the world, but with the end of the final now of the world, not merely with the end, but with the end of the end.[41]

The now of the apocalypse, on this score, is deemed "the first now of the world. Then the beginning of the new heaven and the new earth is the beginning of the universe now beginning. . . . For the first time the I now speaking is apocalyptic."[42] Implicit in this turn is the collapse of the temporal divide for the "not-yet is absolutely now."[43] To heed the imperative of the apocalyptic is to discern that *tomorrow is now because now is tomorrow*, but an absolutely new beginning logically necessitates an absolute ending of the beginning that is now ending. Naturally, Leahy is attentive to this logical possibility, and thus he argues that "this beginning of fully apocalyptic thinking is anticipated in previous conceptions of mind in the history of thought. But precisely because previous thought *anticipated* this beginning of an essentially new form of mind its actuality before now is precluded."[44]

With all due deference to Leahy, I would argue that the pure immediacy of now entails the reiteration of the new that renders the supposition of an absolute novum untenable. Nuancing and further complicating the argument, I would contend that what was before can never be retrieved except as that which has not yet taken place. Here it is apposite to invoke again Heidegger's insistence that repetition is the perpetuation of the identical in a manner that is always different;[45] that is, to repeat is not the continuation of what has been but the retrieval (*wieder-holen*) of the inception that is "begun again more originally [*der Anfang ursprünglicher wieder-angefangen wird*], and with all the strangeness, darkness, insecurity that a genuine inception brings with it."[46] Alternatively expressed, the event of being is calibrated from the standpoint of the originality and uniqueness of being itself—the aggregate that is entirely fragmentary inasmuch as "what is as a whole, as what is, itself demands a grounding in openness,"[47] and, as such, the totality is what it is in virtue of what it is to become—and hence every occurrence is a recurrence of what is yet to be in the fullness of the grounded essence of what has been.[48] Heidegger speaks often of the leap (*Sprung*) that initiates the beginning (*Anfang*) constantly surpassed by the "other beginning" that must always be first, the beginning that begins before the beginning that is unfailingly second,[49] the beginning in which "the truth of beyng must be ventured as grounding, as inventive thought of *Da-sein*."[50]

In "Der Ursprung des Kunstwerkes," Heidegger wrote of the leap as the "suddenness of the beginning" (*Unvermittelte des Anfangs*) that is "always a leaping-ahead [*Vorsprung*], a leaping-ahead in which everything to come is already leapt over [*übersprungen*], even if as something veiled. Concealed within itself, the beginning contains already the end."[51] To the extent that the leap at the beginning is a leap-ahead, the end can be said to be comprised in the beginning. Heidegger distinguishes the "genuine beginning" and that which is "primitive" on the grounds that the latter has no future "because it lacks the bestowing, grounding leap and the leap-ahead."[52] One might suspect a form of temporal determinacy implied in the statement that "everything to come is already leapt over." But, in fact, what Heidegger intends is just the opposite: The unpredictability of the future is upheld by the fact that the having-been in the present is grounded as what is to come; the past is molded by the future that is molded by the past. The distance between the terminus ad quo and the terminus ad quem is bridged by the creative leap, which Heidegger identifies as the poiesis of art, an act that allows truth to arise (*entspringen*) by bringing something into being from the origin (*Ursprung*) by means of the endowing leap (*stiftenden Sprung*).[53]

It is in this sense that Heidegger, partially thinking in the wake of Hegel, can arrogate the transposal of the speculative statement that the result is the beginning: "The beginning must really be made with the result, since the beginning results from that result."[54] We must nevertheless distinguish Heidegger's conception from the uroboric nature of the Hegelian dialectic whereby the end is contained in the beginning as the latter's necessary outcome, since in the end the absolute returns to itself as it was in the beginning. Badiou correctly noted that buttressing this dialectical movement is the "theological circularity which, presupposing the absolute in the seeds of the beginning, leads back to this very beginning once all the stages of its effectuation, its alienation, its-going-outside-itself, and so on, are unfolded. Thus, the dead Son reintegrated into the divisible immanence of the Father *completes* the world-concept of the Christian God, which is the holiness of the Spirit."[55] For Heidegger, by contrast, the realization of the beginning in the end does not presume that the end is nothing but the circular rotation back to the beginning. On the contrary, in a manner more consonant with the Jewish apocalyptic sensibility, the beginning whither one returns in the end is not the beginning whence one set forth toward the end.

Ironically, my contention is supported by Heidegger's comment in the rectoral address concerning the inauguration of Greek science in relation to the mission of the German university in the twentieth century: "The beginning *exists* still [*Der Anfang* ist *noch*]. It does not lie *behind* us as something long past, but it stands *before* us. The beginning has—as the greatest moment, which exists in advance—already passed indifferently over and beyond all that is to come and hence over and beyond us as well. The beginning has invaded our future; it stands there as the distant decree that orders us to recapture it greatness."[56] Heidegger urged his listeners to understand that only by obeying the decree to win back the greatness of the beginning will the pursuit of knowledge again become the means to fulfill the spiritual essence of the German people. However, he already insinuated at this fateful moment that the beginning is a future that has passed *over and beyond all that is to come* and therefore cannot be retrieved as the culmination coiled in the commencement.

In the summer course of 1934, several months after assuming the rectorship, Heidegger elaborated on this theme by noting that the essence of being human is determined from that which is essential in the historical moment, but the latter is experienced on the basis of the self-decision (*Selbstentscheidung*) to become who we want to become in the future, and hence the past—what Heidegger names the "beenness" (*Gewesenheit*)—determines itself from our future. However, as Heidegger is quick to point out, this determination from the future "is not subject to a prediction [*Voraussage*]; it cannot be invented and concocted in a freely suspended manner. It determines itself, rather, from that which essences from earlier on." We come to the structural circularity that induces Heidegger's temporal understanding of tradition (*Überlieferung*) and historicity (*Geschichtlichkeit*):

> That which essences from earlier on determines itself from the future; the future determines itself from what essences since earlier. . . . That which essences from earlier on has its peculiarity to it in that it has always already grasped over [*hinweggegriffen*] every today and now: It *essences as tradition*. . . . That which essences comes up toward us [*kommt auf uns zu*] in this reaching over [*Übergriff*] from the future [*Zukunft*].

The future comes only to one capable of taking over (*zu übernehmen*) the tradition instead of being lost in the bustle of today. We should not conceive of the past as a present that is no longer nor of the future as a present that is not yet; there is only one "*originally singular and proper time*" (ursprünglich einzige und eigentliche Zeit): the future of the beenness into which we are thrown ahead (*Vorausgeworfensein*).[57] The tensiveness of time implied in the ever-evolving tradition consists of a simultaneity of past, present, and future, which I suggest is a hallmark of the temporal swerve at play in the *Lebenswelt* of Jewish apocalypticism.[58]

Coming to the End and the Fragmented Whole

Any thinking that attempts to grapple with the endtime in an age inundated by severe fragmentation needs to engage the problem of the viability of system and the incommensurability of truth that defies incorporation into totality. In contrast to the eminently reasonable observation of Frey that the fragment has meaning only when it is brought into context with the sense of a whole that cannot accommodate it, since the fragment by definition is incomplete and thus is precisely what lacks context,[59] I would submit that the complete incompleteness of the fragment is determinative of the incomplete completeness of the whole. The understanding of the fragment vis-à-vis the whole does not compromise the fragmentariness of the fragment. On the contrary, the fragmentary nature of the fragment is enhanced by the fractional and disjointed nature of the infinite totality. Closer to this ideal is Frey's own observation that the openness of the fragment "leads to a higher closure. If understanding the fragment from inside is now impossible, it becomes nonetheless possible to understand it through the external circumstances that have prevented its completion. . . . Although the fragment is now no longer treated as whole, it is treated as part of the larger structure of meaning from which it cannot be detached."[60] Needless to say, Frey differs to the extent that he posits a finite whole instead of an infinite whole that includes everything and outside of which there is nothing. But the understanding of infinity that I am proffering closes the gap because wholeness implies not an all-encompassing unity of enduring substances but an elaborate web of interrelated processes in which every part can be read as a metonymy for the continually evolving disarray of the whole.[61]

In line with François Laruelle, I would argue that thinking from the perspective of the One does not imply systematic totalization but rather generic fluctuation, that is to say, the generic is rooted in and must always be tested against the unassimilability of the particular.[62] The surmise regarding repeated structures does not imply that the plurality should be subsumed monolithically under the stamp of immutable essences. The perception of totality that the structure sanctions is a unity embodied in multiplicity, a one that is unremittingly configured by the manifold, "a One which does not unify but which remains in-One,"[63] that is, a "unity-becoming"[64] through the array of the many rather than through the unification of the one.

NOTES

1. Hans-Jost Frey, *Interruptions*, trans. and with an introduction by Georgia Albert (Albany: State University of New York Press, 1996), 23.

2. Edward W. Said, *Beginnings: Intention and Method* (New York: Basic Books, 1975), 72–73.

3. Ibid., xvii.

4. Edmund Husserl, *Experience and Judgment: Investigations in a Genealogy of Logic*, rev. and ed. Ludwig Landgrebe, trans. James S. Churchill and Karl Ameriks, introduction by James S. Churchill, afterword by Lothar Eley (London: Routledge & Kegan Paul, 1973), 157.

5. Said, *Beginnings*, 48–49.

6. Edmund Husserl, *On the Phenomenology of the Consciousness of Internal Time (1893–1917)*, translated by John Barnett Brough (Dordrecht: Kluwer Academic, 1990), 9. For an alternative version, see Edmund Husserl, *The Phenomenology of Internal Time-Consciousness*, ed. Martin Heidegger, trans. James S. Churchill, introduction by Calvin O. Schrag (Bloomington: Indiana University Press, 1964), 28.

7. Husserl, *On the Phenomenology*, 9–10. Compare Husserl, *Phenomenology of Internal Time-Consciousness*, 28–29.

8. Edmund Husserl, *The Idea of Phenomenology*, trans. Lee Hardy (Dordrecht: Kluwer Academic, 1999), 33.

9. Ibid., 35.

10. Edmund Husserl, *Phenomenology and the Crisis of Philosophy*, trans. with an introduction by Quentin Lauer (New York: Harper & Row, 1965), 146.

11. John Sallis, *Phenomenology and the Return to Beginnings* (Pittsburgh: Duquesne University Press, 2003), 17.

12. John Sallis, "Doublings," in *Derrida: A Critical Reader*, ed. David Wood (Oxford: Blackwell, 1992), 120.

13. Frey, *Interruptions*, 23. See my similar formulation of the paradox of the temporality of the beginning in Elliot R. Wolfson, *Alef, Mem, Tau: Kabbalistic Musings on Time, Truth, and Death* (Berkeley: University of California Press, 2006), xiii, 131–32.

14. Jacques Derrida, *Specters of Marx: The State of Debt, the Work of Mourning, and the New International*, trans. Peggy Kamuf, introduction by Bernd Magnus and Stephen Cullenberg (New York: Routledge, 1994), 163. See citation and discussion of some other Derridean sources on the nature of the beginning in Elliot R. Wolfson, *Giving beyond the Gift: Apophasis and Overcoming Theomania* (New York: Fordham University Press, 2014), 184–85.

15. Martin Heidegger, *Being and Time*, trans. Joan Stambaugh, rev. and with a foreword by Dennis J. Schmidt (Albany: State University of New York Press, 2010), §65, 314; *Sein und Zeit* (Tübingen: Max Niemeyer, 1993), 329.

16. The view I have expressed here resembles the Deleuzian interpretation of Nietzsche's doctrine of eternal recurrence. See Wolfson, *Giving beyond the Gift*, 12; idem, "Retroactive Not Yet: Linear Circularity and Kabbalistic Temporality," in *Time and Eternity in Jewish Mysticism: That Which Is Before and That Which Is After*, ed. Brian Ogren (Leiden: Brill, 2015), 31–33. A similar interpretation of Nietzsche's eternal return and its relationship to the moment as a subversion of the metaphysical motif of presence is offered by David Wood, *The Deconstruction of Time* (Evanston, Ill.: Northwestern University Press, 2001), 11–35, esp. 26–30.

17. Martin Heidegger, *The Fundamental Concepts of Metaphysics: World, Finitude, Solitude*, trans. William McNeill and Nicholas Walker (Bloomington: Indiana University Press, 1995), 187; *Die Grundbegriffe der Metaphysik: Welt—Endlichkeit—Einsamkeit* [*Gesamtausgabe* (hereafter cited as *GA*) 29/30] (Frankfurt am Main: Vittorio Klostermann, 1983), 276.

18. Heidegger, *Fundamental Concepts of Metaphysics*, 187; *Die Grundbegriffe der Metaphysik*, 276.

19. Ibid.

20. Heidegger, *Fundamental Concepts of Metaphysics*, 183; *Die Grundbegriffe der Metaphysik*, 272.

21. Jacques Derrida, *The Truth in Painting*, trans. Geoff Bennington and Ian McLeod (Chicago: University of Chicago Press, 1987), 32.

22. Ibid., 33.

23. See Wood, *Deconstruction of Time*, 217.

24. Heidegger, *Being and Time*, §74, 366; *Sein und Zeit*, 385.

25. Edmund Husserl, *Cartesian Meditations: An Introduction to Phenomenology*, trans. Dorion Cairns (The Hague: Martinus Nijhoff, 1977), 75 .

26. Heidegger, *Being and Time*, §74, 367; *Sein und Zeit*, 385.

27. Ibid.

28. Heidegger returned to this theme in the 1955–1956 lecture course at the University of Freiburg on the Leibnizian *principium rationis* that "nothing is without reason" (*Nichts ist ohne Grund*). See Martin Heidegger, *The Principle of Reason*, trans. Reginald Lilly (Bloomington: Indiana University Press, 1991), 89 (*Der Satz vom Grund* [*GA* 10] (Frankfurt am Main: Vittorio Klostermann, 1997), 132): "Nevertheless the history of Western thinking shows itself as the *Geschick* of being when and only when we glance back upon the whole of Western thinking *from the point of view of the leap* and when we recollectively preserve it as the *Geschick* of being that has–been. . . . The leap leaves the realm from which one leaps while at the same time recollectively regaining anew what been left such that what has-been becomes, for the first time, something we cannot lose. That into the leap anticipatorily leaps is not

some region of things present at hand into which one can simply step. Rather, it is the realm of what first approaches as worthy of thought. But this approach is also shaped by the traits of what has-been, and only because of this is it discernible."

29. Martin Heidegger, *The Essence of Truth: On Plato's Cave Allegory and Theaetetus*, trans. Ted Sadler (New York: Continuum, 2002), 7; *Vom Wesen der Wahrheit: Zu Platons Höhlengleichnis und Theätet* [*GA* 34] (Frankfurt am Main: Vittorio Klostermann, 1988), 9–10.

30. Martin Heidegger, *Ponderings II–IV: Black Notebooks 1931–1938*, trans. Richard Rojcewicz (Bloomington: Indiana University Press, 2016), 144; *Überlegungen II–VI (Schwarze Hefte 1931–1938)* [*GA* 94] (Frankfurt am Main: Vittorio Klostermann, 2014), 196.

31. Heidegger, *Ponderings II–IV*, 257; *Überlegungen II–VI*, 353.

32. Heidegger, *Ponderings VII–XI*, 201 ; *Überlegungen VII–XI*, 260.

33. Heidegger, *Contributions*, §29, 53; *Beiträge*, 66.

34. Martin Heidegger, *Basic Questions of Philosophy: Selected "Problems" of "Logic,"* translated by Richard Rojcewicz and André Schuwer (Bloomington: Indiana University Press, 1994), 38; *Grundfragen der Philosophie: Ausgewählte "Probleme" der "Logik"* [*GA* 45] (Frankfurt am Main: Vittorio Klostermann, 1992), 40–41.

35. Heidegger, *Contributions*, §33, 58 ; *Beiträge*, 73. For a previous discussion of this aphorism, see Wolfson, *Giving beyond the Gift*, 243–44; idem, "Retroactive Not Yet," 33–34.

36. Martin Heidegger, *Introduction to Metaphysics*, new translation by Gregory Fried and Richard Polt (New Haven: Yale University Press, 2000), 41; *Einführung in die Metaphysik* [*GA* 40] (Frankfurt am Main: Vittorio Klostermann, 1983), 42. See Elliot R. Wolfson, "Revealing and Re/veiling Menaḥem Mendel Schneerson's Messianic Secret," *Kabbalah: Journal for the Study of Jewish Mystical Texts* 26 (2012): 33–34, and the sources that treat the paradox of the repetition of the origin in Heidegger cited op. cit., 34n35. See also Wolfson, *Giving beyond the Gift*, 442–43n116.

37. Heidegger, *Contributions*, §238, 293; *Beiträge*, 371.

38. Martin Heidegger, *On the Way to Language*, trans. Peter D. Hertz (New York: Harper & Row, 1971), 174; *Unterwegs zur Sprache* [*GA* 12] (Frankfurt am Main: Vittorio Klostermann, 1985), 50.

39. Heidegger, *On the Way to Language*, 176; *Unterwegs zur Sprache*, 53.

40. Frey, *Interruptions*, 24.

41. David G. Leahy, *Faith and Philosophy: The Historical Impact* (Burlington, Vt.: Ashgate, 2003), 146.

42. Ibid., 146–47.

43. David G. Leahy, *Beyond Sovereignty: A New Global Ethics and Morality* (Aurora, Colo.: Davies Group, 2010), 232.

44. Leahy, *Faith and Philosophy*, 147.

45. Heidegger, *Contributions*, §28, 52, §39, 65; *Beiträge*, 65, 81–82.

46. Heidegger, *Introduction to Metaphysics*, 4 ; *Einführung in die Metaphysik*, 42. On the paradox of the repetition of the origin in Heidegger, see Paola Marrati, *Genesis and Trace: Derrida Reading Husserl and Heidegger* (Stanford: Stanford University Press, 2005), 109–13. On the "politics of repetition" in Heidegger, see Miguel de Beistegui, *Thinking with Heidegger: Displacements* (Bloomington: Indiana University Press, 2003), 49–60. See also Calvin O. Schrag, "Heidegger on Repetition and Historical Understanding," *Philosophy East and West* 20 (1970): 287–95. On repetition and the experience of poetic language, see William S. Allen, *Ellipsis: Of Poetry and the Experience of Language after Heidegger, Hölderlin, and Blanchot* (Albany: State University of New York Press, 2007), 25–57.

47. Martin Heidegger, *Off the Beaten Track*, ed. and trans. Julian Young and Kenneth Haynes (Cambridge: Cambridge University Press, 2002), 48; *Holzwege* [*GA* 5] (Frankfurt am Main: Vittorio Klostermann, 1977), 64.

48. Heidegger, *Contributions*, §29, 53; *Beiträge*, 66.

49. Heidegger, *Contributions*, §117, 180; *Beiträge*, 228–29.

50. Heidegger, *Contributions*, §117, 181; *Beiträge*, 230.

51. Heidegger, *Off the Beaten Track*, 48; *Holzwege*, 64.

52. Ibid.

53. Heidegger, *Off the Beaten Track*, 49; *Holzwege*, 65–66.

54. Heidegger, *Identity and Difference*, 53; German text, 120.

55. Alain Badiou, *Theory of the Subject*, trans. and introduction by Bruno Bosteels (London: Continuum, 2009), 19.

56. Richard Wolin, ed., *The Heidegger Controversy: A Critical Reader* (Cambridge, Mass.: MIT Press, 1993), 32; *Die Selbstbehauptung der Deutschen Universität: Rede, gehalten bei der feierlichen Übernahme des Rektorats der Universität Freiburg i. Br. am 27.5.1933; Das Rektorat 1933/34: Tatsachen und Gedanken* (Frankfurt am Main: Vittorio Klostermann, 1983), 12–13.

57. Martin Heidegger, *Logic as the Question concerning the Essence of Language*, translated by Wanda Torres Gregory and Yvonne Unna (Albany: State University of New York Press, 2009), 97–98; *Logik als die Frage nach dem Wesen der Sprache* [*GA* 38] (Frankfurt am Main: Vittorio Klostermann, 1998), 117–18.

58. See Elliot R. Wolfson, "Gazing beneath the Veil: Apocalyptic Envisioning the End," in *Reinterpreting Revelation and Tradition: Jews and Christians in Conversation*, ed. and introduction by John T. Pawlikowski, O.S.M., and Hayim Goren Perelmuter (Franklin: Sheed & Ward, 2000), 77–103, esp.

83–86. The simultaneity of the three tenses has figured prominently in my conception of the linear circularity or circular linearity of time, elicited from a philosophical reading of kabbalistic symbolism, and especially as it relates to the compresence of past, present, and future implied in the Tetragrammaton. See Elliot R. Wolfson, *Language, Eros, Being: Kabbalistic Hermeneutics and Poetic Imagination* (New York: Fordham University Press, 2004), xvii, xxviii–xxxi, 38, 88, 428–29n336; *Alef, Mem, Tau*, 69–70, 93, 108–10, 132, 166; *Open Secret: Postmessianic Messianism and the Mystical Revision of Menaḥem Mendel Schneerson* (New York: Columbia University Press, 2009), 85, 99, 127, 164, 277–79, 287–88, 396n66; "Eternal Duration and Temporal Compresence: The Influence of Ḥabad on Joseph B. Soloveitchik," in *The Value of the Particular: Lessons from Judaism and the Modern Jewish Experience—Festschrift for Steven T. Katz on the Occasion of His Seventieth Birthday*, ed. Michael Zank and Ingrid Anderson, with the editorial assistance of Sarah Leventer (Leiden: Brill, 2015), 195–238.

59. Frey, *Interruptions*, 25.

60. Ibid., 26.

61. Ibid., 27: "Wholeness is the order in which everything has its place and in which nothing is missing or excessive. Inside the order of the finite whole everything is a part, which means that everything is recognizable in its relationship to the whole and is therefore read as a metonymy for the whole."

62. François Laruelle, "The Generic as Predicate and Constant: Non-Philosophy and Materialism," in *The Speculative Turn: Continental Materialism and Realism*, ed. Levi Bryant, Nick Srnicek, and Graham Harman (Melbourne: Re.press, 2011), 237–60, and compare the analysis in Anthony Paul Smith, "Thinking from the One: Science and the Ancient Philosophical Figure of the One," in *Laruelle and Non-Philosophy*, ed. John Mullarkey and Anthony Paul Smith (Edinburgh: Edinburgh University Press, 2012), 19–41.

63. François Laruelle, *Principles of Non-Philosophy*, trans. Nicola Rubczak and Anthony Paul Smith (London: Bloomsbury, 2013), 5.

64. Ibid., 43.

JONATHAN BOYARIN (co-editor) is the Diann G. and Thomas A. Mann Professor of Modern Jewish Studies at Cornell University, where he directs the Jewish Studies Program. He was previously Leonard and Tobee Kaplan Professor of Modern Jewish Thought at the University of North Carolina-Chapel Hill and Robert M. Beren Professor of Modern Jewish Studies at the University of Kansas. His most recent monograph is *Jewish Families* (Rutgers University Press, 2013).

SVETLANA BOYM of blessed memory was the Curt Hugo Reisinger Professor of Slavic Languages and Literatures and Comparative Literature at Harvard University. An essayist, photographer, novelist, and playwright as well as the author of myriad scholarly articles, Dr. Boym was best known to a general readership for *The Future of Nostalgia*, her widely praised book of 2001 (Basic Books). In that work, which ranges meditatively over philosophy, history, art, literature, and the experience of displaced persons, she explored the web of memory and mythologizing that underpins the human longing for vanished worlds. In her 2010 *Another Freedom* (the University of Chicago Press), she similarly explores the notion of "freedom." Her preoccupation with these subjects was rooted partly in her own history as a Jewish émigré from the former Soviet Union.

ANDREW BUSH is a professor of Hispanic studies at Vassar College. He earned his PhD in comparative literature from Yale University in 1983. He has published articles on Golden Age Spanish literature, twentieth-century women authors in Spain, and twentieth-century Spanish American literature. He is the author of *The Routes of Modernity: Spanish American Poetry from the Early Eighteenth to the Mid-Nineteenth Century*, from Bucknell University Press (2002), and *Jewish Studies: A Theoretical Introduction* published from Rutgers University Press (2011) in the Key Words in Jewish Studies Series, of which he is a co-editor. He was among a faculty group that designed Jewish studies program for the college, and he served as the program's first director. He has taught courses on Jewish textuality, the

Holocaust, the history of German Jewish culture, and seminars on Jewish culture in Europe and the Americas between the two world wars.

Sergey Dolgopolski is an associate professor in the Departments of Comparative Literature and of Jewish Thought and is the Gordon and Gretchen Gross Professor of Jewish Thought at the University of Buffalo (SUNY). He holds a joint PhD in Jewish studies from UC Berkeley and the Graduate Theological Union, and a Doctor of Philosophical Sciences from the Russian Academy of Sciences. His general area of interest is in philosophy and literature. He is the author of *What Is Talmud? The Art of Disagreement* (Fordham University Press, 2009), *The Open Past: Subjectivity and Remembering in the Talmud* (Fordham University Press, 2012), and *Other Others: The Political after the Talmud* (Fordham University Press, 2018).

Jay Geller is an associate professor of modern Jewish culture at Vanderbilt Divinity School and the Vanderbilt University Jewish Studies Program, and has also taught at the University of Vienna, Bryn Mawr College, Princeton University, Rutgers University, Swarthmore College, and Wesleyan University. He is the author of *On Freud's Jewish Body: Mitigating Circumcisions* (2007), *The Other Jewish Question: Identifying the Jew and Making Sense of Modernity* (2011), and *Bestiarium Judaicum: Unnatural Histories of the Jews* (2018), all from Fordham University Press; and the co-editor of *Reading Freud's Reading* (New York University Press, 1994).

Shai Ginsburg (co-editor) is an associate professor in the Department of Asian and Middle Eastern Studies at Duke University. His work focuses on Israel and its culture in its relation to Jewish nationalism and its variants. He is the author of *Rhetoric and Nation: The Formation of Hebrew National Culture, 1880–1990* (Syracuse University Press, 2014).

Sarah Hammerschlag is director of the MA program and an associate professor of religion and literature, philosophy of religions, and history of Judaism at the University of Chicago Divinity School. She is the author of *The Figural Jew: Politics and Identity in Postwar French Thought* (University of Chicago Press, 2010) and *Broken Tablets: Levinas, Derrida and the Literary Afterlife of Religion* (Columbia University Press, 2016). *The Figural Jew* received an Honorable Mention for the 2012 Jordan Schnitzer Book Award, given by the Association of Jewish Scholars, and was a finalist for the AAR's Best First Book in the History of Religions in 2011.

Hannan Hever is the Jacob and Hilda Blaustein Professor of Judaic Studies and a professor of comparative literature at Yale University. He earned his PhD at the Hebrew University in 1984. In English he published *Producing the Modern Hebrew Canon, Nation Building and Minority Discourse* (New York University Press, 2002) *Nativism, Zionism, and Beyond: Three Essays on Nativist Hebrew Poetry* (Syracuse University, 2014); and *Suddenly the Sight of War: Violence and Nationalism in the Hebrew Poetry of the 1940s* (Stanford University Press, 2017).

Martin Jay is the Sidney Hellman Ehrman Professor of History at the University of California, Berkeley. He is an intellectual historian whose research has included the critical theory of the Frankfurt School, social theory, cultural criticism, and historiography. His many books include most recently *Songs of Experience: Modern American and European Variations on a Universal Theme* (2004); *The Virtues of Mendacity: On Lying in Politics* (2010); *Essays from the Edge: Parerga and Paralipomena* (2011); and *Reason after Its Eclipse: On Late Critical Theory* (2016).

Martin Land (co-editor and contributor) is a senior lecturer in the Department of Computer Science at Hadassah College and the Open University of Israel. With a background in electrical engineering, he teaches computer architecture and issues in computers and society. As a theoretical physicist specializing in foundations of relativity and the theory of time, he serves as president of the International Association for Relativistic Dynamics (IARD). Among his publications in critical theory is *Time and Human Language Now*, with Jonathan Boyarin (Prickly Paradigm Press, 2009).

James I. Porter is Chancellor's Professor in the Departments of Rhetoric and Classics at the University of California at Berkeley. He began teaching at the University of Michigan in Classics and Comparative Literature (1986–2007), and then moved to UC Irvine, Classics and Comparative Literature (2007–2015), where he was director of Critical Theory from 2014 to 2015. He has held visiting professorships at Princeton and Bristol University (UK). His most recent book, *The Sublime in Antiquity* (Cambridge, 2016), was awarded the C. J. Goodwin Award of Merit by the Society for Classical Studies in 2017.

Yehouda Shenhav (PhD, Stanford University, 1985) is a professor of sociology at Tel-Aviv University. His book on the area of history of management, *Manufacturing Rationality: The Engineering Foundations of the Managerial Revolution*, was published by Oxford University Press in 1999. His main work in the area of nationalism, ethnicity, and religion was published in *The Arab Jews: A Postcolonial Reading of Nationalism, Ethnicity, and Religion* (Stanford University Press, 2006). His views on the Israeli-Palestinian conflict appeared in *Beyond the Two-State Solution: A Jewish Political Essay* (Polity Press, 2012).

Elliot R. Wolfson is the Marsha and Jay Glazer Endowed Chair in Jewish Studies in the Department of Religious Studies at the University of California-Santa Barbara. Between 1987 and 2014, he was the Abraham Lieberman Professor of Hebrew and Judaic Studies at New York University. He is the author of *Through a Speculum That Shines: Vision and Imagination in Medieval Jewish Mysticism* (Princeton University Press, 1994); *Language, Eros, Being: Kabbalistic Hermeneutics and Poetic Imagination* (Fordham University Press, 2005); *A Dream Interpreted Within a Dream: Oneiropoiesis and the Prism of Imagination* (Zone Books, 2011); *Giving Beyond the Goft: Apophasis and Overcoming Theomania* (Fordham University Press, 2014); and *The Duplicity of Philosophy's Shadow: Heidegger, Nazism, and the Jewish Other* (Columbia University Press, 2018).

INDEX